319

D0498185

The Pope's Jews

The Pope's Jews

Sam Waagenaar

A Library Press Book
Open Court, La Salle, Illinois

Copyright © 1974 Circle Film Enterprises, Inc.

All rights reserved. No part of this book may be reproduced, stored in a retrieval system, or transmitted, in any form or by any means, electronic, mechanical, photocopying, recording, or otherwise without the prior written permission of the publisher.

Printed in the United States of America

Waagenaar, Sam.
  The Pope's Jews.

  "A Library Press book."
  Bibliography: p.
  1. Jews in Rome (City)—History. I. Title.
DS135.I85R6813 1974   945'.632'004924   73-87739
ISBN 0-912050-49-7

Open Court Publishers, La Salle, Ill. 61301

To Gisele, who believed
—and to Inge

Contents

"We are sorrowed to hear that decrees have been issued against our friends the Jews, which make it impossible for them to live according to their ancestral customs."

Julius Caesar (Circa 50 **B.C.)**

"It is absurd that the Jews, who through their own fault have been condemned by God to everlasting slavery, should claim to be the Christians' equals."

Pope Paul IV (1555)

"Let us extend our hands to our Jewish brothers and repair the damage caused by the outrageous insults they had to endure from those who do not merit the name of Christians."

Massimo d'Azeglio (1848)

"Christians can not possibly have a hand in anti-semitism. Anti-semitism is not admissible. Spiritually we are Semites."

Pope Pius XI (1938)

Foreword

In 1555, when the historic struggle between the Vatican and the Jews of Rome finally resulted in their being shut up behind the walls of a newly-built ghetto, Pope Paul IV believed that this was a just punishment for the Jews' centuries-long resistance to the priests' exhortations to forget about the commands of Moses and to embrace the beliefs of Christ.

During most of the preceding centuries there had been a total misunderstanding between the two communities. The Jews of Rome had for so long fought against hunger, and against the rising waters of the Tiber, but above all against the rules and regulations that flowed forth endlessly from the Vatican. The abyss of misunderstanding that separated the two religious groups often resulted in a battle of wits. The following story, although apocryphal, perfectly illustrates the different ways of thinking that originated within and without the ghetto walls.

It is said that a few years before Columbus set out on the trip that would bring him to America, the Pope decided to ban the

Jews from Rome and from all the territories under his command—unless they succeeded in correctly answering three gestured questions which he would put to them. The Jews quite understandably were alarmed, the more so because the Pope had decreed that anyone who would give the wrong answers would lose his life. Finally, Giuseppe Gobbo, Joseph the Hunchback, also known as Giuseppe Testabuco or Joseph "Hole-in-the-Head" on account of his being the most simple-minded Jew around—finally, it was only Giuseppe Gobbo who had enough courage to face the Pope. The way life was going, he reasoned, it was not worth living anyhow; and thus he preferred a quick clean death in Rome to a death of slow starvation elsewhere.

The Pope, cardinals, and priests all stood on one side, and Giuseppe Gobbo, with only a little moral support from the thousands of Jews behind him on Saint Peter's Square, stood at the proper distance from His Holiness—waiting for the blow to fall.

Gesturing the first question, the Pope spread his hands out in front of him, making slow horizontal movements. Giuseppe thought deeply, then stretched his right arm straight forward, pointing resolutely down to the ground with his index finger. The Pope blanched, the cardinals gasped, and the priests wondered what was going on. The Jews were silent, presuming that apparently one-third of their threatened banishment had been removed.

Now the Pope made ready for the second question. The waiting was painful, especially for Giuseppe Gobbo, who once again felt the noose tightening around his neck. Suddenly the Pope thrust out his arm, his finger directed at Giuseppe's melancholy face. The Jews trembled. The rustling of their clothes continued all the way across the square. Their very existence hung so precariously in the balance, that whenever the Jews up front trembled, they all trembled. Then the fearful shaking stopped, and those in back inquired what had happened.

"Giuseppe pointed two fingers straight back at the Pope," they were told when the rumor from up front reached them. But since no wailing emanated from Giuseppe, it was clear to those

Jews who had to get the news by remote control that question number two also had been answered correctly.

The Pope shook his head. "Amazing!," he said to the immense surprise of the cardinals, who understood as little of what was going on as did the Jews.

Now the Pope sat silently, intently gazing at Giuseppe Hole-in-the-Head. Could it be that the man was not as foolish as he looked? So the Pope brooded a while longer on how to formulate the third and last question, which would decide the fate of the Jews for all time. A hush spread across Rome as if the Messiah were to announce His Blessed Coming. All eyes were on the Pope. What would the third question be, and how would the simple-minded Giuseppe counter it?

Throwing aside the folds of his soutane, the Pope's hand appeared holding an orange. There was a cry of astonishment and horror on the part of the Jews, for to them it was clear that the Pope asked whether they would continue to eat oranges in Italy, or whether they would be doomed to eat them elsewhere—if there would *be* oranges elsewhere! There was little time for meditation though, for within seconds Giuseppe had thrust his own hand under his frayed coat, and when it reappeared, he showed the Pope a *matzoth*—the unleavened Jewish Easter bread.

"Impossible!" cried the Pope. "That man has the wisdom of the Saints!" And to the Jews he said: "Go home, my children, and continue to enjoy Rome. I have lost—but it was well worth it, because I have seen a miracle."

So while the Jews rejoiced and touched Giuseppe's back for good luck, the cardinals and priests were puzzled, for they wondered what kind of questions the Pope had asked, and how the Jew had been able to find the right answers.

"With the first gesture," the Pope explained, "I indicated that the Catholic religion is worldwide. That was the movement my hands made."

"And the answer, Your Holiness?" the cardinals asked.

"The answer," replied the Pope, "the answer was the Jew's finger pointing down, by which he meant to say: 'Yes, but the *center* of Catholicism is right here in *Rome.*'"

"And the second question, Your Holiness?"

"In pointing my finger forward," said the Pope, "I signified that there is only one God. And then the Jew showed *two* fingers, reminding me that as a Christian I should not forget that there is also the Son and the Holy Ghost."

The cardinals agreed that so much arcane knowledge on the part of the Jew could never have been expected.

"But the third question, Your Holiness, what was the meaning of the orange?"

The Pope looked around the circle of eagerly waiting faces.

"It was a visual demonstration of the topic of discussion of our times: the theory that the world is round. But the Jew was clever, for he pulled out his *matzoth* so as to indicate that there are still many who believe the world to be flat."

And so the cardinals walked off, shaking their heads, because to them it was inconceivable that a Pope could be defeated by a Jew.

In the meantime the Jews had not been silent either, and had asked Giuseppe to give *his* version of the gestured duel.

And Giuseppe explained: "You see, when the Pope moved his hands around in circles, he clearly demonstrated what he already previously had threatened—that he was going to scatter us all over the earth. So I pointed down, by which I meant to say: 'No, Your Holiness, we are going to stay right here.'"

"Then, with the second question, when the Pope pointed straight at me, I immediately understood that he wanted to say: 'If you don't follow my orders, I'll have you blinded in one eye.' So I pointed *two* fingers back at him, meaning: 'But Your Holiness, you know that it is written in Exodus—an eye for an eye, a tooth for a tooth.'"

"And the third question," the breathless Jews now asked, "tell us, Giuseppe, what was the third question about—the one with the orange and the *matzoth?*"

"The third question," said Giuseppe Hole-in-the-Head, "the third question was the easiest of all. The Pope showed me his lunch, and I showed him mine."

Chapter 1
The End
of the Jewish Wars

The day had been slow in coming, and it was long after midnight when the last Romans went home. Many of them were slightly drunk on the free wine, and hoped to catch a few hours of sleep before the real fun would begin. Looking down by midmorning from the top of the Marcellus Theater, it seemed as if all of Rome had tried to squeeze into the thoroughfares that ran from the Via Flaminia past the Pantheon and the Theater of Pompey down to the Gate of Octavia. The immense mass of people, densely packed against the walls of the buildings, left barely enough room for the troops which were to appear any moment. Yet this was only a small part of the population, for the crowds extended all over the center of town, having started to reassemble again early in the morning near the Temple of Isis, not far from the tomb of Augustus, where the victorious emperors had spent the night.

The city had gone sublimely mad, a madness still enhanced when the troops finally arrived in its midst. The Romans reveled in admiration of the treasures displayed by the victorious army, carrying along a multi-colored collection of strange objects, rich in gold, jewels, and ivory, yet representing only part of the spoils brought home by Vespasian and Titus.

Ninety-seven thousand prisoners had been taken, many of them sold at the slave markets of the East. The rest were brought home to work at hard labor, but seven hundred of the tallest and strongest Jews were now ready to walk in the triumphal parade, despised by the Romans as the enemy who for so long had kept their legions at bay, yet admired for their proud looks, even in defeat.

To the Jews living in Rome the sight was unbearable. It was the confirmation of the news that at first slowly, then steadily faster, and always more alarmingly had reached the shores of the Tiber, where most of them still lived on the other side of the river just across the Bridge With The Four Heads, built a century earlier in 62 B.C.

At first the news had not been so serious as to upset the Roman Jews more than usually. They were accustomed to trouble in Judaea, and like the Jews in Greece, Syria, and other lands in the East, all those over twenty years of age had quietly continued to send their yearly tax-contribution of half a shekel—two drachmas—to the Temple of Jerusalem.

Then, around the year 67 A.D., two Roman generals—Vespasian and his son Titus—had been despatched by Emperor Nero to Ptolemeus on the coast of Galilae, just north of Mount Carmel, to subdue the Jews. Vespasian had gone overland from Rome via Antioch in Syria, while Titus had first assembled a large army in Egyptian Alexandria. To the Jews of Rome the departure of these two generals for the East had meant an obvious danger to what all of them still considered their homeland.

As his first act in trying to suppress the Jewish rebellion Vespasian had conquered Gabala, a city built by King Herod. Then the Romans laid siege to the city of Jotapata, which was being defended by one of the most capable Jewish generals, Joseph ben Mathias, who had been put in charge of all of Galilae in order to protect it against the advancing Romans.

Instead, when the protracted siege of Jotapata seemed certain to end in a Roman victory, Joseph had deserted his troops and gone over to the enemy (to achieve fame—or notoriety—as Josephus in Rome).

Previously, after having been shouted down when he advised surrender, he valiantly had defended the city, using all his skill, knowledge and ingenuity to keep the Romans out. But then, with the Roman soldiers already on the rampage through the mostly devastated town, Joseph, in order to save his skin, had been obliged to hide with some forty of his followers in an impenetrable cave. Surveying his desperate position, he had craftily suggested to his fellow Jews to draw lots and to kill each other according to the numbers drawn, instead of surrendering. Having somehow managed to be the last one to be killed, Joseph convinced the only remaining soldier of the futility of such action. Thus they both survived, and Joseph was taken before Vespasian by Nicaner, a Roman officer and old friend, from whom he heard that the supreme commander intended to send him to the emperor in Rome. In order to forestall such a move, which might have meant the end of his life, Joseph requested a private audience with Vespasian.

"Do you intend to send me to Nero?" Joseph asked. "And do you expect Nero still to be there when I arrive? You, Vespasian, will be the next emperor. You—and after you: your son Titus! Therefore you may well draw my chains ever tighter around me and keep me with you, for not only will you be emperor, but you will be master of all the seas and of all mankind! And if you believe this prediction to be of my own invention instead of having been inspired by God, then you may keep me in great chains till the event comes true."

Then Vespasian started to make preparations for the siege of Jerusalem, Joseph accompanying him as the not-so-innocent bystander. In the meantime, every new trickle of news aggravated the consternation in Rome. Many Jews were slaves in Rome itself, and thus slavery was nothing new to them. But now it seemed as if all Judaea faced total enslavement, the Jews being picked up in huge batches, to be auctioned off like cattle.

Through the years tens of thousands of them had been sold, and the latest news, after the fall of Jerusalem, had been that there were many offers but few buyers.

Joseph, now back in Rome with the victors, was a free man since his prediction that Vespasian would be proclaimed emperor at Nero's death had come true. Having taken the name of Flavius Josephus in honor of his benefactors who belonged to the Flavian family, he contemplated the Roman legions' victory parade with the cold and observant eye of an historian. Till his death in the year 100 he would claim to have remained a true Jew and a defender of his people and faith, yet he felt glorified by the scene of triumph that unrolled before his eyes on this festive day of decisive Roman supremacy.

Closely he watched the slow progress of masters and slaves heading towards the imperial grandstand in front of the Gate of Octavia, trying to remember every group and unit of the kaleidoscopic pageant, so he would be able to add its details to the history of the siege of Jerusalem he already now was planning to write—in self-defense.

Joseph had been in Rome before. In the year 60 A.D. the Roman procurator Antonius Felix Claudius had allowed some of the Temple's leading priests to go and plead a case before Emperor Nero in Rome. Three years later, at the age of twenty-five, Joseph had been delegated to urge their return from their prolonged compulsory Roman sojourn. That first trip had not been as auspicious as the second, yet it certainly had been more to the Jews' general advantage. Just the same the misfortune that befell Joseph on that earlier voyage had helped him to complete his mission quickly and favorably.

Towards the end of that first journey Joseph had been shipwrecked. He had spent the night in the water, till he was rescued by another vessel. Taken to the port of Pozzuoli on the mainland near Naples, Joseph had met Alituro, a Jewish actor in the service of Nero and his wife Poppaea—herself a great admirer of the Jewish religion. Not only did Joseph succeed with Poppaea's help to procure the priests' release, but on their departure for Jerusalem they were all presented with royal gifts by the delighted empress.

But now Joseph was the supplicant no longer. After all, he had come to Rome on this second trip as a close friend and companion of Titus himself. He had been gracefully received by Vespasian, had been made a citizen of Rome, was allowed to live at the emperor's palace on the Palatine Hill, and was not only awarded for his defection with a generous life-long stipend, but as an important Roman he was given large tracts of land in the country of his birth—a gift which, without feeling any scruples, he gratefully accepted. Josephus no longer belonged to the vanquished, but to the victors. Through it all he was loathed by his Roman co-religionists. But he disdained their feelings and opinions just as he had been impervious to the insults hurled at him from the walls of the beleaguered Jerusalem.

The siege of that city, imprinted with all its horrifying details on the minds of the Jews of Rome, had lasted from March till September of the previous year, 70 A.D. Joseph had been a witness to it all, from the day the first troops had arrived before the walls, till the day the last survivors of the Jewish capital city were massacred. During those intervening months the insurrectionary factions inside the city, under the dual leadership of Simon bar Giora and John of Ghiscala, had thrown their lot together against Rome. By then, neither moaning nor weeping were heard any longer within Jerusalem, for hunger had dried all tears.

When at last the whole of the Temple was burning, the looting Romans in their anger murdered anyone they met, those who continued to oppose them, and those who wanted to surrender. The battle-cries of the attackers matched the shrieking fury of the remaining defenders, trying desperately to save their innermost Sanctum. From the hills around the city the weeping echoed back to the farthest corners of the almost totally destroyed Jerusalem.

The end came on the eighth day of September of that fateful year 70. According to Josephus, survivors later told him and Titus that the number of dead since the beginning of the siege amounted to 115,880. The Roman troops, giving vent to their hatred, plundered and looted so successfully that gold in the bazaars of Syria soon afterwards dropped to half its price. In those same bazaars the surviving Jews commanded no price whatsoever, for Jewish slaves had become a glut on the market.

Yet some of these very same slaves, the ones so carefully selected by Titus for his Roman triumph, were now being led past Josephus, each one of them walking next to, or being carried on, the huge float representing his own city or province of origin. For the Romans had left nothing to imagination. Other slaves, of even lower standing than the momentarily dressed-up Jews, were cowed by the pageantry of the demonstrations of Roman might, making palpable to the citizens of Rome the powers that had been subjugated by their armies, and the beauty and wealth of the cities that had been stormed, taken, ravished, and destroyed.

The loot was staggering. Under the magnificent stage-management of the Senate, the latest treasures from Judaea were being displayed before the enthusiastically gaping Romans, together with trophies taken in previous campaigns. Josephus was careful to take note of it all, planning to use the description in the writing of his justification for his treacherous behaviour. He was standing close to the emperors, who, dressed in precious purple, were sitting on ivory benches on an elevated platform in front of the gate that had been built by Emperor Augustus for his sister Octavia, wife of Marc Antony. Here was the entrance to the temples of Juno and Jupiter, and it was here that they had been received by the members of the Senate.

The guard of honor, all soldiers who had accompanied Vespasian and Titus to Judaea, urged one of their officers to step forward and address the emperors. At first Vespasian listened carefully, then grew distracted. The officer was evidently a better soldier than speaker, and when the words continued to flow endlessly without much meaning, Vespasian caused him to choke on his peroration when he suddenly put up his hand to indicate that he had heard more than he wanted to hear. There was no reason to suffer at the mouth of his own soldiers, after having suffered so much at the hands of the Jews.

The excessive flow of the oratory having been brought to a speechless collapse, Vespasian dismissed the troops, expressing the hope that they would enjoy their victory meal, offered—as was customary—by the emperor. He himself, accompanied by Titus, his second son Domitian, and the notables of Rome, turned to the immediate right, where a sumptuous repast had been prepared for them at the entrance to the Circus Flaminius.*

The repast finished, the emperors and their companions put on again their most elaborate purple to continue with the show. It was an impressive spectacle. Josephus would try to describe it later, but it was almost impossible even to enumerate the many wonderful sights. The embroidered banners, ingeniously depicting the victorious battles and the scenery of the lands taken, shone brilliantly with their gold-interwoven threads before the admiring eyes of the spectators. The jewels were apparently of unimaginable magnificence. The Roman gods were carried along too, statues of immense size made of the costliest materials. Strange and never-before-seen animals, draped with banners and fine cloth that would have done justice to a monarch, were ceremoniously led by. Even the seven hundred Jewish slaves were dressed in costly multicolored raiments for the occasion, and it served to hide their disfigured bodies, emaciated during the long journey from Judaea to the Tiber.

Josephus paid little attention to the prisoners. What impressed him were the floats on which the treasures taken from Jerusalem were displayed. Among them was a solid golden table and an enormous Temple candelabrum. Even Josephus never had seen one this size and of this peculiar shape, for from its golden base emerged a thick shaft (also of gold) which then branched out into seven slender arms, each supporting a gracefully-shaped oil cup, signifying the holiness of the Seventh Day. Then, as the supreme sign of the Jews' subjugation, came the expropriated Scroll of the Law. Behind the spoils rode Vespasian and his two sons astride beautiful horses, the younger son slightly preceding his father and his elder brother.

Down near the foot of the Capitoline Hill the troops came to a halt. Above them stood the great many-pillared temple of Jupiter, whom the Romans had to thank for having allowed them to defeat his rival, the God of the Jews. The immense

*The site, as well as the site of the Gate of Octavia, were prophetic ones, for it was here that many centuries later the Roman ghetto would be established.

crowd grew silent, waiting for the word. Ancient custom decreed that the foreign king or leader who had dared oppose the might of Rome was to be executed near the temple. For the Romans, the man who had been the cause of their long fight was Simon bar Giora (who a year previously had thrown in his lot with that of John of Ghiscala). Josephus considered Simon little more than a bandit who was getting his just desert, while Simon considered Joseph nothing but a traitor. It was an ironic moment of rivalry: the illustrious general would live out his life in despised glory; the career of the soldier who had heroically refused to surrender was at an end.

The crowd had its patience rewarded. From high up on the Tarpean Rock (today a lookout point near the Campidoglio, the Roman city hall), Simon's lifeless body, strangled in the nearby (and still existing) Mamertine prison, was flung into the air, and it dropped silently through sixty feet of emptiness till it thudded on the ground below. The Romans, wild with enthusiasm, burst into thunderous applause. Justice had been done and victory had been sealed according to the rules: the last Jewish leader had paid with his life for his stubborn and insane resistance. The Jews, the most obstinate enemy of Rome, had at long last been brought to their knees.

Josephus thought it a fitting end for the man who had brought disaster on Judaea. The Jews of Rome had different thoughts on the matter. They felt ashamed, disgusted, angry—and afraid. Standing silently in the background, they bent their heads and mumbled their prayer for the dead. There would be no more messengers coming to them from the Temple in Jerusalem, for although the city still existed amidst the shambles, the Temple was no more.

On that afternoon of the year 71 A.D., once Vespasian's and Titus' triumphal entry had come to its trumpeted finale, the Jews of Rome slowly walked across the Bridge With The Four Heads to return to their homes across the river. In their minds they could look back on nothing but ruins. Though their eyes would remain fixed on Judaea, and the saying *Next year in Jerusalem* would carry their hopes through the centuries, Rome on this spring day ceased to be a Jewish outpost, and became a permanent Jewish settlement—their home, their only place of worship, and for all practical purposes the Jewish capital of the world.

For the first time since they had arrived nearly two hundred and thirty years previously, the Jews of Rome were on their own.

Chapter 2
Arrival in Rome

When the first Pope set foot in Rome, the Jews were already there. Two centuries before the arrival of Saint Peter, the earliest Jewish immigrants from Judaea, accompanying a political and military mission, had settled on the other side of the Tiber, immediately across from the island, in that part of the city that is known today as *Trastevere*.

The year was 160 B.C., and the messengers from Jerusalem arrived in Rome in the aftermath of a war with Syria. The Moshe Dayan of those days, who thoroughly trounced the enemy, was named Judah Maccabae. His opponent on the Syrian side had been King Nicanor of Antioch; he did not survive his defeat, and was followed on the throne by Demetrius I. In order to prevent Rome, the great power of those days, from establishing hasty diplomatic relations with the new king, Judah Maccabae thought he would ask the Romans to wait till the dust of the international storm had settled. Although Judaea was smaller in size than Syria, Judah Maccabae felt that Rome might prefer a pact of friendship with a victorious Judaea.

Thus Judah Maccabae sent two of his friends to Rome, Epolaus the son of Jochanan, and Jason, son of Eleazar. The Roman Senate deliberated on the proposal from Jerusalem, decided it had merit, and speedily promised the Maccabaes friendship and cordial relations. Quickly the decision was engraved on tablets that were displayed on the walls of the Senate building, so the outcome of the discussions would leave no doubt in anybody's mind—certainly not in the minds of the Syrians, who would soon hear about it.

"No one who is a subject of or friendly to the Romans," the tablets read, "will make war on the Jews, nor will they supply the Jews' enemies with wheat, ships, or money. If the Jews are nevertheless attacked, the Romans will render them all assistance. And in case the Romans are attacked, the Jews will act similarly. Any change in this agreement will have to be ratified by the People of Rome. Written and signed by Epolaus ben Jochanan and Jason ben Eleazar, during the reign of Judah the High Priest and his brother Simon, in charge of the Armed Forces." Thus ran the First Mutual Assistance Pact between the Jews and the Romans.

The two emissaries returned hastily to Jerusalem, and it took another fourteen years before a second Jewish mission undertook the long voyage from the Jordan to the Tiber. The Syrians, not having paid any attention whatever to Rome's admonitions, invaded Judaea once again. Crying victory where as yet there was none, they scampered back up their hills in the direction of Damascus as soon as the defenders counterattacked. At this point Jonathan felt that the time had come for a renewal of the friendship pact with Rome.

Once again the Roman Senate sent Judaea's emissaries home with warm letters of recommendation. Yet, acting as if Rome never had made this diplomatic gesture, the Syrians attacked again in 130 B.C. This time they advanced as far as Jerusalem, laid siege to the city, and only departed when they were bought off with money dug up from King David's tomb, three thousand talents' worth.

By now the Jews felt that the Romans should honor their obligations as pledged under the mutual assistance pact. Three men went to Rome on this third mission, Simon Disothei, Apollonius Alexander, and Diodorus Jason ("Honest pious men," Flavius Josephus would describe them many years later), and they put their complaints before the Senate. Did the Romans finally feel that they had not entirely lived up to their pact of friendship? Judging from the decisions taken, it would seem that the Senate tried to make up for its own past inaction, and they agreed to instruct the Syrians to return to the Jews Jaffa and Gazara, two cities the Antioch army had occupied.

Evidently the Syrians took the hint, and the Jews took advantage of the lull in the war to attack the Idumaeans, Judaea's neighbour to the south, whom they subjected and subsequently forced to convert to Judaism. If ever a tragic mistake was made, this was one. It brought the Idumaeans into the fold of the Temple, and by the time the last one had left Jerusalem and Rome, the Temple would be in ruins—for with the Idumaeans, Herod Antipater entered into the House of Judaea, and into the life of the Jews of Rome.

In the intermediate years other Jews had started to come to Rome as well, mostly as traders. The treaty of 130 B.C. not only cemented the understanding between the two nations, but it had also opened the Roman door to Judaean businessmen. Some of these came directly from Jerusalem. Others traveled from Alexandria in Egypt, the granary of Rome, where a substantial Jewish colony already existed; and by the year 63 B.C. a fairly large number of Jews had found permanent quarters along the Tiber.

Those who prospered settled close to the Bridge With The Four Heads, then still under construction but opened to traffic a year later. The others, who had drifted along simply because there was a lure to the great city of Rome, had to be content with more simple lodgings. They settled around the pestilential marshes that stretched along the Tiber in the vicinity of the Gianicolo Hill. It was an area that was unhealthy not only on ac-

count of the malarial atmosphere, but also because of its inhabitants. The riff-raff of Rome lived here: slaves, persons who
were in hiding from the regime for political reasons, porters,
tanners (always considered the lowest form of labor on account
of the unbearable stench attached to their profession), and the
descendants of the prisoners taken by the Romans at Capua,
after they had wrested that city back from Hannibal during the
Punic wars. Among these unfortunate pariahs the poorer Jews
were able to live according to their own religious customs. But
soon ominous news filtered back from Jerusalem once again,
and it alarmed all the Jews, rich and poor alike. As could be expected, it was the fault of the Idumaeans.

About eighty years after the first Idumaean converts had
shed their pagan gods to embrace Judaism, Herod Antipater,
son of the governor of Idumaea, felt that greater things were in
store for him. Befriending the Roman legions under Pompey,
Antipater's doings and undoings resulted in the siege of
Jerusalem by the Romans in 63 B.C. The climax was not far off.
On a Sabbath morning in the autumn of that year, when the
Jews refused to take up arms because it was against the Law to
work on the Seventh Day, Pompey and his Romans took
Jerusalem without a fight. The Judaeans were in decline, the
ambitious Idumaeans were moving ahead.

Only a few years later the Jewish colony on the Tiber had
grown so considerably that, emboldened by a mixed feeling of
righteousness and religious fervor, they felt strong enough to
accuse a Roman praetor of theft before the Senate. Valerius
Flaccus, a rather undistinguished Roman governor of Asia
Minor, had embezzled some, if not all, the funds collected from
the local Jews; these were funds that were intended for the Temple in Jerusalem. It was not a small matter. Flaccus had embezzled the gold in various cities—Apamea, Laodicea, Adramyttium,
and Pergamus. The bulk of it weighed some two hundred
Roman pounds, and with every Jew contributing the weight of
two drachmas a year, it meant that the full amount Flaccus had
tried to put in his pocket represented the accumulated con-

tributions of some 75,000 Jews, probably collected from them over several years.

The case not only stirred the Roman Jews, but other Romans as well. It was, after all, not an everyday occurrence to have a praetor accused of theft. The Roman Jews, representing their Middle Eastern co-religionists before the court, had engaged the services of Lelius to defend them. Flaccus, sensing that a good lawyer was a bad case half-won, had asked nobody less than Cicero, Rome's greatest orator, to plead his innocence.

The trial took place in 59 B.C. near the Tribunal of Aurelius (which was just behind today's Campidoglio, below the Capitoline Hill). Cicero took the floor in defense of his client, and accused Lelius of making a play for the massed Jewish crowd instead of for the jury, thus hoping, he said, that their clamor might influence the verdict in their favor. It was clear from Cicero's words that a large number of Jews had come to witness the trial.

"Now let us talk about the case of this stolen gold," Cicero said. "You, Lelius, you well know how many of these people there are in Rome; how they hold together, and how powerful their voice is in the public meetings. I shall therefore speak softly, so as to be heard by the judges only. For you know equally well that a good number of these people would like to incite the public against me, and I have no intention of facilitating their task."

Cicero tried to make short shrift of Lelius' defense. The money, he said, had been collected in the Roman provinces, and it should be known to Lelius that export of gold from the provinces was strictly forbidden. What therefore had Flaccus done? What was he being accused of? Of a complete falsehood, cried Cicero, for he had done nothing but apply the law!

Not so, said Lelius, for if it was so well-known to Cicero that no gold could be exported from the provinces, then it should also be known to him that an exception existed in the case of the Jews. This was "godly" gold, he said, gold intended for Temple offerings. As such it was holy even to the Romans themselves, and exempted from any and all prohibitions as prescribed by law. What Flaccus therefore had done, said Lelius, constituted a crime.

Lelius was on rather safe ground, as was proven a number of years later by Caesar Augustus. Discussing a similar situation, Augustus declared that he permitted the Jews' gold to be sent to Jerusalem, "as had been allowed during the reign of my father Julius Caesar, who proclaimed that the Jews, wherever they might live, were free to send their holy money to the Temple, as had always been permitted, even in earlier times."

As far as Cicero was concerned, there was no reason to discuss the case any further. He pointed out that the gold was not even stolen—it was right there in the treasury. He forgot to mention, of course, that it only happened to be in the treasury because the Jews had lodged their complaint. Had they not done so, then the gold certainly would *not* have been in Rome, or if there, in Flaccus' private purse. And Cicero tried to undermine Lelius' defense by making some pointed and slighting remarks about the people whose religion he called "a barbarian institution."

"Each nation has its religion, Lelius," he said. "We have ours. Even when Jerusalem was still theirs and the Jews lived in peace, the kind of rites they performed badly suited the splendor of our nation, the dignity of Rome, and the laws and institutions of our forefathers. During the last war this nation, taking up arms against us, has shown what it thinks of our friendship. Conquered and brought to servitude, the Jews have been made to understand how little their so-called immortal god bothers about them, since he allowed us to subjugate them."

The verdict in the case is unknown; but a year later Cicero was banned from Rome, and was not to show himself within eighty miles from the city. His punishment had no connection with Flaccus' attempt at embezzlement, but was the result of Cicero having prosecuted Clodius, a wealthy and highly influential Roman—a case Cicero lost. Though he was allowed to return to Rome a year later, his temporary downfall must have caused a certain satisfaction among the Jews of Rome. And one thing was certain: gold continued to be collected among the Jews in all countries around the Mediterranean that were under Roman rule, and continued to be delivered in their name to the Temple in Jerusalem, their spiritual home.

Chapter 3
The Visits of Herod

During the years that followed, there was a constant movement of kings and kingly messengers, sometimes in freedom, at other times as prisoners, to and fro across the Mediterranean, with Roman emperors, praetors and generals—their profession often intermingled—joining the traffic in the opposite direction.

For the next hundred years, therefore, everything that happened in Jerusalem would have its repercussions in Rome. Even though many of its Jews became outwardly latinized, religiously they remained bound to their homeland.

These are turbulent decades of Roman history. Crassus died, and his Triumvirate with Julius Caesar and Pompey disintegrated; the remaining two fought for supreme power.

Caesar, hearing of the difficulties put in the way of the Jews of Delos, the trading center of the Mediterranean, sent a letter from Rome to that Greek island's governor. In it, he expressed his sorrow "to hear that decrees had been issued against our friends, which make it impossible for them to live according to their ancestral customs, and which moreover prohibit them from collecting money for their religious services and Temple offerings." Caesar added that this was all the more disturbing and distressing "because in Rome itself such activities are allowed."

He sent out other letters to the Roman provincial governors, reconfirming his friendship for the Jews, ordering these decrees to be "affixed on the walls of the Capitols of Tyre, Sidon and Ashkelon, and in all the temples in both Greek and Latin." He furthermore reconfirmed the Jewish rights to the city of Jaffa, "which has been Jewish at the time when our first Pact of Friendship was signed." In Italy and elsewhere Caesar allowed the construction of synagogues, threatening with severe punishment all those who damaged the buildings or otherwise hindered religious services.

No wonder that when Julius Caesar was murdered in 44 B.C., the Jews of Rome were deeply shocked, and that for several nights in succession they were seen praying near the imperial pyre. "Amidst that immense public mourning," the Roman historian Suetonius was to write later, "one saw the crowds of foreigners, each lamenting according to its customs, the Jews above all."

The news that reached Rome now was of a continuous series of plots and counterplots. In Judaea, Herod before long had to venture forth without the assistance of his father Antipater, who was poisoned during an otherwise delightful dinner. When this news reached Rome, the talk along the Tiber was full of question-marks. Soon however, the question-marks received answers, when young Herod stepped ashore in Brindisi in the year 40 B.C., to arrive a few days later in Rome.

Why had Herod come to Italy? He believed in Roman might, banked heavily on Antony's esteem for his dead father Antipater, and having no one else to ask favors from, he was perfectly willing to turn Judaea over to the Romans forever, if only they would help him.

Antony listened sympathetically to Herod's story of grief, then took him to Octavian (later emperor Augustus) with whom

Antony at that time was still sharing the government of Rome. Octavian, too, felt that Herod had been sorely tried, and he gave orders to call a plenary session of the Senate, so that Herod could explain what weighed so heavily on his heart, and why. The deliberations did not take long, for Antony pleaded his young friend's case as if it were his own. The result was far more advantageous to Herod than he had ever dared hope. Antony's eloquence moved the Senate beyond his own original intentions, and they proclaimed Herod to be King of Judaea. His wish had finally, and accidentally, come true. All Herod had to do now was to conquer his kingdom.

To make a good start he left the Senate building in the company of Antony and Octavian. Then, the Roman army blowing its trumpets to announce to the world that a new king had been created, Herod, as behooved a good Jewish-king-made-in-Rome, accompanied the two stalwarts of the republic up Capitol Hill, to make an offering in the temple of Jupiter. The Jews of Rome, accustomed to a different kind of religious practice, wondered whether Herod would ever be able to walk alone. His reign, they felt, did not start under a favorable omen.

The Roman Senate had not used idle words. Antony immediately took charge of his protégé, and within a week's time Herod was able to leave the Roman streets behind him and be on his way east, where in 36 B.C.—heavily assisted by a Roman army under Sosius—he succeeded in taking Jerusalem.

Intrigues among several of his sons brought Herod twice back to the capital on the Tiber, in the years 17 and 8 B.C. In the latter year Caesar Augustus was called in as arbiter in the arguments that involved Herod accusing his sons, the sons accusing their father, and brother accusing brother. It appeared a perfect Roman family squabble, and the Jewish inhabitants of the city were kept at a safe distance. Judaea had become an integral part of the Roman Empire, and if there were trouble in the provinces, then it was Roman trouble, to be settled by the emperor. The Jews of Rome were not expected to have any qualms or wishes with regard to government matters, and decisions taken at court only traveled across the Tiber by hearsay. But living among pagans, the Jews of Rome still felt dependent on Judaea, and everything that happened there was of importance to them.

Augustus was genuinely interested in his Jewish subjects, and treated them with much the same respect Julius Caesar had displayed. His letters to the provincial governors had already shown his concern. His preoccupation with Judaism went even so far as to send sacred vessels to the Temple in Jerusalem; and there was a daily offering there, at his expense, of an ox and two rams. If free distribution of corn to the poor—an expedient political move to buy votes—took place on Saturday, then Augustus would give instructions to hand the Jews their share on Sunday. And in his orders not to molest the Jews in the synagogue, Caesar was of the opinion that to steal their holy books was as serious a crime as to rob their money.

Augustus even had adopted a saying by one of Judaea's greatest teachers, Hillel, and had it engraved on the walls of his palace and of a good many buildings in Rome: "That which is hateful to Thee, Thou shalt not do to Thy neighbour." It was said that in times of trouble Augustus had a town crier proclaim Hillel's wisdom in the streets of Rome.

However, if Augustus' interest in the religion of his Jewish subjects was considerable, his knowledge was scant. Writing one day to Tiberius, who was to become emperor at Augustus' death, he clearly showed his misinformation in conveying the idea that on this particular day, which happened to be the Sabbath, he had been as non-industrious as any Jew—he had not worked, and also had not eaten. Augustus wrote: "No Jew could have honored the Sabbath today more rigorously than I did, my dear Tiberius, I have waited till one hour after sundown before eating my first two mouthfuls."

Thus even to Augustus, who knew Herod well, the Jewish religion and its political aspects were nebulous affairs. If therefore he thought that his forced reconciliation between Herod and his sons had ended the troubles in the House of the mixed Idumaeans and Hasmonians, he was sorely mistaken. The disputes that plagued the family, with its many wives becoming mothers to many sons, and many sons eyeing the throne simultaneously, were manifold, complicated, and increasingly intense.

Herod, exasperated by his sons' continued efforts to despatch him to the hereafter before his time was quite due, had his two remaining sons of the Hasmonian bloodline secretly strangled to death. Finally, the son he had favored most during the later years, Antipater, fell out of grace and landed in one of the Jerusalem palace's jails. All the Jews of Rome therefore could do was pray, asking God to stand by them.

Herod himself was in far more immediate need of God's help than the Jews of Rome. He was now almost 70. His body had been ravaged by fevers. He could hardly eat, suffered from stomach ulcers and other intestinal troubles, his feet were so badly swollen he could barely walk, and (according to Flavius Josephus) his genitals "were rotting away and crawling with maggots." Under the circumstances it might have been more expedient for Herod to have suicide on his mind instead of murder. Yet it was the latter thought that kept his wits active.

Hoping to alleviate his physical agony, Herod went to the other side of the river Jordan to take hot medical baths. As a change from these, the doctors decided to lower him into a tub filled with warm olive oil, hoping *that* would help. The result was disappointing, except probably to those who wished he were gone. Herod fainted dead away, and only the frightened shouts of his servants, amplified by the agonized wailing of the doctors who thought they had killed him, brought the king back to his senses.

He returned to Jerusalem and asked for a knife with which to cut an apple. But his grandson Achyab, thinking that Herod wanted to do himself some injury, kept him from whatever useful purpose he wanted to put the knife to, his agonized outcries spreading such fearful panic through the palace that everybody imagined Herod already dead.

Antipater, hearing the lamentations, also thought his father departed and tried to bribe his jailer to let him go free, in order that he could take over the reins of government. But the jailer had his doubts, went out to reconnoiter and, finding the king still alive, told him about Antipater's proposition. It was too much for Herod. He flew into the last rage of his life and ordered Antipater killed before he could try any more trickery.

Five days later Herod himself was dead. It was the fourth year before the start of the Christian era. Till the very end there were complex ironies. Augustus heard about Antipater's execution, and with quite innocent disregard for Jewish eating habits he wrote the pithy epitaph for Herod's tomb: "He treated his sons worse than his pigs."

Chapter 4
The False Alexander

Towards the end (in their traditional calendars) of their Fourth Millennium—about the time Herod died—Jews had been constant visitors and residents of Rome for well over a century. Yet the Romans had only the vaguest ideas about the religion of these people whom they still looked upon as foreigners only. They knew that the Sabbath was holy. Jewish slaves steadfastly refused to do any work on that day, no matter how they were threatened or how severely they were pressed, and not a few were freed by their masters. There were plenty of other slaves available in Rome, so why should anyone keep Jews who regularly caused nothing but trouble one day a week?

These former slaves were those Jews—or at least part of them—who then settled across the Tiber not far from the island. Others went to live a bit farther away, at a place known as Mons Vaticanus—the Vatican Mount—a site that later would lure other expatriates from Jerusalem, who would occupy it permanently.

Known as *libertini*, liberated slaves, the early Jewish settlers built their first synagogue close by, not far from the present day's Piazza di Santa Cecilia and the narrow street known as the Vicolo di Santa Maria in Cappella. It was called the synagogue of the Augustesians, and Philo, an Egyptian Jew, mentions in his writings that "it was full on the Sabbath."

All these Jews in later years would cross the Tiber from Trastevere to the "civilized" side of the river via the Bridge With The Four Heads, one of the many entrances to as well as exits from Rome. The bridge probably derived its name from the four-faced statue of either Janus, god and protector of doors and entrance gates, or of Terminus, the god of boundaries. (The statues adorn the bridge's parapets till this very day.)

Originally the bridge, which would play such an all-important part in the life of the Jews of Rome, was known as the Bridge of Fabricius, named after the *Curator Viarum* or Road Inspector of Rome, who had built it. As part of the ancient inscription still explains, he inspected the bridge after completion in the company of Rome's two mayors—Q. Lepidus, son of Marcilius, and Marcus Lollius, the son of Marcus. Having agreed, after due consultation, that it was a job well done, the trio of experts declared the bridge safe for pedestrians and chariots, and open to traffic. It was not an empty ceremonial phrase, but a sound judgment, for two thousand years later the bridge still stands, still open to pedestrians (and to a kind of heavy traffic that would have made Fabricius' hair stand even more on end than it does a modern Roman's).

Nowadays so very much in the heart of Rome, the bridge forever remained near the center of Jewish activities—the huge modern synagogue (opened to services in 1904) is only a few steps away. Through the centuries Jewish feet have trodden its ancient pavement millions of times, and Jewish eyes have looked at the Four Heads with smiles of joy and gratification, and with tears of sorrow and desolation.

In our own age, Catholic Romans consider Jews simply as fellow Romans. "In our country," as author-politician Luigi Barzini once remarked, "all Italians look like Jews, and all Jews look like Italians." But when the bridge was still young, the mystery of Judaism was widespread among the Romans, and the basic conception of what the Jews believed in was lost to even its most erudite citizens. The Jews' strong belief in their God and the ways His rules and laws governed their lives were subjects of constant astonishment and incomprehension. The difference in the Jewish and Roman way of thinking is fairly well explained by the story of Rabbi Samuel ben Sufsarti. One day he came to Rome and happened to find some jewelry belonging to the empress. Instead of returning it immediately, he only announced his find thirty days later. He was asked whether he had not been in Rome for over a month already, and the Rabbi confirmed it. "Then why did you not return the jewelry immediately?" he was asked. "You must have known that a reward was offered for its return within thirty days, but after thirty days the finder would lose his head!"

"If I had returned the jewelry within thirty days," answered the Rabbi, "it might have been said that I had given it back in fear of punishment. Now that the thirty days have passed, it is clear that I returned it trusting in God."

The Roman intellectuals did not understand the Jews and their way of life any better than did the empress, nor did they know what this way of life actually meant, or how it involved the day's every action. The Sabbath to many of them was taken to mean a day of fasting, rather than the day of rest.

Obviously the Romans who sympathized with the Jews were as little understood by their friends as were the Jews themselves, and once again the idea of the Sabbath as a day of compulsory non-eating became confounded with the idea of non-working. Horace, the contemporary of Emperor Augustus, relates a meeting with a friend of his, Fuscus Aristius, a fellow poet to whom Horace had dedicated several of his writings. In describing the meeting and its conversation, Horace evinced total confusion.

Fuscus was in a hurry when Horace stopped him. "You wanted to tell me something," Horace reminded his friend. "Indeed I did," answered Fuscus, "but couldn't it wait till some other time? Today is the thirtieth Sabbath, and you would not like to make fun of a converted Jew, would you?'' Horace remarked that he did not mind waiting, but that after all, he was not superstitious. ''But I am,'' said Fuscus, ''I'll talk to you some other day.''

Not eating on Saturday was also the idea put forward by Persius Flaccus, a satirical poet living around the year 50 of the first century. To him the Jews of Rome seemed rather pale-faced towards the end of the Sabbath—which he called the ''day of Herod''—when they ''slowly and silently move their lips in prayer'' before starting the evening meal, so ardently awaited. The ''oily lamps in the window, well aligned and surrounded by flowers, have vomited their thick smoke,'' Persius wrote, ''and while the pitcher is being filled with wine, the tail of a tuna fish swims in its sauce at the bottom of a red earthen plate.'' The end had come, of course, to the ''day of fasting''; and, according to Persius, the Jews finally were allowed to eat again.

The ''thick smoke'' which Persius alluded to did not for various reasons find grace in the eyes and nose of Seneca either. ''Let us forbid them to light their lamps on the day of the Sabbath,'' he wrote, ''because gods do not need any light, and men do not like the smell of smoke.''

Valerius Maximus, a contemporary of Emperor Tiberius, completely embroiled Judaism with paganism by calling it the ''cult of Jupiter Sabathius''; again, the Jewish religion was disapproved because of that seventh day of rest. The idea of doing nothing for one whole day was evidently repulsive to Valerius Maximus. Seneca, who died 65 A.D., was also fairly violent on the subject. He condemned the Sabbath as ''an annoying practice, because doing nothing every seventh day means the loss of the seventh part of one's whole life, and a great many pressing interests suffer from it.'' Seneca considered it an imposition, but had to admit that the idea was attracting followers. ''The practices of this villainous nation have become so important,'' he wrote, ''that they are being imitated in the whole world.'' And inasmuch as during his lifetime Judaea had become an integral part of the Roman Empire, Seneca concluded that "the vanquished have given their laws to the victors."

Still another Roman author was of the opinion that the Jews, in "spending one day out of every seven in shameful idleness, in imitation of their tired god," propagated a religious idea "which not even children would believe in." And in a despairing outburst, he wailed that "Heaven would be grateful if Judaea never had been subjugated by Pompey."

Flavius Josephus, always the careful observer and chronicler of things Jewish in Rome, wrote that there was no city in the empire where the sanctification of the Sabbath had not penetrated among non-Jews. In Rome itself Jews enjoyed such tolerance that they could not be called upon for the performance of any function on Saturday, even when they happened to hold official positions.

This peaceful situation in Rome did not find a replica in Jerusalem, where Herod during the five days that had elapsed between the murder of his son Antipater and his own death had quickly made a new will. In a final change of heart he had promoted his son Archelaus to king. That is, he would be king if the emperor in Rome, who had the final word in the matter of royal Jewish succession, would agree.

Archelaus set off for Rome accompanied by more than half his family. His aunt Salome was in the party, taking along her own son Antipater. Of Archelaus' immediate relatives, his two brothers Philip and Antipas were members of the group, plus children, uncles, nephews, and hangers-on. It was a family expedition large enough to wipe out all of the Idumaean descendants, now called the Herodians, if a storm had sunk the ship—and probably no one in Rome would have wept.

In Italy the domestic Jews were solidly opposed to Archelaus' claims, and the would-be king, feeling full of confidence before Emperor Augustus, had a rude awakening. Nearly all of his accompanying relatives (on whose support to win the throne he had counted so heavily) changed sides as soon as they found themselves in the imperial presence, ready to convince Caesar that Antipas, Archelaus' brother, was the only one fit to become the country's ruler.

In the middle of this royal crisis, a mission of fifty Jews suddenly arrived from Jerusalem. They came to beg the emperor not to let his Roman generals interfere any longer with their religious way of life. At this point the interest of the Jews of Rome was far more aroused. Royal succession in Jerusalem was a matter of politics, and it would influence their lives only little; but a decision on religious freedom struck far closer to home. A huge crowd of eight thousand Jews accompanied the fifty emissaries to the temple of Apollo near the Palatine Hill. Here the drawn-out dispute dragged on, requiring Solomonic wisdom on the part of Caesar to keep the peace in his disturbed Jewish royal house. The only way Augustus felt he could solve the dilemma was to divide the country, and to some extent the Jews of Rome could not care less. As long as the Temple and their religion remained untouched, the land itself could be cut up.

Augustus did not have to wait long for the next episode in the restless life of his Jewish subjects. They received news of such importance that for a while the thoughts of the Jews of Rome were occupied with little else. The exhilarating announcement was sure to upset Augustus' recent decisions and might well result in the reunification of Israel under its rightful king from the House of the Hasmonians.

Alexander, son of Herod, who (together with his brother Aristobolus) was supposedly murdered at his father's instructions, was alive. Not only was he alive, but he was on his way to Rome to claim his rightful heritage, the throne of Israel. He had already traveled via Cyprus to Crete and Malta, collecting enthusiastic supporters and goodly sums of money on the way. Arriving in Italy's Pozzuoli, the crowds hailed him as the new and rightful king. On he went to Rome, where his imminent arrival stopped all activities in the Jewish colony. People rushed out of the city to acclaim a beloved prince. A triumphal entry was organized, and the exalted crowds carried Alexander on a portable throne through the streets of Rome. The honor of old

Judaea was saved, and all that was needed was Caesar's recognition of the prince's legitimate claims.

Augustus, who was hurriedly informed about the sensational turn of events, felt confirmed in his opinion that Herod had treated his sons worse than his pigs.

In order to get first-hand information, Caesar sent one of his freedmen, a certain Celadum who had known Alexander well, to get further details, and to bring the resurrected prince to him. Celadum did so, and he and the emperor were struck by the still royal bearing and the good health of the prince they had thought dead. The Jews of Rome were jubilant; they crowded together in front of the palace and quickly made elaborate plans to celebrate the happy and unexpected occasion.

Then Caesar looked at Alexander's hands, coarse, work-hardened hands. His body, although beautiful, was not as delicately formed as that of the royally-pampered Alexander, whom Caesar had known.

The emperor asked questions. Alexander gave plausible answers: the years spent in hiding had changed him and Aristobolus. Aristobolus? Had he been saved as well? Yes, said Alexander, their father's soldiers had taken pity on both of them, and two other men had been killed and buried in their place. Then why had Aristobolus not accompanied Alexander to Rome, so as to claim his own royal rights? That would have been risky, replied Alexander. If they had departed together from Cyprus, where they had spent these intervening years, and a storm had demolished the ship on which they were to travel, it would have brought the House of the Hasmonians to an implacable and definitive end. So Aristobolus had stayed behind to wait for the confirmation of his brother's safe arrival in Rome.

The emperor thought it a weak explanation, and took Alexander aside. "Now let us have the true story," he is supposed to have said. "If you tell me who put you up to this, I will save your life; if not, you will lose it. I have known Alexander well, and although there is a great resemblance between you and him, I am sure that you are not the dead prince. So tell the full story."

The supposed Alexander now realized that he could fool the Jews of Crete, of Malta, of Pozzuoli and those of Rome, but that the throne and fortune he had visualized were quickly evaporating under the mounting anger of the imperial interrogation. He confessed to have been put up to the whole affair by a slave who had been freed by his Roman master in Sidon.

Caesar was true to his word: the false Alexander kept his life, but was sent to the galleys. As to the Sidonese instigator of the fraud, he lost his life; and there were nothing but other losses all around. The Cretans and Maltese who had financed the trip and who had accompanied Alexander to Rome, had forfeited their money. But the Jews of Rome had lost something of far greater value—their hopes and illusions. They returned to their homes, a prince poorer, an experience richer, cursing Archelaus, and looking forward to what they hoped would be his miserable end.

They had to wait nine more years. By then the situation in Judaea had worsened to such an extent that a joint mission of Jews and Samaritans decided to put their complaints before Caesar himself. Nothing could have pleased the Jews of Rome more. Augustus found the charges fully justified, called Archelaus to Rome, and banned him and his wife for the rest of their lives to the Rhone Valley of France.

Augustus died shortly after these events and was enshrined close to the Tiber in the mausoleum he himself had built. It had twelve entrances, a white marble interior, and a statue of the emperor on top. What is left of it today on the Piazza Augusto Imperatore is impressive enough to convince us that at the time of his death the Romans, and the Roman Jews who had lived quite undisturbed under his reign, must have been struck by its magnificence. With Augustus gone, and Tiberius taking his place, the Jews of Rome could only hope for a continuation of the benevolent rule.

But if a false Alexander had been able to stir their enthusiasm while only bringing harm to himself, in the fifth year of the reign of Tiberius—the year 19 A.D.—another falsehood was perpetrated that had far more serious consequences. By now the Jewish population of Rome had increased to between fifty and sixty thousand; and the influence of their religion among the Roman upper classes was considerable. There was admiration for its mysticism, for its belief in a Being who could not be seen, and for the Jews' unshakeable trust in its rules which were so implicitly followed. Though the Jewish princes who came to Rome nearly all lived and behaved like Romans, the local Jews were significantly different. Their mysticism, moreover, was somehow surrounded by an atmosphere of knowledge of the future, which held great fascination for the Roman women, the more so because they could practice this attractive religion without being circumcized, a compulsory operation for converted men. It was this fanciful love for Judaism that caused the financial downfall of Fulvia, wife of the Roman aristocrat and Senator Saturninus. Her predicament created panic among the Jews of Rome, resulting in their first wholesale banishment on the European continent.

Fulvia, who had taken to the various attractions and sobrieties of Judaism, had started to receive instruction in her newly-accepted faith from a seemingly devout but actually rather unsavory character, who had been obliged to leave his native Judaea for obscure but certainly not laudatory reasons. More versed in circumventing legality than in the teaching of Jewish law, the pseudo-scholar took three similarly oriented brigands as his accomplices. Among them they planned a neat act of extortion, extolling their virtues before Fulvia and posing as the ideal persons to forward her gifts to the Temple in Jerusalem. Of course Fulvia, as a woman of high social standing, had to make quite substantial offerings—gold, jewelry, and expensive purple cloth. Fulvia readily accepted the proposal, and the foursome as readily accepted the gifts—for their own benefit.

Fulvia, probably feeling herself as little blessed afterwards as before, told her husband about the swindle. Saturninus went to see Sejanus, Tiberius' left and right hand, a somewhat sinister character who ran a private army of informers and was something of a specialist in intrigue, sycophancy, flattery, intimidation and torture. He had been busy trying to ward off the influence of foreign and principally Egyptian religious movements which were makng dangerous inroads on Roman paganism. To Sejanus Judaism was just another foreign religion that had to be equally combatted, and the case of Fulvia gave him a lead in that direction. On his advice Tiberius punished not only the four culprits, but the whole Jewish population of the city. Those who would not take up Roman arms were to leave immediately. The others were given a certain transition period to abjure their religion, at the end of which, if their decision were negative, they would have to leave as well. And in order to set an immediate example to all, Tiberius—again at Sejanus' suggestion—had the city magistrates select four thousand of the strongest Jewish males, and he shipped them off to a life of hard labor (and some bandit killing) on Sardinia, not the healthiest place off the Italian coast. Indeed it was so unhealthy, that Tacitus, retelling the history of this period, remarked that "if these liberated slaves of military age, infected as they were by their superstitious belief, had died in Sardinia on account of the bad climate, their loss would have been very little regretted."

In 31 A.D. Sejanus' ambitious plans included the assassination of the emperor. Warned in time, Tiberius judged that Sejanus' influence in the affairs of state was becoming too awkard. Sejanus was executed, and his body was thrown from the Tarpeian Rock and flung into the Tiber—the usual practice. Now suspicious of Sejanus' past actions as well, Tiberius reviewed the case of Fulvia. He quickly discovered that only four Jews had been involved, and that all others had been victims of slander on the part of Sejanus. Tiberius rescinded his earlier act of banishment, recalled the Jews from Sardinia, and ordered that henceforth they be left in peace. Not only this, but he promulgated a new order to be affixed on tablets and displayed clearly on the walls of all temples:

"We find it just that the Jews be not restricted anywhere in their privileges, not even in the Greek cities, since the Divine Augustus ordered it that way. We therefore find it equitable that the Jews fully enjoy their national customs everywhere in our empire, without any restrictions. We want this our edict to be engraved on tablets by the magistrates of all cities and colonies, in Italy and elsewhere, also by all kings and princes in our realm, through their appointed officers, and we desire this edict to be exposed for thirty days in a place where it can easily be read."

Chapter 5
The Jew Who Saved the Roman Empire

The black sheep of the Herodians, and yet a Jew who would play a key role in one of the upcoming succession fights within the Imperial Roman hierarchy, was Agrippa, son of the murdered Aristobolus and his wife Berenice. Brought up mostly in Italy, Agrippa was in his youth a Roman first and a Jew second. He was moreover the perfect Tiberean aristocrat, spending small and often large fortunes that usually were not his own, while he was always able to get his hands on more. Traveling back and forth between Rome and the country of his birth, escaping debtors in one place while borrowing elsewhere to refund a third party, he had been a playmate of several of the Roman imperial family's children—including Tiberius' son Drusus, who died in 23 A.D. when Agrippa was about 33 years old.

On one of his trips Agrippa landed near Naples and heard that Tiberius was in Capri, where by then he was spending most of his time. Agrippa sent him a note and was immediately invited to come over and enjoy the pleasures of the island.

One day, when Agrippa and young Caligula—whose tutor and older companion Agrippa had been when Caligula was a child—were being driven around in their carriage, Agrippa told his young friend that he hoped Tiberius would die soon, so Caligula could become emperor. The imprudent talk was overheard by Caligula's servant Eutyclus, who went to tell the emperor. Thus Agrippa, whose dangerous words did not please Tiberius in the least, soon found himself in jail. Once again a Jewish prince, no favorite with the Jews of the capital, was a prisoner of the Romans.

However, Tiberius by now was close to eighty years old, and by the time Agrippa had been in prison for six months, Caesar died. Hardly had Agrippa's Jewish servant Marsius heard the news, he rushed to bring the happy tidings to his master. Not wanting the guard to hear about the event that was still being kept a secret, Marsius yelled in Hebrew: "The lion is dead!"

Caligula, age 25, took over from the dead Tiberius in 37 A.D., and before long Agrippa, by now about 47, was once again dressed in purple. After spending another twelve months in pleasurable Roman fashion, he departed in August of the year 38—wearing a crown bestowed upon him by his friend Caligula—for his lands, that part of Israel that was inhabited mostly by non-Jews.

During the few years of Caligula's reign his mania for kingly adoration turned into megalomania, which made him look upon himself as a god, one of the major ones. His horse, also elevated to godly stature, was only slightly less important. As a god, his image obviously had to be adored by the multitude, and among the many-gods-adoring Romans and other subjects it was simply a matter of adding one more statue. To the Jews, however, it was about the greatest sacrilege they would commit since the adoration of the golden calf.

In the capital the promulgation of Caligula's order showed up an early Roman tendency of breaking the law that would continue through the Middle Ages and to our own days; law would be rigorously applied in the provinces, but in Rome itself—and sometimes even elsewhere—they would be circumvented with all the ingenuity that the inhabitants felt was their right and their duty. Thus the Jews of Rome, for the moment at least, were not disturbed, and their synagogues were unspoiled by images of the emperor. In Jerusalem and Alexandria, however, things were different. While in Rome the Jews were part of the indigenous population, Judaea and Egypt were subjugated countries and as such their inhabitants were compelled blindly to follow orders issued by the emperor.

The dispute, started in Alexandria, soon would be diverted to Rome to be put before Caligula himself. As elsewhere, the Jewish Alexandrians had opposed the emperor's orders, and the Greeks in the city, believing that in helping to enforce the order they might obtain certain privileges for themselves, were among the staunchest supporters of the Roman commanders. The Jews, not to be intimidated, decided to send a delegation of three men to Rome, and as soon as the Greeks heard about this plan, they countered with a delegation of their own, headed by one of their most prominent citizens, Apion. A would-be philosopher who had traveled extensively in Greece and the Middle East, Apion was said to be "always blowing his own horn," and to place himself on a level with the best Greek philosophers.

The Jews delegated Philo as head of their mission, a Greek-educated gentleman of about 55, whose knowledge and use of the sages was such that it was said of him: "It is not sure whether Philo platonizes, or whether Plato philonizes."

To the Jews of Rome the discussions were of the highest interest. Even though Caligula's orders had not yet been enforced locally, the Sardinian exile was still fresh in their minds, and a possible repetition was talked about in whispers only. So it was with fear and trembling that they awaited the outcome of the controversy to be enacted before the emperor.

Caligula obviously was on the side of the Greek Alexandrians, who were there to plead his own case, and Apion used his most biting words to depict the Jews as vile, depraved, and ungrateful human beings. These Jews, said Apion, who certainly was the most violent anti-Semite of the first century, each year had offered a live Greek to their dead God. Moreover, he argued in a case which he obviously was going to win hands down before the emperor, their refusal to honor Caligula as a god was treason, and any opposition therefore should be suppressed by force.

Caligula liked that, turned his back on the Jews and walked off into the garden, trailed by Philo and his Roman supporters. Theirs was a lost case, yet Philo, the devil's advocate, tried his best, at the same time trying to keep pace with the uninterested, apathetic and bored emperor. Philo reminded Caesar of Augustus' favorable attitude towards the Jews, of his allowing them to send money to Jerusalem and of all the other honors Augustus had showered upon them. But he might as well have stayed home playing anagrams with his alexandrines and hexameters. One can not argue with the gods, and Caligula considered himself as such.

The emperor violently reproached Philo that the Jews preferred an invisible God to a live one. Philo defended his people in saying that three times they had made offerings to their God in favor of Caesar—when he was crowned, when he was ill, and after a much vaunted victory over the Germans. Caligula cut him short: "Those were offerings *for* me, not *to* me." And with that he walked off.

Philo, an optimist, turned to his companions. "Let us be happy at these words," he said, "for now that Caesar is angry, God will protect us." With that the controversy came to an end, and the two delegations returned to Alexandria. The outcome had been in favor of the Greeks, who now wondered how they were going to exploit their victory, since not even the Roman army had been able to enforce Caligula's command.

The case thus remaining undecided in Alexandria, today's Middle East—and more specifically Jerusalem—became the next place of conflict. Orders went out to have a statue of Caligula put up in the Temple. The horror of this news echoed far and wide, with reverberations that shook the nervous system of Jews everywhere.

Their protests seemed absurd to the local Roman commander. If the Jews, as a conquered people, accepted the laws of the

Romans, then why in Jupiter's name did they constantly make such a fuss about the victors' gods? Everybody else had accepted them, and some Romans, including Emperor Augustus himself, had equanimously included the Supreme Being of the Jews in his own range of gods in sending gifts to the Temple. So why all the commotion about adding just one more god, the great and exalted Caligula, to their Own? It did not make sense, and any trouble the Jews made would have to be crushed mercilessly. And such, exactly, were Caligula's orders.

In this year 41 Agrippa happened to be back in Rome on one of his usual trips. Having been king for almost four years, the dissipating impulses of his youth had made room for a more serious contemplation of his duties, and Agrippa, now fifty years old, had greatly matured and had become a conscientious king. In appearance still a Roman, his religious outlook had undergone a change. Although remaining a staunch and patriotic Roman vassal, he had also become a good Jew, who fully understood his subjects' frenzied objection to Caligula's demands.

An excellent politician, Agrippa invited Caligula to a sumptuous meal, and the emperor, not yet entirely crazy, mellowed under the influence of food and wine. He regarded his friend and mentor, about twenty years his senior, with benevolent eyes and promised him greater power, more lands, and even more women if that were his wish. Agrippa felt flattered, waited patiently while more dishes and glasses were emptied, and then sprung his surprise—all he wanted from the emperor was his order to call off the erection of his statue in the Jerusalem Temple.

Caligula was torn between godly superiority and earthly friendship, and after silently considering the daring request, he decided on a compromise. If actual preparations for the placing of the statue had not yet been made, the whole thing could be called off.

But as Philo has predicted about a year previously—in 40—God apparently *was* ready to protect the Jews, for Caligula was murdered. His statue would not be on display in the Temple in Jerusalem, nor in the synagogues in Rome, and the sudden turn of events placed Agrippa, king of the Jews, right in the middle of the succession to Caesar's throne.

When the news of Caligula's murder spread through Rome, his German bodyguard, according to Flavius Josephus a group of "angry Barbarians with nothing but muscular strength and empty heads," were out for revenge. Not being able to find the dead emperor nor his murderers, they did what they considered the next best thing. They pulled Caligula's uncle Claudius out of the little room he had fled to in his fear of being killed too, and proclaimed him the new Caesar. The Senate, hearing of the development, was in an uproar, for the right to name a new ruler belonged to *them*, and not to the army.

In the middle of this melee stood Agrippa, a friend of the dead Caligula, and equally a friend of the kind but frightened Claudius. By now the situation was getting hopelessly out of hand, and even in the Senate the confusion went crescendo. Agrippa, the only man who did not lose his head, saved the situation. He went to see Claudius and encouraged him to take the crown. He then walked over to the Senate and, in an effort to quiet its members, he explained that Claudius had no intention to continue Caligula's reign of crazy terror. On the contrary, he planned to rule with kindness, and his first thoughts and care would be for the Senate and the populace of Rome.

Back to Claudius Agrippa went, only to discover that in the meantime the soldiers had hoisted the new emperor on their shoulders, ready to carry him in triumph to the Forum. They arrived just when their fellow German guards were leaving the Senate building to go and kill Claudius anyhow. But on meeting their countrymen carrying the new Caesar, the Germans all embraced and were delighted to have a new leader.

Agrippa, the Jew who to some extent had saved the Roman Empire, was not sent home empty-handed. Claudius reconfirmed him in the lands he already governed, and moreover added Judaea and Samaria, thus making him king in the agglomerated territories that once were ruled by his grandfather, Herod the Great. This was not all, and the Jews of Rome, formerly not too enthusiastic about Agrippa's behaviour, now had reason to praise him. For at his suggestion Claudius sent letters to Alexandria and to all praetors and governors of the Roman Empire, reconfirming the Jews' freedom of religion and cancelling all edicts of godliness as claimed by Caligula. In Rome the Jews thanked Claudius, hailed Agrippa, and spent some extra hours in prayer in the synagogues of Trastevere.

Claudius dictated his letters of tolerance even before Agrippa left for home: "I, Tiberius Claudius Augustus Germanicus, High Priest and Ruler of the People, twice proclaimed Caesar, at the request of my two good friends the Kings Agrippa and Herod*, hereby reconfirm the Jews in all their rights. As we have done already for those Jews living in Alexandria, we also reconfirm, not because we are asked to but because we consider these rights due to them, that none of the Greek cities will violate these rights, which the Jews already enjoyed under the reign of Caesar Augustus. Thus the Jews, wherever they may sojourn in Our Empire, will be allowed to live according to the laws of their forefathers. It is moreover not necessary for them to honor Caligula as a god as ordered by him, since this is against their religion. And this my edict will be communicated to all within thirty days by the kings and governments in Our lands, so it may be read by all people on earth."

The good Claudius came to an untoward end when he was poisoned in 54 by his wife Agrippina II. Yet notwithstanding his initial kind attitude to the Jews in general, Claudius was not too tearfully mourned by those in Rome. Some rather unfortunate disturbances had taken place in the city about five years before his premature end, disturbances which had resulted in a temporary second banishment of some local Jews. And so these Jews of Rome could wonder what the future would hold for them under the next emperor—Nero.

Their worry turned out to have been unnecessary. As far as they were concerned, his reign on the whole turned out to be a period of providential tranquillity and even prosperity, for Judaism found ever more followers among the Roman

*King of Chalcis, Agrippa's brother, and husband of Agrippa's daughter Berenice.

aristocracy, with Nero's erstwhile mistress and later wife, empress Poppaea, setting the tone.

But while flirting with the God of the Jews in Heaven, Poppaea's life on earth was not exactly blameless. She urged Nero to murder his mother Agrippina, caused the death of Seneca and of Nero's first wife Octavia, and finally is said to have enervated Nero to such an extent that one year after the fire of Rome he precipitated her death with a precisely-footed kick. With that, Nero's soft spot for the Jews was superseded by his wish to have peace in the land, that is—peace along the lines dictated by Nero. Within a few years, the Jerusalem Jews' increasing opposition to the Romans would herald the beginning of the end.

Chapter 6
The Arc of Titus

When one stands in front of the Colosseum and looks along the Via Sacra towards the Roman Forum, the Triumphal Arch of the first Christian emperor Constantine is on the left. Straight ahead, with the ruined fragments of a civilization between them, stand two other arches, both of them built long before Constantine was even born. Down towards the end of the Forum, just below the Capitoline Hill, is the Arch of Septimus Severus who in the year 202 suppressed yet another revolt in Judaea for which the Senate of Rome accorded him a "Jewish Triumph." Closer to the Colosseum rises the arch belonging to the man who thought he had settled the fate of Jerusalem for all time—Titus.

Dominating the Forum in its entire length, Titus' arch is in modern eyes usually taken as simply another sign of the glory that was Rome. To the Jews of the city it meant something different. For a thousand years and more it was the painful reminder of the destruction and profanation of the place they considered the holiest on earth. And they would refuse to pass under it, or even to go near it.

The Arch of Septimus Severus carries no embellishment nor even an inscription that reminds one of Jerusalem, because its erection was intended to commemorate this emperor's entire life and glorious deeds. Titus' arch was built with a different idea in mind. It was to show the great achievement of Vespasian's son in the destruction and annihilation of the Jews and their strongholds. Therefore its statuary had to imprint deeply the destruction of the Temple on the minds of the Romans as an everlasting tribute to Caesar.

The Arch as we see it today is not the original one, which had been built as a gateway to the Circus Maximus while Titus was still alive. He was crowned in the year 79 at the death of Vespasian, and died in 81. According to one legend a mosquito had settled in his brain and bore through it for seven years as punishment for his misdeeds in Jerusalem. The outlines of the Circus Maximus are still with us on the other side of the Palatine Hill (opposite the United Nations' FAO building) but the arch has disappeared forever. Domitian, Titus' brother and successor to the throne, had the present arch constructed at the entrance to the Roman Forum, and it bore a text that was shorter than the one which had illustrated the original monument. Then Titus had been praised with the inscription: "The Senate and the People of Rome—to Emperor Titus, Father of the Fatherland, their Caesar, who with the help and advice of Vespasian subdued the Jews and destroyed the city of Jerusalem, which before him had withstood the onslaught of generals, kings, and peoples."

Domitian apparently was of the opinion that a shorter text would serve as well, and perhaps he also thought that his brother (whom he himself had poisoned) should not be over-praised. The second arch therefore simply informed the Romans—and still informs us—that the monument was put up as a memorial offered by "The Senate and People of Rome to the Divine Titus, son of the Divine Vespasian." But if the words are limited in their adoration, the sculpture inside the arch reminded the Jews all the more of their defeat.

Protected from rain and shine, and somehow having escaped the acts of destruction by Vandals and early Popes who stripped the ancient city to construct their palaces and churches with its marble columns and sculpture, the structure was used during the Middle Ages as a fortress by the Frangipani family (who owned this part of Rome, including the Colosseum).

Under the vaulted arch the high-reliefs show, on one side, Titus on his victory chariot, guided by one goddess and crowned by another. But it is the opposite side that made the Jews bend their heads whenever they were forced to go near it. A replica of the triumphal parade that was witnessed by Flavius Josephus, it shows with documentary clarity the Jewish slaves carrying various Temple appliances, above all the seven-branched candelabrum. The gold it was made of must have been heavy, for the sculpture indicates that eight men were needed to carry the precious trophy.

Vespasian put great value on his son's spoils, and displayed them in the Temple of Peace, dedicated in the year 75. It stood halfway between the present Piazza Venezia and the Colosseum on the Via dei Fori Imperiali built by Mussolini, right next to what is left of the Basilica di Massenzio. Not all the spoils went into the Peace Temple. Vespasian had more practical use for the Temple curtains which he hung in his own palace on the Palatine Hill, where he also kept the Scroll of the Law.

Nothing is left of the candelabrum and of the golden table which in 191 were moved elsewhere in Rome, after an earthquake followed by fire had destroyed the Peace Temple. In 410 when the Empire was moving towards extinction, the Visigoth King Alaric I is said to have taken part of the Temple treasures with him after he sacked Rome. The rest, including the candelabrum, was moved to North Africa's Carthage in 455 by Gaiseric, king of the Vandals, after yet another sacking of the city. The dispersal of the Jewish treasures was not over yet. In 534 Belisarius, general of the East Roman Emperor Justinian I, on his way to reconquer Rome from the Ostrogoths who by then were masters of Italy, took Carthage from the Vandals and moved the candelabrum and other objects to Constantinople.

So close, and yet so far. One Jew in the city on the Bosphorus told Justinian that the candelabrum had brought bad luck everywhere. Rome had been sacked twice by Alaric and Gaiseric, and invincible Carthage too had been destroyed. If Justinian wanted to save Constantinople from a similar fate, it would be advisable to move the candelabrum back to Jerusalem. Justinian is said to have been impressed by the argument, and orders were given for its transport back to Judaea. According to one story the various objects were deposited in a church; according to another report they never reached Jerusalem. Whatever happened to them, the only early and exact reproduction of the candelabrum still in existence is the one to be seen on the Arch of Titus.

Vespasian, who would reign for another nine years after the memorable defeat of the Jews, was of the opinion that any God was a god, and any Temple a temple. Quite naturally he saw an important source of revenue in the Jews' regular contribution to the upkeep of the Sanctuary in Jerusalem. Once it was destroyed, there was no reason to relinquish the money. To Vespasian there was no difference between the voluntary tribute to the Temple in Judaea and a compulsory tax in Rome. He ordered the Jews to pay their half shekel in future to the temple of Jupiter, the one that stood on top of the Capitoline Hill, where Herod had started his kingship in the company of Antony and Octavian.

Special coins to commemorate the event were minted too, with the inscription IUDAEA DEVICTA, IUDAEA CAPTA—*Judaea conquered, Judaea captured*. Of course the Jews protested, but the collection of the *Fiscus Judaeicus* was strict, not only in Rome but in the whole empire. Suetonius mentions how "when I was very young, I saw an old man of ninety being examined by the procurator before a large committee, to find out whether he was circumcized."

The collection of the temple tax was eased by Emperor Nerva, who reigned only for two years (96 to 98). Under him a new coin was issued with an inscription that partly obliterated the previous one: FISCI IUDAICI CALUMNIA SUBLATA—*Easing of the indignity of the Jewish tax*. Yet it would take another two-and-a-half centuries before a definitive end came to the collecting of the *didrachmon;* and it required the act of the most pagan among all pagan Roman emperors—Julian the Apostate, who reigned from 360 to 363. Trying to revive paganism as a state cult, he fought Christians but favored Judaism.

In a letter addressed "To the Jews," Julian gave vent to his indignation and explained that not only had he ordered the tax stopped, but he had also burned all incriminating documents. Julian wrote: "I have seen a great deal of your misery, of which I learned even more when I found the registers which were used against you. I have thrown these registers into the fire, so that such an infamous tax can no longer be collected. Thus you will live untroubled in all parts of our lands, enjoying peace, and you will address even more fervent prayers in favor of my empire to your Almighty Creator and God."

The original taxing of the Jews in Rome brought no discomfort to Flavius Josephus, to whom half a shekel meant nothing, and who moreover considered himself far too much a Roman even to bother. Besides, he felt no pity for his former countrymen in Judaea and elsewhere, nor for the Jews in Rome. His feelings were entirely shared by the last Herodian king, Agrippa II. An ineffectual monarch who had been educated in Rome at the court of Claudius, he was crowned at the age of twenty-four, and was a loyal pro-Roman collaborator long before Flavius Josephus (whose friend he became) went over to the enemy. He and his elder sister Berenice dutifully and even gladly followed Titus back to Italy. But if Agrippa's trip to Rome was the result of inclination and political necessity, Berenice's crossing of the Mediterranean had a far more personal reason, for she was in love with Titus. Although she was a Jewess whose religious fervor in later years would certainly not have reignited Moses' burning bush, Berenice repeatedly had begged the Roman procurator in Judaea for clemency in his implacable persecution of the Jews. But when she met Titus, her own fall preceded that of the city of Jerusalem. When she was first established as Titus' mistress, a Greek philosopher once remarked that Berenice would destroy Titus as he himself had destroyed Jerusalem.

In the end Berenice did not destroy Titus; he effectively set her aside. For the time being, however, the attraction was durable and in 75, four years after the lovers' return to Rome, the affair was still happily on. Berenice probably died late in the century, and with her and her brother Agrippa's death, the Jews of Rome had seen the last of the Idumaeans' descendants.

With the Temple gone, the very cradle of Judaism destroyed and its holiest remains put on show to demonstrate pagan superiority over Judaism, it might have been expected that Romans would turn away from this religion which, in pagan terms, had been so cruelly let down by its so-called Almighty God. The reverse is true. With the disintegration of the Jewish state, its religion found more and more admirers in Rome. The Caesars had destroyed the land, but they had not been able to subvert the faith.

In Judaea, before the destruction of the Temple, there had been certain rumblings. In a period of great national stress a great many Jews had emerged who claimed they were able to lead the nation as its Messiah, its Anointed Saviour, the Guiding Spirit known to the Greeks as *Christós*. Especially one of them, a learned rabbi by the name of Joshua—which in Greek, the *lingua franca* of the Middle East, was translated as *Iesus*—had found many followers, some of whom had even come to Rome. Flavius Josephus felt that he should mention this movement in his massive history of his people; but as a Jew living in pagan Rome, the new faith—in the beginning simply considered a deviation from Judaism—neither attracted him, nor did he find it worthwhile to dedicate much space to it.

"Around that time," Josephus wrote, "there lived a man called Joshua, a wise man who performed many miracles and the teacher of those who gladly accepted the truth, and he found followers among both Jews and pagans. He was considered the Messiah, and after he had been accused by some of the important men among our people, he was crucified at Pilate's orders." Josephus then went on to say that Joshua was said to have returned among the living after three days, and "the Christians who took their name from him still live on."

That, according to Flavius Josephus, was all there was to it. It was of no further importance amidst the intensified Jewish life of the Roman capital, where so many pagans already had embraced the religion of his—Josephus'—forefathers.

The writers of the time could scarcely understand it. Tacitus was particularly upset by his countrymen who admired Judaism to the extent of being converted. "Those who adopt their religion," he wrote, "are told to despise our gods, to swear off their country, to forget parents, brothers, children. And yet they take good care to increase their population. They even consider it a crime to kill just one of their children at birth. From the Egyptians they have borrowed the system of rolling their dead in cloth instead of burning them.* Their God is a supreme and eternal Being, who can neither be imitated nor perish."

Juvenal, the satirical poet, was as much at a loss as Tacitus. Nothing of the Jewish faith followed by the apostate pagans meant anything to him:

"When a child happens to have a father who celebrates the
    Sabbath,
Soon he too will honor only the divinity of clouds and
    heaven;
He will not eat pork, as if it were meat of humans
Because his father does so neither; and so he will cut off his
    foreskin.
Educated in the contempt of Roman laws, he learns
Observes and reveres nothing but the Laws of the Jews
Which Moses once transmitted to his followers in a
    mysterious book;
He will guide only those who practice his religion,
Indicating the water in the cool well only to the circumcised;

---

*Even today this ritual has not changed in Rome. The Jewish dead are still swathed in cloth, not unlike Egyptian mummies.

And all this because his father celebrated the seventh day
In not fulfilling his obligations in life."

Making fun of the new Roman Jews, Juvenal chided them about
their "cooking cases" in which they kept the food warm on the
Sabbath. And meeting a friend who seemed to be in a hurry, his
first question was: "What synagogue can I find you in?"

A correct answer could not be easily guessed. The synagogues had multiplied over the years, and towards the second
half of the first century ten of them were in existence, the
number soon afterwards to grow to thirteen, and perhaps even
seventeen. Many of them being patronized by freed slaves,
they took their names from their deliverers: the already mentioned synagogue of the Augustesians (Caesar Augustus),
Agrippesians (Agrippa), Volumnesians (after Procurator
Volumnius), and one even named after Herod. Another one
carried the direct name of its worshippers—the Synagogue of
the Vernaclesians, from *Vernaculus*—liberated slaves.

Three synagogues were named after sections of Rome, like
Campo Marzio and the synagogue of the Calcaresians (the Lime
Burners); and still others after the countries the members came
from, like the Tripolitans. The combined congregations were
under the supervision of an Archsynagogus, a term so widespread and so generally understood that Emperor Alexander
Severus (222-235)—who was very favorably inclined to the
Jews, and who had paintings of Abraham, Orpheus, and Christ
in his palace—was known by that nickname.

No traces have been found of any of these synagogues. Yet
the religion had spread constantly; and in 1961 the remains of a
synagogue whose foundation dates back to the end of the first
century, and which remained in use till approximately the year
400, were discovered in Ostia Antica, the ancient port of Rome.
Its fairly tall columns, its prayer hall, and nearby bakery-oven
can be seen from the old main road between Rome and its
Fiumicino airport, and it offers proof of the existence of a thriving Jewish community just outside the capital, and perhaps too
of its mystifying lure which attracted ever more Romans
(especially among the women).

Chapter 7
Jewish-Christian Arguments

Fortune-telling was greatly in vogue in Rome in those years. Women would have their future (and its possible love affairs) prophesied by Jews, often bedraggled poor human beings recognizable by their basket of hay and straw that was the symbol of the beggar. They could always be found at the gates of Rome, including the Bridge With The Four Heads, to warn and guide the travelers on their fortunes (and misfortunes) outside the town or—for the newly-arrived—within the city. Again it is Juvenal who has left us a useful description. An encounter took place between a friend and a beggar woman near the Porta Capena, the Capena Gate; this stood right opposite the first Arch of Titus at the place where the Via Appia (Antica) then began, and now embellished by the obelisk of Axum. It was the site where in former days Numa Pompilius who, according to legend, was the second King of Rome after Romulus, used to meet his mistress nightly near the temple and its holy well.

Apparently Juvenal's friend had already been approached by another unfortunate woman, a pagan, whom he had given some coins. "Then an old Jewish woman arrived," Juvenal wrote, "having put aside her basket and hay. She was trembling, and whispered imploringly into his ear. She was one of those women who interpret the words spoken by the priestess of these trees, the true messenger of the secrets of heaven. She too got her hand filled, but less generously—the Jews sell their visions at a discount."

The non-necessity of circumcision made it far easier for women than for men to turn Jewish, because all they had to do was to be immersed in water in order to be cleansed of previous sins. When during the reigns of Domitian and Hadrian circumcision was considered a crime (it was confounded with castration), this still did not prohibit conversion to Judaism for women.

However, women evidently were not considered important under Domitian and their conversion probably was only taken as a female fancy. It was different with men, whose "crime" was punished by the confiscation of all worldly goods. The same sentence was reserved for those who had instigated the conversion. But such was the confusion that reigned about Judaism, that when a great many books were destroyed by the fire of the Capitol in the year 83, advice from a Jew was sought on how to replenish the library. He suggested to bring other ancient books from Erythrae in Asia Minor, which on arrival were found to be written, curiously enough, in Hebrew.

None of this was to Domitian's liking. Efforts by Roman Jews to make converts were strenuously opposed, and proselytizing became a dangerous activity, which finally in 204 under Septimus Severus was entirely forbidden. Domitian had some reason—at least a family reason—to combat Judaism and its inroads on Roman paganism. His father's and brother's struggles in Judaea were closed chapters. The Jews had been subjugated. Those who lived in Rome were not seen as hostile elements, as enemies of the state. But *joining* them in their religion was a different matter, for to some extent this meant going over to the enemy. As long as the conversions were kept far from the imperial family, even though they often reached into the inner circles of Roman aristocracy, they caused no direct trouble to the government. But when Domitian discovered that a nephew of his, Clemens Flavius, had gone over to the Jewish faith together with his wife Domittila, he felt that things were going too far. A defeated enemy appeared to be lurking at the gates, and had to be dealt with. Domitian's decision was swift and harsh: Clemens was executed in 95 A.D. and Domittila banished.

Something more than that appeared to bother the Romans in connection with conversions to Judaism. The difficulties with Jewish slaves, refusing as they did to work on the Sabbath, had plagued them for many years. But it was an old and familiar irritation. They had accepted it for what it was, and unreliable slaves were freed. But now the Romans themselves and through them their other slaves became "interested"; and now it was becoming a matter of freeing slaves who were not born as Jews. The enticement to a slave to become a Jew was an obvious one. So was the concern to the government, which could detect the breezes of Judaism wafting through Roman society with a monotheistic force. It was not even necessary to become a one hundred percent Jew, a concession that had not existed before and would not exist again. Conversion could be partial, and only involved the acceptance of most—but not necessarily all—of the Jewish rules and commandments. These *menuentes*, or partial Jews, were neither fish nor fowl, but they meant trouble to Domitian just the same.

The new converts were not the only source of religious agitation that plagued Domitian. In the year 45 A.D. one of the early followers of that Jewish Messiah called Joshua had come to Rome to convince the Jews of the righteous claim of his Master. He had been born in the Galilaean village of Capernaum on Lake Genasaret as Simon, and Joshua had bestowed the name of Peter on him. It was normal that on his arrival in Rome his first visit would be to the Jews of the city, the sons of his fathers. Those Roman Jews whom he convinced that Joshua was indeed the true Messiah quickly rallied to his side, for they rejoiced in the Messianic coming. But others were violently opposed and they argued long with Peter-Simon in their barbarous Greek, their knowledge of Aramaic having disappeared over the generations.

The disagreement between Jews who opposed the new movement and those who accepted the ideas of Joshua the Messiah or Iesus Christós became far more accentuated when Saul of Tarsus, the aggressive propagandist of the new faith, arrived on the Tiber in the year 61. Where Peter had softly persuaded, Saul came on a war path. Still, Saul's first steps in Rome were also directed to his own people, to the Jews across the Bridge With The Four Heads on the other side of the Tiber. For as Saul himself had announced in his letter to the Romans, "it is the power of God unto salvation to every one that believeth; to the Jew first." And elsewhere in this same epistle he remarked, "for circumcision verily profiteth, if thou keep the law."

The Jews had their own tribunal in Trastevere, the Beth Dem or House of the Law, its central office of rules and regulations. As had happened before to Peter, Saul did not make very much headway. Any arrival of the real Messiah, the Jews argued, had to be announced and confirmed by Jerusalem. They had received no such information. Consequently they could not accept Saul's assertion that He had come. It was basically very simple: no confirmation, no Messiah.

The new creed spread nevertheless, especially after Saul (now named Paul) decided that circumcision was no longer necessary to follow the Jewish Messiah. The Roman government, however, became thoroughly weary of the violent discussions that raged through the Jewish colony. To them Judaism was a *religio licita*, a religion that had been permitted for well over a century, and had official status in the empire. The new creed of those followers of Iesus Christós, was something else again. The enthusiasts were obsessed beyond Roman endurance. Had not Rome had enough trouble with the Jews, now to have more trouble with a splinter group?

Under Nero, the non-Jewish and sometimes anti-Jewish followers of the Messiah came in for severe punishment. The Colosseum with its 87,000 seats, started by Vespasian and finished five years later by Titus, had become the showplace of Rome. Its cost had been ten million denari, and thousands of Jewish slaves (brought home by Titus) had been pressed to work and die on its construction. The Christian troublemakers were easy and cheap human resources for circuses and games. But they in turn, particularly attracted to their assigned role in the gruesome theatre, often hid their paganism-cum-Christianity under the guise of Judaism—a protected and allowed religion.

The Jews had heavily participated in the construction of the Colosseum, but they were never much in evidence while the games (sometimes spectacular and exciting but, mostly, hideous and revolting) were in progress. Jewish Law forbade their being a witness to spectacles that were of a pagan nature and which, more often than not, ended in a bloodbath or in scenes of carousing debauchery. And blood, except when defending their faith—at which time they could and would become fanatics—was usually far from their mind. Rabbi Mathis ben Heresh, who arrived in Rome early in the second century to start teaching the Law, made a telling remark about Jewish behaviour when he said, "It is better to be the tail of a lion, than the head of a fox." Yet under Nero and under the later Caesars the line of recognizable difference between Jews and the new Christians was at times very thin; the lions were altogether too much with them.

In the upheaval caused in Rome by the propagation of the new faith, the necessary intensification of the study of Judaism was logically explained by the famous Rabbi Akiba. One day he was discovered teaching the Law openly. Emperor Hadrian—who had been a great general, a highly efficient administrator, and a scourge to the Jews (for which reason his mausoleum along the Tiber, today known as the Castel Sant' Angelo, was looked upon with wrath and revulsion)—had forbidden the Torah's study. When asked how he dare oppose the emperor's orders, Rabbi Akiba related the story of the foxes and the fishes. A hungry fox was voraciously eyeing the fishes careening through the water. Inquiring why they moved so haphazardly, the fishes explained that they were trying to escape the nets, set out to catch them. The fox then slyly suggested that they seek the safety of the shore. But the fishes objected, for having enough trouble in their own element, they felt that they would only encounter more if they left it. The wise rabbi thought it was much the same with the Jews. They were persecuted when they studied the Law—how much more would they have to suffer if they neglected it!

Later on, other rabbis came to Rome; and their impressions were sometimes favorable, sometimes not. Rabbi Joshua ben Levi wrote in admiration that Rome had become the capital of Judaism; and when someone asked him where God was, he answered: "In the great city of Rome." It was the city that was despised for its attempts to destroy Judaea. But it was respected as a world capital—a grand centre which was supposed to have 365 squares, one for every day of the year, and on each square stood 365 palaces with great staircases that had 365 steps.

Several years later, when Marcus Aurelius was emperor, Rabbi Simon ben Johai came to Rome in the company of Rabbi Eleasar ben Jose, to see whether Emperor Hadrian's harsh anti-Jewish measures might be softened or perhaps even entirely revoked. They were shown candelabra and other holy treasures in the Temple of Peace, after which they were brought into Marcus Aurelius' presence. The emperor received them graciously. Having been informed that the two rabbis were renowned for their wisdom, he asked them to cure his daughter from an apparently incurable disease.

Rabbi ben Johai spoke one word into the girl's ear, after which she evidently recovered miraculously and instantly. The emperor was so impressed that he allowed the rabbis to choose any document they wanted from the imperial archives. They did not have to search for long. They took away with them the hated anti-Jewish laws.

Though the rabbis were well treated by the emperor, and were highly praised by the Jews of Rome, their impression of the famed city itself was unfavorable. It was a city of decadence, they thought, in which the Romans had "built brothels and sumptuous baths to satisfy their lusts, and had built bridges only to collect tolls. . . ."

Some decades later an equally unfavorable opinion was delivered by yet another rabbi. When Joseph ben Levi visited Rome during the first half of the third century, he found a disagreeable and degenerate city "where they protect the buildings, but leave the poor to die."

Under such conditions Rome's pagan religion had hardly any attraction for the Jews. Shortly after Joseph ben Levi, another leading rabbi, Tanhum ben Hanilai, also visited Rome. He too had a conversation with the emperor. Caesar, in a good mood, felt that it would not be too difficult to end the centuries-old Roman-Jewish animosity. The easiest way to accomplish this, he suggested, would be to unite in the same religion.

The rabbi judged it to be a brilliant plan, but he had second thoughts on how to carry it out. "A splendid idea," he told the emperor, "but since the Jews unfortunately already have been circumcized, and the pagans are not, it will be far easier for all concerned if *your* people were to join *ours*. . . ."

Chapter 8
The Jewish Catacombs

During the next eight centuries of turbulent history Rome blossomed majestically, declined miserably, was attacked and invaded, and finally its lifeblood ran through its efficient system of gutters and sewers as if oozing from a beetle crushed under the heels of the ravaging Visigoths, Vandals, and Ostragoths. Its emperors disappeared. Theodoric the Great, the mighty king of the East Goths took their place for a while; its population of well over a million slowly dwindled to a negligible 28,000; its inhabitants turned Christian; the city became a Papacy. And through it all its Jews continued to live and die as Jews, their ranks at first enlarged by pagans who joined their religion, then reduced by others whose inclinations were different or changeable.

They were buried in the cemeteries and catacombs which were discovered centuries later to reveal so much of Jewish history. We might have known much more about these early Jews of Rome, if necrophagous adventurers through the ages had not plundered the tombs. Towards the end of the twelfth century the thievery became so extensive that Popes Gregory VIII and Clement III had to prohibit "the plunder and digging up of Jewish graves and cemeteries." Certainly the thieves were faultily inspired, for if they expected to find golden masks and precious jewelry, they were far off the mark. In some respects rich Roman Jews may well have followed the ways of life of their contemporary pagan friends; but when it came to their burial arrangements, they were neither ancient Egyptians nor Etruscans.

Hundreds of tombs have been brought to light since Antonio Bosio, the earliest of many frenetic Roman catacomb-explorers discovered in 1602 the first Jewish cemetery, at a place near today's Roman Flea Market between the Porta Portese and Porta Portuense. These tombs show that, in some manner, a few of the early Jews had already deviated from the strictly orthodox way of life of their forefathers, and were following some of the pagan Roman customs. Instead of only the names and other biographical details as prescribed by Jewish custom, a good many of the tombstones are embellished with pictures of Hebrew objects like ram's horns and candelabra. Other tombs show less religious designs of fruit baskets, chickens, and even a cow and calf, while two sarcophagi must have belonged to actresses (one with flowing hair, the other sarcophagus bears two actors' faces)—unless these stone caskets (as sometimes happened) had served a pagan Roman before its Jewish occupant, or were simply bought ready-made.

The inscriptions bear out the fact that the early Jews of Rome indeed spoke Greek nearly exclusively; for the great majority of the more than 530 discovered stones show inscriptions in that language, others turn to Latin; and not till the eighth century was the distinction between Christians and Jews so severely drawn that Hebrew was used exclusively to commemorate the dead. Of the ancient stones of these early centuries, only a very few are inscribed in Hebrew.

In the catacombs below the Villa Torlonia on the Via Nomentana—during the period of fascism the private residence of

Benito Mussolini—the oldest part dates back to the second century A.D. One of the best preserved and illustrated tombs shows not only a beautiful candelabrum, but also a striking design that can be seen on the collapsed friezes of the fourth century synagogue at Israel's Capernaum (where, according to legend, Joshua Christós preached his first sermon): the swastika. Originally taken to denote a Sanskrit word meaning "well-being," its intricate contours were probably exported to Judaea at an early stage. It was similarly used as a good luck sign in China, on phallic stones in Japan, as a branding mark on Indian cattle and, of course, by the German Nazis.

Rich Jews joined their deceased Roman friends on the Via Appia, where the ruins of the ancient tombs provide in our day the beautifully picturesque background for Roman outings. A certain Zabda and Akiba are found to be buried here. Jews were also buried at the cemetery of the Porta Portuense and in the catacombs under the Villa Torlonia; they found last resting places in the catacombs of the Via Appia's Vigna Randanini—still in existence—and at the large cemetery of Monteverde and the small one on the Via Labicana (now Via Casilina) outside the Porta Maggiore, both of which have since been destroyed.

Neither the catacombs under the Villa Torlonia (containing lovely wall-paintings and beautiful sarcophagi) nor those on the Via Appia are under the supervision of the Jewish community. According to the 1929 Concordat between the Italian government and the Vatican, they are "owned" and semi-protected by the Pontifical Commission on Sacred Archaeology, which holds the keys to the entrance gates—and both catacombs are closed to the public. (Those under the Via Appia's Vigna Randanini constitute a vast agglomeration of endless subterranean corridors; they are only partly excavated and remain without any lights, in contrast to the nearby Christian catacombs which are electrically illuminated, neatly cleaned up, and perfectly guided.) Here and there a leftover tombstone in Greek or Latin, sometimes embellished by a seven-branched candelabrum, has been cemented back into the black stone-and-earthen walls in which the thousands of tombs have been dug; a few still contain bits and pieces of two-thousand-year-old bones. Of outstanding interest in the labyrinthine Appian city of the dead are two connecting burial chambers of obviously well-to-do Jewish families, the walls and ceilings elaborately decorated with colored paintings of humans, angels, and animals. There were evidently professors as well as sailors among these people, and all kinds of craftsmen and shopkeepers found in busy working communities, *e.g.* butchers, tent-makers. There were also bankers who used to finance trade via the ports of Ostia and even Pozzuoli. Their names often were Latinized: such as Tullio, Aurelio, Giuliano, although I found typically biblical names like Samul (Samuel), Aster (Esther) and Jonata (Jonathan) present in fairly considerable large numbers.

They married young, these early Jews of Rome. According to inscriptions found on the tombs, one woman died at the age of eighteen, after three years of marriage. A certain Venerosa had already been a bride for fifteen months when she passed away at the age of seventeen. A man by the name of Anteros was only sixteen when he entered upon the state of matrimony, to die six years later at the age of twenty-two.

One of the dead is reminded by his family that *"No One Is Immortal,"* which must have been of only slight consolation to the poor man. Elsewhere we read that *"Even The Departed Have The Power Of Love,"* perhaps indicating a vow by the surviving spouse not to remarry too quickly.

Also among them was a "sausage maker, a good man, and friend of all"; an immigrant from Laodicea in Asia Minor "who lived for 85 years" (she did not do as well as "Pancharius, Father of the Eleia Synagogue, who was 110 years old"). One man described himself on his tombstone as *archon* or leader of the community: "I, Zotikos, archon, I rest here, having lived an exemplary life, friend of all and known to all for his distinction, his virile character, and his constant willingness to be of service. May his sleep be with the Righteous."

A certain Asteria was "the orthodox and blameless head of the synagogue" (without mentioning which one). Two other families were more careful to let posterity know what houses of prayer their beloved had attended. One was "Eirina Parthenike, wife of Clodius, father of the Campensian synagogue." The other one was "Menophilos, father of the synagogue of the Carcaresians, who lived well as a Jew, spent 34 years with his wife, and witnessed his grandchildren." The inscription was found on the tombstone of his daughter, whose name was twice mentioned on the grave, once at the beginning of her father's biography, and once at the end: "Here lies Cattia Ammias."

A certain Mannacius memorialized his sister Crysidi as "the sweet proselite." Another son who had gone over to Judaism expressed his love for his "mother Sateria, *menuente* of the Jewish religion" (evidently one of those pagans who had only partly embraced Judaism, yet was close enough to her new faith to be entombed at the Jewish cemetery).

About 135 of the ancient tombstones have until recently been preserved in a wall of the "Jewish Room" at the Basilica di San Giovanni from where they have now been removed to a new addition to the Vatican museum, which will be opened to the public, as explained by Professor Iosi, its director, "some time before Holy Year 1975." The small museum belonging to the Rome synagogue, which has expressed its eagerness to have just a few of the original tombstones, has to make do with some plaster copies of the originals.

Under the remaining Roman emperors, the fate of the Jews of Rome outwardly suffered only a few slight ups-and-downs. Caracalla in 212 made all inhabitants of his lands full-fledged citizens, which therefore included the Jews.

By then, for over two centuries, Jews and their Christianizing half-brothers had steadily grown apart, the separation mostly caused by the followers of Christ. If, at first, there was not much difference between the two factions (at least not from a pagan-Roman point of view, although the Christians were more persecuted than the Jews), between the two groups themselves the breach had widened constantly.

Christian anti-Semitic feeling in Rome had started with the conversion of the first pagans. About two centuries after

Flavius Josephus had closed his book on *The Jewish Wars*, a Greek-Christian writer (probably a converted Judaean Jew) by the name of Egesippus reopened it and looked at the Jewish wars and their aftermath from a Christian angle. Although Egesippus can not be called an anti-Semite, the Jews came off badly in his treatise on *The Destruction of the City of Jerusalem*, most of which he copied from Flavius Josephus. According to Egesippus' interpretation the fault lay wholly with the Jews, and whatever happened to them was entirely deserved. Egesippus' attitude, later elaborated, set the tone for centuries of anti-Semitism.

In the beginning the new Christian religion was propagated quietly and persuasively, with arguments of goodwill and kindness and the engaging watchword "We are right." But quite soon another slogan, this one of a militant nature and specifically directed against the Jews, was added to it: "You are wrong." Then the religion which had started out in the spirit of tolerance developed an angry intolerance towards the Jews. An offspring of common traditions, the new religion behaved like offspring often do—turning against its origins, and the reproach that the old did not submit to young ideas. With that conflict an historic hostility began.

For the time being Christianity was not yet an official or state religion, which it would not be till 375 when paganism was officially abandoned. In 303 Emperor Galerius prohibited the practicing of the new creed, then relented, and together with his Roman co-emperor Licinius and the aspiring West-Roman emperor Constantine it was decided in 311—just before Galerius' death—to allow the observance of the Christian faith all over the Roman Empire, in both East and West. It was tolerated, but was not yet official; nearly three centuries after the death of Christ, a new religious movement was on the eve of a great temporal victory.

Two years later, in 313, Licinius and Constantine issued the Edict of Milan, proclaiming total freedom of religion for all. Judaism was no longer the only *"religio licita."* The idea, of course, was great; an adventurous one, and its consequences were not without complexities.

Officially Constantine was still a pagan, but soon he started to act officiously as a Christian and began to look askance at the religion Christ himself had originally belonged to. As a first prohibition Jews were no longer allowed to make converts, because from now on this field of action among the pagans was exclusively reserved for Christians. If a Jew himself turned towards the new faith, his fellow Jews were not to hinder him. The Jews of Rome had done just that in bringing a certain Joseph forcibly back to the synagogue, where a committee of elders then condemned him to be whipped. Jews, moreover, were no longer to keep slaves; and if a pagan did embrace Judaism, both he and his sponsor would lose all their possessions. Marriages between Christians and Jews were forbidden, and soon were to be punished by death. When before long Judaism joined paganism as a faith that had to be fought tooth and nail, the tragic conflict deepened.

It took Constantine a few more years before he himself was baptized, a step that was only undertaken in 337 when he was already on his death-bed. But if history records his conversion that way, legend tells us a different story. It was said that Constantine's conversion was due to his suffering from leprosy. In a dream he saw Saint Peter and Saint Paul. They advised him to pay a visit to Sylvester I, who had become Bishop of Rome in 313. When Sylvester restored him to his health, it was clear to Constantine that a faith which could perform such miracles was join-worthy. Receiving the news, Constantine's mother, Queen—the later Saint—Helena, was shocked. Unlike her son, she herself had for many years been attracted to Judaism. She wrote Constantine that if he did feel the need to change religions, he would have done much better to turn to the original faith of Moses instead of to a changed version propagated by Christ.

Constantine was apparently not only upset by the motherly rebuke, but also shaken in his convictions. He went to see the Bishop of Rome, who suggested talking the whole matter over before a group composed of Christians and Jews. The course of the disputation would prove decisive. Twelve Roman rabbis were assembled before Sylvester and Constantine, who was assisted by two prominent pagans, the philosopher Craton and Zenophil, mayor of Rome.

Sylvester and the rabbis discussed paganism, God, Christ, and the Ten Commandments, with Constantine putting in a word here and there to make the balance go down in favor of Sylvester. The two pagan spokesmen were really not overly interested, because they knew beforehand they were going to lose, *whoever* was the winner. The leading rabbi by the name of Zamberi, feeling especially strong in his faith in God, was prepared to perform a miracle. He approached an ox and softly pronounced the name of Jehovah into the animal's ear. The beast, evidently unaccustomed to religious discussions of such high nature, promptly dropped dead. At this the Bishop of Rome in a stentorian voice called out the name of Christ—and the ox, possibly no longer frightened to death, came back to life. Thus was Constantine reaffirmed in his new faith. His two assistants had to join him in his new affiliation—as did the twelve rabbis, three thousand Jews of Rome, and four hundred thousand assorted pagans.

If the tale is not entirely true, it is—as the Italians have been saying for centuries—*ben trovato:* it still makes a good story. But true or not, a 13th-century wall painting in the church of San Silvestro in Tivoli near Rome pictures for us the scene of the conversation before Sylvester I, the Pope dimly outlined, two oxen up front, the rabbis looking rather perturbed, and an anxious Queen Helena pondering the fate of her son.

Chapter 9
Troubles and Tribulations

Until the year 476, when the last Roman emperor, Romulus Augustulus, was deposed—for once there was no political murder, as he was allowed to retire peacefully to a villa near Naples—the road traveled by the Jews of Rome was a difficult, downhill one. They were more and more excluded from government posts, and slowly lost all civil and political rights except as teachers, physicians, and *"militia togata"* or lawyers. The various laws, rules, and edicts that were enforced by these early Christian rulers would remain in effect for well over a thousand years—and then would not improve, but worsen.

Although the first Ecumenical Council of Nicaea in 325 took place far from Rome, its decisions were all the more felt among the Roman Jews. A definite break was made with the celebration of Easter; henceforth it was to be on a different date from the Jewish Passover, a festival that was too closely related to the days when Christ had been known only as Joshua the Messiah. Far more important, and far worse for Christian behaviour during the next sixteen centuries, was the decision that Christians "should have nothing to do with the murderers of the Lord."

The result was vituperation, and it became worse with the passing of the years. The greatest pulpit orator of the East, (Saint) John Chrysostom, declared the synagogue to be synonymous with a whorehouse. Voices in the West were less sexual in tone, but this did not mean that the admonishments of the Jews were any more elevated in tone. Roman Senator Flavius Cassiodorus, a 6th-century statesman who in later life became a monk and established a monastery, fulminated against the Jews. "Listen, you Jews!" he thundered, "listen, you obstinates! Whom do you wish to honor if you don't even know the words of your own prophet?" He meant, of course, Cassiodorus' prophet: Christ. "Come and listen to our priests, so your ears may be opened and so you may evade deafness through the grace of our Lord!"

Discovering, apparently to his surprise, that the Jews did not run as they were told, Cassiodorus exhausted his rich and extensive vocabulary in addressing them with a nomenclature that went from scorpions to wild asses, from dogs to unicorns (perhaps because they were so hard-headed).

Jews were also attacked for their rare but occasionally still practiced polygamy, which in France existed as late as the 13th century. In Rome Saint Hieronymus reproached them for seeking beautiful women (a habit still assiduously followed by the Catholic Romans of our own generation). Yet, on the whole, monogamy was the rule, with no adverse effects on the growth of the tribe. Jewish children continued to make their appearance in Trastevere with the regularity ordained by God; and then, of course, subjected to the vigorous insults by the scandalized clergy.

What did the Jews do about it? Nothing, for the new patterns of Roman power were beginning to assert themselves. Verbally assaulted and flagellated by priests, they were protected by the worldly rulers who came after the Roman emperors. Theodoric the Great, the Ostrogoth who towards the very end of the fifth century became master of all of Italy, was an Arian Christian belonging to the East-European branch of the followers of

Christ, strongly opposed to the Roman doctrine. As such he was fairly indifferent to any Roman Christian opinion regarding the Jews. He treated them benevolently, decreeing that "Jews should not be hindered or restricted by any laws."

Half a century later Emperor Justinian forbade the Jews to have Christian servants or slaves, and the situation rather reverted to the one that had existed several centuries before. In his position as temporal head of the Church, Justinian took it upon himself to advance the power of Christ. Any Jew in Rome who dared declare against the actions of a resurrection or a last judgment, or even that angels were not divine creatures, had to leave under penalty of death. The only thing for the Jews to do was to keep silent, which was difficult when openly provoked. It was a hopeless but not unfamiliar situation, in which the Jews were kicked when they were up, and kicked when they were down.

But help was in sight, and it came from a quarter it was least expected—from the Pope. Gregory the Great, from 590 and during all the fourteen years he sat on the throne of Saint Peter, suddenly made life much easier for the Jews. For the first time since Theodoric the Great, the pendulum was swinging in the opposite direction. Intervention for Jews in other countries was made via the Jews of Rome—again the Jewish capital of the world.

Gregory was the first Pope who fell back on the original teachings of the Church Fathers: "We must gain the Jews' confidence and support through our kindness, our love and benevolence, our earnest appeal. Threats and violence only will alienate them." In principle it meant that although Jews would not be allowed any new or additional rights, already-existing laws were to be honoured and observed. In reality there was not much for the Jews to hold on to, but at least there was a promise that the few rights and means of support they still had, would not be taken away. "We forbid to vilify the Jews," wrote the Pope. "We allow them to live as Romans and to have full authority over their possessions."

Pope Gregory, again through the intermediary of the Jews of Rome, interceded on several occasions. In Naples, where citizens had been exhorted to disturb the Jewish Sabbath service, he quieted down the militant spirits. When the Bishop of Palermo in an excessive act of religious zeal confiscated several synagogues, poor-houses and schools, the Pope again intervened and righted the wrongs. That is, he had them corrected as far as the schools and the houses for the poor were concerned. Since the synagogues already had been converted into churches, Gregory ordered the Jewish congregation to be paid damages. It would have been easier to turn the buildings back, and the Pope's gesture, as well-intentioned as it was, set a precedent that would be followed time and again elsewhere.

In Sardinian Gagliari, things were about just as bad and, as so often would happen later when Jews became converted to Christianity, it was an apostate Jew who started the trouble. A day after his conversion this Jewish heretic rushed into the local synagogue and put a picture of Christ in front of the *haron akodesh*, the holy Ark in which the Torah rolls are kept. It was a calamitous event for the Jewish congregation, but again the Pope came to the rescue. This time the synagogue was not handed over to the priest with damages to be paid to the Jews; instead the priest and the new convert were rebuked.

The ninth century started most propitiously for the Jews of Rome. On Christmas day of the year 800 Charlemagne was crowned Roman emperor by Pope Leo III. Among his retinue was a Jewish doctor by the name of Isaac. He would not be the first medical advisor to keep either emperor or Pope in good health, and to the Jews of Rome it was a hopeful sign of perhaps better times to come.* There was more than one Jew in his immediate entourage, Charlemagne having been attracted to a famous rabbi, Moses ben Kalomynos.

If a few Jews were converted to Christianity, the reverse—although rarely—also happened. In 838 the private chaplain of King Louis the Pious, a priest by the name of Bodo, felt the need to abjure the extravagance and decadence of the French court.

---

*The doctor was not the only Isaac in Charlemagne's service. In 797 he had sent a Jewish merchant from Aachen, also named Isaac, as guide and interpreter with an imperial mission to Caliph Harun al Rashid. Four years later Isaac was the only member of the group to return, the others having died from hardship on the way home.

Having copiously participated in the charmed life of the palace, he decided that a pilgrimage to Rome would serve his purpose twofold—he would lead an ascetic life en route, and once in Rome he would pray for absolution.

Louis the Pious agreed wholeheartedly with his chaplain's plans and took advantage of his trip to send presents to the Pope and various churches in the Holy City. Arriving on the other side of the Alps, Chaplain Bodo met a number of Jews—*"enemies of humanity"* a chronicler calls them—whose views on religious affairs rather interested him. It could well be that the daughter of one of his new companions also caught his fancy, because later on he did marry a Jewess. For the time being, however, he decided that his life had been totally in error and that Judaism was the only religion that could put him on a sounder, purer path.

Bodo continued to Rome without delivering his presents. Instead he sold his slaves to pagans (which was even worse than selling them to Christians), and he and his nephew who accompanied him both turned Jew. On 23 June 838 they had themselves circumcized, and let hair and beard grow. Bodo then took the name of Eleazar and married his Jewish love; and the story, not unexpectedly, created a storm in Christian and Jewish Rome, as well as throughout the rest of Europe.

Twenty years after the Bodo incident the Jews of Rome could point to another astonishing sphere of influence. In 858 Pope Nicholas I woke up one morning to find that Jewish sartorial style had invaded the Church. The Bishop of Orta, a city north of Rome, had ordered his clerics to wear fur coats that were exact copies of those worn by the Jews. Since the Pope was only too well aware that Chaplain Bodo's fairly recent conversion had started with simply *looking* at Jewish clothes—although perhaps with a woman inside—he took energetic steps to quell the new fashion, and ordered his bishop "to swear off the dress of the heretics."

The Jews of Rome now had been waiting for a long time without any apparent indication of the coming of the Messiah, that is, their own approved or "official" one. Still they were patient, because there was a consoling legend that promised the arrival of the Messiah 990 years after the destruction of the Temple, which therefore would be in 1060. Towards the end of the tenth century, therefore, they began searching for signs, because the Messiah certainly would not arrive in their midst without prior warning.

The expectations of the Messiah's arrival went hand in hand with a variety of mysterious and very involved stories. Reading like written versions of a Hieronymus Bosch painting, they told of dreams in which souls (looking rather like human arteries) were painlessly extracted from good people, while causing infinite suffering to evil ones.

More down-to-earth Jews of the tenth century preferred realistic praying in their Roman synagogues to any belief in nebulous dreams. "Those who fell under David, before the Temple was built, died because they did not press on enough for its *con*struction," they said. "Then how much more should we pray today—after its *de*struction." Somehow the wisdom of this thought had an echo of the story of the foxes and the fishes.

Instead of the Messiah, German Emperor Otto II set foot in Rome in 980 to reinstate Pope Benedict VII, whose predecessor had been set to flight by a Roman aristocrat named Crescentius. Having accomplished his task, Otto continued his way down the peninsula, where in 982 he defeated the Saracens in a great battle in Calabria, only to be disastrously ambushed by them shortly afterwards.

Otto II had to run for his life, and it is recorded that a certain Kalonymos, a Jew with the same name as the rabbi who had accompanied Charlemagne, lent Otto his horse.

Thus, in Rome, the tenth century could be said to have come to a fitting close. The Jews were still in residence, the first French Pope, Sylvester II, now sat on the throne of Saint Peter, and deep below the church lay Otto II, buried with the proper religious honors—a German emperor who had been saved by a Jewish horse.

Chapter 10
Love, Sex, and Prostitution

The Millennium of the thousand-year-Reich, that Jewish apocalyptic utopia which Hitler would appropriate as his own, did not get off to a propitious start in Rome after the year one thousand. Hardly had the first century of the second millennium begun, when the Jews were accused of a grave mischief—of having caused the flooding of the city. It was neither the first nor the last time that rivers would break their dikes, but when the Tiber ran wild in 1021, the Jews had done it. Nor was that all: in the same year they were also accused of having caused an earthquake. If the second accusation did not make any more sense than the first, at least it showed consistency: anyone capable of causing a river to overflow would surely only have to lift a finger to make the earth tremble. In fact it was not quite a hand-movement, but the flickering of an eyelid. A Jew was supposed to have looked at a passing crucifix—or it could also be that he had *not* looked at it; in the search for any kind of reason to beat up a Jew or two, the argument could be put both ways. And since the crucifix had to be resanctified one way or the other, the Jews were beaten up in either case.

Jews had evidently worked strange wonders with the weather and terrestrial catastrophes before. In 1017 a violent storm raged through Rome and its countryside. The Pope and the citizens were in despair, cursing the elements and praying to have the wind stop. Then someone had a luminous idea. Who had done it? A Jew, of course! So a wretched devil was picked up, and after having been put through a certain number of inquisitorial exercises, he readily confessed to have insulted the image of Christ. Persecutions made Jews excellent human barometers—they often (but, unfortunately, not often enough), saw the storm coming. In 1017 the culprit first had been hanged, then burned at the stake. Rome was perhaps a shade grateful to that tortured eleventh-century Jew, for the very moment he confessed, the storm had abated. Had he not done so, who knows how long the hurricane would have gone on blowing?

The Roman Jews fared better in 1349. The black plague was decimating thousands upon thousands of people in Europe, and according to Vatican records "the Jews were burned all over Germany." In Rome, however, Pope Clement VI held out a protecting hand. There were anarchic conditions in town and the plague did hit Italy, but the Jews were kept from being persecuted because the Pope declared that contrary to the widespread German accusations, the Jews had *not* poisoned the wells.

In a later crisis Rome did not get off so easily. The plague hit the city brutally in 1468. Who—or what—was at fault? The Jews suffered with the rest of the inhabitants. Every day between forty and fifty people died in the streets, and finally the Pope himself had to leave Rome to save himself. In 1470, it was the Tiber that struck again. Its waters rose and covered the city as far as the Corso. There was little time—or logic—to accuse the Jews this time, because by now a great many of them had permanently crossed the Bridge With The Four Heads and were living on the opposite side of the river, where they themselves were the first victims of the devastation.

The move to the other side of the Tiber had started several centuries earlier. A fairly important number of Jews did remain in Trastevere, where in the fourteenth century a good many Jewish doctors lived near the Rome Medical School. But on the left bank of the Tiber they grouped together in that part of town which later would be known as "The Ghetto." Not only had the Bridge With The Four Heads now taken on the name of *Pons Judaeorum*, or "Jewish Bridge," but there was already a *Platea Judaeorum* and *Ruga Judaeorum*, or Jewish Square and Jewish Street, appellations that would be found all over Europe then and later. (In Amsterdam Rembrandt used to live on the *Jodenbreestraat*, the *Broad Street of the Jews*.) Yet the bridge area was not a compulsory Jewish section of Rome. Jews also lived elsewhere, in places of their own choice—there was even a Jewish neighbourhood near the Porta Nomentana, not far from the early catacombs under the Villa Torlonia.

The more than a dozen ancient synagogues that had existed for a thousand years, had all disappeared. After the synagogue in Trastevere burned down in 1268 with the loss of twenty-one Torah rolls—which prompted the Trasteverini to destroy the nearby Jewish cemetery—new prayer houses, some four in number, were constructed amidst the growing community on the other side of the Tiber. Several centuries later the Spanish Jews bought either the nearby Cenci Palace, a building very much in the center of Roman Jewish life, or a house right next door, and made it into the Aragonese synagogue.*

Food was an important item in Roman Jewish life, and dishes were prepared with great care even then. Spices such as cinnamon and ginger were frequently used. *Pasta*, the modern staple food of the Italians, had yet to be brought back in the form of spaghetti from China by Marco Polo, but many other dishes that are found on Italian tables today, were already known. Fish was a delicacy, and probably as expensive in Rome

---

*The Palazzo Cenci nowadays houses the Pompiere restaurant, and nearby, on the Via Monte dé Cenci, is the equally well-known Piperno establishment. Both excell in *carciofi alla Giudia*—"Jewish artichokes"—a crisp oil-fried Roman specialty of which the origin probably goes back to those early times when the Jews, already experts in good cooking, moved to this part of town.

then as it is now. At festivals wine was made into a grog by adding honey and spices. There were fluffy pastries filled with fish, rice, or cheese, like our own Roman *pasta sfoglia* or the thready—and not so light—*supplì*. In food there is seemingly little new under the Italian sun.

When eating at home, knives used to be covered with a napkin before saying grace. Apparently the idea had started when an especially sensitive religious Jew was so overcome with melancholia as he recalled the destruction of the Temple while pronouncing the words "And next year in Jerusalem," that in a sudden attack of total despair he grabbed the knife nearest to him and committed suicide. Life and appetites, if not religious melodrama, were better served by the new arrangement.

Thus life was livable enough during these first centuries of the second millennium. Being able to reside wherever they wanted to, homes—at least those of the well-to-do Jews—were often comfortable and large. Street dress was important, and fashions were followed with great attention. Women wore blouses embellished with flowers and bird designs. Elaborately embroidered belts were *très à la mode*, holding tight the long trains flowing down from the blouse. Veils also were in fashion, and so were gold- and silver-threaded hair nets. Another female piece of jewelry was the house key, which—in order not to forget it—was cleverly made into a broach, an idea that as yet has not been rediscovered by modern jewelers.

Subsequently, a self-restricting anti-luxury role on clothes was adopted by a council of Italian rabbis. Extravagance became taboo, and anyone who felt that fashion was more important, was fined—the husband being made responsible for his wife's frivolity. Out went dresses that showed colored lining through narrow slits which rhythmically opened and closed with the swinging movement of the body; short sleeves which presented too much naked flesh to the curious eye were henceforth forbidden; velvet and silk were frowned upon. Brides could wear the lovely golden hairnet for one month only—then back to the drudgery of the veil; silver buckles on men's belts were to weigh no more than six ounces, and similar female accessories were restricted to a maximum of about twice that weight. A man could wear one ring, women no more than three (but there were no limits as to size). On the other hand that luxurious object known as a handkerchief—a rare item—was allowed, on condition that it was sewn onto the sleeve.

Roman engagements usually lasted from six months to a year. The groom-to-be was allowed to visit his betrothed, but as Rodocanachi has remarked *sans en abuser*—without taking advantage of her. The luxury restrictions were equally applied to the giving of presents—the girl was allowed to give her fiancé two handkerchiefs, two shirts, and a prayer shawl. The man's presents were of a somewhat more intimate nature—a pair of slippers, stockings, and a pair of garters.

At weddings, where tables were laden with ducks, pheasants, and much other game, no more than twenty men, plus ten married and five unmarried women, could be invited over and above the members of the family, who were not to exceed beyond the range of second cousins. Given the traditional connubiality of both town and tribe, one wonders how the festive gatherings could have been kept so restricted among Roman Jews.

In the beginning weddings were allowed even on Saturdays. Much later—towards the year 1600—Tuesdays were often preferred, because then on a Thursday the groom could complain to the Council of Rabbis in case his bride turned out not to have been a virgin. If the wedding therefore involved a widow, Thursday was a lucky day, for only rarely would the widow have a maiden-like constitution. It was also advisable to marry at the age of eighteen, because any Jew who was still unmarried at twenty was automatically suspected of having a mistress with whom he lived in sin.

Musicians at weddings were never Jews—Christians were hired for that purpose. Dancing pleased everybody, and even though mixed couples were frowned upon by the rabbis, sexless twirling was even more frowned upon by the participants themselves. To keep the betrothed apart during the last week before the wedding, there would be separate parties for the sexes every evening.* Gambling and chess were widespread, but betting was supposed to be a low activity. Gambling was allowed on Saturday, but not for money, and anyone who discovered betting for stakes was to inform the Elders. The culprit would then be fined; but there is no evidence that the Elders' treasury waxed prosperous on this arrangement. Another habit frowned upon was the singing of worldly melodies in mixed company. But on this point at least there was little difference between Roman Jews and Christians, and despite synagogue and church, the amateurs of vocal harmony and perhaps even ribaldry usually won out against the straight-faced Elders.

Indeed the Elders in fact had to worry about things that were a little more serious than Italian songs of amusing if dubious meaning. How to keep the faithful on an altogether straight-and-narrow path? The *fattori* or magistrates of the Jewish community were increasingly disturbed. The rich got richer, poverty spread among the lower classes and soon prostitution came more and more into the open. In a field where the twain shall always meet, the law of offer and demand made equal inroads among Jews and Christians, for as always has been the case, sex knew no religion.

Early in the fifteenth century the Jewish magistrates proclaimed that Jewish men should not have intercourse with prostitutes *or* with Christian women; nor should they otherwise behave immorally. (The phraseology makes one wonder whether the prostitutes were Jewish and whether the Christian women were strictly honorable!) The matter of the virginal bride also came under close scrutiny. It was decided that an engaged couple were not to meet before the wedding day, nor were they to be allowed even to see each other.

Of course, Rome even then was a fairly large and lax city, and the Vatican did not exactly set a high and holy tone of decency. While still a cardinal, the later Pope Alexander Borgia had four children (including the famous Lucrezia)—with his mistress. Mores were rather loose all around. Church Fathers were even more worried than the Jewish Elders. It could happen that a

*Such separate or sexually *apartheid*-dancing-parties are still customary at Yemenite weddings in Israel.

Jewish male might sleep with an honorable Christian prostitute "by mistake."

If not occasionally encouraged by a smile, Jewish prostitutes had nothing more to fear from their co-religionists than dirty looks. But once the Church Fathers had made their decision, greater dangers set in. Under Alexander III fifty Jewish prostitutes were condemned to be burned at the stake. In 1498 a Jew was literally cut to pieces because he had intercourse with a Christian woman. A tragically confused case was brought to light early in the sixteenth century. After a prostitute had been arrested and condemned to be whipped, someone mentioned that she was "Jewish." The punishment promptly was changed to burning at the stake, and the sentence was duly and swiftly carried out. Now religion got mixed up in the proceedings, because it was discovered that the presumably Jewish prostitute actually had been baptised, making her a good, albeit not entirely pure Christian. So the people's fury turned against the evil-tongued informer who was cruelly manhandled. Was there a Roman moral to be learned from this story—namely, that if a Jewish woman wanted to ply safely the prostitute's trade, it was advisable for her to turn Christian first?

Pietro Aretino, a satirist of the early sixteenth century, wrote about a baptized Jewish prostitute by the name of Niccolosa who used the various Roman churches as her hunting ground and playing field. She never ended up at the stake, nor did she have to undergo any other type of official punishment. The charming seductress used to wander through nave and transept with one pious eye in her jeweled Bible, the other eye roaming with a come-hither look to catch the flesh of the occasional devil, all the while loudly intoning the saintly liturgy with an air of virtuous and devotional piety. The strategem worked miracles, and as Aretino informs us, there were princes and dukes, prelates, lawyers, merchants, and cardinals among her admirers, accosting her in holy whispers that deftly used the love-thy-neighbor theme to promote a possible rendezvous.

A Dutch visitor to Rome, who spent some time in the holy city towards the beginning or the middle of the sixteenth century has left us a vivid impression of the role of public sex and society which he witnessed. In a series of epigrams which he published under the title of *Trias Romana*, he had the following to say about prostitution along the Tiber:

Three groups are well-dressed in Rome:
Popes, mules, and prostitutes.

Three things are prevalent in Rome:
Lust, church clothes, and dishonor.

Three things one learns in Rome:
Never to fast, to whore around, and to be disobedient.

With three items one does business in Rome:
Christ, religious lives, and women.

Three things one finds in Rome in all shapes and conditions:
Holy places, ruins, and whores.

We do not know why this Dutchman was so set upon telling his countrymen all about Roman lewdness, but it is obvious that to him there was no difference between prostitutes of Jewish and those of any other faith. Nor was there, one may presume, among the Romans. Sexual allures of the most conspicuous kind were, then as now, enjoyed irrespective of nationality, color, or cult. The appreciation of certain Jewish women penetrated into the highest circles of the city, and when it became known to Pope Sixtus V that the son of the Duke of Parma had lost his heart to a Roman Jewish beauty, the papal wrath decreed that the young man should be punished by death. Christian Rome was aghast and outraged, for there was (perhaps as there always is) a difference of opinion on the subject of sex between the people and the clergy. The young man's execution was set for two o'clock in the afternoon. The Roman ruse was to put all the official clocks of the city one hour forward. At the stroke of two the Pope relented, and gave the victim *a posteriori* pardon, being sure that by now justice had already been done. The prince was saved, and on this agonizing note the recorded tale ends. What the historian of the Pope's Jews would also like to know is what happened to the lovely signorina.

Chapter 11
The Jewish Pope

All through the beginning and middle of the eleventh century, Papal candidates and triumphant Popes were constantly at odds with each other. Pope fought Pope, family fought family, faction fought faction, and (as a side line, and often main line) Pope fought Emperor.

In 1077 Gregory VII forced German Emperor Henry IV to visit him in Canossa and to ask forgiveness for having opposed him so violently. Henry took revenge in 1084 when he besieged his papal enemy on his own homegrounds. Gregory had to abandon the city and flee to Salerno. (Before he died there a year later he passed on a bit of imperial advice and informed the King of Spain that it was entirely wrong to let Jews hold more important posts than Christians, because this would mean "oppressing the Church of Christ and elevating the synagogue of the heathen.")

The story was repeated many times over. Through it all, Rome slowly became subdivided into a certain number of family enclaves, private cities within the city, owned and governed by the Orsinis, Colonnas, Vitelleschis, Frangipanis, and others, all with their own private armies. For centuries these families and groups would play musico-clerical chairs, with the difference that it cost fortunes in the effort to occupy—and to hold—the Holy Seat.

Some of the money involved was supplied by the son of a man whose name had been Baruch, the Hebrew word for *Blessed*. Baruch, of course, was not the first Jew to be converted. Others before him had accepted the faith of Christ as his or her own, including (as we have seen) Jewish ladies of easy virtue or virtuous ladies who were Jewish, and turned to Christianity to save their own skin (or perhaps, that of their beloved). But there were also many who had changed faith in all sincerity. One of these semi-honest converts—"semi" because money was involved—was Baruch. After his baptism he did not look for an entirely new Christian name, but took the Italian-Latin literal translation of his own—*Benedictus*.*

After his conversion Baruch had been fully accepted by Roman society as a rich new Christian, and he had been allowed to marry a lady with a noble bloodline. Their son, Leo de Benedictus Cristiano—*Leo, son of Baruch the Christian*—became one of the wealthiest men of Rome, and was still living in Trastevere in 1058.

The family influence then spread. Around 1080 Leo's son Petrus Leonis, whose name was to become that of the family (Pierleoni), and who owned the whole island in the Tiber, moved across the Bridge With The Four Heads to live in a fortified home on top of the ruins of the Theater of Marcellus. When in 1099 Pope Urban II had to flee from the Vatican, pursued by yet another German-created anti-pope Clement III, he rushed to the fortress-home of his friend Pierleoni and died there in comfort.

Petrus Leonis kept on siding with the right Popes, and at one time shared the government of all of Rome with a member of

*Much later other Italian Jews known as Cohn, Cohen or Coen (meaning *High Priest*) would italianize their name to *Sacerdoti* (or priest), without being converted.

the influential Frangipani family. Later on, in 1119, he fought those same Frangipanis when they imprisoned the Pierleoni-supported Pope Gelasius II. Those were auspicious times, for having abandoned the religion of the people who supplied the very first Pope, the Pierleonis now could more or less create their own. It was not Petrus Leonis' fault that he never succeeded in accomplishing this during his lifetime. Under his guidance his son had become a cardinal, and twice he had tried to get him elected to the papacy, only to fail each time. Yet after his death, this son in 1130 climbed to the Church's highest post and took the name of Anacletus II.

With that event, grave consequences ensued. While Anacletus was crowned by the majority of cardinals, a minority faction elected Innocent II, also a Roman by birth, and in doing so created a situation that tore the Church asunder. Innocent had to leave Rome, went to France and was received as the official Pope by the enormously influential Bernard de Clairvaux, later a Saint. Bernard immediately set out to win support for Innocent, leaving no stone unturned to blacken Anacletus who was called every name in the book, and one that wasn't: "the Jewish Pope." Bernard accused him, moreover, of all imaginable evil including an incestuous relationship with his sister.

Certainly Anacletus' great-grandfather had been a Jew, but he himself had served the church well, and in 1123 had presided over the Church Councils in Beauvais and Chartres. But some men never could be reconciled with a Jewish family presiding over the whole Church. His antagonists, of course, overlooked that Josua Christós had come from a similar family, and that Saint Peter and Saint Paul had not been born as Christians. But in the historic struggle for power in the Church, during those centuries more influenced by worldly than by ecclesiastical ideals, many of the combatants seemed to forget a great many things which were self-evident to others. The campaign against Anacletus grew more vicious. Anacletus' ancestors had an unblemished name both as Jews and Christians—unblemished as far as this was possible in a society where all were engaged in a brutish battle for power and money—and a 19th-century French author, Bedarride, even used the words "Peter the Good" when discussing Anacletus' father.

Shortly after "the Jewish Pope's" death in 1138 the Pierleonis switched sides; and Anacletus' brother Jordan, who had been elected virtual dictator of Rome in 1143, came into violent conflict with Eugene III. The Pope countered the attack with his most bloodless but also most severe weapon: he excommunicated the great-grandson of the apostate Jew Baruch. Yet in the end Jordan and the people of Rome gained supremacy; and in 1149 the Pope was obliged to leave Rome for the second time, to die in France four years later. Whether Jordan Pierleoni remained excommunicated is an unanswered question, but he certainly did not complete the circle in returning to the faith of his forefathers. Yet the Church must have forgiven Jordan, for the quayside along the Tiber—not far from the modern synagogue today—is called the Lungotevere dei Pierleoni, in commemoration of the family that brought forth Anacletus.

From a religious point of view the presence of a "Jewish Pope" in Rome left the Jews of the city totally indifferent. To them an apostate Jew was an execrable human being. Yet at the same time the Pope was their Master, and as such the tradition of the Baruch family, represented by the Pierleonis, carried a certain weight. The story of the Jewish Pope therefore lived on along the Tiber, and turned up now and again in different forms, creating a series of legends that were told and retold through the ages.

One version had it that the Pope was the son of the famous German Rabbi Simon ben Isaac ben Adun of Mainz. Sometimes this son's name is given as Andreas, at other times the boy was called Elhanan—"On whom God has Mercy." Having been forcefully baptised as a babe, the intelligent child rose quickly in the Christian hierarchy and crowned his career as Pope. At that point doubts about his religion and his family started to torment him, and he finally threatened to kill his servants if they continued to decline to reveal the circumstances of his birth. When the secret and the whole truth came out, the Pope sent for Rabbi

Simon and inquired about his children. All were accounted for—except one, and the Rabbi did not mention him. The Pope pressed him and at long last the Rabbi from Mainz had to confess—many years before one of his children had been kidnapped. Birthmarks and other signs as indicated by the Rabbi—the Jewish youngster after all had been circumcised—checked entirely with those of the Pope. He was now convinced there was only one thing left for him to do: abdicate. So he called the Romans together in front of the Vatican tower and made an impassioned speech against Christianity, which had evolved from Judaism—the only True Faith. The cardinals, taken aback by this peculiar turn of events, thought the Pontiff mad. By now the Pope was beyond Christian argumentation. He looked around him and disconcertedly noticed the precariousness of his situation: he was standing all alone high up on a tower. An angry group of cardinals raged down below. An endless number of stairs stretched under his feet to the ground. The Pope resolved all difficulties by throwing himself across the parapets. Some say he disappeared into thin air. In any event, with his leap into the Unknown, the story ends.

A variant of this papal Jewish legend starts out the same way—once again the boy is stolen by a Christian maid-servant. She has him baptised; he is brought up by the priests; but then, at an already advanced age, she informs him about his antecedents. The Pope, who had been puzzled for years about his *petite différence* from other priests, now had good reason to start wondering even more. A clever man, he ordered the persecution of the Jews of Mainz, knowing full well that a delegation would be sent to him promptly to try and buy off the threat, a money-making manipulation that was often practiced by Popes during the Middle Ages. Even though the Pope was not yet blessed by infallibility, his premonition turned out to be right.

In due time Rabbi Simon arrived in Rome at the head of the Jewish Mainzer Elders, pleading their case. They were surprised by the Pope's ready acceptance of their arguments; but they gave it no further thought, happy to have circumvented the danger. That night the Pope, an excellent chess player, invited Rabbi Simon to come to him for a little game. The Rabbi, a renowned master in his own town, realized he might lose if he would not attack with an ingenious series of moves of which he alone knew the secret. "Check," said the Rabbi. But the Pope's divine inspiration must have warned him about his opponent's highly intricate technique; for he nullified the Rabbi's advance by an even more skilful move. The result was obvious—father recognized son, and son recognized father. This time the story did not end with a flying descent from the tower, but with a stealthy departure for Mainz in the dark of night. According to legend the Romans never did find out what happened to their Pope. Some thought, and a few are even said to have said, that he had simply slipped away to the house of his mistress, since this would not have been the first time that such a thing had happened.

The Popes, of course, were often strange and unpredictable personalities during the Middle Ages, and in their treatment of the Jews they were quite erratic. As Popes and anti-Popes fought each other, the Jews often became a pawn in the middle. Some Popes decided everybody should be Christian, and if the Jews did not want to change religions the easy way, then they should be forced. The most amazing statement of this time was pronounced when German King Henry IV decided that all forcibly baptized Jews would be allowed to change over again. "Treason!" thundered Clement III in 1097, himself an anti-Pope; and he angrily added that "the sacrament of the baptism is being violated by the Jews!" Force having been used to baptize them in the first place, the best one can say about this papal statement is that it had the usual logic of hypocrisy.

The papal zeal of persecution often turned with the political wind. When the Vicar of Christ was threatened by war, he would be benevolent to the Jews. At other times he would fulminate from Rome or from any of the other cities he was voluntarily or forcibly sojourning in, simply to show that he had not forgotten the evil Jewish heathens. The Jews of Rome—and sometimes the Jews all over the world—would be threatened with hell on earth. It was, as we know, not always empty rhetoric. Perhaps the Roman Jews already were so italianized that they, too, had become past masters in the art of *adattarsi:* a new proclamation is recognized, the details are circumvented, the dangers are aborted, shoulders are shrugged—it was all meant for someone else.

Was there ever a time in this great transitional period when the Jews of Rome were not in a peculiar and difficult position? The good Popes were sometimes bad, and the bad Popes sometimes good. In 1073 Alexander II complimented the Vicomte de Béranger in southern France for protecting the Jews: "We have seen with pleasure that you have protected the Jews from the death that threatened them. God does not rejoice in the spilling of blood in His name."

Nicholas IV, no friend of the "heathens," declared in 1291: "Recently the Jews of Rome asked for protection when they were insulted and threatened by the clergy. We do not want Christian love to be so inflamed as to result in insults and injuries to the Jews. We hereby declare that they are protected by us against torture, and that those who act against our wishes will be punished."

But the times were turbulent. In 1095 the crusades had started in the name of the Glory of Christ; unfortunately they often degenerated into expeditions for personal glory only. A century later one of the worst possible Popes—from a Jewish point of view—Innocent III, dealt European Jewry one of its deadliest blows with his Bull of 1215. In it he reiterated and more or less reconfirmed all previously enacted anti-Jewish decisions, setting a powerful example that would not be abrogated until the French Revolution of 1789 enacted legislation which re-established human liberty and dignity. The Bull, moreover, decreed that crusaders would not have to pay interest on money borrowed from the Jews, which was an ingenious way to get money at cost-price; and to make matters worse, Innocent made the rule retroactive.

Yet once again the miracle of Rome manifested itself. The Popes decreed, the priests everywhere readily applied the law more severely than its text indicated, and then in Rome itself the Popes relented, not infrequently after accepting bribes simulated as heavy taxes. Money could always be used by the Popes, either for private or for religious purposes—and especially after the crusades had started, large sums were always welcome.

Pope Alexander II was one of the first to extol the virtue of fighting the Moslems. At the same time, once again, a good word was put in for the Jews: "It is the duty of all good Christians to fight the Saracens who persecute the true believers, and to save the Jews, who are peaceful and inoffensive."

Urban II who, as we have seen, in the end died so peacefully at the home of the Pierleonis, in 1095 could never have dreamt that his exhortation to reconquer the Holy Land from Islam would have had such disastrous effects for the Jews. Killing with God's blessing became the watchword of the century, to be repeated every time the organisation of a new crusade needed some militant enthusiasm. Starting with the first crusade in 1096, the priests would shout their orations from pulpit and street corner, promising a special place in Heaven to anyone joining the armies that set off for the East.

There were, of course, thousands of poor people who were only too glad to leave a miserable life in Europe, and to look forward to adventure, freedom, and financial gain at the expense of the Moslem. They joined up in droves, many of them doubtless with a purely religious idea in mind. There were others, priests and monks among them, who in their eagerness indulged in their crusading spirit even before leaving for Jerusalem.

While the Popes tried to keep the Roman movement peaceful, disciples in Germany and France felt that the fiery cause called on their immediate services. "You are off to Jerusalem to fight infidels," they cried, "and you forget that the Jews, those archenemies of Christ, are right among us? Why let them live in peace as long as you are out to get the unbeliever? Let a glorious feat of arms crown your efforts before leaving to fight the other heathens! *Let's get the Jews!* . . ."

Even after the crusades were over, the idea lingered on. In 1298 a German nobleman with the name of Rindfleisch took up the cry for Jewish extermination, and an estimated hundred thousand Jews were enthusiastically massacred.*

*Later another German grasped the idea of making the Jew the scapegoat for everything that was wrong with the world. His henchmen were identified by armbands, and they followed their leader with such dumb devotion that untold thousands of Jews were victimized. The leader of this rabble was not a house painter, but a village tavern owner, who went by the name of *König der Armleder*—King of the Leather Armbanders. He ranted and murdered between 1336 and 1338, some six hundred years before Hitler.

Chapter 12
Talmud Burnings

To be sure, there were and always had been certain Jews who refused to accept the monks' and priests' anti-Jewish speeches. They were neither gospel truth nor irresistible. If the Church tried to convert the Jews, then the Jews would try to convert the Church, even though it was a slightly uneven contest. After the first huge upswing of pro-Jewish sentiment under the early Romans, there had been a thousand years of quiet in Jewish proselytizing. During the 13th century there were some efforts to impress the Christian world, to speak out, to convince the Christians that not everything was bad about the religion which even Christ had practiced. But Pope Gregory IX, who was to excommunicate Emperor Frederick II, put an immediate stop to it when he was crowned in 1227 at the age of 82. After that the Jews already felt pleased enough when they were simply allowed to breathe, and it was not till the end of that same century that a Jew arrived in Rome who took up the great challenge. In 1280 Abulafia tried nothing less than to convert the Pope.

Born Abraham ben Samuel Abu'lafia, in Spain, in the round-figured Jewish year 5000 which corresponds to 1240 A.D., Abulafia had a full life behind him when he arrived in Rome at the age of forty. Brought up in the country of his birth, the "Godly Spirit" had seized him when he was twenty. He traveled extensively through Greece and the Middle East, trying to find—among other marvels—the mythical river Sambation. The river had already intrigued Flavius Josephus, who wrote that for six days the river bed was dry, but that every Seventh Day the water flowed abundantly.

Twice Abulafia had a vision in which God ordered him to go to Rome. It took him about ten years of constant wandering to reach the Tiber; but once there, he did not lose much time. His reasoning was quite plausible; if he could persuade the Pope to accept Judaism, all of Christianity would follow.

The Pope, Nicholas III, was resident at Soriano, a small town near Viterbo, north of Rome. Driven on by his mystical belief, Abulafia made his way up the Via Cassia and entered the castle courtyard. He never got any further. The Pope, who had been informed about Abulafia's plans, had given standing orders to throw him into prison as soon as the Papal guards set eyes on him. Even failing that, Abulafia's plan would have been in vain. Four days before he reached Soriano, Nicholas III had died.

But if the Pope did not turn Jew, more than a few Jews had turned Christian through the years. Some of them accepted the new faith in all sincerity and even with humility. Yet there were others who felt that an excessive show of apostolic zeal was necessary and proper to prove their devotional enthusiasm.

A good many such "Ultras" existed through the ages. They were the apostates whose first act as a new Christian would be to profane the synagogue by putting up pictures of the Virgin Mary within its walls. Usually their actions were merely of local nuisance value only, resulting in some minor communal upset without any wider repercussions. The renegade in those cases would not be taken too seriously.

In the early part of the 13th century there was, however, a French apostate Jew whose missionary zeal had invidious and lasting effects. Nicolas Donin was without any doubt an extraordinary man of the most despicable character. He was, as a Christian, a monstrous Christian, and if he had remained a Jew, he would have been a monstrous Jew.

In France, Donin had raged against the Jews, and as the Dominican defender of Christ, he had participated in one of the century's most infamous religious discussions between members of the two faiths. Then the monk came to Rome. Aware of how Donin had been trying to get the Talmud openly burned in Paris, the Jews of Rome had more than an inkling of what to expect. The Pope at this time was still Gregory IX, now close to 95 years of age. He had already decided against a delegation of French Jews who had come to Rome to beg the Holy Father to take some action to countermand Donin's Talmud-burning activities.

The Roman Jews decided on a day of fasting. But how would empty stomachs serve as an adequate weapon against Donin's propaganda? A special prayer dates back to these days:

> Destroy, Oh Lord, the dastard villain,
> Who accusingly speaks against Thy Law,
> The Law he broke and honors not,
> The Law that comforts and gives Life.

> See, Oh Lord, how he mocks Thy name,
> And threatens Israel with the oppressor's lash,
> My voice cries out to my Lord for help,
> The enemy is after my life.

> His angry cries I hear in panic,
> Caught I am, yes, caught in his net,
> "I am not after your possessions," he shouts,
> "I am after your very life!"

But Donin's words weighed far heavier with the Pope than the Jews' prayer, and on June 20, 1239 Gregory IX ordered the burning of the Talmud. Perhaps it was the Pope's old age that caused the execution of the order to be postponed. It was certainly not due to a sudden change of mind on the part of the

French apostate. Five years later Innocent IV reconfirmed the order, and the triumphant campaign of the ex-Jew Nicolas Donin set off a series of *autos-da-fé* that would light up the skies through the ages.

There were Talmuds burned under Innocent IV in 1244, and more were burned under Clement IV in 1265, and under Honorius IV in 1285—for some mysterious or accidental reason all of them the fourth Pope in order of name-succession. But it was not until about eighty years after Nicolas Donin's infamous initiative that the Jews of Rome found themselves faced by an even stronger movement to burn their books. This time the initiative came from a woman, named Sanga or Sancha, the wife of King Robert of Naples. Her feelings about the Jews, were, if anything, no less intense than Donin's. It was said of her that "in her hate she resembled Haman"* and that she favored the idea of having "the name of the Jews never again mentioned on this earth." Her deeds matched her words, and even though she lived in Naples, it was Rome that would bear the brunt of her campaign.

Encouraged by his wife, Robert did all he could to get the Jewish religion suppressed and, if possible, to have the Jews banned from the city. It was said that the Jewish community of Rome offered the Pope—who at the time was still in Avignon—anywhere between 20,000 and 100,000 pieces of gold, if he would rescind the order. In point of fact a Jewish delegation from Rome did go to Avignon. Yet nothing helped. In 1322 on the eve of the Jewish harvest festival of *Shevuoth*, (which is celebrated seven weeks after Easter, and more or less coincides with Whitsun) the Talmud was ordered to be solemnly and triumphantly burned. To heighten the festivities, at least one Jew was burned with the books. The Pope at the time was John XXII. (It would take six more centuries before the next Pope who took the name of John, John XXIII, would wipe out the bitterness that had stuck to his namesake.)

*The villain in the Book of Esther, who had suggested that all Jews be hanged.

Twenty-five years later there was another burning in Rome, and again the Jews were involved. This time, however, neither they nor their books were destroyed. The burning instead involved a man who had been admired and helped by the Jews—Cola di Rienzo.

At the corner of the Via San Bartolomeo de' Vaccinari and the Via del Progresso, right in the very heart of the Roman ghetto, a plaque was unveiled in 1872 commemorating *"The birth near here of the last tribune* COLA DI RIENZO*."* Two years previously Italy had been unified, and the nation created as we know it today. An end had been made to the existence of the Papal States; the Pope was no longer the Ruler of Rome; and the word "liberty" had taken on a physical meaning in the city. The memory of Cola di Rienzo, who for a great part of his life had dreamt of liberty and who had tried to make the Pope submissive to the worldly ruler of Rome (for a short time Cola himself)—finally was celebrated openly by its citizens. A street too was named after him. It runs straight from the Tiber to the Vatican which he had tried to make the city's servant.

Before 1870 Cola di Rienzo was probably the only ruler of Rome who had had an intimate knowledge of how the Jews lived. Brought up amidst Jews, his youth was certainly as poor as that of the youngsters he knew and probably played with as a boy. His mother was a washerwoman, who also sold buckets of water from door to door. The house she lived in stood between the later-built Church of Saint Thomas and the principle synagogue. (The church is now closed, and the synagogue has disappeared.)

An imaginative youth, Cola di Rienzo, after some miserable and frustrated years, finally began to make his way and was named a tribune by Pope Clement VI. His youthful dream of power was strengthened by a night of prayer at the Church of Sant' Angelo in Pescheria—the church of "The Holy Angel in the Fish Market" which stands stone to stone with the Gate of Octavia where Vespasian and Titus had celebrated the downfall of Jerusalem. The next morning Cola di Rienzo walked over to the Campidoglio and without a fight took possession of the city in May 1347.

Seven months (and innumerable festivities of extravagant pomp) later, Cola had misused his power to such an extent that he had to flee from Rome. He had dissipated its civic wealth (or whatever there was left of it when he took power), and with hunger and poverty abroad in the land, the enthusiasm of the Romans had cooled. Cola's enemies, marshalled and guided by the Neapolitan Count Giovanni Pipino di Altamura and by that most Roman of all Roman aristocrats Stefano Colonna, stormed and took the capital, one stronghold after another. The final attack came in the very early morning of December 15, 1347.

While Cola had been on his way up, the Jews of Rome had acclaimed him as much as all other citizens. Perhaps even more so, because with the Pope removed from the government of Rome, their position might have improved. With Cola on his way down, it was still a Jew who tried to help. In the dark of night he rushed to a nearby church and rang its bells to warn Cola of imminent danger. The church in the Jewish neighbourhood was, again, Sant'Angelo in Pescheria where Cola had prayed so fervently seven months previously. The event is duly recorded in his biography *The Life of Nicolai Laurentii* (Cola's family name): "During the night the alarm bell was rung to call the Romans to arms. It was rung by a *Jew!*"

The Jew's assistance hardly did Cola any good. Weary of a liberator who had turned dictator, not a Roman came to his rescue. He first fled to Castel Sant'Angelo, then fled the city. Yet a little over six years later, in August 1354, Cola returned triumphantly. The Romans suffered under ever-increasing want during the intervening years, and were direly threatened by the plague that already ravaged the rest of Europe; they revolted in 1353. On February 16 of that year they had driven a small army of dukes, princes, counts, and barons out of town.

It is unknown whether the Jews—it happened on the Sabbath—took part in the uprising. One can hazard a guess that ever since those legendary times when Pompey took Jerusalem without a fight on a Saturday, the Jews had thought twice before doing nothing in defense of their lives. One thing we do know: they did take part in the warm welcome the city prepared for Cola di Rienzo one year later.

Again the citizens' enthusiasm cooled quickly, perhaps even more quickly. Two months after the highly-lauded entry, on October 3, 1354, Cola met his death at the hands of his enemies, once more led by the Colonnas. His body was left hanging for forty-eight hours from a wall, to be reviled by those who previously had acclaimed him. It was then taken to the Piazza Augusto Imperatore, where the Colonna brothers, Giugurtha and Sciaretta, ordered the Jews to burn it.

Why the lugubrious honor fell to the Jews is unknown. Maybe it was the Colonnas' revenge for the ringing of the church bell, that alarm in the night. They built a funeral pyre from autumn-dry thistles, and kept adding fuel to the flames till nothing but some scarred bones was left of the man who had breathed their own insalubrious air in his youth. The glory gone, his ashes were thrown into the Tiber.

Chapter 13
A Torah for the Pope

Between the years 1000 and 1555, the year of the start of the Roman ghetto, there were ninety-eight Popes, including seventeen anti-Popes. The latter, although opposed by the "official" ones, usually governed happily or unhappily, efficiently or inefficiently as the case might be—from Rome. Most of the absent Popes spent their time in Avignon. Others whiled away the hours in places like Orvieto, Florence, Anagni or Pisa, protected by kings and emperors, and kept at a safe distance from the Vatican by other kings and emperors, by anti-Popes, and once even by the people who forced Eugene IV out of the city in 1434 (he went to Florence and stayed away nine years) to declare a republic. Popes and anti-Popes, holy men all, just did not get along.

Some Popes lived exemplary lives, were honest and God-fearing, and their attitude towards the Jews ranged from lukewarm to fair, from good to excellent. Other Popes, as is well-known, were decadent and corrupt, but they too dealt with the

Jews in a way that went from lukewarm to fair, from good to excellent. Many Popes, the corrupt as well as the God-fearing ones, treated the Jews like dirt.

Leo X, an able member of the Medici family who loved music, art and luxury, was made a cardinal at the tender age of seventeen. Once he was supreme in the Vatican he was perfectly willing to create anyone else a cardinal too, as long as he was well renumerated. Secularly he reigned so grandiosely that during the years of his Papacy the population of Rome more than doubled to 90,000. His favourable treatment of the Jews was such that during the last year of his life they even sent a delegation from Rome to Jerusalem to find out whether under these conditions the Messiah could not be hiding somewhere, only waiting to make an early appearance. A similar voyage had taken place in 1419 under Martin V, a member of the Colonna family and a most excellent Pope for the Jews. Rumors had reached Rome—again the result of the blossoming atmosphere of well-being—that the Ten Tribes had reunited and were ready to free their exiled brothers everywhere. When the three emissaries reached the Holy City, it turned out to be only a rumor. But the Roman Jews were not overly disappointed: the messianic deliverance was not at the moment urgent.

Other Popes, like Sixtus IV and Paul III, were past masters in nepotism, and the former consistently sold religious favors and lucrative posts. Paul, closely rivalling the earlier Sixtus, was a magnificently pro-Jewish Pope. He bestowed many personal favors on them; he also stopped the Passion Play performances at the Colosseum, which usually heated the spectators' religious feelings to such an extent that the evening never finished without attacks on Jews. Alexander VI, the Borgia Pope with four children, in 1514 created a Hebrew Chair at the University of Rome. The Chief Rabbi was then a frequent visitor at the Vatican, and the Jewish population of the city practically doubled during his regime, mostly due to the arrival of the Jews fleeing from the Spanish Inquisition, saved by the efforts of the Pope.

Different as these Popes might be, they were all greeted in the same way by the Roman Jews on being crowned or on entering the city for the first time. On such an occasion they would be offered a Torah. The historical record mentions Eugene III as the first Pope to be received in that way, but the ceremony apparently had originated shortly after the year 1000, when the Jewish community for the first time accompanied the standard request for renewal of their permission to stay in Rome with the offering of one of their Scrolls of the Law.

Many of the offered Torahs were kept by the Popes, and a Dutch guidebook to Italy dated 1665 mentions in its chapter on "How To Visit Rome In Four Days" that "the keeper of the key to the Vatican library, on being offered some drink-money, will gladly open the door that leads to the seven rooms. With admiration one sees the great many noble books, all written by hand, some of them with golden letters that seem to be poured unto the parchment—and he will also show you a scroll with the Law of Moyses."*

Those Popes who were elected far from Rome and who would then make their way laboriously down the Via Cassia towards the Eternal City, were met in the early days outside town on Monte Mario, (in the vicinity of the present-day Hilton Hotel). The greeting ceremony dealt with more than just the presentation of the Torah. The Jews were paid twenty *scudi* by the Apostolic Chamber, and according to custom the papal authorities were then handed one pound of pepper and two pounds of cinnamon.**

---

*What happened to the many Torahs is a mystery. Often they were disdainfully returned to the supplicants, but in view of the numerous Popes who kept them, one would expect the Vatican to have a large collection. Yet today there are only two scrolls left in the manuscript section of the Vatican Library. There are also some handwritten copies of the Pentateuch bound in regular book form, probably copied by monks.

**Though spices arrived early, Jewish cooking did not come to Monte Mario till much later. During the 1963 Ecumenical Council I observed an American priest getting up from among a group of colleagues sitting in the lobby of the Hilton Hotel, saying: "Well, I guess I'll go and get something to eat." "Hey—Jack!," cried one of the other priests after him, "Try their *matzoth*-ball soup—it's delicious!"

At times the Jews were in a dilemma as to whom to offer their Torah; this was the case in 1130 when Innocent II and Pierleoni-Anacletus were elected together in unbrotherly love. The Christians not being able to make up their mind about who was who, both Popes were offered a scroll. But in the stormy aftermath Innocent was still angry by the time he reached the sanctuary of France. When the Jews of Paris followed in the footsteps of the Jews of Rome and offered the exiled Pope a second Torah, he threw aside the velvet covering with the harsh words: "May the omnipotent God in similar fashion take away the covering of your hearts!"

In 1165 Alexander III—during whose reign there were no less than four successive anti-Popes—ruled again in Rome on *his* return from exile in France. A large welcoming committee was waiting for him with flagbearers, notables, judges, and rabbis, the latter of course carrying the Torah. In the next century Boniface VIII was the last "official" Pope to receive such a festive though not happy welcome in Rome (the Popes who came after him spent their long exile in Avignon). The news of Boniface's death in 1303 can not have been too unhappy an announcement for the Jews of Rome, for under his reign Chief Rabbi Elia de Pomis ben Samuel (a friend of the anti-Boniface Colonna family) had died at the stake. Even at the very beginning of his reign Boniface had not been exactly encouraging when he accepted the Torah during the welcoming ceremony. "Formerly you were a nation loved by God," he said, "but now you are His enemies. Because, while other nations gather around, you continue to close your eyes to the True Faith. Christ has shed his blood for you, yet you refuse to recognize Him as your Saviour!"

Nearly all other Popes pronounced their Torah-acceptance speeches in the same vein. The words might be different, but it was always the same fearful attitude of reproaching the Jews for their incredible stubbornness in not recognizing Christ. The Pope's message indicated that he honored the Law of the Jews, but that he condemned their interpretation of it. One of the standard perorations was: "The One of Whom you say He will

View of the island in the Tiber and the Bridge With The Four Heads—from a model at the Rome National Museum at EUR.

(Sam Waagenaar)

The Bridge With The Four Heads as it looks today. In the background the Roman synagogue, opened in 1904.

(Sam Waagenaar)

Titus coins with the inscription Judaea Capta. (Note figure of victorious Roman soldier on one coin, and enslaved Jew on the other.)   (Sam Waagenaar)

High-relief under the Arch of Titus, showing the captured Jews carrying the Ten candelabrum and other holy objects. (Sam Waagenaar)

Triumphal entry of Caesar in Rome. (Sam Waagenaar)

*One of the columns of the Ostia synagogue, with
design of candelabrum. (Sam Waagenaar)*

The Jewish catacombs on the Via Appia—the first of two fairly intact burial chambers. The catacombs, "owned" by the Vatican, are closed to the public.

The front of a Jewish sarcophogus, now in the Rome National Museum at the Baths of Diocletian.

(Sam Waagenaar)

Wall paintings inside the Jewish catacombs below the Villa Torlonia on the Via Nomentana.

Wall-painting inside the Church of San Silvestro in Tivoli, showing discussion during the 4th century before Pope Sylvester between King Constantine and Roman Rabbis. (The Pope is partly visible behind cow that was resurrected by him. Pope is holding staff.)

(Sam Waagenaar)

An early print of the Theater of Marcellus, right next to the Jewish section of Rome. It was the home of Baruch, grandfather of the "Jewish Pope" Anacletus. (Sam Waagenaar)

The first Church of St. Peter and the Vatican buildings, which were visited by David Reubeni. (Sam Waagenaar)

Jews in the Trent synagogue at the time of the murder of the later "San" Simonino.

The Jews of Trent are being tortured and executed in the presence of priests.

Religious discussion between Rabbi and Capuchin monk—17th century. Drawing is based on proverb: One always sees the splinter in someone else's eye, but never the beam in one's own.

Pope Martin V bestows his benediction
on a group of Jews during the Ecumenical Council
of Constance (1414-1418).

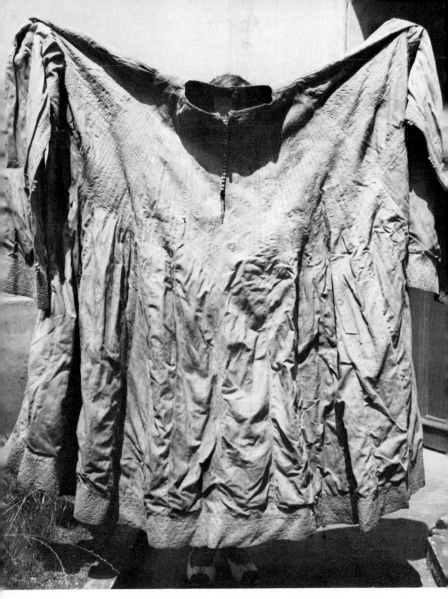

(Sam Waagenaar)

Flag and coat of
Schelomoh Molcho,
which he carried and
wore on his way to
visit Charles V in
Regensburg shortly
after 1530. Both objects
are now in the
Jewish Museum in
Prague.

Schelomoh Molcho's
cabalistic signature.

1555—Pope Paul IV orders the Jews to live inside a walled part of
Rome. One of the earliest maps of the ghetto by DuPerac-Laffery
(1577). There are only two entrance gates in the ghetto wall, one
on the Piazza Giudia, the other one near the Gate of Octavia. The
round building on the lower left is the Theater of Marcellus. The
ghetto had not yet been extended to the bank of the Tiber.

(Courtesy Rosenthaliana Library, Amsterdam

*Winnowing of grain
in the preparation of
flour to bake matzoth
with.*

*Cleaning and
purifying of plates
and dishes.*

*Kneading of the
dough to be used for
the matzoth.*

*Rolling and cutting
the dough for
matzoth.*

(Courtesy Rosenthaliana Library, Amsterdam

come, already *has* come—our Lord Jesus Christ—as the Church and the Bible tell us."

Was it simply a matter of interpretation and misinterpretation? After all, according to the Synagogue and the Old Testament, and contrary to the Church and the New Testament, the Saviour of course had *not* come yet. It would take more than six hundred years, actually till the liberal reign of the humane and understanding Pope John XXIII, before there would be a beginning of a compassionate thaw in the Vatican rulers' attitude about this unbendable Jewish conviction.

At the end of the Avignon exile, new Torahs were prepared by the Roman community. But when Innocent VII finally arrived in the city, he returned his gift to the Jews "over his shoulder," a gesture which usually indicated disdain. One year later yet another set of papal Torahs were being offered in a mad rush all over Europe. Gregory VII was offered one in Rome, Benedict XIII received his in Avignon (now the seat of the anti-Popes) and to make matters even more complicated, a third Pope was elected in Pisa, Alexander V. The Jews really did not know any longer whether a Pope was coming or going; and the picture was not much clearer to the Christians themselves who had their own difficulties to figure out who was Pope and who was not. A settlement was finally reached in 1417 with Gregory's abdication and the election of Martin V. Following the example of the now somewhat bewildered Gregory, Martin insisted on keeping the Torah for good, a custom that had not always been followed before then.

The new Pope turned out to be a God-send to the Jews. He accepted the Torah with the words, "the past is gone, the present is everything." But he did more. Having been elected in Constance by the Council that had brought the chaotic Gregory-Benedict-Alexander episode to a close, Martin already had sent a message to Rome while he was still in Florence. Of course he made it clear that the Jews were in the wrong and the Church in the right, but his letter was not menacing in tone.

"The Jews in their blindness remain stubbornly opposed to the words of the Holy Writ which would make them accept the

Christian belief," the message said. "Yet we do not want to keep
Our Christian love from them, so they may understand their
mistake and come to recognize the true Light of Love, who is
Christ." Martin then went on to admonish the Christians who
"had forfeited the right to be called such," because many of
them "did everything in their power to oppress the Jews."

It was a perfect beginning to a quite civilized relationship,
and for once the Jews of Rome must have thought that the
Torah had worked its wonders even on a Pope. Pope Martin
took it upon himself to take the Jews "under his paternal
protection against unjust vexations on the part of the Christians
and against false accusations resulting from hypocritical
religious zeal. . . ." The Jews were on the eve of a new era of
good feelings, and it is not surprising that the previously-
mentioned delegation went to Jerusalem to check on the arrival
of the Messiah. This seemed especially plausible after Martin
had made a simple statement of fact which must have sounded
like heresy to a good many of the subordinate priests.

Martin V said: "Jews are created like other men in the image
of God, and in order to protect their future, they must not be
molested in their synagogues, nor hindered in their commercial
relations with Christians." This, of course, was quite a
revolutionary pronouncement after all the ugly words the Jews
had been hearing from certain Popes among Martin's
predecessors. Martin went even further than that in his declaration of 1417. The laws of the Jews should not be impaired, he
decreed, they should not be obliged to undergo forced baptism,
nor to keep Christian holidays. It amounted to a whole series of
"hands off" regulations, which fell upon the Roman Jews like
the proverbial manna from Heaven.

But the Torah scrolls did not always work wonders. Three
Popes later, the holy Torah ceremony ran into trouble. The
presentation until now had usually taken place at Monte Giordano, located a short distance from the Tiber (the square still exists); and with the exception of some of the Popes' occasional
rude remarks, there never had been any serious incidents to mar
the occasion. Not so with Calixtus III. When he arrived at

Monte Giordano in 1455, the Jewish delegation stood ready to hand the Pope the Torah, an especially beautiful specimen, richly ornamented with precious metals. Was the huge crowd touched by gold fever? Crowd psychology is always difficult to explain. Something happened: the Pope had great trouble simply holding on to his present, enthused or excited Romans nearly ran him underfoot, the confusion was such that cardinals and Pope could hardly be extricated from a milling mass of people. Three days afterwards, it was reported, the 77-year-old Pope was still trembling. It was decided that in future no more risks should be taken with such ceremonies. It gave the Romans a possibility to air their enthusiasm for the Pontiff but also to give vent to latent anti-Semitism. There had been anti-Semitic shouts and gestures. The location of the Torah offering was removed to the safety of the entrance to the Castel Sant'Angelo.

Towards the end of the 15th century the whole Torah ceremony was discontinued, perhaps to protect the Pope from further possible incidents. Instead the Jews were obliged to decorate a part of the Forum and the Arch of Septimus Severus every time the Pope would go from the Vatican to the Church of San Giovanni in Laterano, of which the Pontiff, as Bishop of Rome, was the head.

Chapter 14
The Badge of Shame

Though the bunting which was put on Arch and Forum did not carry a Jewish inscription or trade mark, the Romans knew of course that it had been supplied by the Jews. Even if they had not known this, they would easily have recognized the Jews as they were hanging up the draperies, for anyone by then could see who was a Jew and who was not.

When Hitler put the yellow Star of David on the Jews of Europe, he invented nothing new—he simply picked a new design that put German civilization back seven hundred years. If he had gone back three more centuries, Hitler would have found that the marked Jews were in astonishing company. Towards the end of the ninth century Jews *and* Christians were wearing distinctive bits of clothing in southern Italy—where Caliph Matewakal had prescribed a leather or woollen yellow waistband for members of both religions, thus distinguishing them from the True Believers. The otherwise perfectly civilized Caliph also had signs put on Christian and Jewish doorposts.

In 1215 the Fourth Lateran Council had decreed that all Jews should wear a bit of cloth in the form of the letter 0, which would make it easy to detect them. The Roman Jews were by now fairly good Italians, and they obviously expected to delay the execution of the government's order for a while. Not till 1360 did the mark of distinction appear in public. Pope Innocent III, the inventor of the degrading badge, hoped that it would or at least *might* prevent "accidental sexual intercourse" between Jews and Christians. It was as good a reason as any, for the main idea was to set the Jews apart from the rest of the world.

By 1360 all Roman male Jews had to wear a red domino over their clothes. For women a specially colored extra skirt, a sort of apron, was prescribed. Anyone infringing on the rule was fined, and half the money was paid to the informer. It placed prostitutional trespassers in special jeopardy. The Christian male would have a difficult time to discover whether his partner was Jewish or not; but motivated complaints from Christian females could cause imprisonment or worse.

In 1402 a new rule came into force which indicated exactly the streets on which the Jews were allowed to appear without their red capes or skirts. Most of these Roman streets were close to the Bridge With The Four Heads. But to cross the river for a visit to friends or relatives on the other side, the extra piece of clothing had to be worn again. Out-of-town Jewish visitors were given a ten-day period of grace before having to conform to the Vatican rule.

Various countries had different forms for the initial badge; it was some times square and sometimes round, its colors varied from red and yellow, to half-white half-red. In some cities the badge was later on replaced by a red or green hat, long and pointed. In Rome yellow was much preferred. With acquired Italian ingenuity, the Jews slowly added a small quantity of orange and then red dye to the cloth the hats were made of, till at last the original yellow had a beautiful deep red hue and all Jews seemed to look like Cardinals. Evidently the high church dignitaries did not quite appreciate the shared distinction, and two cardinals kept on recording their protests until the Jewish hat went back to its original yellow.*

Towards the latter part of the fifteenth century there was another change, especially appreciated by women—all that was required were two bits of blue ribbon attached to the veil. The only Jews who during all these centuries were hardly ever pressed to wear any distinctive mark at all were the doctors, probably because they were frequent visitors at the Vatican, often desperately trying to keep aging Popes alive.

The need for Jewish doctors appeared to be an obvious one for the Heads of the Christian Church. Were they better, more skilled than doctors brought up as non-Jews? Their frequent knowledge of Arabic was of a tremendous advantage in studying and translating important medical works into Latin. In later years, when the Inquisition in Spain made life unbearable for Jews and descendents of Jews ("Marranos"), many of them came to Italy. So to the Popes it was a matter of elementary logic: they wanted the best medical attention they could get, and with Christ already taking care of the soul, a Jewish doctor would take care of the body.

Being Jews, and being close to the Popes, many doctors were called upon to try and soften the blows which the Vatican might from time to time mete out to the Roman community. With the "good" Popes this was a simple matter, or at least not especially difficult. With the "bad" ones, the diplomatic task became more strenuous. Still it worked at times. When Nicholas IV was living in Orvieto towards the end of the 13th century and the situation for the Jews in Rome became precarious due to a sordid game of financial blackmail which was being played to perfection by the clergy, they sent in desperation a group of prominent Jews to the Pope. Nicholas was receptive to the complaints, and in 1291 he pointed out to the priests that the Jews were under his protection. His decision may well have been influenced by his

---

*In some countries the Jewish hat became a sign of a proudly accepted distinction. When as a result of the French Revolution the wearing of the yellow hat was prohibited in Avignon in 1792, the local Jews were so attached to their headgear that they had to be threatened with a fine of 12 *livres* if caught wearing them!

Jewish doctor, known at court as Maestro Gajo, but called Yitzhak ben Mordehai by his family.

A hundred years later two Jewish doctors were especially honored by Popes. In 1392 Boniface IX promoted "his beloved son Angelo di Manuele (Angel ben Manuel), a Jew from Trastevere, his doctor and trusted friend" to be his personal physician and *"familiaris"* (member of the household) "under the protection of the holy Peter and Paul, so that under this patronage of the Holy See you can profit more and shall benefit from all honors." The protection of the two Apostles must indeed have been of great help to the Jewish doctor from Trastevere.

In 1406, Elia di Sabato, who had been practicing in Rome among the city's aristocracy, received a curious letter from Innocent VII who liked him, honored him, yet could not do so without pointing out that not everything about Elia was entirely to his satisfaction. "The faithlessness of the Jews has to be condemned," wrote the Pope, "and the stubborn opposition to our Belief is to be tread upon. Yet in a certain way their maintenance at court is useful and necessary to the Christians. So since you not only heal Our own citizens but even foreign travelers, We make you, judging your presence necessary to the health of the Romans and others, a Roman citizen." It was a reluctantly bestowed and yet a tremendous honor for a Jew; for besides the honor itself and the salary of twenty gold ducats a year that went with it, Elia was allowed to carry arms and could go about without any Jewish badge or other recognizable racial sign of discrimination.

Another Jewish doctor who was treated benignly by a Pope was Samuel Zarphati, the first of a number of Zarphatis who would play important medical roles. Samuel got his start at the Vatican as private physician to that pro-Jewish Borgia Pope Alexander VI, and was subsequently reconfirmed by his immediate successor Julius II. As personal attendant to the Pope, he was permitted to treat Christians; he and his family could live wherever they wanted to; they were allowed the free and unhindered profession of their religion; and, again, no blue ribbons, red cloak, or other Jewish badge had to be worn. For some Jews such honors were rather inducive to conversion to Christianity. This in fact did happen to some of the later Zarphatis, who not only turned Christian but who, at the same time, became violently anti-Semitic.

Samuel's son followed in his father's footsteps and took up as Pope Julius' private doctor when his father died. A third Zarphati, Isaac, was named *"familiaris"* of Clement VII in 1530, and he too was allowed to treat Christians in their homes. The new Pope was obviously quite partial to Jewish doctors, but with the best of intentions, the results at times were sometimes unfortunate. In November 1526 Clement asked another physician, a certain Abraham Arje, also known as Abraham Porteleone, to rush to his good friend Giovanni de Medici. The patient was famous as Giovanni With The Black Armor, and he had been wounded in battle, a game he pursued all his life with spectacular results. Abraham did his very best. On November 24 he amputated a gangrened leg; but five days later Giovanni was no more. Here was a famous soldier, and the doctor was a Jew—surely the true cause of his death was easily detectable to those who saw Jews only in a dark light.

Under the benevolent Martin V, during that early 15th-century era of good feelings, Jewish doctors had the run of the Vatican. This situation continued under Alexander VI, one of whose private physicians was Bonet de Lattes, an immigrant from the French Provence, where he was born in Lattes near Montpelier. Bonet was not only an efficient doctor but shortly after taking up his duties with the Pope he was appointed Chief Rabbi of the community. He was also an astrologer who invented an instrument with which to calculate the position of the sun at any time of the day. Armed with this little apparatus and his strong belief in the Old Testament, Bonet—whose Jewish name was Rabbi Jacob ben Immanuel Provincial—figured out that when the sun would come up on a certain day in 1505, the Messiah would come along with it. He must have realized that his calculations were somewhat off the mark, for when Bonet de Lattes died towards the end of 1514, the great day had not yet dawned.

Under Paul III the medical profession at the Papal court probably reached its zenith. Jacob Mantino, born in Spain, came to Rome after having spent some time in Venice. An able philosopher as well as a Talmudist, he dedicated his "Comment on the Republic of Plato" to the Pope. In 1539 the Pope named Mantino to a chair of medicine at the Roman University, a singular occurrence in those days, all the more unusual because Mantino had been obliged to leave his native Spain under the anti-Semitic persecutions of the Inquisition. Jacopo Sadoleto, a cardinal when Mantino was appointed to the university, painted a true if somewhat exaggerated picture of the situation when he wrote: "No Christians have been favored under the Papacy of Paul III as the Jews, who not only have been promoted to posts of honor, but have been armed by Him! . . . "

Indeed the position of the Jewish doctor of medicine in Rome never again reached so high a status. A few years after Mantino's career, changes occurred in Rome which until as late as 1870 would make it impossible for Jewish doctors to practice anywhere but among their co-religionists, and even this rarely. It went so far that the Jewish doctor had to swear not to come to the aid of a Christian, not even in rescue cases of extreme emergency.

Mantino's arrival in Rome exposed one of the enigmas of the Christian world, and reconfirmed the trend of Roman liberty for the Jews even when things were going badly elsewhere. When in 1492 Ferdinand and Isabella with a stroke of the pen brought an end to the existence of the great Jewish communities in Spain (and, subsequently, in southern Italy and Sicily which also belonged to the Spanish Crown), some nine thousand Jews arrived in Italy where they hoped to find asylum with the magnanimous—in some ways—Pope Alexander VI. Among the fugitives were a good many "Marranos," Jews or descendants of Jews who had been forcibly baptized and who even after several generations still rebelled against their conversion. The name "Marranos" had been given them by the Spaniards, who after the acceptance of the Christian faith by the Jews continued to look upon the converts as *Marranos*, a colloquial Spanish word for pigs—they were unclean.

In Rome the Jewish community was afraid of the influx of this mass of Jews from the Iberian peninsula. Living under the benevolent rule of the Borgia Pope, and being only too well aware that such happy circumstances might easily change again at Alexander's death, the Roman Jews took a most unusual step. They asked Alexander to refuse entry to the Spanish Jews and the "Marranos." Alexander was properly aghast, even more so when the community offered him one thousand ducats if he would accede to their request. Of course, being a Pope who could always use funds, Alexander's scorn went hand in hand with an ingenious financial scheme. He was angry at the Jews and fined them twice the amount they had offered him. With Alexander financial trifling was out of the question.

It was, therefore, not surprising that the Pope soon afterwards deftly blended his humanitarian weakness with religious fervor, mixed in turn by the political need not to antagonize Ferdinand and Isabella. The "Marranos," who lived not in Rome proper but just outside the Appian Gate, could enter the city only secretly. Soon a goodly number of them—including "Marranos" from Portugal—found themselves in jail, and were freed only after they abjured the religion for the preservation of which they had left the country of their birth.

In one incident some eighty "Marranos" were put behind bars. The Pope had all their belongings confiscated, including money, carriages, and horses. He then told the confused half-Jews that all those who confessed their true religion would have their possessions returned. Knowing full well that such confessions would probably cost them their lives, none of the victims stepped forward. They were then freed with a grand, benevolent gesture, and were back where they had started from—only dead poor. The Venetian ambassador in Rome probably made an astute assessment of the situation when he

wrote in one of his reports that "these days the attitude of the
Pope towards the Marranos has grown more severe, some say to
please their Spanish Majesties, others claim in order to
strengthen His coffers! . . . "

In 1498 Alexander went to the extraordinary lengths of im-
prisoning in Castel Sant'Angelo the Spanish Bishop of
Calahorra, Piero d'Arando, and his bastard son. The Bishop was
accused of being a "Marrano." It was another one of the
astounding Church exercises in theological ambivalence. Jews
were constantly pressed to swear off Judaism and embrace the
teachings of Christ. When they did, no one would trust them.

Yet, on the whole, these appear to be happy centuries for "the
Pope's Jews." Despite the occasional beating, hanging, or
burning, the Jews of Rome lived and worked in relative content-
ment. As early as the late twelfth century, that intrepid Jewish
traveler Benjamin of Tudela already had found two hundred
quite satisfied Jewish families in Rome, "well-established people who are not paying tribute to anyone, some of them even
close advisors of Alexander III, Chief Pontiff of the whole
Christian religion." The Spanish-born Benjamin, traveling
through the Near East, Persia, and India, is said to have reached
the borders of China and Tibet a full hundred years before Marco Polo. Criss-crossing Italy, he was in Rome around 1166,
where apparently he did not meet with the less fortunate Jews.
Some of these bedraggled sons of David, whose compulsory
and exclusive occupation it was to act as hangmen for the city
magistrates, were certainly not among the two hundred well-to-
do families Benjamin wrote about.

In his travel memoirs, which were first published in Constantinople in 1543, Benjamin of Tudela mentions a certain Jehiel
among the Roman Jewish aristocrats. Jehiel was a financial ad-
viser of Pope Alexander, a "young, elegant and intelligent man"
who also administered the Pope's private domain. Jehiel is identified as the grandson of Nathan ben Jehiel, another famous
Roman, the author of one of the best Hebrew Lexicons of all
time. He, too, was a member of the happy Two Hundred

Families, all of whom lived (according to Benjamin of Tudela) in Trastevere.

Besides reporting on the Jews of Rome, Benjamin made an entry in his book that would serve posterity as a Roman landmark. "Near the palace of the empress stood two columns from the Temple of Solomon," Benjamin wrote, "and the Jews of Rome told me that every year on the ninth of the month of Ab (the day the Temple was destroyed) these columns sweated water."

If we may believe Benjamin, then half the temple columns were brought to Rome from Jerusalem; for inside Saint Peter's, immediately behind the railing that guards Michelangelo's *Pietà*, stood a spiral column which is supposed to have come from the same Temple, brought to Rome in 1338. A plaque explained that "against this column Our Lord Jesus Christ was leaning while preaching to the people." Along with eleven other columns (the plaque further specified) the one in Saint Peter's was brought to Rome from the ruins of the Temple of Solomon. Once in Italy, it was celebrated for "driving out the demons and evil spirits."

The Roman Jews did not need such miraculous columns, sweating or not, to remind them of the ancient days when Solomon's Temple was the pride and glory of Jerusalem. Under the invigorating cultural influence of the Renaissance, Jewish writing flourished, and Jewish themes did not neglect Solomon.

An early and lonely figure in Jewish literature was Immanuel ben Solomon Rossi. Though he did not spend all his life in Rome, he was known as Manoello, Immanuel Romano and Immanuel Giudeo (Immanuel the Jew). He was a contemporary of Dante, perhaps even knew him, and like Dante he wrote erotic literature about hell and paradise, women and wine in the form of a Hebrew *Divina Commedia*.

In the middle of the 15th century Moses ben Isaac from Rieti who, as so often happened, combined medicine with literature, described the Torah as "The City of God." He too coupled his literary work with the task of Chief Rabbi of the community, at the same time putting his extensive medical knowledge at the service of various Popes. He finally became private physician to Julius II. This Pontiff, in his earlier days, had been a court poet of Emperor Frederick III, and no doubt he could enjoy the good company of the literary doctor from Rieti. While Moses ben Isaac and many other doctors managed to get along famously with the Masters of the Vatican ever since Martin V had arrived from the Council of Constance, there was in 1417 one man who took the Papal-Jewish friendship as a terrible indictment against the teachings of Christ. He was a great orator, a militant, an awesome threat to unbelievers, and a later saint whose memory is venerated at one of the main altars in the Church of Santa Maria in Ara Coeli in Rome. His name was Giovanni di Capistrano, or John Capistran—and he was one of the most fanatical Jew-baiters ever.

Chapter 15
Ritual Murder

Giovanni di Capistrano was a member of the Order of the Franciscans. The Franciscans tried to help the poor, and the poor could always use alms. During the 12th century, Italian Christians were usually the ones who were happy to supply their less fortunate brothers with funds on a profitable basis, that is—against payment of interest. The practice started in the north, where the Lombards were well-known for their money-lending activities. Then in 1179 the Vatican decided to excommunicate all Christians who lent money against interest. The Holy See was convinced that banking as a form of usury was an un-Christian activity.*

---

*The Lombards went across the Alps and eventually reached Holland and England. A pawnshop in the Netherlands is still known as the *lommerd*, an obvious derivation from the word *Lombard*, and in London *Lombard Street* is right in the center of the financial district of The City. Of course, the Vatican ultimately changed its mind. It is today a minority stockholder, yet an important one, in the Banca di Roma and the Banca di Santo Spirito ("Bank of The Holy Spirit"), two of the most powerful institutions in Italy.

To be sure, the Popes themselves at times used the Jews as debt-collectors. As far as money-lending was concerned, several Italian cities asked for permission to allow Jews to open official loan banks. And the Jews, to whom most other professions time and again were forbidden by the Vatican, were undoubtedly glad to have at least this possibility to make a living. Moreover, money-lending had a special communal advantage: one was able to take cash along whenever the Pope or city magistrates made some sudden expulsion order, as so often happened. The trouble, then, was to try and collect.

When the Jews, often at the Christians' own request, took over where the Lombards left off, they were always welcome when money was needed. But when the time came for the money to be refunded (or else the original owner would forfeit his property) the picture became different. There was an obviously special tension between creditor and debtor. To create a somewhat happier relationship, the Christian money-lenders were sometimes called back in various places. It was of little avail. Under benevolent Christian management the interest rates often went higher than ever; and once again it was the turn of the Jews to take over.

There seemed to be no end to the vicious circle, and this is where Giovanni di Capistrano came in. The Jews were the cause of all poverty and all evil. Once again there was only one way out: *out with the Jews!* The Franciscan monk devoted himself to the accomplishment of this comprehensive solution to the ills of life and society.

Giovanni di Capistrano fulminated incessantly. In fact, the erudite monk ranted against anything and everything that did not fit in perfectly with the rules of the Franciscan Order and Christianity as he saw it; and the Jews were definitely not among those who suited his ideal order of things. Giovanni even suggested to Pope Eugene IV an easy way to get rid of the Jewish scourge—put all of them on ships and send them across the sea (*anywhere* across the sea), as long as they would be out of Rome and out of Italy.

When during the Holy Year of 1450 yet another plague spread a depressed atmosphere through Rome, some bright event was needed to lighten the dispirited souls and help a celebratory mood. Giovanni di Capistrano hit upon the idea of arranging a public "Christian-Jewish discussion." The confrontation was a great success. As could have been predicted, the principal compulsory participant, a certain Roman Jew by the name of Gamaliel, was forcibly baptized. So were forty other Jews who had been forced to be present. According to reports dating from that period, Giovanni di Capistrano was elated with the results, which had somehow convinced him of the "visual truth of Christianity."

Until the appearance of Giovanni di Capistrano, the preceding years were on the whole, as we have seen, a fairly happy time for the Roman Jews, if one does not take into account the hunger, the pestilence, the occasional earthquake, and flooding of the Tiber. As long as there were some funds available, there was always the possibility of buying off the threat of the worst political or religious disasters. In Northern Europe, the fanatacism of the oppression was always more rigorous, more complete. Especially in Germany, the Jews often were obliged to give up most of their possessions against the most paltry and spurious of promises. This never happened in Rome, at least not as tragically. Rome was a special case.

The prosperity of the Roman Jews during that 14th century is proven by the heavy (and often quite impossible) financial levies that were put upon them. If Jews, as Juvenal had written during the first century A.D., "sold their visions at a discount," it turned out that Jewish life in later centuries was "sold" (or, if you will, preserved) only at a high price. Whether governed by emperor, prince, or Pope, the physical body of the Jew became a valuable piece of property. Only by gold could it be protected.

When German Emperor Henry VII left Rome after having been crowned there in 1312 (at the Church of San Giovanni in Laterano) by a special emissary from the Pope, he ordered the Romans to pay him a "Crowning Tax." The amount was paid—but exclusively by the Jews.

In 1321 the Roman Jews had tried to buy off the burning of their holy books by offering the Pope a large amount of money, which again suggests their relative wealth. In 1328 King Louis the Bavarian, after his crowning in Rome, asked for 30,000 gold pieces from the city. One-third was to be paid by the (Christian) citizens, one-third by the clergy, and one-third by the Jews. Inasmuch as the Jews were a small minority, the three thirds seemed rather unevenly divided.

During the next century Giovanni di Capistrano had made a valiant effort to change all this, and he had received excellent support from Pope Eugene IV. From Florence, where he had fled in 1434, the Pope, whose anti-Jewish decrees always promptly nullified his pro-Jewish statements, had done his best to bring all Jewish well-being to an end. They were forbidden to ply just about every trade; they were not allowed to be collectors of taxes, administrators of Christian domains, middle-men of any kind, brokers (including marriage-brokers), nor were their women permitted to exercise the profession of midwife. To make matters worse, Eugene ordered the Jews to live in a certain part of town only; they were not to have Christian servants; nor could they initiate law suits against non-Jews. No Christian could leave money to a Jew in his will.

To be sure, Eugene in Florence was at his wits' end. Abroad the Turks were besieging Constantinople, and before his departure from Rome the city had rebelled against him. He had endless troubles with King-Emperor Sigismund of Germany, and his nine years of forced exile from the Vatican were not apt to increase his good humour. The Pope was looking for a cause in which he could be victorious. Would not the anti-Jewish decrees—which he fervently supported anyhow—provide the easiest way out? After all, *someone* had to be punished, so why not the Jews?

In 1442, a year before his return to the Vatican, Eugene ordered a certain number of important Jewish citizens to leave Rome. The results were ruinous for the community, which became so impoverished that financial assistance had to be asked for from Jews in other cities. Then, with the temperamental change of his otherwise quite straightforward mind, Eugene "forgave" the Jews when he finally did return to Rome. One only wonders what, under the circumstances, there was to forgive.

As to the impoverishment of his Jewish subjects, Eugene discovered that they were not the only ones who had suffered. The city was destitute. Faces and streets looked transformed. Its physical aspect as well as that of its inhabitants was such that Roberto degli Roberti, a member of a famous Florentine family, wrote in 1443: "All Romans look like shepherds to me, and the city itself hardly gives the impression of being a city any longer. . . ."

In these years Giovanni di Capistrano had been doing his job well, and he had also found diligent pupils. The most effective of these (and, consequently, the worst as far as the Jews were concerned) was Fra Bernardino da Feltre or Brother Bernard from Feltre, a little town in the Dolomites north of Venice where he was born. In a probably honest effort to protect the simple citizens from paying extravagant interest on loans, he preached the establishment of special banks. But he overlooked that Christians at times had asked for far higher interest than Jews and his rancor was directed against Jewish usurers exclusively.

The Jews, of course, did ask for high interest payments. The risk was great, far greater for the Jewish money-lender than for his Christian counterpart. Loans and lenders both could at times be abolished.* Loans to the simple townsmen were usually on a short-term basis only, and these simple folk were the ones whom Bernardino da Feltre wanted to protect.

To convince the citizens of the honesty of his endeavour, Fra Bernardino traveled the length and width of Italy, extolling the virtue of his plan and the wickedness of the Jew. Things could not, should not, go on as they were. The poor people had to be liberated from the clutches of these Jews who, at least according to crusading Brother Bernard, were ruining them. Fra Bernar-

---

*The idea of cancelling Jewish debts outright was an ingenious invention. In 1223 Louis VIII of France decided unilaterally that all debts that were over five years old were automatically null and void.

dino's idea was that the poor people should be able to borrow money without paying any interest whatsoever. The institution that would do this work would be a Bank for the Needy or for the Poor—the *Monte di Pietà*.

Bernardino da Feltre succeeded magnificently. His loan banks mushroomed, especially in the north. His method was simple. Speeches to arouse the enthusiasm of the poor (and the sympathy of the rich) would be interfused with violent attacks on the depravity of the Jews and on their profit-taking. Towards the end of the mass meeting the rich would be asked to put a certain amount of gift-money at the disposal of the multitude. From this free fund the first small loans would then be made.

Fra Bernardino organized parades, and used all the fanfare of the circus and of the barker at a fair to arouse his listeners. He foretold the future to these eagerly receptive crowds, predicting events which he knew would definitely come true. This often involved playing upon the credulity and superstition of the crowd, but then the happy end would after all justify the unhappy plot.

In Brother Bernard's campaign the "plot" was ritual murder. This pernicious story has been used to melodramatic advantage through the ages, notwithstanding occasional very strong opposition from Popes and others. According to the propagandists of the story, the Jews needed Christian blood—preferably taken from a child—in the preparation of their unleavened Passover bread or *matzoth*. It was a lunatic story, under the cover of sanctity, and simple folk who at times are apt to follow a crazed leader, were ready to go on a rampage. The "ritual murderer" had to be found and destroyed.

Gregory X in the early part of the 13th century decreed that such stories should not even be considered by the tribunals, and that no Jew could be jailed on such an accusation. Since the crowd often took justice into their own hands, jailing of course was hardly ever necessary; usually the Jew was already dead before he could be accused.

The ritual-murder prophecy was eminently used in 1475 by Brother Bernard. The results were fatal to Jews everywhere, including those in Rome. On one occasion, there was the conventional propaganda speech for the establishment of a *Monte di Pietà*, and the site was the town of Trent in northern Italy. The saintly Brother prophesied a ritual murder to take place just before the Jewish Easter Festival. It obviously had to be Easter, for how otherwise could the Jews ever bake their *matzoth*?

To suggest that Brother Bernard had foreknowledge of the disappearance of young Simon Unverdorben would probably be going too far. Yet the disappearance of exactly *this* boy, whose family name means *Simon the Unblemished* or *Simon the Pure* (the literal translation of *Unverdorben*), may well have been a providentially accidental stroke. As it happened, little Simon, the two-year-old son of Andreas Unverdorben, disappeared from his home on March 23. Mindful of Brother Bernard's prophecy, the rumor immediately spread that "the Jews had done it." Done what? Murdered the child, of course.

The Jews of Trent felt the strangling sensation of panic, but as luck would have it, three days later, on March 26, two Jews saw a body floating in the river. A sense of boundless relief swept through the Jewish community. The Passover Festival would after all be celebrated without disturbances, and all minds could be at rest. The authorities were quickly notified of the tragic yet alleviating discovery. The body of little Simon was retrieved from the water; and the two Jews were promptly thrown into the local jail. The murderers themselves—said the city fathers of Trent, vociferously supported by the local priests—had brought the body home.

Help for the campaign came from an unexpected source. The old men who had spotted the body were not the only Jews in jail. There was also a baptized Jew by the name of Israel sharing their miserable cell, and he was serving a long-term sentence. Might not siding with the Christians bring a fortunate change in his own dismal future? So this renegade Jew informed the local bishop that there was no doubt whatever about the Jews' guilt. He confirmed it: they *always* used a young child's blood to bake their *matzoth*. This testimony finalized the case; more proof was superfluous. In fact, as far as the local priests were concerned, *no* proof was needed.

On March 28 the trial began. Torture, of course, was included in the efforts to persuade the accused tell the truth, and any denials quite naturally were considered nothing less than blatant lies. At last one of the arrested Jews, eighty years of age, could not stand the pain any longer and "confessed." Justice had triumphed. Thirteen Jews were executed, some burned at the stake, some beheaded, and the whole Jewish community were forever expelled from Trent. For good measure, Israel, the baptized Jewish perjurer was put to the wheel.

The Jews of Rome, in the meantime, had not been idle in unconcern. Pope Sixtus IV, in August 1475, had sent the Papal delegate from Ventimiglia to Trent to start an investigation. He reported that, in his view, local Christians had killed little Simon in connivance with the Bishop of Trent, whose name was Hinterbach. Among them they planned to confiscate all the Jews' possessions prior to their expulsion.

By then, however, the good burghers of Trent had completed their case on the poor boy's death, and before long they started to see miraculous happenings near the statue that had been erected to commemorate Simon's innocent suffering.

Yet the Pope did not give up. He charged a committee to investigate the trial. Unfortunately he named at its head a priest who was a close friend of Brother Bernard from Feltre, the prophet who had predicted it all. On 20 June 1478 the committee's report was sent to the Pope. The trial, it indicated, had been *rite et recte factum*—it had all been done justly and rightly.

In Trent the local priests continued to acclaim the wondrous miracles that took place in the name and under the influence of Simon Unverdorben, now regarded as a true martyr. Finally the Vatican not only acquiesced in what had happened; under popular pressure, Pope Sixtus V in 1588 gave in to the constant urging of the Archbishop of Trent, Cardinal Madruzzo. Fra Bernardino da Feltre henceforth was to be regarded a prophet, and the innocent little boy who had been used to extol Christian virtue and to vilify Jewish machinations was to be known in Trent as a saint.

From that day onward San Simonino ("Holy Little Simon") as he was named, was officially acclaimed, adored, and asked for special favors under the auspices of the Church. To honor the Protector of Trent, every year on his nameday a procession was held in the city. In the street that was named after him, the Via San Simonino, a chapel was built on the ground floor of a mansion. Above its doors stands a charming baroque statue of Simon, looking divinely up to Heaven. A little higher up, painted on the outer wall of the chapel, is another picture. On both sides of this fresco, part of an inscription can still be deciphered. I could still make out the recognizable fragments to read: " . . . .147 [?]. . . .*by the Jews.* . . . "

Four centuries later the Vatican decided to simplify the diocesan holy calendars, which were cluttered up with too many saints' days. Rechecking the procedures that had made a saint out of many a local martyr, they decided that all those regional saints whose antecedents were rather nebulous were, to a certain extent, to be written off the calendar.

In 1961 the scrutinized findings of the Vatican were completed. They were disastrous for many a provincial saint, including the beloved Saint Simon of Trent. His chapel was dutifully closed. Little Simon was a saint no more,—not, at least, a real, proper, officially recognized saint—and no more processions were to be held in his honor. Or that, at least, was what the newspapers reported at the time.

In 1967 the Vatican, being asked for clarification and verification by the author of this book, corrected the story. "Newspapers always get these things wrong," explained Monsignore Frutats, one of the priests in charge of the Vatican's *Sacra Congregatio Rituum*, the historical office that had conducted the investigation. Simon actually had never been canonized, he said. He was just a *Santo Popolare*, who had been "tolerated under a *culto locale permesso*," a locally permitted religious belief.

"There is *such* a difference between real saints who have suffered endlessly for the Church, and those local or provincial saints whose past is quite obscure. Of course, I presume that in the case of Simon of Trent the story may have been kept alive by the Jews," the very pleasant Monsignore said to me.

It was reassuring to hear that only the Jews had kept the story alive. Brother Bernard, the local priests, and Cardinal Madruzzo, who had insisted on the saintly comportment of Little Simon, evidently had never been at fault. It could have meant that Simon should never have been regarded as a real saint, which the people in the province of Trent considered (and consider him) and which his name—Saint Simon of Trent—still indicates. It could also mean, of course, that the Jews should never have been killed.

Chapter 16
Carnival Races

To the Jews of Rome, living in the shadow of the Vatican, the struggle between Popes who occasionally protected them, and ex-Jews and priests who constantly attacked them, was like the ebb and flow of life itself. They never knew when the flood would rise high enough to drown them.

Sixtus IV, nepotically distributing papal favors while building the Sistine Chapel as a monument to Christianity, had been the strong defender of the Jews in the Trent murder case. Yet he allowed the Spanish Inquisition to start, the reports of which swiftly reached the alarmed Jews of Rome; then he admonished Ferdinand and Isabella to go slow in their extreme anti-Jewish measures. (Could it have been the personal influence of his doctor who was, of course, a Jew, a certain Maestro Salamone?) He persisted in his efforts to counteract the lurid accusations of the zealous baptized Jews, most conspicuously in the case of a certain Guillermo Siculus. This monk had declared in a violent speech in Rome that he "had discovered most of the Jews' secrets, from which it was clear that they continued obstinately to hold on to their shameful beliefs. . . . " For an ex-Jew this could not have been an altogether surprising discovery.

Then suddenly a Christian emerged who went into open battle in defense of Judaism, although perhaps not directly for the continued existence of the Jewish community as such. Still, his struggle for the freedom of the *knowledge* of Judaism and the Hebrew language was so valiant that it finally shook the very walls of the Vatican, and as such helped to prepare the way for the Protestant Reformation and Protestantism.

In 1492, at the age of thirty-seven—and possibly shocked by the Spanish Inquisition—Johann Reuchlein, a German jurist who next to Erasmus was probably Europe's greatest Humanist, began to study Hebrew. Till then the old biblical writings had been perused in Greek and Latin only. Reuchlein's search for the Jewish confirmation of the coming of Christ started him off on a detailed study of the Kabbalah, on which he wrote several learned treatises. Continuing his extraordinary research, considered at the time pure heresy ("Anyone studying Hebrew," one priest stated, "becomes automatically a Jew") his work led him in 1506 to the composition of the first Hebrew grammar ever made by a Christian. For this he was strongly attacked by the Dominicans.

Before the scene shifted to Rome, Reuchlein had to defend himself in his native Germany against the prior of the Dominican Order in Cologne, Jacob van Hoogstraeten. In his campaign to defeat the study of Hebrew, van Hoogstraeten used an apostate Jew, a thoroughly ignorant fellow who had been a butcher by trade. After his conversion Johann Joseph Pfefferkorn became a willing tool in the hands of his Dominican masters. He was acclaimed as an expert on Hebrew and on the wickedness of Jewish religion, its practices, and several ghostwritten pamphlets were published under his name. All of them—with titles like "The Jewish Confession" and "The Jewish Mirror"—described the danger of Jewishness and extolled the holiness that would come with the final destruction of the Talmud. Of all the apostates we have encountered Pfefferkorn was indeed a Jewish renegade *par excellence.*

In this campaign an effort was made to engage the help of Reuchlein, who by then—around 1510—had become a recognized authority on the Hebrew language and on Jewish life in general. Behind him lay two years which he had spent in Rome—from 1498 to 1500—where in association with Jewish scholars he had perfected his knowledge of Judaism and of Hebrew. A cultured man of stern good character, Reuchlein declined to have anything to do with Pfefferkorn's scheme. In fact, when he was requested by the emperor to give his opinion on the apostate's planned (and partly executed) activities, Reuchlein submitted a devastating report. The Dominicans were outraged, and published another pamphlet under Pfefferkorn's name, this one sharply criticizing Reuchlein. Reuchlein countered the Dominicans' intemperate accusations in 1511 with an exposé of what they were after in a publication he entitled *Der Augenspiegel,* "The Eye's Mirror." A few years later the controversy had gone so far and had grown so bitter that Reuchlein wanted to appeal to Leo X, at whose court a small but select number of Jews played a special role.

Leo was quite a pious man, yet his life left a legacy that points up his artistic achievements far more than his religious temperament. He was a patron of the arts, and sponsored Raphael's career. Raphael in turn employed one of the Pope's favorite Jewish musicians, Jacopo di Sansecondo (Jacob the Unmatched)—his personal beauty caused as much comment as his music—as his model for the painting of Apollo on Mount Parnassus.*

The Exquisite Jacopo was only one of the group of Jews in the Vatican circle. Another was Giovanni Maria, a highly gifted flutist (later perhaps baptized), who travelled between the Vatican and Venice, where he became *Pifaro dil Doxio* or Flutist to the Doge. Giovanni's art delighted the Pope to such an extent that he made him Count of Verrutium, giving him at the same time a special allowance of twenty-three gold ducats. The third

*A work known as "Parnassus" and now in the Vatican Museum in Rome.

in the musical trio at Leo's court was a Jew of Spanish descent, Angelo Mordechai, who was known as *Galantuomo*, a man of his word, straight and uncorruptible, on whose assistance one could always count. His family name later became Galante.

These ministered to the Pope's soul. His body was in the hands of a Jewish doctor whom we have met before, Jacob ben Immanuel Provinciale, rabbi at the principal Roman synagogue, Papal physician under Alexander VI and Julius II, and better known as Bonet de Lattes.

Reuchlein, rather than make his appeal directly to the Pope, decided to approach him through the intermediary of his physician. This seemed more advisable to him than the choice of the musical trio, whose appeal to the Pope might not have been so effective. The erudite German was a cautious man. He sent the doctor a letter composed in his careful Hebrew, requesting an introduction and recommendation to Leo X, "who had entrusted His holy body to him."

Bonet de Lattes duly transmitted Reuchlein's request. Leo was of the opinion that all this trouble in Germany between Dominicans and Franciscans on one side and Martin Luther on the other—a struggle that went hand in hand with the Reuchlein-Pfefferkorn-Van Hoogstraeten dispute—was "nothing but a quarrel between monks." Still he ordered an investigation.

The Lateran Council decided against the Dominicans and defended Reuchlein, part-champion of the Jewish cause. Among the Jewish community in Rome the decision was naturally hailed as a triumph, not so much a triumph of Jewish influence at Court, but far more as an example of the just and humane attitude of the Pope.

Van Hoogstraeten, Pfefferkorn's mentor, could not comprehend the Vatican's attitude. Jews were evil, Hebrew was evil, but how was it possible that the Vatican could be evil? He came to Rome and posted an attack against Reuchlein on the walls of the city and on a wooden statue in Trastevere (which was specifically used for such purposes) protesting the decision. A surprising thing happened. The Romans, probably not out of sympathy with the Jews but more likely as the result of an antipathy for the Dominicans, tore off the German protestnotes—and van Hoogstraeten left Rome in defeat.

Yet these were the years of such blissful well-being that the Roman Jews decided, as I have already recounted, to send the delegation to Jerusalem to inquire whether the Messiah was to make his appearance. The extraordinary feeling of freedom had started already under Leo's predecessor, Julius II, another art-loving Pope. He laid the cornerstone for the new Saint Peter's, and had Raphael redecorate some of the rooms of the Vatican. Julius' commission to Michelangelo to create for him an appropriately sumptuous tomb, resulted in the magnificent statue of Moses (the tomb was never finished), which now stands in Rome's Church of Saint Peter in Chains. When Michelangelo completed it after Julius' death the spectacle of his chisel at work became the greatest attraction for Jews of all ages, as they marvelled at a piece of Old Testament come to life. They also discussed a question which has occupied art critics for centuries:* Why did the Jewish Moses have horns on his head?

The mistake goes back all the way to the first Torah translation into Greek by Aquila Ponticus in the second century. Mistaking the Hebrew word *karan* (shining, or ray of light) for *keren* (horns), Aquila wrote that Moses had horns, instead of translating that his face *was shining*. The four-language taped oral information that foreign tourists can listen to today inside the Roman church, does not offer any explanation. Moses was given horns by Michelangelo, and his popular image will probably have horns till the end of time.

In this period the living conditions of the Jews made them spread out from the area near the Bridge With The Four Heads. Many of them went to live in the neighbourhood of the Piazza Farnese, where Michelangelo was completing the building which now houses the French embassy. Even today a great many shops in the nearby Via dei Giubbonari—the Street of the

*For a recent scholarly work, see: Ruth Mellinhoff, *The Horned Moses* (University of California Press, 1970). See also Edouard Roditi discussion of St. Jerome's Latin translation of *Exodus 34:29* and the whole medieval tradition of horned helmets (*Commentary*, November 1971, pp. 92-93).

Coatmakers—are Jewish-owned. Tailoring had become an important Jewish profession. Other Jews were pharmacists, and this kept them in close touch with Jewish doctors. The guild system seemed to have gained a foothold too, and for a while there was even a *Master of the Baking of Matzoth*.

Yet the overall situation in Rome had deteriorated. Leo X had spent enormous sums for the beautification of the city, but the people had gone from riches to rags. When Leo died in 1521 a Dutchman born in Utrecht succeeded, and he became the last non-Italian Pope ever to reign. He reigned for only twenty months, and it was Adrian VI, who had been the tutor of King-Emperor Charles V, who had to clean up the financial crises left by Leo. He had neither the time to do it, nor were general social circumstances in his favor. Life in Rome had reached a new low. Prostitution was widespread, and it was reported that an average of six people were found murdered in the street every morning. The ever-recurrent plague afflicted the city. According to one report, nearly twenty-eight thousand people died. Only God, or perhaps His Son and the Virgin Mary, were expected to be able to turn the tide of misery. Anyone who did not honor the cross as the symbol of Christianity was asking for trouble. A Jewish woman who was said to have diverted her eyes from a passing crucifix was forcibly blinded for her nonchalance. The Romans living in Trastevere—for centuries the turbulent neighbourhood of Rome—felt that a good brawl might help, and in staging it they included an assault on the homes of the Jews across the bridge near the Piazza Giudea, where four Jews were killed.

In his series of *"Trias Romana"* epigrams, the outraged Dutch visitor to Rome (he has already given us his opinion on prostitution), pointedly completed his semi-poetical description of the city with lines that suggestively depict Rome as it was during the time when its government was for a brief period in the hands of his countryman, Adrian:

> Of Three Things there is plenty in Rome:
> Fever, Pest, and Poor People.

Three Things exist in Rome:
Expenses, Foul Air, and Adultery.

Three Things are needed in Rome:
Bribes, Good Connections, and Lies.

Three Things everyone wants in Rome:
A Short Mass, a Full Purse, and a Good Time.

Three Things are hardly seen in Rome:
Gold, the Pope, and Humility.

Three Things are needed for success in Rome:
Brute Force, Holiness, and Cunning.

With Three Things one returns from Rome:
An Outraged Conscience, an Angry Stomach, and an Empty Pocket.

And then, in a final mood of disgust, our descriptive visitor to the Holy City gave vent to his disappointment in a few well-chosen lines which suggest perhaps that nothing much has changed in Rome over the centuries:

Three Things adorn Rome:
Old Homes, Crooked Streets, and Confusion.

and lastly,

Three Things one does not do gladly in Rome:
Pray, Pay, and Get out of the Way.

There was, however, one event for which the Romans gladly did get out of the way, and from its inception they continued to do so for two centuries to the detriment of the Jews.

It had all started off rather gaily and pleasantly. Pope Paul II, who had been made a cardinal at the age of twenty-two by his uncle Eugene IV, was a kind Pope in many ways. On the whole the Jews did not have much to complain about. Wanting to enliven the city a bit during carnival time, Pope Paul decided to add a new attraction to the revelry.

The added program-number was "races for two- and four-legged animals," which would start on Monday for boys of fifteen and over. Their prize was a pair of stockings. The following day was reserved for Jews, and the prize went up to three lengths of beautiful cloth. Every other day of the week a new category would compete. Wednesday was reserved for men over seventy. The four-legged category included bulls on Saturday, races for buffaloes and donkeys, and much later—in 1663—there was a special race for hunchbacks and other cripples which must have caused much grotesque hilarity. But by then, of course, Pope Paul's original idea of having really nothing but some good clean fun had been reduced to a festival that took on certain very nasty aspects.

In the beginning the Jews were as pleased with the idea as any other Romans. Their participation had nothing onerous about it. On the contrary, it established them as part of the Roman population, with the only segregated exception that they were to race separately. But that was all. Their part of the expenses covering the races was established at 1130 *fiorini*—1100 for the actual cost, and thirty as a belated compensation for the number of pieces of silver Judas had received for betraying Christ.

It was not until several years had passed that the Romans decided that the running of Jews, especially of old men, was side-splittingly funny, all the more so if before the race they were forced to over-eat, and then had to hop along nearly naked. When, finally, riders on horseback were added to chase them on, the amusement of the populace was almost complete. They might also be pelted by whatever came to hand. Throwing things at defenseless people is always a release, possibly also a safety valve for over-excited tensions, and the appealing idea therefore found instantaneous acclaim.

But all this was only to come later. The start of the races on February 9 1466 was a great festive day for the Romans. Pope Paul, who had just had completed his new palace, the Palazzo Venezia (its construction had started while he was still a cardinal), decided to move the carnival parade from the Piazza Navona to the Via Lata, which at the time was a section of the street in the center of Rome that today is known as the Via del Corso. The new races were to take place here. The start was at the triumphal arch of Marc Antony*, and the finish line was practically under the windows of the palazzo, on the Piazza San Marco right opposite the present-day Victor Emmanuel monument. Eight Jews took part in the race, and this would continue to be their minimum number till the humiliating event was bought off by the Jews in 1667.

It was not the first time Jews had participated in Roman games in Rome. During the fourteenth century a festival had taken place on the Piazza Navona in which they already had played their part—ignominiously. It was known as the "Hunting Game," and the Jews were ridden piggyback. Shortly afterwards, at Monte Testaccio—a huge garbage heap dating back to early Roman times—it is recorded that the same game was played by officers of the army.

Monte Testaccio was the site of still another game in which Jews participated. An unfortunate victim would be put inside a barrel, then would be rolled down the slope, where at the foot the members of the Jewish community were allowed to extricate the poor man. Whether he was dead or alive appeared to be of no special importance.

The races were usually held during carnival, but were sometimes also held in December, on Santo Stefano or second Christmas day. Winter in Rome often being as wet and chilly as anywhere in the north of Europe, these races, especially when run in mere loin-cloths, were an extra incitement to the citizens to cheer the participants on. But the real sight to behold was, of course, the Corso races in the late winter or early spring, when masked crowds frolicked down the streets before and after the sporting event.

The Jews took part in the races but were forbidden to wear masks during the carnival period. Any Jew who could not resist joining the fun was promptly punished by a flogger who was held in readiness in the nearby Via Cavalletto.

For ten days the people living along the Corso would put their windows at the disposal of friends or of the highest bidder. The pavement was strewn with yellow sand, and the houses and

*In 1667 Pope Alexander VII dismantled the arch in order to widen the Corso.

palaces of the rich were hung with tapestries (still today a Roman way of festoonery during state visits). Flower stands were everywhere, and bouquets, flower petals and confetti would be tossed onto the gay crowds. In 1487 a Spanish Jew won the race, barely outrunning a competitor who happened to be knocked down by a horse. It supplied the Romans with an extra day of Jewish fun, because the competition had to be re-run.

Under Julius II the races took on as sumptuous a form as everything else that was done by this stylish Pope. The parade that preceded the game was like the entry of bullfighters into the arena, calling for the best in costume and finery. The runners were dressed in white coats and embroidered capes that hung halfway down their legs. They held lances and halberds, and wore "bizarre hats" (about which the chronicler did not give any detailed description). Thus they paraded in front of the papal palace, the crowds cheering with the usual Italian enthusiasm. The start in that year took place near the great sewer of Santa Lucia, and the moment the trumpets blasted the signal and the rope was pulled away, "the Jews dashed off, pushed on by the covetous will-power to win. . . ."

Towards the end of the sixteenth century whatever gaiety the Jews enjoyed must have dwindled considerably. The course, which frequently was changed, was extended to Castel Sant'Angelo, and the report of an eye-witness indicates that the Jews would have needed a super-extra dose of optimism and enthusiasm to have run with a "covetous will-power"—except to reach the finish line in one piece.

"Last Monday," reads the report, "the Jews had the gratification of running against a strong wind, in a cold rain worthy of that perfidious people. When they arrived at the finish they were obscenely dirty and covered with mud from head to foot."

The phraseology does not exactly indicate sporting feeling. Times had changed in more ways than one, and the Jew had become an objectionable figure that just by chance happened to be composed of flesh, bones, and fairly thin blood. In 1547 one Jewish competitor died during the race. Whether death was caused by old age, by a running horse, a well-directed stone, or a simple heart attack is not known. One thing may be surmised—it was not caused by the will to win.

The harsh fact of the matter is that the races, which had started with the Jews on a more or less equal footing, had degenerated into a week of fun in which the running of the Jews had become the *pièce de résistance*, the high point of the festivities for which everybody waited. It was the day that obscenities could be shouted at frightened and exhausted men, who became the targets of anything that was foul and that could be hurled—verbally or materially. The Jews clutched their sides for protection; the public did the same for laughter.

In 1667, two centuries after the races had started, the Jewish community bought off its compulsory participation for 300 scudi. As a further gesture of goodwill the Jews offered to decorate every year, the small grandstand on the Corso where the judges sat. The races from then on would be run without the Jews. The offer was gladly accepted.

The cost of the decorations amounted to about 29 scudi a year. But with the passing of time the city's demands became such that the Jews had to go out and buy or rent new furnishings for the one-week display. This ran the expenses up to 95 scudi, no small sum. A century later the total amount of income tax paid by the Jews to their own Central Office came to just over 2500 scudi. Between the 300 scudi paid for the buying-off tax, still regularly due, and the hundred scudi required for the embellishment of the jury boxes, the community had to spend one-sixth of its total income in order to be allowed *not* to participate in the festive races.

In 1668, when "Jewish races" were for the first time suspended, and the Jews only had to deliver eight *palii* or banners to be put on the winning horses (one gold, one silver, two velvet, and four made of brocade), the carnival itself went on almost as usual. Even though the Jews were no longer active participants, there was still plenty of opportunity for special fun. The annual ceremony of the opening parade was replaced by a more modest assemblage in the largest reception room of the City Hall on Capitol Hill, as had been decreed by Pope Clement IX in January of that year. The Chief Rabbi of Rome, accompanied by several of the community's Elders, was to offer a bouquet of flowers to the three city magistrates. Hidden inside the bouquet would be an envelope containing twenty scudi, the amount needed for the construction of still another small grandstand, from which the city fathers would view the races.

The speech to be made by the rabbi on that occasion was always more or less the same. Bending slightly forward as a sign of submission, homage, and deference, the rabbi would start by saying that "with a feeling of deep observance and devotion, we the Chief Rabbi and governors of the wretched Jewish community come to you to offer you in the name of that community a humble gift."

The rabbi, furthermore, would assure the magistrates that they would pray the Almighty "for a long and peaceful reign by the Supreme Pontiff." This done, the city magistrate would accept the flowers, take the money, and (according to tradition) he would then pronounce the word "*Go!*"—at the same time giving the stooped rabbi a magisterial kick.

The Jewish delegation, by Supreme Order dressed in ceremonial attire, would then walk the short distance from the Campidoglio back to their nearby homes, jeered at by the Roman populace. When a few years later the city fathers demanded that the rabbi should go down on his knees when addressing them, the community drew the line. Going down on one's knees one only does "before the Almighty," they said, not before just the Mighty. A compromise was reached; the rabbi would only have to bend one knee.

The ceremonial clothes, so inviting for insults, were later on changed for regular street attire. It was not of much help. The Romans knew where and when the ceremony would take place—on the Sabbath, as had been ordered by Clement IX. The rabbi, moreover, could easily be recognized, and the route back home was a known one. Insults and spittle would continue to rain on the heads of the Jewish delegation for a great many years. It was not till 1848 that the objectionable ceremony was abolished. By then a temporary end had come to the Papal powers in Rome. Mazzini and Garibaldi had set up their short-lived Roman Republic, and Pius IX had fled from the Vatican to seek safety at Gaeta in the south.*

But during the nearly two hundred years that the Campidoglio ceremony did take place, the lusty Roman carnival itself had continued its merriment. And with the Jews no longer spending their days at the races, other opportunities for amusement and laughter had to be contrived.

The Roman fishpeddlers, working right next to the Portico d'Ottavia which remained the center of Jewish life and activities, were the cleverest among these new impresarios. They built huge floats to be displayed during the carnival parade, and the Jews were the constant object of their ridicule. Grotesque figures, wildly gyrating while putting on phylacteries in the name of Jehovah, provided some fun. Making a comedy out of the solemn prayers for the dead at funerals could also be diverting, the more so when the dressed-up pseudo-rabbi appeared to drop dead from a heart attack while officiating his travesty. A miniature stage was erected in the center of the Campo Vaccino (just around the corner from where the Jews lived), and a rude play enacted in which Moses and the rabbis appeared as half-man-half-pig. Hilarity was recorded.

The community objected time and again—to the Vatican, to the city magistrates, to anyone who had any power or influence. To little avail. The Jews used Christian agents to give them advance information on the floats the fishmongers were putting together behind closed doors and fences. Year after year a humble but wounded letter of protest would be sent to the Supreme Pontiff, who was their Lord and Master. Quite often the Pope intervened, but the next year the offending displays would be rebuilt. Making fun of the Jews was, after all, not a serious matter. Insults could do no bodily harm.

*On the Pope's return in 1850, the ceremony partly resumed. Gregorovius, the German historian, reports that "today (that is: 1856) the Jews still come to the Capitol on the eve of carnival, to offer their *palii* for the horses."

One of the many protest notes, dating from the early eighteenth century and preserved at the library of the Jewish community in Rome, gives a good example of what went on. The fishmongers, wrote the Chief Rabbi to the Congregation of the Holy Office, continued to display offensive scenes on their carnival floats, "making fun of circumcision, of the unleavened bread, of the wedding ceremony, and of many other Mosaic rites."

The Vatican gave in to the protest and forbade such tasteless demonstrations. Unfortunately, that year—1709—the Polish prince Alexander Sobiesky happened to be in Rome. He had been told about the hilarious shenanigans, especially the funeral float which parodied the death of a rabbi, and the prince requested a repeat performance under his palace windows. Such a royal request could not be set aside by the Vatican, and the show went on. Indeed it inspired the fishpeddlers, and the next year they arranged a parade of a hundred fictitious Jews riding donkeys, preceded by a rabbi riding backwards, waving a Torah.

In the Papal States things changed only very slowly. The four centuries from 1466 to 1848 often were turbulent—for the Jews, for Rome, and for the Pope. As far as the Jews were concerned, one of the high points occurred about sixty years after the footraces had started. It was the arrival in their midst in 1524 of a man who by some was hailed as a King of the Jews (by others as the brother of the King of some of the Jews), and of whom all, including the Pope, thought he would fight for Christians and Jews together to free the Holy Land from the Moslem invader.

The mysterious visitor, who raised hopes in the hearts of many when abstract hope was the only reality to help keep alive, was David ben Shelomoh of the Tribe of Rueben. And not since the arrival of the false prince Alexander under Caesar Augustus had expectations run so high among the Jews of Rome.

Chapter 17
The Jewish Crusader

The time was ripe for it. The sense of happiness and freedom that always filled the Jewish community when there was no direct attack on their religion, had reached a new high under Leo X. There was poverty in Rome, yes—and misery. The Jews, as far as welfare was concerned, were not any better off than the rest of the Romans. But as far as life and liberty were concerned, hardly a Jew was killed simply because he was a Jew. As for religion itself, to be allowed *to profess* that religion, which to the Jews had always constituted a necessity far greater and more valuable than life itself, that freedom existed under Leo X. And even if, now and then, there were encroachments, there was always the Pope as the last instance —and a protest would get a hearing.

Of course, as so often happens, the intense religious life suffered under such circumstances. It was not that the Roman Jew was less of a Jew than before, but the freedom he felt would lead a younger generation to depart from the very rigorous rules that were supposed to govern daily life. As would be the case later (and as still happens in the twentieth century), there was a distinct difference between the often intense feeling of *being* a Jew, and the outer formal display of that feeling.

A good many Roman Jewish youngsters were allowed to go to the university in those happy days. In some cases their knowledge of Latin was often greater than that of Hebrew. The study of the Greek philosophers held a stronger attraction than the study of the Talmud. A future as doctor, or some other free profession, promised higher remuneration and a better worldly life than the future as a teacher of Hebrew. Many men did go to the synagogue on Saturday. But many others preferred a pleasant stroll, especially when the Roman sun was shining, and young men and women were about on the streets.

Would the Messiah really appear? The news brought back from Jerusalem had been negative. Yet did this matter so very much? After all, it was mostly in times of *stress* that the Jews would ardently pray for the coming of the Messiah, who was then to deliver them from their life of hardship. These were the moments of urgent hope, the anxious waiting for the event that would bring relief from oppression and subjugation. But when life was good or joyful or fairly happy, then the Messiah would be expected in a different way—as the crowning glory of exactly that state of benevolence, the final and all-englobing confirmation and culmination of the Paradise to come.

Little troubles within the community did not appear to matter much during good years; and even the big troubles, although they were not to be brushed aside, were sure to be settled somehow. The antithesis that had slowly developed among the old Roman Jews, the *Italiani*, and the newcomers from Spain, Portugal, the Provence, and Sicily, known as the *Tramontani* (those from across the mountains) had split the community into several factions. Yet even this did not affect the sense of well-being, it was far more the *result* of it. Opposed from the outside, the Jews would stand together. With no one on the outside overly bothering them, troubles were apt to develop on the inside.

Pope Clement called in a friend to reorganize the community's governing rules. He was Rabbi Donzeille from Pisa, also known as Rabbi Daniel ben Isaac, a rich banker who was held in much esteem by both Christians and Jews. The wise rabbi acquitted himself brilliantly. Three *fattori* or administrators were named, and they would be responsible to the Papal Court for everything connected with life inside the Jewish community. They were to be assisted by a council of sixty members, to be chosen half and half from among the poor and the rich. Towards the end of 1524 the rules drawn up by Rabbi Daniel were confirmed by the Pope, and everybody, wherever he came from, seemed to be satisfied. Addressing himself "to the Jews, the Romans as well as those from the other side of the mountains," Clement VII confirmed their rights and decreed that they "should be observed by all for all times." The Pope, of course, was an optimist.

Yet in 1524 the Jews of Rome were jubilant. It had been an extraordinary year. If the Messiah had not yet made his appearance, a highly promising advance guard had arrived in their midst—that mysterious envoy from across the seas, who had roamed the deserts of Arabia with his 300,000 nomadic Jewish companions, the reborn members of the dispersed Tribe of Reuben, governed by the envoy's brother Joseph, King of the Jews. The Thousand Year Realm was surely approaching, and David ben Shelomoh of the Tribe of Reuben, to be known forever after as David Reubeni, enthralled the Roman Jews.

News of his arrival had come from Venice early in 1524. His ship, on which he had sailed from Alexandria, had dropped anchor in January, and soon the Venetian Jews spread his fame all over the country. The story he told about his past seemed indisputable. He was a tanned, small, sinewy person, looking "very much like an Arab," was an excellent horseman, and spoke fluent Hebrew and Arabic. His knowledge of both the Talmud and the Kabbalah was considerable.

Whether the tales about his childhood are true has never been ascertained. Max Brod in his novel *Reubeni, King of the Jews*, makes him an obvious imposter who was supposed to have been born in Poland or Russia. An imposter he probably was, and a magnificent one, but he must also have been a great utopian dreamer, honestly convinced of the feasibility of his grand schemes. It is fair to assume that David Reubeni was born somewhere in the Middle East, although his knowledge of those countries at times seemed to emerge from the haze of a *fata morgana*.

The information that reached Rome was that of a childhood spent around Mount Tabor, and of a brother who was king of the nomadic Jews roaming around the countryside between Medina and Damascus, centering on the oasis of Khaibar.* In his thirties when he arrived in Venice, Reubeni claimed that he had left his homeland at an early age, to cross the Red Sea from Jidda to Suakin, a famous Sudanese slave port (it is still used by Mohametans from all over Africa on their *hadj* to Mecca and—as some claim—is still a slave port). From Suakin Reubeni had continued his trip to visit those dispersed Jews in the country of Prester John. This is the legendary king of a legendary kingdom, often located in Africa, and taken at times for the kingdom of Abyssinia or Ethiopia. It is possible that Reubeni mixed his fantasies with facts about the actual Jewish "Fallasha" tribe living north of Lake Tana.

The Venetian Jews had to absorb this exhilarating news in a hurry, because that was the condition Reubeni himself was in —he wanted to rush on to Rome to see the Pope. His fame had preceded him, and he was surrounded by multitudes when he crossed the city on horseback on his way to see Cardinal Egidio of Viterbo. This cardinal was known as a great friend of the Jews and as an expert on the Hebrew language. Reubeni found him in the company of one of his Jewish teachers, Joseph Ashkenazi—an auspicious beginning indeed.

The accompanying Jews stood back, but remained close enough to hear the conversation. Could they believe their ears?

*In Reubeni's own memoirs the place is indicated as Tabor, which in Hebrew easily can be misread for Kabor—hence Khaibar, an oasis about 100 miles north of Medina in Saudi Arabia, predominantly Jewish, partly-nomadic settlement. Mohammed conquered Khaibar in the year 628.

If the plans they heard Reubeni propose could be carried out, would not the Ten Commandments be put back on Mount Sinai, and might not the Vatican proclaim David Reubeni a bona fide Jewish saint? What Reubeni proposed was nothing less than a Jewish crusade to reconquer the Holy Land, with weapons to be furnished by various Christian countries, plus some ordnance experts to teach his 300,000 Bedouin Jews how to make gunpowder and all the practical instruments of war.

Evidently the Cardinal was impressed, even if the Jews present could not quite comprehend. Reubeni remained firm and poised through it all. This was what he had come for, this was what he proposed, this was what he would do—it was a fair proposition of mutual interest. Where half-a-dozen major and an even greater number of minor Christian crusades had failed, where the Knights Hospitalers and Templars had been defeated, there the Jews would succeed. Their fast horses would lead them from Arabia to Acre to Jerusalem, the coveted summit of Mount Zion would be peacefully shared by Christians and Jews, and the Moslems would be crushed forever.

That weekend David spent at the homes of the Cardinal and of Rabbi Ashkenazi, while the Jews of Rome spread the word about the incredible Messiah. The synagogues were full that Saturday. There were many who, after the religious services, hoped to catch a glance of the would-be warrior and perhaps even touch him, surely as close to God's own blessing as any Jew could get that day. Towards evening another bit of news spread through the streets near the Bridge With The Four Heads like flames through tinderwood: at the request of Cardinal Egidio, Pope Clement VII would receive David Reubeni the next morning. The holy Kiddush wine that evening was sipped with all eyes directed towards Jerusalem, where—who could know?—a new Temple might soon be built.

The joy was even more intense the next morning when David, accompanied by an official group of Elders and an unofficial group of just about everybody, was introduced to Clement VII by the obliging cardinal. The Pope was most gracious. Since the Turkish danger in the Balkans was growing worse, a diver-

sion caused by a Jewish attack through Islam's back door might
well temporarily diminish, and perhaps even altogether end the
threat of a further invasion of Europe.

Reubeni explained that it would be simple to transport
weapons and men across the Red Sea to Arabia. The best way to
do this would be to load men and materiel on ships belonging to
the King of Portugal, the Portuguese being the most intrepid
mariners of the day. The Pope, whose relations with the 22-
year-old King John III in Lisbon were excellent, promised a
letter of introduction. Requesting royal help in Papal under-
takings was simple in those days when the worldly power of the
Vatican was so great. With new lands to be conquered or
reconquered during the coming Jewish crusade, the Pope was
sure King John III would think twice before refusing—the more
so because the Portuguese for several years had been exploring
the lands of the mythical Prester John—Abyssinia—which
Reubeni claimed to have visited.

What commotion! From the Piazza Giudea to the Piazza di
Pescaria, and from the Campo de' Fiori to the Bridge With The
Four Heads, the conversation that evening could hardly have
touched upon anything else. Not only the Jews were intrigued,
excited, hopeful, but the minds of the various diplomatic envoys in Rome were at equally feverish pitch. Reubeni's
proposals, if realized, might well change the whole map of the
Middle East; any seafaring and trading nation had better look
out for its interests.

The Venetian ambassador in Rome was involved in the
speculation, and in March 1524 he sent off a report to the
Doge. Informing him of David Reubeni's arrival and reception at the Vatican, he explained how the Pope had been told
about the 300,000 nomadic Jews who only lacked the necessary
weapons in order to go to war. "The use of guns is unknown to
them," the envoy wrote, "that is why Reubeni would like some
specialists who are familiar with the manufacture of rifles and
gunpowder to accompany him." He added the remark that this
was the only skill in which the Jews were inferior to the
Mohametans, the enemies of the Pope.

Reubeni stayed on in Rome for about a year, and his stature appeared to be constantly growing. When Cardinal Egidio had to leave the city for two months, David asked Rabbi Daniel of Pisa—still at work on his reorganisation of the Jewish community—to be his interpreter with His Holiness, "inasmuch as he sees the Pope frequently, lives near the Papal palace, and is rich, learned, and esteemed." The rabbi was delighted to serve such a noble person and, through him, such a noble purpose. He entertained his guest at his home.

The Pope arranged for visits to all the sights of Rome, and it was said that he even allowed Reubeni to enter Saint Peter's on horseback to inspect the main altar. On another occasion the Papal trumpeteers offered the Jewish envoy a serenade in front of the rabbi's home. Clement, under Reubeni's influence (and perhaps to strengthen him in his project to go to Portugal), even allowed some Portuguese Marranos in Rome to reconvert to Judaism, an unheard-of favor. Wherever David went, enthusiastic crowds would follow and acclaim him. And so, when his star had finally risen to its zenith and its messianic glow illuminated the Roman skies, Reubeni judged that the time had come for him to leave for Lisbon. Accompanied by Rabbi Daniel, he paid another visit to the Pope in February 1525.

Clement VII had the promised letters of introduction ready for him, not only to King John III, but also to the King of Abyssinia (whose name also happened to be David). The Pope informed the African king that he already had been in touch with his regal equal, the King of Portugal. He requested all possible help and guidance for Reubeni, since the countries he planned to conquer were closer to Abyssinia than to Italy, and consequently would be better known to King David.

With that, and with ten gold scudi plus a heraldic shield as a farewell present from the Pope, David Reubeni on March 15, 1525 started on his triumphal parade through Italy in the direction of Livorno; there he was to set sail for Portugal. Jews and non-Jews in every city he passed through hailed him as if he were a general whose campaign had already proved victorious. Christianity and Judaism were on the march, hand in hand, personified in the figure of a great Jewish warrior. The Messiah, or at least his shock troop, was on the way.

Passing through Pisa, news reached Reubeni that John III was eagerly looking forward to his arrival. The Pope had organized the trip in all its details, including a ship full of war gear, manned by a perfect ecumenical crew—half Jewish, half Christian. Off they sailed, and the blessings from every Jewish community in Italy accompanied them.

The reception in Lisbon was monumental. The King received him royally, a miracle in a country which so recently had let the Inquisition loose on Jew and ex-Jew alike; the arrival of the Jewish Knight in Armor also created a sensation among the Marranos. Had David been a quarter- or half-Messiah to the Jews in Rome, the Inquisition-terrified Portuguese Marranos hailed him as the True Deliverer. His was the Jewish Kingdom-Come, and they were more than ready to share it.

Things moved more slowly in Lisbon after the King's first enthusiasm had cooled off. The conquest of Arabia had a great religious appeal. But sending ships to fertile Brazil and around the Cape of Good Hope to spice-rich India—Vasco da Gama at that very moment was off on his third trip to the new Far-Eastern colonies, now as viceroy—was a far more lucrative business. Reubeni could wait, and wait he did—for about a year-and-a-half. Slowly his patience began to run out. There were also difficulties in his relations with the Marrano community.

Especially the constant appeals made to Reubeni by one Diego Pires, a Marrano scribe at a Lisbon tribunal (and possibly a private secretary to King John), made Reubeni feel highly uneasy. He sensed the precariousness of his position as a supplicating Jew, even though supported by the Pope. He was a guest at a definitely anti-Jewish court, and he tried to keep as far removed from the Marranos as politeness and religious decency permitted. Unfortunately young Pires was insistent to the point of discomfort.

Diego Pires was about twenty years old at the time. Born from forcibly baptized parents who secretly had held on to their former religion, Diego's enthusiasm for David Reubeni was unlimited, and he confided his intentions to David—he wanted openly to re-embrace the religion of his forefathers. This obviously would have been a disaster for Reubeni. Perhaps in order to get rid of him, or perhaps even in the young man's own interest, David advised him to leave Portugal and to go east. Wanting to be not only a Jew, but a complete Jew as well, Diego Pires circumcized himself before his departure; no doctor in the shadow of the Inquisition country would be willing to perform such an operation. Shedding his name with his foreskin, he stealthily left Portugal as Shelomoh (Solomon) Molcho; so he would be known from then on. Shelomoh slowly found his way to Saloniki, Adrianople, and Palestine, constantly studying Hebrew, the Talmud, and the Kabbalah.

David Reubeni decided to leave Portugal and to return to Rome. His trip back took a little longer than his outbound voyage, since he no longer had a papal ship at his disposal. He took the overland route through Spain, and was moreover detained for two years in Avignon. When he resumed his travels, Reubeni returned to Italy, still the grand seigneur, but no longer so certain that an army under his own and his brother's command would ever cross the Red Sea on Portuguese ships. He apparently stayed again for a short while in Rome, and then emerged in the autumn of 1530 in Venice, his point of departure six years previously.

What had happened to Shelomoh Pires or Molcho in the meantime? He had soaked up Jewish lore and knowledge in Palestine, where he stayed for a while in Safed. He heard about the sacking of Rome in 1527 by troops allied to Charles V. To him this could only mean the destruction of the Christian land of Idumaea, the Edom which had been subjugated by the Jews so many centuries earlier; and it would also be a sign that the Messiah's coming was near. It had taken the news a while to reach the Middle East from Rome, and it took Shelomoh a while to reach Rome from the Middle East. But towards the end of 1529 one report has him sitting at the foot of the Bridge With The Four Heads, dressed in rags, mingling with the beggars. Alternating between this Jewish bridge and the one in front of the Castel Sant' Angelo, he tried to get the feeling of what was going on in the Papal City.

Immersed in his kabbalistic dreams, and his wits sharpened by the misery he saw around him (and doubtless by his own hunger), Shelomoh began to have visions. He saw catastrophes for all of Europe looming on the Christian horizon, especially in those two centers of Christian power that had been governing his life and that of his fellow Marranos—Portugal and Rome. In February 1530 the vague visions took on a piercing sharpness and Shelomoh clearly saw a tremendous flood in Rome (and also in the Lowlands which were ruled by that most Catholic of all Catholic emperors, Charles V). Portugal was to be struck by a possibly worse fate, an earthquake that would devastate the whole countryside. After that the skies would clear, according to Shelomoh's visions, and a new star would appear in the heavens.

It was too important a message to keep to himself; and there was only one person with whom he wanted to share his knowledge—the *pro tem* Master of the World, the Pope. Clement VII was not unimpressed by the predictions; and, as had happened with Reubeni several years before, Shelomoh's name spread magically through the Jewish community. Participating in an intense Jewish life for the first time since he had left the East, Shelomoh became one of the most fervent members of the largest Roman synagogue, where he preached every Saturday to the congregation. They were all impressed by his fire, his dreams, by his impassioned Jewish feeling.

As for David Reubeni, he had taken up in Venice where he had left off in Rome. Again the Jewish community was swept along by his tales about the liberation of the lands of their forefathers. The messianic feeling David spread around himself made the Venetian Jews look up to him as the leader who would be able to free them from their chains. The chains had been put on them securely, for since 1516 the Doge had enclosed the Venetian Jews inside a ghetto.

When Shelomoh Molcho heard that the person he revered and idolized so much was in Venice, he rushed up from Rome.

The meeting between the two men who had not seen each other since one of them had not even been a "full Jew," was warm and tempestuous. Their identical views on the future of Israel strengthened and stimulated their individual dynamism. Yet there was a difference in their attitudes. Both were men of high pressured energy. But David's ideas could be said to be of a more practical nature; Shelomoh's feelings were more in the visionary realm of prophetic religion. Still, it appears that he rather liked the somewhat ostentatious life Reubeni was leading in Venice, the magnificent clothes he wore, and the number of servants (five in all) who were at his disposal.

David asked the city authorities to be allowed to live outside the ghetto, where his quietude was constantly disturbed. At this point the Doge thought he would like to find out a little more about the man who, for the second time, was filling the minds of the Venetian Jews with messianic expectations. One of their most brilliant citizens, the author Gian-Batista Ramusio, was requested to have a talk with Reubeni. The conversation was a wide-ranging one and Reubeni told Ramusio about his visit to the country of Prester John. But when pressed for geographical details—with which Ramusio was familiar—there were some strange gaps in his knowledge. Yet David's rhetorical display, full of supernatural kabbalistic pronouncements, greatly impressed the Venetian interrogator. Still, he suspected that behind the messianic facade an imposter might be hiding; with his dark complexion—as he informed the governors of the city—he might even be an Arab or an Abyssinian.

The Doge did not need much time to make up his mind. Reubeni was to be allowed to live outside the ghetto, on condition that it would be very far out. He was kindly but urgently requested to pack his bags and decamp with his five servants to other regions. It was a bitter blow for Reubeni, but rather less upsetting to Shelomoh Molcho, who had been busy elsewhere while Reubeni was being investigated.

Shelomoh had gotten himself somehow involved in a royal marriage, that of King Henry VIII of England. The king, at odds with the Vatican on the subject of his divorce from his first

wife, Catharine of Aragon, had tried to get support from wise
men all over Europe in his attempts to sway the Pope to let him
marry his new love, Anne Boleyn. The king's emissary in
Venice had managed to embroil two famous Jews in the matter,
whose opposing opinions—for and against the divorce—made
for an embittered confrontation. In this legal struggle Shelomoh
Molcho took the side of Elia Halfon against Jacob Mantino, an
immensely influential physician with excellent connections at
the Vatican. (Mantino's subsequent role in Shelomoh's life
revealed the darker side of his character.)

There was still another and more personal reason that made
Shelomoh temporarily overlook the Venetian expulsion order
against his closest friend. The first of his predictions had come
true! Early in October 1530 the Tiber had risen higher than ever
before, and had flooded large sections of the city. Shelomoh,
wanting to see with his eyes what his mind had prophesied,
rushed back to Rome. He was soon convinced of the drama that
had happened. The Tiber had flooded a huge part of Rome,
causing three hundred people to lose their lives, but thanks to
Molcho's early warning the Pope had been able to seek safety in
nearby Ostia.

Clement was naturally impressed by the Jewish clairvoyant's
vision, and took him under his personal protection. His esteem
for Shelomoh increased even more when the second and third
prophesy also turned into reality: there was an earthquake in
Portugal early in 1531, and in the autumn of that same year a
bright light streaked through the sky (it later became known as
Halley's comet, named after the English astronomer who had
tracked its course). Shelomoh, one might say, was sitting on
Papal velvet.

Yet, for all the successes, there was still the obstacle of Jacob
Mantino, the physician who would neither forgive nor forget.
Shelomoh's opposition to him in the King's divorce case had
made him vindictive and irresponsible: and he, a Jew, came to
Rome to accuse Shelomoh Molcho, another Jew, before the Inquisition. Mantino discovered, however, that he had a far
mightier opponent in the Pope than in the reconverted Por-

tuguese Marrano. So the doctor tried a different attack. He obtained one way or another some correspondence between Shelomoh and one of his Jewish teachers in Saloniki, and Mantino charged—on the basis of a translation done by himself—that Shelomoh had made disparaging remarks about Christianity. This was considered by the Inquisition to be far worse than blasphemy or Protestantism, since the remarks were made by an ex-Marrano who had dared to forsake the true Christian faith. This was unforgivable, and not even the Pope could save his protegé from being burned at the stake.

It was a hasty sentence, and it was carried out even more hastily. Once the flames had consumed the last fibers of Shelomoh's body, the members of the Inquisition proceeded to the Pope to announce the accomplishment of their purification rite. The Pope beckoned to open the door to the next room. Out stepped. . . . Shelomoh Molcho, who had been hidden by His Holiness in defiance of the Inquisition. The black-clad Inquisitors blanched and discovered too late that they had picked up a man who looked astonishingly like their intended victim, and that they had burned some totally innocent fellow in Molcho's place.

The Jews of Rome, hearing about "the new miracle," tried to defend and protect Shelomoh, to have his life saved a second time. Yet the power of the Inquisition was not to be denied. Having once rescued Molcho from certain death, there was little else even the Pope could do but to make special arrangements for him to flee the city. For the Jewish community, first enthralled by Reubeni, then by Molcho's astonishing predictions, and finally by the miraculous way he had escaped from torture at the stake, Molcho's departure seemed to herald the end of an era of supernatural good fortune.

Traveling north, Shelomoh once again joined forces with David Reubeni. Together again, the utopian political pretender and the apocalyptical religious zealot devised a plan, and it would convince the only man in Europe who had as much, if not more, power than the Pope.

Charles V was in Regensburg in Upper Bavaria, presiding

over a Diet of all the German princes. The King-Emperor was their last resort, and they took pains to be dressed properly, to make an impression. When they reached Regensburg, Shelomoh Molcho, wearing a long cape, also carried his own personal triangular flag,* shaped like the open beak of a bird. The flag's cloth is fully embroidered with silver and golden now partly-faded Hebrew letters, many of which seem to have no meaning at all, although they may have had a mystical significance for Shelomoh Molcho. Next to the single letters there is a still readable inscription, also in Hebrew: "The Eternal is King, was King, and will remain King in all eternity." It was said that in order to flatter Charles V, a pennant was attached to the flag with the words: "Who is equal to You among the Gods, O Lord?"—but it seems highly improbable that such additional text would have been penned by a man as devout as Shelomoh.

Unfortunately neither the garb nor the flag carried much weight with the Emperor. Charles did not trust either of the two men, had them put in chains, and took them back with him to Bologna, where he had another meeting with the Pope. (The first meeting had taken place in Bologna when Clement reluctantly crowned Charles there in 1530.)

January 1533 saw the conclusion of the spectacular adventure that had started nine years earlier in Rome. The Italian mail, which even then was not famed for postal speed, had finally caught up with events. An answer to an inquiry by the King of Portugal arrived from the King of Abyssinia, with a copy addressed to Clement VII. There was no definitive yes or no, but no matter what the King of Kings and Lion of Judah might have decided at such a late hour, it was too late to save the neck of Reubeni, King of the Jews.

The Inquisition had its moment of triumph. There was keen interest in Reubeni, but even more so in Shelomoh—the Jew who had dared turn his back on Christianity. In Mantova, Shelomoh Molcho, ex-Diego Pires, was condemned for the second time to be burned at the stake.

---

*Flag and cape are extant. They are preserved in the Jewish Museum of Prague, where the author has seen and photographed them. (See illustrations.)

A special envoy from Charles V arrived on horseback, having covered the seventy miles that separate Mantova from Bologna. It seemed to be a race with death, for there is reason to believe that the courier was sent at the instigation of the Pope in a last-minute effort to save the life of the man he had admired so much and protected for so long. The message the courier brought resulted in the putting of a simple but crucial question. Would Molcho recant? If he would swear off his Jewish religion, couldn't his life be spared? But surely it was a useless question to put to a man who had performed his own circumcision and who had now spent nearly ten years of his adult life as a deeply religious and even fanatical Jew.

The mission to Mantova failed. Nearly sixty years earlier, eighty miles north of Mantova as the crow flies, little Simon of Trent had been killed and been made a saint. The Jews, of course, have no saints. Shelomoh Molcho simply perished, a man who had roamed the world in search of truth, and who paid for his quest with his life.

It may be assumed that David Reubeni's end did not come much later. He was taken to Spain, where he was turned over to the Inquisition at Llerano in the Estremadura.

In Rome the news of the passing of the two men was received with sadness and resignation. Yet another prophet was gone, yet another hopeful Messiah had turned out to be the wrong one. The rising of the Jewish Bedouins remained a dream beyond the seas, and David Reubeni became a memory. Only the Marranos wept. They wept for the loss of a man who till the bitter end had dared to stand up for the convictions of all of them.

Chapter 18
The Inquisition

In 1528, when Shelomoh Molcho made his belated, hectic trip
from the Middle East to Rome because he felt that Edom had
been razed and good news for the Jews was in the air, he found
that the situation was not as bad as he had thought (or perhaps
even had hoped).

French and German troops, fighting on the side of Charles V,
had plundered the city for three weeks; and good Pope Clement
VII (who had sent Reubeni on his way to Portugal) first saved
himself inside Castel Sant'Angelo, then fled to Orvieto. The
enemy had killed many in Rome, and hunger and pestilence
took care of many more. The total number of victims is said to
have surpassed 100,000. And since in a non-religious war
soldiers usually make very little difference between circumcized
and uncircumcized enemies, the Roman Jews had suffered with
the other citizens.

The Pope fared badly, some of his cardinals fared worse. The
kind Egidio of Viterbo, who had introduced Reubeni to His

Holiness, lost his precious library and all other possessions, as did Elia Levita, his teacher of Hebrew. Elia has left us some lines of verse with his impressions of the siege and its aftermath:

> That year it was in the air
> That Rome, a city great and fair,
> Would be destroyed, of all bereft,
> And without a single penny left.
> It was a time of great distress,
> No food to eat, no clothes to dress. . . .

For an author who was known to put a lot of deep thought into his writing, this short description of the situation was rather thin in philosophical range. But perhaps Levita, who was also known as Elia ben Asher Halevi the German (he was born in Neustadt, not far from Nuremburg, but spent most of his life in Italy), only got through the holocaust because he was fortified by a sense of humor and a casual indifference. He was, at his best, one of the finest Jewish poets of that period, whose literary works, later translated in various languages, were printed on one of the first Jewish presses allowed in Rome by the Pope. The press was situated on the Piazza Montanara, close to the heart of the Jewish section (the Via Montanara still exists), and it is reported that Elia Levita would often come there in the company of his friend the cardinal, to proofread his writings.

Rome collapses, Rome recovers. If Elia Levita and even some of the cardinals had lost all their belongings in 1527, it did not take too many years for the general economic situation of Rome to return to fairly normal. When Pope Paul III took over from Clement VII in 1534, the great last years of the Renaissance made Rome blossom. A Farnese by birth, the Pope built the magnificent palace that bears his name (today the French embassy), and as one of his greatest artistic legacies he had Michelangelo decorate the Sistine Chapel.

The Roman Jews for a while blossomed with the times. So much so, that Cardinal Jacopo Sadoleto, who did his best to bring the dissident European Protestants back into the fold of the Church, wrote in 1539: "How is it possible to see the

Protestants persecuted in the name of religion, when at the same time the Jews are tolerated? . . . " The cardinal was clearly no partisan on the side of the Pope in this matter. "Never before," in his opinion, "have Christians been patronized as the Jews have been under Paul III."

Even though the Jewish community thrived under this partly-benevolent Pope, their wealth was not quite of the order that allowed them to build palaces and arrange sumptuous gardens. Elia Levita, for one, was highly critical of the newly-rich Christians he saw around him. He wrote:

> My heart looks in disgust at the prevaricator,
> Who sells his soul to increase his wealth,
> Who embellishes his garden for himself alone,
> And builds palaces on the earth that is not his.
> Hew to the truth and ban the lie,
> For it is on truth only that peace is built,
> Deceit is mother and daughter of dissension.

Indeed dissension was rife all over Europe. The schism in the Church of Rome was spreading, and the Church was beginning to fight back. Kind and good as Pope Paul might have been in many ways, there were others around him who considered any method fair, as long as it preserved the unity of Roman theological thought and authority. Under the influence of Cardinal Carafa, the Church's greatest militant against heretics and Jews, the Pope in 1542 officially instituted the Holy Office, better known as the Office of the Roman Inquisition. It was not the only cloud on the Jewish horizon. Other signs were already darkening the sky.

Using his purse for the beautification of Rome, Pope Paul simultaneously began to use his temporal power to support the measures that soon would throttle the life of the Jewish community. It was, perhaps, not his intention to do so. Yet the various institutions which he consented to establish would quietly, quickly, and with sinister intent develop into instruments of moral and physical torture of the Jews.

The first Roman loan bank was opened in 1539. One year

later the Pope gave his consent to the organisation started by Ignatius of Loyola as the Society of Jesus, and which would be known henceforth as the Order of the Jesuits. Based on a humanitarian principle (to follow both the doctrine and the simplicity of life as propagated by Christ), some of its most ardent followers soon would make the existence of the Jews an unmitigated hell.

In 1543 the Jesuits received permission from the Pope to establish two homes in Rome for Jews who wanted to convert to Christianity—one for men, the other for women.* The idea was to reserve these homes, the *Case di Catecumeni* or Homes for Catechumen, for those Jews who freely wanted to change their religion; but before long Jews who had no intention whatever to exchange the Star of David for the Star of Bethlehem, were to be dragged through its doors.

Under pressure from the Jesuits, the Jewish converts or neophytes were to break off all relationship with their families. At the same time these families were prohibited from any act of disinheritance. On top of this, it was decided in 1554 under Pope Julius III that the upkeep of the two homes was to be supported by the Jews themselves at the rate of ten ducats per synagogue. When, in later years, Papal pressures had drastically reduced the number of synagogues, the total amount which at first had been paid by the earlier synagogues, some 115 in number, finally became the financial burden of the Roman Jews exclusively. Thus the Jewish community along the Tiber was faced with a struggle on two fronts—one religious, one financial. As had been the case before, the religious attacks sometimes were staved off with money; but soon money was of no avail, nor even available.

It was the factor of financial gain that, to a great extent, brought about the downfall of the Jews. But the money-making effort was, however, a Christian effort, and, most incongruously, the profit was to come from the sale of Jewish literature.

In Venice two Christian publishers had discovered that the

*At number 82 in the *Via in Celci* in Rome is the Monastery of the *Clarisse di Lorenzo in Panisperna*, one of the original homes of female Jewish neophytes.

printing of Jewish books, especially of the Talmud, could be a lucrative affair. Both Marcantonio Giustiniani and his competitor Alvise Bragadini were set on obtaining exclusive rights. In the literary rivalry that followed, each printer accused the other of publishing material that was detrimental to the interests of the Church. But who could read Hebrew and therefore be a judge? Converted Jews, of course.

Thus both parties sent emissaries to Rome to plead their own cause and attack that of the opposition. Julius III was at something of a loss, because in general his feeling for the Jews was not unfriendly. He had been most lenient in the case of forced baptism, and had imposed a fine of one thousand ducats on any Christian who baptized a Jewish child against the wish of its parents. But could he be lenient when a war was being waged on Christian learning? Enough of these attacks already were taking place outside Italy. The Reformation movement set into historic motion by Luther in Germany had found independent fellow remonstrants in Calvin in the French-speaking world, and in Zwingli in Switzerland. The British Protestants had seceded, and the whole movement was greatly helped by the invention of printing which made the cheaply reproduced dissident word available to all. The Pope therefore had enough trouble to combat this ever-spreading anti-Church movement outside Italy, and he certainly could not allow offensive statements against the Church to be published in Italy itself, within or outside the Papal States.

Among the converted Jews who came to plead the case of the Venetian printers was one rather notable figure—the former Shelomoh Romano, now known as Vittorio Eliano. His second name came from Elia, and the Elia from whom he descended was none other than Elia Levita, his grandfather, the stalwart of Jewish thought in Rome and teacher of Hebrew to cardinals.

Another of the apostates was Joseph Moro Zarphati who had taken the Christian name of Andreas del Monte, in honor of the family of Pope Julius III. He, too, had a famous Jew as a grandfather, Joseph ben Samuel Zarphati, who had been private physician to Julius II. Some of Joseph's children had wandered off to the Near East and Africa, and Andreas del Monte's original middle-name of *Moro* (the *Moor*) clearly indicates his African background. (He came, indeed, from Fez.)

The ex-Zarphati and ex-Levita, helped by some other apostates, did all they could to convince the Pope of the pernicious influence the Jewish printed word would have on the Christian religion, whether published by Giustiniani or by Bragadini. Their efforts were greatly enhanced by the example of a certain Cornelio di Montalcino, a Franciscan monk who had recently converted to Judaism. If the Jewish word could have such a disorienting influence, argued the devout apostates, then the Jewish word should be burned. To set a more proper example, the unfortunate monk was burned first.

Soon the commercial matter was taken out of the hands of the competing Venetian printers, and handed to a committee of cardinals, many of whom could not read Hebrew either. But with the Counter-Reformation on the offensive, a clear or expert understanding of what it was all about was not really necessary—even if it was, as the outraged Flemish Humanist Andreas Maes wrote to one of the cardinals, "like asking blind men to judge colors." But then Jewish apostates were always available to offer their own special expertise.

The Church was persuaded, and the Pope in 1553 sent instructions to all bishops, worldly rulers, and other magistrates to confiscate the Talmud. But since the magistrates (and most others) understood even less Hebrew than the cardinals themselves, *all* Jewish writing was considered offensive, and the Papal order degenerated into the indiscriminate confiscation of Jewish books. In Rome the action was crowned by a special festival that took place on what was considered to be a most appropriate date: 9 September 1553, the Jewish New Year. On the Campo de' Fiori—only two steps from the Papal Farnese Palace, and today better known for its colorful market—a huge auto-da-fé took place in which the accumulated achievement of so many Jewish writers and thinkers went up in smoke.

Andreas Maes, who already registered his objections to the choice of the cardinals who had to judge what was and was not offensive in the Talmud, wrote another letter, in which he gave vent to his disappointment and anger about the blatant improprieties. "I feel the pains of torture," he wrote, "that simply as the result of complaints by two printers who acted from greed only, you have come to a conclusion that will everlastingly stain the Apostolic Chair."

The opinion of the Jews themselves was still more heartrending. One of them from Verona wrote: "It was like burning the Holy God Himself." Jews continued to protest, but the evil was already done. Afraid of worse measures that might follow, they decided in 1554 to hold a conference in Ferrara. Two members of the Roman community were delegated, and a firm kind of self-censorship was agreed. No Jewish books could henceforth be printed without the authorization from a committee of three prominent Jews.

If the Jewish apostates were delighted, still they considered the measures far from complete. More Catholic than the pope himself, they went on calling for stricter and more far-reaching action against their former co-religionists. If grandfather Elia Levita had created Hebrew literature, his grandson was perfectly happy to destroy it. Andrea del Monte's zealotry was even greater, and in time he would develop into a highly accomplished Jew-baiter. When, in 1557, he happened to discover one left-over Hebrew book in the Ashkenazi synagogue in Rome, Jews were arrested, the synagogue was closed, and the community was fined the enormous sum of one thousand ducats.

The pattern for the confiscation and burning of Jewish books was now set, and before long a Papal Index came into existence, which included "the Talmud of the Jews, with all notes, remarks, interpretations, and explanations." . . . . All during the second half of the sixteenth century new orders would be issued by the Vatican, to be rightly or wrongly interpreted by cardinals, bishops, and priests; and book-burning would continue nearly as fast as audacious or foolhardy printers could supply the market. In 1559 Pope Paul IV ordered all Jewish books burned. Pope Pius V burned 20,000 copies of the Talmud.

Towards the end of that century Pope Clement VIII prohibited the printing of any Talmudic, Kabbalistic, or other books "which contain heresies or mistakes directed at church customs, priests, and neophytes, or" (a curious detail) "which contain dirty stories." In 1601 the same Pope had Jewish books burned in the center of Saint Peter's Square.

The Papal opposition to Hebrew thought and printing would continue for centuries with the usual ups-and-downs. In 1753 a cleaning-out of Jewish homes in Rome resulted in a harvest of thirty-eight wagon-loads of books; and when the Vatican finally judged such action no longer necessary, Hitler tore a page from the Index and widened the issue. Finding a most receptive audience in Germany itself, his henchmen in Italy took advantage of the situation to plunder the library of the Roman synagogue.

Since good Popes were often followed by bad ones, the Roman Jews were looking forward to better times when Julius III died on March 23, 1555. A cardinal known for his excellent knowledge of Hebrew was elected as the new Pope on April 10—Marcellus II. His reign might be kindly, the Jews thought, and in any case it could hardly be more trying than that of his predecessor. Unfortunately the Pope's possible good intentions were cut short. Three weeks after he had been crowned, he was dead.

Still a cardinal, the later Pope Sixtus V, on his way to Rome to pay a formal visit to the new Pope, heard about his untimely death while two days from the city. His reaction to the announcement was, "If all Popes die that fast, then even I may have a chance one day. . . ."

A quite different reaction to the Pope's death came from one of the foremost members of the Jewish community in Rome who exclaimed: "May God help us—the noble soul is dead!" The Jew who in such distressed tones mourned the Pope's early demise (Marcellus was only 54 years old), Rabbi Elia ben Shabtai, had every reason to feel deep concern. The Jewish community had barely escaped utter destruction, due to another threat of ritual murder that had held the city in an uproar during the short reign of Marcellus.

The body of a young boy had been found in the center of a Roman cemetery, nailed to a cross. As was usual under these dark circumstances, the Jews were promptly accused. One of Andrea del Monte's apostate colleagues, Chanalel of Foligno, who already had been a protagonist in the ban-the-Talmud struggle, jumped unhesitatingly into the matter, for nothing could play more into the hands of the anti-Jew than a dramatic "ritual murder" case. Speeches were held at the street corners of Rome, and when Cardinal Alessandro Farnese, grandson of Pope Paul III, intervened in favor of the Jews, the revengeful Chanalel doubled his efforts to have them accused and evicted —or worse.

The cardinal employed a notable strategem: he spread the false report that the Pope had canonized the little boy. The Roman crowds, as the cardinal had expected, assembled for prayers to pay homage to the new saint. Before long someone identified the child as the ward of a Spanish-Arabic lawyer, and he had in fact murdered the boy in connivance with his mistress in order to get his hands on the child's fortune. Traces of blood were found at the lawyer's home; and while Chanalel still refused to give ground, his confrontation with the chief members of the Jewish community soon established the real reason for his nauseous action. Indeed the Pope, "the noble soul," could die in peace. His reign had been short, but he would long be remembered by the Jews of his earthly kingdom.

The Jews now would have little time left to be joyous. The Chair that became vacant on the departure of Marcellus II, was filled on 23 May 1555 by 79-year-old Gian Pietro Carafa, who took the name of Paul IV. Having been the power behind the establishment of the Roman Inquisition, which he had led with an iron hand, his ascension to the throne of Saint Peter was witnessed by the Roman Jews with apprehension. Implacable in his persecution while still a cardinal, it could only be expected that he would be more zealous as Pope.

The waiting period did not last long. Paul put on the tiara, and seven weeks later, on July 12, he published his Bull that started with the words *"Cum Nimis Absurdum."*

The Bull contained a series of orders of which the most important ones may well be grouped as the Ten Anti-Commandments. Eleven days later, on July 23, all Jewish males were to start wearing the yellow hat, the women a five-foot-long yellow scarf. The following day instructions were posted all over Rome, ordering the Jews to gather together in one special part of the city. Within forty-eight hours the order was put into effect. That same day a beginning was made on the building of a wall around the area. It was July 26, 1555, the day the Roman ghetto was born. Just to make sure that the Vatican would not lose any money on the new arrangement, the Jews themselves had to pay for the construction of the wall.

Chapter 19
The Ghetto

"Since it is absurd," Pope Paul had written, "that the Jews, through their own fault have been condemned by God to everlasting slavery, should claim that Christians love them and accept to live with them in close proximity, while in reality they are so ungrateful to the Christians that they repay their kindness with insults—and since instead of resigning themselves to a humble existence, they act as if they are the Christians' equals—and since . . . "—and from here on the Pope registered a whole series of complaints against the Jews. Not only did they push their insolence so far as to live close to Christian churches, but they dared to do so without dressing differently from their Christian neighbours. Worse yet, the Pope wrote, the Jews had had the impertinence to live in some of the best parts of the city, and some of them even had the timerity to purchase the homes they lived in. Most odious, obnoxious and infamous of all, they had Christian nurses for their children, and Christian servants for their homes. Such a situation obviously could neither be endured nor tolerated any longer, the Holy Father concluded, and stringent and long-overdue measures were indicated to curtail this nefarious Jewish expansion into Christian neighbourhoods, and to protect Rome from evil Jewish contamination.

Evidently it had taken the Pope close to eighty years finally to unburden himself, and now that the moment had come, and knowing full well that not even he would be allowed another eighty summers, there was no time to lose. His long-term objective required short-term execution, and to get his Ten Anti-Commandments translated from paper plans to iron-clad reality, immediate action was on the agenda.

The ghetto wall was already being built; the rest would have to follow without delay. There was no "total" or "final" perspective of extermination of the Jews yet envisioned, but there was always the possibility of the Jews being starved out of existence. No trade was allowed any longer, nor any other economic activity, except rag picking. The consequences would inevitably be a crisis of subsistence. Visible emaciation would do. Christian servants, of course, were prohibited. So were Christian nurses, and all other relationships with Christians.

If the Jews chose not to work on Saturdays, that was their affair; in that case, including Sunday, they would have to take two days off. To be sure, having all work forbidden them, an extra day to do nothing was not actually excessive. Under the circumstances it was perhaps the only measure taken by Pope Paul that somehow had a tragic absurdity.

All synagogues outside the ghetto area were to be destroyed, and only one house of prayer would be allowed inside the walls. The Jews solved this problem for their different national groups by combining five synagogues under one roof. As to privately-owned property outside the ghetto, it would have to be disposed of within six months; as an order with a time limit, the Papal injunction created genuine bargains in real estate for the Roman Christians.

Health and medicine were other "religious issues" that were now resolved. In the future Romans would have to be cured by

Christian physicians only; the Jewish doctors, of whom there were now a considerable number, were restricted to keeping their own people alive. This rule also had a grotesque logic about it, for inasmuch as the Roman Jews from now on were to live in an area that was just about large enough for one-tenth of their population, hardship and sickness would soon be matters for all medical hands; at least Jewish doctors could be sure to find work to do.

One other thing—since slaves and beggars—which was the level the Jews were, in effect, being degraded to—could hardly expect to be called *Signore*, it was ruled that no Jew could any longer be addressed as such by his Christian masters and fellow men. Actually, as things stood, there would not be much opportunity for him to meet any of these fellow men, for the Pope also decreed that one entrance and one exit would be sufficient to let the occasional Jew make an occasional exit from the ghetto to go and pick up his rags and second-hand clothes.

Where did the word *ghetto* come from? This has been much disputed. Not that the Roman Jews of 1555 cared very much for the semantics of their tribulations. The fact that their Venetian brothers had been living behind closed walls for close to forty years was hardly a consolation. In Venice it was first known as the *Serraglio degli Ebrei*, the Jewish Enclosure. It is thought by some that the word ghetto came from the nearby (Venetian) iron foundry, known as the *giètto* or *gètto*. In the Rome of 1555 the Jewish section had no name; it was just a restricted part of town as indicated by the Pope. Not till 1562 did Pope Pius IV use the word *ghectus* for the first time.

There has been a suggestion that ghetto comes from the Hebrew word *get*, a document made up in case of divorce, and therefore a separation, a paper that cuts one person off from another. The *Enciclopedia Cattolica* finds this a faulty etymological deduction, which it probably is. But for some strange reason this authoritative Church Encyclopedia believes that the word may come from the English *gate*, "because the gate which was closed at night constituted the true character of the ghetto. . . ." And thus not even the Catholic Church, which originated it, seems to know where the word came from. Perhaps the sources of words for hateful things are best left in confused obscurity.

The "living space" was a minuscule one—hardly three acres in size. The whole rearrangement was actually hectic in organization, hastily ordered by the aging Pope, a make-shift set-up that took no serious social problems into consideration. It was, to some extent, a concentration camp tempered by a modicum of haphazard liberties.

Even today one can easily retrace the area of the ghetto. A leisurely stroll around the original perimeters takes about seven minutes. The Via del Portico d'Ottavia, which earlier was called the Rua Pescheria, formed the extreme at one end, (in reality the location of today's street was already just *outside* the area). The wall continued here as far as the Via de' Cenci, which due to its minimum dimensions has since been renamed the *Vicolo* or Alley de' Cenci, continuing more or less towards the river along what we know now as the Via Beatrice Cenci. That was all there was of it.

Parallel to the Rua Pescheria ran the Tiber, everlastingly ready to flood the neighbourhood. Consequently, as time went by, the poorer Jews would live close to the river, where they were more often troubled by the rising waters, and the more well-to-do Jews would move to the "uptown" section—a hundred yards away. The "frontiers" here indicated were already an improvement over the original ones and were made possible by the magnanimity of Pope Sixtus V, thirty years after Paul IV had announced the first enclosure. By then (in fact since 1557)—the two original gates had been augmented by three others. But the main entrance remained near the Palazzo Cenci on the Piazza Giudea Fuori Del Ghetto, the Jewish Square outside the ghetto, (today it is a square without a name, a widening of the Via del Progresso, with a fountain in the center). This communicated via the main gate with the Jewish Square *inside* the walls. In the center of the ghetto was the Piazza Macello or Slaughterhouse Square, and very close by (although *everything* was close-by in that restricted area) was the Via delle Azimelle, the Street of the Matzoth Bakers. The gates were closed at sundown, by which time the Jews had to be home.

The proximity of the Tiber constituted, as I have suggested, a menace of its own. If one considers that even today when the snow starts melting on the Appenines, the houses in Trastevere are sometimes flooded, then it is easy to imagine what the troubles must have been like four centuries ago. The first time the Tiber waters flooded the ghetto was in 1557. In 1598, during one of the worst floods, fifteen hundred Romans drowned. For once the ghetto escaped miraculously: the waters were reported to reach the top of the door to the synagogue, and then stopped. Clement VIII, who was Pope at that time, refused to credit the story of such clemency on the part of the angels. An eye-witness had to convince him; the confirmation must have come as something of a theological shock.

The Tiber took revenge in 1660, when water inside the ghetto rose to the third floor of the brick-cemented yet rickety dwellings. And if one looks at a line drawn on one of the buildings on the Piazza Navona (opposite the Church of Sant'Agnese) and notes that in 1870 the water rose to about eight feet above street level, then it is easy to form a picture of the annual threat to the lower-lying Jewish neighbourhood.

Pope Paul's ghetto order, of course, created havoc among the Jews. It was an unprecedented turn of events. Had there ever been, within human memory (and even going back to the trouble-laden legends that were told and retold), anything comparable, any order that could be compared to the one resulting from the *Cum Nimis Absurdum* Bull? Rich and poor were suddenly thrown together on a kind of human scrap heap; hygiene, or whatever there was of it at the time, became an impossibility; education, momentarily, came to a standstill; sexual relationships became problematical.

There was a detail which the Pope absent-mindedly had overlooked—the churches within the area—and these had to be closed; and several of them would be destroyed in later years. Christians had to move out of the designated space, and they too objected to the new rule. One of the Jews, David Ascoli, protested vigorously and wrote an *Apologia Hebraeorum*. His protest was disregarded, his punishment a jail sentence. As is the case under any dictatorship, one was only allowed to accept—disagreement was strictly forbidden.

In a burst of illumination the Christian owners of the homes now occupied by Jews saw a special ray of hope. Since the Jews could not move out, rents could be pushed sky-high. But soon a second illumination came—inasmuch as they could not be evicted, the Jews refused to accede to the increasing demands. A long stalemate developed, until finally—more than a century later—the Jewish community as a whole was made responsible for all rents in the ghetto, whether the houses were occupied or not. But already in 1567 the situation had become so involved, and charges and counter-charges between lessor and lessee became so vociferous, that soon rents were frozen and could only be raised 5 percent for "necessary repairs" (which hardly ever took place). The system turned out to be a boon to home owners, inasmuch as the rent paid within the ghetto could be counted on for generations—forever, as far as the Vatican was concerned. The Jews considered the situation on the same bases as the *Chasaka*. This is known in criminal and civil rabbinical law as a circumstance that becomes legal after having been in continued existence over a period of three years. The Romans, too, were willing to accept it as such because it allowed ownership to continue even if the house ceased to exist. Before long it became known in Roman law as the *Jus Gazaga*, a "property" that could be left to children in a will, sold to strangers, used as a dowry or for whatever other financial transaction the owner could think of.

While during the following centuries the status of the Roman Jew would undergo manifold changes, sometimes for the better but mostly for the worse, the ghetto itself would never rise above the original depressed standard of its creation. Poverty was its emblem, and pauperism its reason for existence. Three centuries after its establishment, in 1848, the Italian statesman Massimo d'Azeglio, one of the leaders of the *Risorgimento*, had this to say about the living conditions in the ghetto as he had seen them: "It is a formless mass of houses and hovels that are badly kept up, in constant need of repairs and falling half apart. In it vegetates a population of 3,900 souls, in a space where even half that many would live badly. The narrow streets, which are choked with people, the lack of air, the constant dirt which is the inevitable result of forced overcrowding, all of these factors constitute to make this area sad, ill-smelling and unhealthy. Families sometimes live more than one to a single room, without discrimination of sex, age, and health. They live crowded on every floor, in the attics and even in the subterranean holes which in more fortunate homes only serve as cellars. . . ."

Around the same time the German historian Gregorovius visited the ghetto. The rag-picking, ordered by Pope Paul IV, was still the main occupation of its inhabitants, and Gregorovius remarked that he had "never seen such a gigantic mass of rubbish. There was enough to enable the Jews to outfit the Creation and to dress up the whole world with colorful rags like a buffoon."

Very little had changed since Pope Paul had first ordered the Jews confined in 1555. His intentions, so far as preserving the interests of the Catholic Church was concerned, had been excellent. The only trouble was that no one apparently appreciated his efforts, not even the Catholics in Rome.

The Church, fighting for its own life, indiscriminately took that of others. Burning of heretics became commonplace, and the burning of Marranos received special attention. In 1556, one year after Paul IV had succeeded to the Papacy, he ordered all Jews and Marranos arriving from Portugal to be burned alive. This prompted the Venetian ambassador to write to his Doge, "He is zealous in everything, especially in the Inquisition." Three years later, in 1559, the Pope—by then eighty-three years old—condemned to death all kings and princes who fell out with the Catholic Church. Death was too much with him, and ruin and destruction. Even before the Pope expired, the news of his imminent passing had set frayed Roman tempers on edge. When word finally came that the Pope was gone, an immense crowd went on a rampage, destroying Papal statues. Crests and escutcheons of the Pope and his family were smashed; homes were ransacked, especially those of the members of the Inquisition. Fire was put to the headquarters of that hated institution; and some of its members, cardinals in rank, were manhandled. As far as these Romans were concerned, they had finished with the Papal Inquisition.

As for the Jews, they too profited from the erupting revolutionary spirit. There is always a "Jewish problem" in such populistic outbursts: they themselves might fall victim to the excited populace. It took them five days before they decided to wreck their ghetto gates and storm into town. By then some of the younger Jews already had joined the boisterous crowds in their jubilation over the death of a Pope of whom it was said that he had sinned against the city and against the whole world.

To Jews everywhere the announcement of this Pope's death came as a welcome event. They could not know what was in store for them, but surely they could expect only an improvement. A Jew in the city of Modena summed up the general and quite festive mood: "We have today received the news," he wrote, "of the death of Pope Paul, who during his lifetime convulsed the earth, spread fear throughout the world, made kingdoms fall, started wars, and brought great misfortune over Italy, and especially over our Jewish brethren, as has not happened since the destruction of the second Temple. May God bring us a new Pope who is favorably inclined to Israel, and who will be able to heal our wounds. . . ."

Four months later his prayer appeared to be having an auspicious hearing.

Chapter 20
Tolerance and Intolerance

With the arrival of Pope Pius IV the ghetto did not disappear, and the temporarily unhinged gates soon were properly in place again. Yet the new Pope, sixty years old when elected, was in nearly every way the opposite of Paul. The antagonistic feeling among the Romans against the Papacy soon quieted down; both Jews and Christians began to breathe easier. The new Pope was known to be no great partisan of the stringent rules of the Inquisition.

Yet a certain new strictness was on the order of the day in Rome. Pius IV felt that the social situation under Paul had been disastrous, and that it would be necessary to clean the "pool of vice," as he called it, that had developed during the preceding years. To a great extent that pool had been created by the former Pope's relatives, especially by some of the nephews whom Paul had promoted to high posts (including the Papal Secretary of State).

Pope Pius was appalled. He was crowned the day after Christmas of that year 1559, and at the beginning of next June, having taken stock of the situation, he issued orders to assemble all the relatives who went by the name of Carafa and to place them in jail. It was a kind of Inquisition of insiders and for once the Jews would feel the papal wrath less than some of the Christians.

Having cleaned house among the Carafas, the Pope could now look more closely into the problem of the Jews who had been wondering whether the ghetto gates would ever open again. Pius took a mild view of the problem. There was no reason, he found, to keep the Jews cooped up forever behind their walls, at least not during the day. Ragpicking, after that, suddenly became a profession of secondary importance; and before long Jewish shops were opening up again between the Piazza Venezia and the Piazza Colonna. The only condition the good Pope put to the Jews was that by nightfall they would be back within the walls of the ghetto; the gates were to be securely closed by dark.

Even though their freedom remained considerably curtailed, the Jews could not complain too much. Living in closer proximity than ever, the Jews' religious life became more intense, especially when the Pope allowed them to print Hebrew books "that would not be injurious to the Christian religion."

But, of course, things would not just continue. In 1564 Pope Pius had a first brush with death when four Christian assassins made an attempt to shorten his reign and his life, only to falter at the last moment. His passing one year later was a blow to Christian and Jew alike: but as it would soon turn out—a more serious blow to the latter.

Bad Pope, good Pope—good Pope, bad Pope. The pendulum had to swing in the opposite direction in order to keep the tragic balance straight. It took only one month to get the next Pope elected, and in January 1566 there was another Pius on the throne—the Fifth. The Fourth having been "good," the new Pope obviously had to be "bad." Indeed he was, certainly in the opinion of his Jewish subjects.

Extolling the virtues of Catholicism and the extreme dangers of anything Protestant, the Pope soon saw religious wars break out all over Europe under his prodding. Philip II of Spain began his battles with the Dutch, Emperor Maximilian II was threatened with demission if he would not oppose Protestantism more diligently, Catherine de Medici fought the Huguenots in France, and Queen Elizabeth was told that she "had lost all her imagined rights to the throne"—an order to which (to the Pope's chagrin) Good Queen Bess paid no attention whatsoever.

As a Christian, the Pope is said to have been an examplary person. But having been head of the Holy Office while still a cardinal, he did not take long before re-introducing the traditional methods of the Inquisition. It began to be said of him that "God has resurrected Paul IV." Two months after Pius V had started his rule, not a few of Paul's old edicts were in full force again. The shops on the Corso, on the Piazza San Marco and the Piazza Colonna were boarded up again, and the locks on the ghetto gates were checked and double-checked.

The new Pope's ideas about the Jews were rather strange and confused. They were not to be plagued illegally, he said—only legally. He ordered the Romans "not to disturb the Jews." But whatever property the Jews had been able to regain under the clement rule of Pius IV, now was ordered to be resold. In case it were to be discovered that such a sale was actually only a subterfuge, the Jews were threatened with total confiscation—half of it for the benefit of the *Case di Catecumeni*, the other half to be handed to the *Monte di Pietà*.

Under the circumstances a small number of Jews thought that it might be as well to "go over," to become Catholic. Those who did were received with open arms and with baptismal festivities at Saint Peter's. Most of the Jews, however, disliked this way out. With the "oddness" that has become proverbial ("How odd of God to choose the Jews. . ."), they preferred to be treated as pariahs. They continued to live quiet lives of desperation and semi-starvation. But soon even this path was narrowed when the Pope decided to change the usual Roman market day from Wednesday to Saturday. On Saturday, of course, no Jew would work.

What could still be done to make the Jews' life impossible?

There were, in the sad Jewish phrase, "only two possibilities"—death or exile. The "lesser evil" seemed to be more promising. The Pope decided upon expulsion of the Jews, a plan that began to take on reality by February 1569. All Jews would have to leave Italy. But since the Pope was not master of the whole country as we know it, the expulsion rule for the moment would be enforced within the Papal States only. Everywhere in the Papal States? Of course not—because in at least two cities the Jews were still needed. In the first place, in Rome proper; so the Vatican would have at least *one* city where the valuable tax-revenue of the to-be-closed synagogues could be collected; and, secondly, in that important Adriatic port of Ancona. For if the Jews were to be turned out, Christian trade with overseas territories would suffer. So the Ancona Jews were allowed to stay, or rather—after an initial hasty forced departure they were even more hastily called back when the Vatican discovered, to its unworldly surprise, that it had expelled the Jews who were collecting its golden revenue.

The retaining of the Jews in Ancona made to some extent good sense, at least from the pecuniary standpoint of the Vatican's finances and its trade with the Orient. But why did none of these violently anti-Jewish Popes ever think of suppressing the Jews in Rome proper? Time and again they were banned from Italian cities; and time and again, under Vatican pressure, they were forced to leave other countries of Europe. In 1290 they were chased out of England; in 1395 from France; in 1492 from Spain. The 16th century saw them expelled—not for the first time—from such Italian cities as Naples and Genova; in Venice it was a game of in-again, out-again. Bavaria prohibited Jews from residence in 1276. In 1360 Hungary followed suit, and that same century saw wholesale expulsions in Germany. Prague and Bohemia pushed the Jews out in 1542. The story was not very much different elsewhere (except in such Protestant lands as the Netherlands where they were welcome).

What reason was there for their permanent sojourn in Rome? Why were they allowed to stay for centuries, albeit under pressure, constraint, and within the confines of a ghetto? It was certainly not as the result of some secret influence on the Pope; for most of the time—even when the situation seemed favorable on the surface—they were reduced to the permanent status of supplicants. I suspect that the explanation lies in the sphere of materialist utilitarianism. The only answer (if there *is* an answer) seems to be money. The Vatican always needed it, and there was always the chance of pressing another few thousand golden ducats out of the Jewish lemon, if one only pressed hard enough. Certainly the Jews' continued residence in Rome was not due to a sentiment of humanitarianism on the part of the Popes (most definitely not on the part of such Popes as Paul IV* and Pius V*).

Yet times changed, especially when, after the harsh Pius V, a man from Bologna by the name of Ugo Buoncompagni—(obviously a lover of good food and good company) took over the reign of papal government as Gregory XIII. In fact time changed in more ways than one, for it was Gregory who eliminated ten days from everybody's life in 1582, when he changed the calendar. The Popes and indeed the world at large had fallen "behind the times," and losing ten days was the only way to get even with the sun. To the Jews the revolutionary change did not mean much. They had started counting from a much earlier "year zero," and were perfectly content to plod along in their own fifty-third century.

According to all reports Gregory was mismanaging papal government in the states under his jurisdiction. For the Roman Jews this was at times the very breath of relief. Still, the Inquisition was made more powerful in its punitive privileges. And the financial situation of the Jewish community reached a new low, caused by cumulative taxes, by the departure of some rich residents from the ghetto, by increased payments for the upkeep of the *Case di Catecumeni*, and by stricter supervision on legacies. If the Jewish doctors lost money because once again they were not allowed to treat Christians, then they managed to

*Such feelings for life as there were proved themselves to be "inner-directed." It was said that under Paul IV, the instigator of the ghetto, "the hat of the Jewish physician was more often visible in the Papal antichamber than that of the cardinal."

save money because they were not allowed to rent carriages and horses from Christians (or to employ Christians to drive their own).

Perhaps it could be taken as a sign of progressive tolerance that so few Marranos were killed during Gregory's reign. In 1578, after a preliminary public hanging on the bridge in front of the Castel Sant'Angelo, the inert bodies of several of these unfortunates were burned at the stake at the Porta Latina. This was followed in 1583 by the burning (this time alive) of two Portuguese Marranos by the names of Diego Lopes and Gabriel Henriques, one of those edifying spectacles for the multitude. Especially Henriques had "sinned greatly," for he had evidently succeeded in convincing hundreds of newly-arrived Marranos to return to Judaism. To the Inquisition there was hardly a greater crime.

In 1585 the Pope was eighty-three years old, and for some time some of the more active cardinals had been canvassing to see whom they might put in his place when the time would come. The time did come that year, and the cardinal who was now elected was one of the strangest and least promising princes of the Church ever to sit on the throne of Saint Peter—the ex-Cardinal Montalto, sharp of tongue, and thought to be the least offensive and most amenable of human beings. None of the electing cardinals apparently had listened with any attention to their colleague's statements during his many years in Rome. Or perhaps Montalto's quiet life during Gregory XIII's reign had been deceptive, for he and the Pope had not seen eye-to-eye ever since they had had a falling-out twenty years earlier on a journey to Spain, when both were still only cardinals.

Montalto's early life had been a most simple one. As Felice Peretti he was a miserably poor farm boy in the province of the Marche; at the age of nine he was the village's swine herd. From there to the exalted position of Pope was social mobility indeed. His election, in fact, was one of those compromise affairs stage-managed by a few cardinals who expected they would be able to manage the Pope himself as easily as his election.

The Jews of Rome, once he was elected, would live better and more pleasantly than any of them could remember, for the Pope turned out to be a far stronger and better person than they had expected. One of his first differences of opinion on a Jewish subject took place during a conversation with the Spanish envoy in Rome, who came to protest in the name of King Philip II against the publication of the Latin translation of the Old Testament by the Apostolic Printing Establishment. The ambassador, the Count of Olivares, lamented for more than an hour, and insisted on receiving a reply for his King. "Your Holiness, You do not answer," he complained repeatedly. "What is Your Beatitude thinking about?" "About two things," said the Pope. "In the first place the printing was done especially for your illustrious King—because he does not understand Hebrew." "And secondly?" inquired the solicitous ambassador. "Secondly," said the Pope, "secondly, I am thinking about having you thrown out of the window, in order to teach you how to talk to the Pope. . . ."

When Sixtus was crowned, he found his city riddled with manipulators of all kinds, and with an unholy group of monks and priests. For notwithstanding Pius IV's efforts to stamp out the "pool of vice," it had obstinately persisted. At one of the city's religious palaces eight superiors had introduced an equal number of prostitutes into their quarters, to live with them in happy concubinage. Sixtus soon had his troops put an end to it, but lost all of the eight culprits; they and their ladies escaped. The only victims of the mêlée were two guards and one lay-brother, virtuous souls all.

No one had expected such hard-handed action from such a seemingly soft-handed and soft-spoken cardinal. Certainly not the cardinals who had done everything they could to get him elected. All during the conclave Sixtus had seemed to be acting the feeble old man, leaning on his walking stick from which he had not been separated for years; most of the time he remained in his room. Some of the cardinals, it was recalled, actually wondered whether he was still alive.

The surprise was not long in coming. Hardly had the votes gone his way when Montalto threw down his stick, straightened his shoulders and "looking a lot taller than usual, spat against the ceiling." Although it was a fairly low ceiling, one of his chroniclers would write that "a young man of thirty would have had trouble to spit that high with so much vigor."

Astonished cardinals sought an explanation. "Simple," as the new Pope informed his closest collaborators. "When We were still a cardinal only, We walked with bent head and shoulders, looking for the keys of the kingdom. Now that We have found them, We look up to Heaven because We have nothing more to seek on earth." And with that, the new Pope started the *Te Deum*. The cardinals wondered why they had called him "the ass from the Marche" for so long.

If it had turned out to be a bad day for the hoodwinked cardinals, it seemed to be a fine day for the Romans and to augur well for the Jews. The new Pope was all set to reform and renovate Rome, to revitalize its *mores*, and to restore the Vatican's prosperity. To a considerable extent he intended to employ Jews to help him achieve this. They would be a source of funds, and of services, crafts, and general ingenuity.

People used to say: "Don't forget—*Sixtus* is Pope!" And with that they expressed their admiration for the Pope as well as their view that certain things simply could not be done, or perpetrated, so long as he directed the affairs of the Vatican. Some little verses made the rounds of Rome at this time: "We have seen how a little priest/ changed Rome and enriched the Castle/ at the very least. . . ." In fact, when Sixtus died, there were some five million scudi left behind in the papal coffers. In five years the Pope had accomplished quite extraordinary feats of Vatican policy.

The Pope's motto seemed to have been: "We must respect and protect the Jews, if We are to tax them. . . ." The Jews were glad to oblige, as they always had been. But this time at least they received value for money. It was a welcome change. Not one single Jew was killed during these five prosperous years; and a good many Jewish families, who had fled from the shores of the Tiber's ghetto, now returned. After all—*Sixtus* was Pope. Two Jewish physicians were engaged to attend to the Pope's health. The task of taking care of the growing finances was put into the able hands of a Marrano-ex-Catholic, a certain Lopes.

Sixtus' interest in Hebrew was such that David de Pomis, a Jewish physician and author, dedicated a Hebrew Talmudic dictionary to him. For de Pomis it was a good thing finally to have a Pope who was receptive to things Jewish, inasmuch as Paul IV previously had made de Pomis' life miserable in more ways than one.

Sixtus, although an expensive Pope, was a righteous one for the Jews. One Roman, a servant of Prince Conti, was punished when he grabbed a Jew's hat in the ghetto and threw it into the Tiber.* Other Christians who had maltreated Jews were horse-whipped from one end of the Corso to the other, considered a perfectly normal punishment in those days: Only it had not happened often—in fact never—for the misdemeanor of tormenting a Jew. The Romans' eyes must have bulged at the sight.

Sixtus was totally revolutionizing the edicts, Bulls, and prohibitions of earlier Popes. The Jews suddenly were allowed to settle anywhere again and do business with whomever they wanted. Even the reopening of Jewish loan banks was favored by the Pope. Synagogues could be rebuilt, schools freely established, and no more Jewish hats or veils had to be worn. If new cemeteries were needed, ground was made available—and a new wall was constructed for the cemetery in Rome near the Porta Portese, perhaps to keep out marauders. The yearly carnival races which still took place, and which for so long had been a terrifying occasion, became a kind of joint Christian-Jewish celebration, a simple folk festival to be enjoyed by all. Under these happy living conditions not only the cemeteries, but also the ghetto itself had to be enlarged. The Pope instructed one of his favorite architects, Domenico Fontana, who had erected the obelisk (still standing) on the Piazza San Pietro, to

*A religious "crime," inasmuch as Jews had to keep their head covered at all times.

build new homes right along the Tiber. In a word, the Jews for once were being treated as fellow human beings.

Always open to new suggestions that might be helpful to enrich the Vatican's coffers—and incidently the coffers of the Pope's family and friends—Sixtus was especially attentive when two Jews, Meir di Gabriele di Magino from Venice and Giovanni Corcione from Naples, came forward with a plan to establish a silk factory in Rome. The Vatican itself needed considerable supplies of silk, and sales from the increased production would be beneficial to the Holy See. But how could one induce an innocuous silk worm to spin more silk? Magino had the answer to that too. He had found a method that made the worm spin two cocoons a year, thus doubling the raw material. Sixtus was delighted, and in a special decree dated June 4, 1587—a great privilege to be extended to a Jew—the Pope gave the Venetian specialist the right to exploit his invention, and to receive its benefits for a period of seventy years. It was, in fact, a kind of patent.

There were, of course, shrewd special conditions on the Vatican side. The Pope's sister, Camilla Peretti-Maginucci, was to receive half the profits from the silk factory. Unfortunately for Magino, the Pope would not be there for all of those seventy years to enforce the financial obligations; and some of the later Popes would have (once again) rather different ideas about Jewish business enterprise.

For the time being, however, things went well. Civic problems were faced, festivities were great, the Jews were happy, and justice was done and seen to be done as never, or hardly ever, before. Strange as it may seem, without this historic context, Shakespeare probably might never have written his *Merchant of Venice*. For it was a Christian-Jewish affair before Sixtus V that provided Shakespeare, via various literary sources, with the inspiration for a play involving "a pound of flesh"—Shakespeare, of course, taking a few literary liberties.

During the third year of the reign of Sixtus, the story* in-

*As retold by Giuseppe Levi, Italian author and pedagogue, in his book *Cristiani ed Ebrei nel Medio Evo*, published in Florence in 1866. Levi, in turn, had copied the story from Gregorio Leti's much earlier biography *The Life of Sixtus V*.

forms us, the news spread through Rome that one of Queen Elizabeth's admirals, Francesco Drago (Sir Francis Drake), had sacked the city of San Domingo. Paolo Maria Secchi, a rich Roman merchant, was disturbed about this British act of piracy, since he had several properties and other interests on the island of Hispaniola. He called on his Jewish insurance agent Sansone (Samson) Ceceda, and asked him to be indemnified for the loss. Not yet having received any confirmation of the British victory, Sansone said that he would like to wait, because after all the story might not be true. "But if it *is* true," said the unconvinced Sansone rather mockingly, "then I'll allow you to cut a pound of flesh from my body." Secchi, who thought that he was right in the first place and that therefore he had nothing to lose, replied: "And I bet you a thousand ducats that what I told you *is* true."

Sansone wondered: nowhere in the world could there be a pound of meat that would not be worth a thousand ducats; and he willingly extended his hand, offering to sign and seal the deal, black on white. To make sure that neither of them were to be left empty-handed, the contract was made up immediately and countersigned by two witnesses, one Christian, one Jewish. But unhappiness of all unhappinesses—before three months had gone by, the news was confirmed. Sir Francis indeed had sacked the city. Secchi had won; Sansone was out of luck. Soon he probably would be out of his misery too, if Secchi were to insist literally on the cutting of his pound of flesh—which Secchi did. "Take a thousand ducats instead," Sansone begged, but Secchi could not be moved. He had his promise on paper, black on white, and was ready to sharpen his knife.

Sansone's wits had their own sharpness, and he went to see the cardinal who was Sixtus' governor of Rome. The cardinal was a bit shaken by the details of the strange wager, and thought he would do well to inform the Pontiff. Sixtus, who was greatly upset to find that two of his subjects had been ready to make a grotesque deal involving part of their bodies, proceeded to instruct them in ethical religious proprieties.

"When one bets," he said, "one should be prepared to lose and pay, and We wish to make sure that your bet be executed in full. So you, Secchi, go and bring your knife, and in Our presence you will cut one pound of flesh from that part of our subject Sansone Ceneda's body which seems most appropriate to you for that purpose. But We warn you. Cut one pound only and not one *drachma's* weight more, or We will have you sentenced to death by hanging. So go now to prepare yourself, and be sure to bring back a pair of scales."

Secchi's distress was great at these words, for what would be the use of one pound of his insurance agent's flesh, if in getting it he would surely lose all of his own? He flung himself down at Sixtus' feet, exclaiming that the only thing he wanted to be cut up now was the piece of paper on which the wager had been made official. If that were done, he said, he would be perfectly happy.

"And you," said the Pope to Sansone, "would that make you happy too?" Sansone replied that indeed nothing would make him happier, and winner and loser were ready to walk off to celebrate the narrow escape. But Sixtus went on with increasing severity.

"*You* may be happy," said the Pope, "but We are not. Our subjects are the owners of their bodies and their lives, but they can sell neither the whole or any part of it without Our permission."

At this both men were thrown into jail. A few days later, and after paying two thousand ducats each into the Papal treasury, they were allowed to rejoin their families. All of which some ten years later became one of the sources for Shakespeare's story of the *Merchant of Venice*. Shakespeare transferred the locale to Venice, and instead of having the Christian insist on getting his pound of flesh, he made the Jew Shylock do this. In those days, as is well known, it was difficult for a Jew to be presented as a sympathetic character.

In 1590 the Pope fell ill. On the Piazza Navona, where—thanks to Sixtus—the market again took place on Wednesday instead of on Saturday, the news spread as early as July that the Pope was dying. Knowing only too well that "bad times" might start again even before a new Pope were to be elected, the Jewish merchants hurriedly picked up their wares, closed their stalls, and fled behind the relative safety of the ghetto wall. The move turned out to be premature; but towards the end of August rumours sadly fulfilled themselves. Sixtus was no more, and no one knew what the future might bring. Had they known how long it would take before another friendly Pope would come along, the Jewish community on the Tiber might well have vanished from Rome to take up residence in a more benevolent land.

Chapter 21
Forced Sermons

Right across the Bridge With The Four Heads, half-facing the Tiber, stands the small church of the *Congregazione della Madonna della Divina Pietà*. Not so very long ago one of the gates of the ghetto was just opposite this house of prayer. Above its door, written in Hebrew and in Latin, is a quite extraordinary inscription, a rare statement in Hebrew on a non-Jewish building, and certainly the only one to be found in Rome on a Catholic church. Taken from Isaiah (65:2), the passers-by are reminded that this great Jewish prophet once wrote: "I have spread out my hands all the day unto a rebellious people, which walketh in a way that was not good, after their own thoughts."*

Above the inscription is not a painting of Isaiah, but a picture of Christ Crucified. Obviously Isaiah's words were not intended to encourage the Jews (who lived in the ghetto right opposite) to stay true to their religion; but, instead, they were to remind

*King James version as published by the New York Bible Society.

them that they were still "a rebellious people," stiffly walking in a "way that was not good," and that it would be better for them to make up their minds and join the Catholic Church.

Originally, the words of this admonishment were on display on a huge cross that stood in front of the Church of Sant'Angelo in Pescheria, just behind the Gate of Octavia. It was destroyed at some unknown date, and one of those converted Jews who thought that all should follow his own example had the verse repeated in 1858 (when the ghetto was still in existence) on the church where it is today. Is it a relic of times past? or is the message still very relevant? Although today the spirit of ecumenism has, to a certain extent, taken hold of the Catholic Church, and the idea of peaceful religious coexistence has been one of the main points of discussion at the Vatican Councils of 1962-1965, it was not always like that. For some two thousand years the Church had been an embattled militant force, and the priests—certainly many of them—had wildly orated, first against the pagans, then against the Jews, after a while against the Moslems, then against the Protestants, successively against the heathen on various continents, and through and during it all, always and uppermost, against the Jews. Popes and cardinals could beget children; priests could flout each and every rule of the Apostles; the Church as a whole, at times, could be thoroughly corrupt; but the idea of religious righteousness was always supreme in the mind of the Vatican. It was not that tolerance was an unknown word, but it was an unknown *fact*, and that (as the saying goes) everybody was out of step but the Church of Rome—with the Jews more spiritually out of step than anybody.

So the Jews were to repent, and to embrace the Church. And if they did not choose to do it peacefully, then just about every other means of persuasion would be acceptable—from fire at the stake to poverty in the ghetto. Should stubborn and even bellicose Jews still not want to accommodate themselves, then there were compulsory sermons, forced baptism, and the *Case dei Catechumeni* for Neophytes as alternatives. A cruel pattern was set: if things were not accomplished willingly, then they would have to be enforced unwillingly.

Sermons for—which is also to say, against—the Jews had of course always existed. But it was not till September 1577 that Pope Gregory XIII decided that trying to convert the Jews the easy way did not bring the required results. Prompted by that zealous convert Andrea del Monte, the former Joseph (Giuseppe) Zarphati from Fez, Gregory made the Jews' presence at these sermons compulsory from then on. An accomplished and intelligent speaker, Andrea told his listeners—those few who did listen—that they were hopelessly wrong, because the Messiah had already come. Why wait any longer? Joining the religious bandwagon seemed on the order of the day. The only trouble was that the Jews were bad joiners.

At the outset some sixty members of the community were to listen to Andrea, a number he had insisted upon when he found that only very few Jews freely consented to spend their Saturday afternoon listening to arguments they rejected. To be sure, a few Jews did appear to agree, although they may not have been entirely convinced. They often were seduced by the financial gains that were held out to them. There were some who felt it better to follow Christ on a full stomach than to hunger with Moses.

Later on, the sermons—most of which took place in the Church of Sant'Angelo in Pescheria, conveniently located right outside the ghetto—had to be listened to by an even larger captive audience: one hundred men and fifty women. In rotating the members of the community, every Jew over the age of twelve had to be present at some time. Still the results were rather meager, certainly in comparison to the effort that was put into the campaign. God, or so the Jews must have reasoned, was neither on the side of the bigger battalions nor the most persistent pulpits.

Montaigne, the French philosopher, gives a description of one of the compulsory sermons he witnessed in Rome in 1580. Montaigne was evidently quite impressed with the intelligence of the speaker, Andrea del Monte, and with his thorough knowledge of the subject.

"The apostate rabbi was an excellent preacher," he wrote. "There were several learned men among his audience of about sixty people, whose beliefs he combatted. Speaking both Hebrew and Italian, he was quite admirable."

Before witnessing the scene of Andrea del Monte's effort to convert his former co-religionists, Montaigne already had paid a visit on a Saturday morning to a synagogue, one of the five inside the ghetto that had been constructed under a common roof. His somewhat astonished description of what he saw, twenty-five years after the enclosure had been started, suggests that only little has changed between a Roman Jewish religious service then and now.

"They sing totally discordinately," wrote Montaigne, "the way they do in Calvinist churches, chanting their Hebrew prayers with a certain cadence, but in extreme dissonance. They seem to pay no more attention to their prayers than we do to ours, nor do they pay great reverence to the mysterious words. Before entering the synagogue they wash their hands, and once inside, taking off their head-cover would be an execration. On their shoulders or on their head they wear a kind of sheet with fringes attached—it would take too long to try and understand why. After the service the learned men among them explain the part of the Torah they have read. Then they choose one or more men in the congregation to argue about it. The main speaker we heard seemed to have great eloquence and wisdom."

It must have been a trying experience for the priests who, for centuries, continued to bombard the Jews with all the force of their logic and their reason, to find that so very few could be swayed. Between 1636 and 1700 a total of 1195 Jews were baptized in Rome, an average of nineteen a year. The average number subsequently dropped to fourteen a year during the next century. Since the ghetto-population during these centuries was, on the average, around 6,000—and since, moreover, a considerable number of Jews from elsewhere, who were es-

pecially brought to Rome for "showcase" baptism were also included in these convert figures—the percentage of Jews who
embraced Catholicism was numerically therefore fairly negligible, probably not more than one-sixth of one percent at the
most.

Between 1800 and 1870 there were years of respite whenever
the Pope was stripped of his worldly power, as happened during
the Napoleonic upheaval, and during the short-lived Roman
Republic. But as soon as the situation changed back again to its
papal normalcy, the Vatican immediately reverted to its original
proselytizing inspiration, and the forced sermons were
reinstituted.

The Jews, of course, could hardly be considered obedient and
attentive pupils at these Saturday afternoon sessions. It was
supposed to be their day of rest; and instead of being able to
take a walk or a nap, they had to sit in a church, where from the
pulpit an incessant flow of words of an alien theology would
pour forth. For some these words went in one ear and out the
other; others would hold their hands over their ears, or stuff
them with wax. Dozing was not allowed, and the papal *sbirri*
used to walk up and down the aisle to rouse the culprits from
their slumber with a blow of their stick. The same chastisement
was meted out to those Jews who chatted, or who yawned aloud.
But from the evidence it appears that the Jews were great at
yawning at these sessions, and at talking about business,
forthcoming marriages, *bar mitzvahs*, and the like, all subjects
considered of far greater importance than the words of even the
most eloquent priest. The cacophonic obstruction often was
such that the priest's words hardly could be understood by the
orator himself. Perhaps for the Jews, this was just the kind of
effect they were after.

The scene was not without its comic aspect—in the audience,
Jews, staging a tremendous tumult talking, gesticulating, surreptitiously putting the wax back into their ears whenever they
were ordered to remove it, elsewhere Jews snoring in unison; in
the aisle, official guards dashing up and down swinging their

sticks to enforce theological attention; and up front, the desperate priest trying in vain to make his voice heard above the unceremonious din.

As if this débacle were not enough, visits to the synagogues on the part of Christian Romans appeared to hold out such an attraction that at one point the Vatican decided to fine every non-Jew twenty-five scudi whenever he was found inside a Jewish house of prayer.

Again it was Massimo d'Azeglio, one of the formidable Italian critics of papal government, who in 1848 defended the liberal cause of the Jews, who has left us a vivid description of what must have been happening "emotionally" during the forced sermons.

"Let us try and imagine what must be the Jew's feelings," he wrote. "Sitting in the church under the constant surveillance of the *carabinieri*, he hears the words Charity and Peace which, to him, mean nothing but mockery and insult. It is probably not unnatural that, pushed by indignation and by a disgust which he must hide, he has only one satisfaction left, saying in his heart: 'You may well oblige me to listen to you, but not in all eternity shall you have the joy of seeing me convinced!' "

Yet the Church during all these centuries did not leave off in its efforts to make what it considered decent human beings out of the Jews. The imperfect system worked perfectly. First came the sermons, then the transitionary period of instruction at the House of the Catechumen. During the time of his or her internment, the Jewish Community had to pay for upkeep at the rate of thirty *baiòcchi* a day; the Church was certainly not going to risk its own money on the not yet fully transcended Jew. If after the required forty days' stay the aspiring neo-Christian decided that remaining a Jew was after all just as well, and chose to leave the House of Catechism, then the repenting pupil had to pay a fine—with money which usually he did not have. At this point once again the Jewish Community would be made responsible for the required funds. There seemed to be no way *not* to pay the Vatican its never-ending levy of dues.

In the archives of the Jewish Community in Rome I have seen

one of the best examples of this money-refunding system as it was carefully practiced by the Home for Catechumen. Dealing with a most recalcitrant young Jewish woman, who refused to accept the religion of Christ in exchange for her own, the ghetto authorities in 1823 were obliged to pay for her upkeep. "Received from the *Monsignori Fattori* (regents) of the ghetto, through the hands of *Avvocato* Arcangeli the amount of 13 scudi and 80 *baiòcchi* for food supplied to the obstinate Jewess Flaminia Toscana, who returned to the ghetto." Signed: "*Filippo Colonna, Rector of the Catechumen.*"

The neighbourhood of the Catechumen Home was forbidden territory for the Jews who, from within a distance of two hundred feet, were not allowed to look up at its windows. Those Jews who did cast a forbidden look from within the prohibited area were fined one hundred scudi, and were moreover whipped. Jews were also punished for trying to help organize escape attempts, and for harboring those who did take unauthorized leave before the end of the forty-day trial period. Turning Christian was not without its risks and dangers.

Children, of course, presented less of a problem for the Church. In 1604 Joshua Ascarelli, Chief Rabbi of Rome, was taken by force to the House of the Catechumen at the order of its Superior. Accompanying him were his wife and four children. After forty-three days—the three extra days probably added on for desperate last-minute conversion efforts—the rabbi still could not be convinced that the New Testament provided better divine guidance than the Old, and he was set free. But all the four children were supposed to have declared that they wanted to be baptized. Twelve-year old Camilla made this soul-searching decision after ten days; eight-year old Bellucia needed less, only eight. Young Judah, six years old, was convinced after five days; and the Benjamin of the family, Manuele, needed still less—four days, being at the time he took this decision all of four years of age.

Children under twelve (in other periods, under seven) for a time needed their parents' consent to be baptized. Those over that age could decide for themselves. For minors, that is for those minors under the seven (or twelve) year age-limit, Pope Innocent XI found a way out. If the child were abandoned by its parents, which surely was a rare enough case in the closely-knit Jewish family, then it could make its own decision—under duress if need be. Another case of "extreme necessity" would be a child dying in the presence of a Christian nurse (when these nurses, due to slackening Vatican control, from time to time could be engaged again). This papal decision would give rise to a certain number of baptisms performed by zealous nannies who often considered the slightest cough or sneeze as sure signs of a malady that needed undelayed extreme unction. One nurse, watching over the infant Isacco Finzi in 1725, made haste to take care of both body and soul. Dipping her hands into a pail of water, she made the sign of the cross over the child's body and pronounced it baptized. This legalized the procedure entirely, and the child was handed over to the House for the Catechumen.

But no matter how and under what circumstances the hasty baptism ritual was performed—with or without parental consent, on a pale hollow-cheeked sickly child or a youngster bursting with health—once the ritual had taken place there was no power on earth that could nullify the deed except the Vatican. In December 1746 a certain Antonia Viviani, armed with a bucket of water, entered the Jewish home of the Misani family in the ghetto. She rushed around hectically, cascaded drops hither and thither on the three small daughters, and then probably tripped. For, according to the record, she suddenly was out of water for the fourth child, a boy. By the time she came back with her replenished bucket, there was no boy to be found. With this random act of water-splashing three daughters were lost to the family. The mother, of course, protested vigorously and went to see the archbishop-governor of Rome. Not only did he refuse to help, but he reported to the Pope on "the great deed" that had been performed in the best interests of the Church.

Pope Benedict XIV did not entirely share the enthusiasm of his monsignore. There was, he felt, a limit to such cases; and a year later, in 1747, he published a guiding rule *"On the Baptism of Hebrews, Children and Adults."* If a child—under seven, that is—were brought to a priest for baptism by a stranger, then it should be returned forthwith to its parents. But suppose it had already been baptized, as in the case of the Misani children? Then nothing could be done about it (as was clearly pronounced in the decisions of the Council of Toledo, back—two full centuries—in 1565). But assume that the child, once grown up, wanted to return to its original religion? By then this act would be declared heresy, and would be dealt with as such: which could mean that the poor soul would end up at the stake. Why? Because that was what Pope Boniface VIII had decreed some four centuries ago. The burden of the centuries was heavy, and there was no escaping history; evolution and modernization in the Church was slow, and a rule was a rule.

Human ingenuity and private deviousness played a role. There were more ways than one to use baptism to personal advantage or to the disadvantage of others. An irate Jewish husband whose wife would not want to accept a divorce could go over to the Catholic Church, which was very accommodating in a case like this. If the spouse did not want to follow along this (as she might consider it) misdirected religious path, then the Church could declare the union dissolved because mixed marriages were forbidden, and the husband by now was a Catholic. A soul would thus be won, a woman's heart lost, and the man could remarry and live happily ever after outside the ghetto.

In other cases of difference of opinion between members of the same family, the person who had decided to embrace Catholicism could denounce any of his relatives, including those of minor age. He could claim that others wanted to follow his example. He could testify that the willing persons were being held back from taking this step by still other kinsmen. The papal police could then invade the ghetto in an effort to weed out the lost sheep. Daytime searches being usually fruitless, a special system developed (which, in much later times, would be dreaded in Hitler's Germany and Stalin's Russia)—the knock on the door at midnight. If, again, the looked-for child were un-available, the governors of the ghetto would be given twenty-four hours to present the refugee, or the governors themselves would be imprisoned. It became, also, a routine game of peren-nial hide-and-seek. There were no hiding places, and the seekers would usually win in the end.

In 1787 a Roman Jew who certainly could not foresee the consequences of his act, went over to the Catholic faith. There were two orphans among his relatives, he said, who also were eager to take this step. A search was instituted, but to no avail—the children were carefully hidden. So sixty other youngsters were picked up at random in the ghetto as hostages, of whom the elder ones were tortured till they betrayed the hiding places. The children were found and were dragged to the House of the Catechumen, notwithstanding the protests of the community. The ghetto was fined for its unbecoming behaviour.

Making the Jews pay for those who had abandoned their faith was standard Vatican policy. They paid for those who were at the House for the Catechumen; they paid for those who came back; they were fined for the things they did and for the things they refused to do; and sometimes they were even fined for no discernible reason whatever.

In 1629 Pope Urban VIII devised another financial duty for the already heavily-burdened community. Ten years previously a Jew, a certain Francesco Masserano by his new name, had em-braced Catholicism. Having become a perhaps not too devout Catholic but certainly a most violent anti-Jew, he wrote a treatise on the errors of his former religion. The Pope, in order to compensate him for this noble work, decided that he and his family should be paid a yearly subsistence fee of 1200 scudi for life. The money, of course, was not to come out of the papal treasury. Instead it was decided that the Jews in the ghetto should provide for their renegade. When Masserano finally drew his last breath, the governors of the community requested to be acquitted of the onerous tax. It was not a difficult question to be put to the Vatican which promptly deemed that the money could serve another purpose as honourably from then on, and every year the 1200 scudi had to be paid to the House for the Catechumen. In a tradition that apparently has been inherited by the present-day Italian Internal Revenue Bureau, a refund from the Vatican was absolutely out of the question. It would have required an Act of God; and God, though evidently still interested in the fate of His Chosen People, seemed to take no interest in its material welfare, at least not in the specific financial interests of His Tribe on the Tiber. To the *Case dei Catecumeni* the money was supposed to go, and to the *Case dei Catecumeni* the money went—for on earth the power of the Vatican was still supreme.

To demonstrate this supremacy, the Church would exploit the new Christian convert's change of faith to the fullest. The neophyte would be paraded through the city streets for about two weeks as the perfect example of beatific magnificence, true devotion, submission, and holy servitude. The convert was usually dressed in white, and a cardinal frequently would act as godfather. Showered with presents, he would soon have a suitable marriage arranged, and more than one of today's prominent Papal and aristocratic Italian families have, somewhere in their past, Jewish blood in their veins, the watered-down result of a forced baptism that took place during the centuries when the Church considered itself as the relentless defender of the faith at all costs.

Chapter 22
Forced Baptism

It should not surprise us, at this stage of our history, that the aggressive campaign to convince the Jews of the superiority of the Catholic religion gave rise, time and again, to ugly rumors of ritual murder. Through the centuries the Church, and more frequently some over-zealous priest or monk would dig up this *canard* and use it for the familiar dark purposes: branding the Jews as murderers, simultaneously frightening some others into abandoning a religion that proclaimed such bloody exercises as a necessary accessory to the development of its holy services.

The case of Saint Simon of Trent in 1475 had been investigated by the Pope, and was found to be a nonsensical invention. However, it had taken quite a few centuries to convince the clergy. The Vatican, always in the center of re-emerging ritual murder controversies, decided once more to make its voice heard in 1758, when a thorough inquiry declared a ritual murder charge in Poland as totally invalid. Every time such a statement was issued by the Vatican, the Jews of Rome could breathe a bit easier. Anxiety returned in 1840 when news reached the ghetto that Jews in Damascus had murdered a Capuchin monk (by the name of Tomasso di Calangiano, born in Sassari on the island of Sardinia as the son of the family Fossa). Fear spread through the narrow ghetto streets; repercussions in Rome itself were expected.

The murder case developed slowly, but it would soon engulf all of Europe and even spread to the other side of the Atlantic (American Jews held a meeting in Philadelphia). From then on the case would be known as "The Damascus Affair." Looking back at it after more than a century, it is amazing to discover that until very recently the alleged events were given complete credence by the Order of the *Frati Minori* of the Capuchins. A detailed report in the Capuchin Lexicon of 1957 (referred to as a reprint) states without any further comment that Tomaso "was barbarously killed by the Jews on February 5, 1840." Then, here and elsewhere, the details are given of this case which finally brought one prominent French Jew and a well-known British Jew, Adolphe Crémieux and Sir Moses Montefiore, to Cairo. They hoped to plead the case of the innocently imprisoned Jews with the Turkish Viceroy of Egypt, Mohammed Ali, who was also in charge of Damascus. It also brought Baron James de Rothschild from Paris to Rome to plead the case with Pope Gregory XVI.

This is how the Damascus affair reads in volume number 5 of "The Missions of the Capuchins,"* published in 1919 and recording "the truth" about the so-called ritual murder:

"Father Thomas frequented the Jews of Damascus and was very kind to them, putting his faith in the Divine Providence to be able to bring them closer to God, as he had said more than once."

The details of what happened in Damascus on the days preceding the monk's murder (and I continue to use the 1919 version of the Capuchin Mission throughout), are these:

A Damascus rabbi by the name of Kakam Jacob Elantabi was brooding on how to get the necessary human blood with which

*"Le Missione dei Minori Cappuccini."

to bake his *matzoth* for the approaching Passover festival. Discussing the recipe ingredients "with seven of the most boastful or most corruptible Jews in town," they decided upon Thomas, who as a practicing doctor, visited their streets regularly.

According to plan they gagged and bound the unsuspecting Thomas, and while "the Jewish barber Soliman held his beard, they stabbed him and collected his blood in a silver vase, because it had to be used for the Passover festival." The monk's clothes were then burned, and his cut-up body was sewn into a coffee sack, which was deposited in a gutter-stream.

The next day people found the convent closed, the food ready on the table for a meal that was never consumed; and they immediately went to bring the monk's absence to the attention of the French consul, whose name was De Ratti-Menton. The consul, who would vigorously continue to support the ritual murder charge, informed the Sherif Pasha who sent his chief of police to the Jewish sector. The barber Soliman was suspected, arrested and tortured, after which he readily "confessed" and named his accomplices.

During the trial two of the men died; one of the accused turned Moslem; three were acquitted; and the others were to be executed when sentence was pronounced on September 5, 1840.

By now news of the case had spread as far as Europe. The Roman Jews tried to get help from Pope Gregory XVI who was one of the less anti-Jewish pontiffs. From London Sir Moses Montefiore left for Egypt, picking up his companion Crémieux in Paris on the way. James de Rothschild had, in the meantime, traveled to Rome. In Cairo the two prominent European Jews asked Mohammed Ali for a retrial, emphasizing the absurdity of the charge. This, in the view of the troubled Middle Eastern Viceroy, might even aggravate the situation further; instead he simply ordered all the condemned men to be freed. Rothschild, while this was going on, had some interesting financial discussions with the Pope.*

*Inquiring about details of the conversation from the Rothschild family in Paris, the author was informed by Baron Edmond that "unfortunately there are no details on this encounter in my archives."

If the Damascus Affair roused agitated interest on both sides of the Atlantic and especially in Rome, eighteen years later a storm broke which brought the Rome ghetto to a state of frenzy, and shook the Vatican—standing like a rock. Attacked by kings, emperors, and heads of state, by Protestants and by Jews, Pope Pius IX and the Holy Office calmly pointed their fingers at the statutes of the Homes for the Catechumen and at the Vatican rules: A baptized child is a Catholic, no matter under what circumstances the baptism took place. And if, moreover, anyone declared that the child was baptized during its last gasps of life, then the case was even more perfect, and everything was legal and theologically proper. Which, according to the Vatican, it was by definition.

It took six years for the affair to unfold; because when the act in question took place, no one knew about it but the maid who secretly performed the haphazard ritual. The Jewish child, Edgardo Mortara, born in Bologna on August 27, 1851, was eleven months old when it happened; and, obviously, whatever statements he made during later life were not dictated by childhood memories but by hearsay.

The maid, Anna Morisi, who had acted at the instigation of a nearby druggist named Lepari, carried her secret well; Edgardo developed into a vigorous young boy, his fictitious brush with death before his first birthday not having brought him to his early grave. Then the maid one day talked openly to a girlfriend, and as a consequence the story was told in confession to a priest. The Vatican was quickly informed: a baptized Catholic boy was still being raised as a Jew; it mustered its forces and went into action.

On the 20th of June 1858, at eight o'clock in the evening, five papal policemen, guided by a monk, entered the home of the Mortara family in Bologna, and without further ado or explanation, and to the understandable consternation of the parents, took young Edgardo with them. Was this kidnapping? The Vatican did not consider it as such. The boy immediately was taken to Rome and its Home for Catechumen. The chapter, for the Vatican, was closed; but the curtain went up on world indignation.

The panic-stricken parents got in touch with their Bologna rabbi who contacted his colleagues in Rome. These in turn protested to the Vatican. The Roman Jews were, after all, no longer living in the Middle Ages, this was the vaunted nineteenth century—and they had even tasted a short period of complete emancipation ten years previously under the Roman Republic. The Pope, however, was indignant. The Jews were "interfering" in the internal affairs of the Vatican State, as they were told by a Vatican spokesman. This was clearly a matter for Catholics only—for that was the religion of the boy. But the boy was Jewish! Not any longer, stated the Vatican, citing the decision of Toledo three centuries earlier. Once the act of baptism was performed, no matter how or under what conditions or circumstances, the ceremony was valid, and the Jews had best return to their ghetto and forget the matter. The same message was transmitted to the parents; the father, Mamolo Mortara, had travelled to Rome to plead the case.

Back to their homes the Jews went, but far from forgetting about it, they sounded the alarm and sought help from Jewish centers abroad. Committees were formed everywhere; and (as would happen in similar cases in Holland and France after the Second World War) world public opinion responded instantaneously. Hundreds of letters started to pour in to Rome, where they are still being carefully kept at the archives of the Jewish Community.

Again, protest meetings were held and requests for a reversal of the Vatican decision came in from Emperor Franz Joseph and from Napoleon III (who had just concluded an agreement with Cavour and this had already brought him in opposition to the Pope). A liberal-inclined emperor, the nephew of Napoleon Bonaparte, who during his youth had scuttled back and forth in exile between America, England, and Switzerland, and who moreover had spent some time in a French jail, he was prepared to join the cause of the unfortunate Mortara parents, and to come to the support of the Jews of Rome.

An adventurous English Jew by the name of Charles Alexander Scott—*né* Blumenthal, devised a plan by which he and some fellow conspirators would disguise themselves as monks, travel to Rome, and re-kidnap the boy. What the Vatican could bring off as a monkish coup, the valiant Britons certainly could do better. But the heroic school-boy plan never quite materialized. Scott stayed in England* and Edgardo Mortara remained in Rome, where the Vatican paraded the little boy through the streets of the ghetto as a living example of what the combined force of Catholic faith and papal police could accomplish.

The Roman rabbinate prepared a dossier on the case, and after much editing and rewriting sent a carefully-worded memorandum to the Pope. It pointed out that there had never been any danger of death when the boy was so irresponsibly baptized by Anna Morisi. The boy, as was confirmed in a statement from Dr. Pasquale Saragoni who treated the Mortara family, had had an attack of *semplice febbre verminosa*, a simple fever caused by worms. This was a frequent children's disease, the doctor added, "with nothing to worry about." And, said Dr. Saragoni in his medical report, he would "be willing to swear as to the accuracy and truth of his statement"—there had never been any grounds for "baptism *in extremis.*"

The maid, the memorandum went on to point out, had not yet been sixteen years old when she baptized the boy, and was known—sworn statements from Bologna citizens were attached—to have been of rather loose morals; she had been found *in flagrante delicto* sleeping with Austrian soldiers. This corroboration, of course, did not contribute to the strengthening of the rabbinate's case, for Anna's youthful promiscuity could not affect any spiritual good work she might do as a good Catholic.

Then the cautious lawyers of the Roman ghetto went into the past history of cases of forced baptism—there were precedents where the Vatican was understanding and subsequently relented. There was such a case in 1429; a good number of other examples were found on yellowed papers in the community's archives. In 1840 "the armed forces had entered the home of a French family by the name of Crémieux in Rome, and had asked

*He later joined Garibaldi, and died in 1866 in Venice as the result of wounds received in battle.

for a new-born baby which was presumed to have been baptized in Fiumicino." The child had not been handed over; and the Vatican had not made further representations.

In the year 1852 the family Pincherle (as it happens, this is the original family name of novelist Alberto Moravia) at Verona had been asked for a five-year-old girl, presumably baptized by her nurse-maid. The parents refused, and an agreement was reached by which the girl would be turned over to the Home for the Catechumen at the age of fourteen, at which time the choice of religion would be left to her.

The Mortara memorandum concluded by pointing out "the desolation of a father and the distraught fear of a mother at this loss of their son." The community hoped that "the charity which is embedded in the mind and the heart of the Magnanimous Pontiff and His worthy ministers" would cause them "to decree the requested restitution" of the child.

A personal letter from the boy's parents accompanied the memorandum. Addressed to the *Beatissimo Padre* and referring to the loss of their son two months previously, Mamolo and Marianna Mortara "once again implored his return."

The Pope did not answer the letter, nor reply to the memorandum. The only concession granted by the Vatican was to allow Mamolo to pay a visit to his son at the Home for Catechumen. Worldwide indignation kept mounting while these contacts between community and Vatican remained stalemated. The Jewish citizens of Metz wondered how such things could happen—"in France the Jews are entirely free." The Amsterdam Jews wrote that the Mortara case soon would be discussed by the Council of Ministers. The French sent a letter to the Duc de Grammont, minister to the Holy See, asking for his intervention.

Again it was Sir Moses Montefiore who came to Rome to plead the return of Edgardo to his bereft parents. From Paris Adolphe Crémieux (it was said that it was his relatives who had been requested to give up that new-born baby in Rome eighteen years previously, during the year of the Damascus Affair) added his voice to the growing chorus of world opinion. But evidently nothing could shake the decision of the Vatican and Pope Pius. In Germany a 26-page pamphlet was published during that year of the papal kidnapping, entitled "The Violent Bologna Kidnap Case" (1858). It was intended "as a word of warning to all friends of the *Concordat*," namely, supporters of the various agreements signed by the Vatican and other countries, regulating the prerogatives between church and state. Mamolo Mortara himself had been persisting in his pleas to the ecclesiastic authorities. According to the German pamphlet, the only answer the father had received was: "Become a Roman Catholic yourself and you'll get back your child."

The Vatican tried to justify its case by disseminating sentimental tales about young Edgardo and his happy life at the religious home. They were apparently written by a priest with a naive literary talent; his sugar-coated tales took no account of the factor of parental anguish, and hence of the strong personal emotions which had seized readers everywhere. *L'Armonia*, the diocesan daily newspaper of Turin, printed the following account of Edgardo's celestial bliss on 16 October 1858, four months after the child had been kidnapped:

"We have just received news about the Mortara boy. He entered the Hospice of the Catechumen with extraordinary happiness, and as soon as he had set foot in the hall of his new home, he saw a statue of the *Madonna Addolorata*, and asked: 'Why is she crying?' Answered his guardian: 'Because the Jews do not want to be converted—because they do not want to recognize the Divine Son.' 'In that case,' said the boy, 'in that case she is crying for my father and mother.' "

"These were the first words the boy spoke," the newspaper explained. "He has these ideas deep in his mind, and even more so in his heart—the blessing to be a Christian and the singular grace he received through the baptism, which enables him to face the immense misfortune of his parents who want to be and who want to remain Jews. The little Mortara boy is as strong in his belief as a little apostle. When he was asked 'Who is the Pope?,' he answered: 'The Vicar of Jesus Christ.' And to the question: 'Who is Jesus Christ?' he answered: 'The Saviour of men, who was crucified by the Jews.' "

After this report of the most unlikely theological dialogue of the day came the crucial question: The newspaper asked: "And then there are people who would be ready to send a boy with such deep-seated faith back to the ghetto?" It was a rhetorical question; they waited not for an answer.

The storm of anger, as storms usually do, abated. Edgardo did not go back to the ghetto but remained in the custody of the well-organized Home for the Catechumen till he was ready for the priesthood. Having become a member of the Order of the Augustins, Edgardo then spent the rest of his life spreading the word of Christ. On 25 April 1900, interviewed by the Paris newspaper *Le Matin* (he answered the interviewing questions by mail), Edgardo, by then 48-years-old, revealed the virtues of a thorough indoctrination. The son of Mamolo Mortara wrote: "I was baptized when I was hardly eleven months old, in great danger of death, by a Christian servant who was in the employ of my parents in Bologna, where I was born in 1851. After my baptism I remained with my parents for seven years. In June 1858, by order of Pope Pius IX, I was taken to Rome, where the same Pope had me educated as a Catholic . . . "

Some six months after the outbreak of the Second World War, during which millions of his parents' co-believers would find their premature death, and a month before Belgium was overrun by the German *Wehrmacht*, Edgardo Mortara died in Liège, on 17 April 1940, at the age of 89. By then the popularity of the forced baptism in Rome had necessarily become a thing of the past, for in the meantime an end had come to the existence of the Papal States as independent Vatican territories.

Chapter 23
The False Messiah

All through the Middle Ages and the Renaissance and for centuries afterwards, especially since they were enclosed behind the walls of the ghetto, the Roman Jews' pursuit of happiness had been more quest than fulfilment. Jewish joy in Rome was always short-lived. It should surprise no one that the idea of the Coming of the Messiah was an "eternal recurrence." His arrival had been promised for so long, surely some day the prediction would *have* to come true. The greater the misery, the more intense the yearning: and we have already seen it in the case of David Reubeni in the early sixteenth century.

Still, Reubeni had not been looked upon as the Messiah; he was rather taken more as a liberator—who did not quite fulfil an historic task. Since then there had been nobody. Yet good news was in the offing, for according to both Christians and Jews the middle of the seventeenth century would bring a Great Event. The Kabbalists had calculated the date as the year 1648. The Christians gave the momentous upheaval a little more time—1666 was to be the world-shaking year. (It is strange that the Kabbalists had not chosen 1666 as well, since between that year and the year of the start of the Roman ghetto, 1555, there might have been all kinds of seductive supernatural numerical comparisons.) No one was sure how the Event would come about or what its result would be, but everybody felt certain that it was imminent and inevitable. A kind of messianic hope and apocalyptic desperation gripped the Roman Jewish community as the time for the Coming drew closer. The sense of excitement was palpable.

If misery were the sole requisite for the arrival of the Messiah, then it was clear that He must be on his way. The situation *was* bad: it was not a Jewish mind-set. The financial situation of the Roman Community (or *Università* as it was then called) was kept on an artificial level of near-bankruptcy, with only new loans from the Papal *Monte di Pietà* and a kind of refinancing by the Vatican keeping the ghetto from total insolvency. The refinancing meant that the Jews' previous debts were all converted into one huge debt with a unified interest rate which, in the end, left the community in as dire straits as ever. Pope Innocent X was not a hostile ruler, but circumstances that were even beyond *his* control had made living conditions in Rome nearly impossible. The year 1647 brought repeated floods of the Tiber; bread became unobtainable; figs and herbs had taken the place of staple foods.

Elsewhere in Europe, especially in Poland, the situation was far worse. The Cossack *hetman* Bogdan Chmielnicki massacred Jews wherever he found them; and the Swedes, who shortly afterwards entered into the Polish political and territorial conflict, gave him a helping hand. Hence the news that reached Rome from abroad dampened whatever little political hope there was left. Could Israel be so punished without even a ray of new hope? The year 1648 came and went—disappointingly. Where was the Messiah?

The "Messiah" was in the East, as well he should be. He was born in Smyrna in 1626. Very poor but highly intelligent, he was a Kabbalistic scholar at the age of fifteen, and some years after he turned to asceticism. So ascetic indeed that he divorced his wives—for somehow there were two of them (whether simultaneously or progressively seems to be in doubt). Evidently the Messiah-to-be did not go into any absolute seclusion, for he took an interest in the events in Poland and elsewhere in Europe. His fame as a holy man began to spread westward, and European Jewry began to take an interest in him.

His name was Sabbathai Zwi. According to various etchings that exist, his appearance mixed the features of an Eastern potentate and a Dutch aristocrat, with well-trimmed beard, wavy moustache, starched lace collar and Rembrandt-like beret. His final legacy would be nil, but before the end his influence reached tremendous heights. His was a meteoric messianism which would evoke tremblings of expectation, mass hysteria, and an understandable concern in the Vatican. It would also bring the Jews of Rome to a state of religious frenzy.

When Sabbathai heard about the Polish pogroms, he declared them to be the birth-pains of the Messiah; because, after all, things first had to reach an all-time low before the Messiah could make an appearance. Sabbathai felt himself growing in strength, determination, and religious power. If 1648 had passed, 1666 was still looming up ahead—and by 1651 the aspiring Messiah felt that the time had now a fullness and a ripeness.

After considerable travel in the Middle East, Sabbathai arrived in Cairo, where before long—his asceticism behind him—he took a third wife unto himself. It was a union perfectly in harmony with the high ideals of messianism and holy matrimony, for the wife was none but a woman who had been told in a dream that she was destined to marry the Messiah. Sabbathai Zwi's fame having reached Rome and Livorno, where the girl had been spending some time, she speedily set off to persuade her husband-to-be.

She was no (nor could she be) plain ordinary person—she had to have a special background; and Sarah, the woman in question, indeed could look back on a fairly checkered past. She had been born in Poland, and had lost her family in one of the Chmielnicki raids. Taken to a convent, she fled to that haven

for the persecuted—Holland. From there she slowly drifted to
Livorno, a drifter. It was a flash of revelation when Sarah heard
about Sabbathai the Messiah; here was her future, and it certainly seemed to guarantee her better and more solid prospects
than the odd jobs in the streets of Livorno.

The news of the Cairo wedding soon spread back to Italy,
Sarah's past by now undoubtedly being buried in the back-
alleys of Livorno. The Jewish communities started to rise to the
occasion, and in Rome the enthusiasm was great. The time had
come. The Messiah was on his way. Wise Jews from all over
Europe set sail for the East. They found Sabbathai back in his
home town, Smyrna, where the Jewish New Year festival of
1665 (so very close to the longed-for Year of the Coming, 1666)
became a day of immense rejoicing.

Hallucinations play a certain part in the proceedings.
Wherever they were, far or near, and whatever it was that they
saw, the visionary spectacle was of Sabbathai as the Messiah.
Eye-witness reports about the great scene in the East brought
the European Jews to a state of divine paroxysm. The Vatican
could not remain uninterested, even though it had other
apocalyptic problems in this mystical year. If the year 1666 were
to bring what Jewish messianic optimism said it would bring, at
the very least Jews would no longer be third-rate citizens along
the Tiber, and what would happen to the ghetto? Everything
might well come into flux.

The Italian Jewish communities began to make immediate
plans on how to celebrate the great event. Who could know
what preparations had to be made for the day after?

His followers now urged Sabbathai to start on his way to
Europe, where the dispersed Jews had to be reunited into one
great rejuvenated People of Israel. In Rome the Tribe on the
Tiber would no longer stand alone. It would join the tribes from
the Danube, the Nile, and even those of the dispersed Jews near
the Ganges in India and of the Marranos who had left Portugal
to settle north of the Rio de la Plata in South America. (These
were four rivers made famous in Rome by Bernini, who had im-

mortalized them fifteen years previously in his great fountain in the center of the Piazza Navona, so close to the ghetto.)

To reach his flock, Sabbathai and an ever-growing band of fervent believers left Smyrna and set off for the West, for who could doubt that Jews everywhere would with gladness form a revitalized nation around the figure of the Messiah? Only in Rome there might be trouble. The Pope, perhaps, might not be so easily persuaded to let his people go.

On his arrival in Constantinople, Sabbathai was detained. The Pope was not the only person who was disturbed about the possible ramifications if it turned out that it was the Jews who were finally getting their Messiah. The Mohametan world too was beginning to take a concerned view of the new movement. To gain time, the Grand Vizier in Constantinople put the new Messiah in jail, removing him soon afterwards to the castle of Abydos on the Hellespont. Here Sabbathai was made quite comfortable in what his followers started to refer to as the "Tower of Power." He had several rooms at his disposal, could receive friends and missions from abroad; and he held court as if he were the veritable ruler of Judaism.

Before long the Grand Vizier transferred the Messiah-claimant off to Adrianople, where Sabbathai was a step nearer to his goal of Western Europe. But the strenuous course left him seriously ill and only the intervention of the Grand Vizier's physician (a Jew who had turned Moslem) saved him. There was one condition attached to the cure: Sabbathai, too, would have to embrace Islam, a proposition which he readily accepted.

The one-time Messiah's precipitous move from Moses to Mohamed and from Mount Sinai to Mecca was a move followed by the faithful. Sarah, his wife, joined him, and so did a good number of his followers. The year was the fateful 1666, and since *something* important had to happen, the astonishing conversion of the Jewish Messiah to the role of Turkish Keeper of the Door—which was the job the new-named Nehmed Effendi was assigned—was dramatic enough. Yet it was no longer a purely Jewish drama.

The fever and fervor of the messianic movement had been too strong to die down quickly. Europe remained in a religious turmoil, and the Roman Jews with it. Sabbathai Zwi, alias Nehmed Effendi, remained a name to be reckoned with, and the Sabbathaian movement would continue to obsess the European Jews for years to come.

Thirty-eight years after Sabbathai Zwi's death, in 1714, another religious zealot made his impact in Rome—Nehemia Ghia Chayon, born in 1650 in Sarajevo. A Kabbalistic dreamer with a highly fanatical and persuasive manner, he had been able to get his controversial religious books printed in various European cities. He was soon repudiated as yet another false prophet. One of his visionary ideas was a Jewish Holy Trinity, and the schisms he caused in learned Jewish circles with this extravagant theological notion would need years to heal.

In Vienna Emperor Charles VI had supplied Nehemia with a letter of introduction that would open a great many European doors, including—Nehemia hoped—the door of the Vatican. But in Rome he found that not only the door leading to the Pope was closed to him, but even the gates of the ghetto, symbolically at least. Claiming alternately to be a Moslem, a devout rabbi, and a pretender to the empty Sabbathaian messianic throne, his dream-like confusions had no effective message for Jewish realities. He died on a journey to North Africa, around 1736, a disillusioned old man without any clear or coherent religious legacy.

By this time there had been, and still were, several Popes by the name of Clement—the XII, the XIII, and the XIV. As with so many earlier Clements, the XIIth was far from what his name suggested. Yet with the crowning of the XIIIth and XIVth, a happier spirit pervaded the walls of the Roman ghetto.

Sabbathai Zwi, the Messiah who had failed, had been unable to convince the Jews of his claims. Yet he may well have influenced one of the "more clement of the Clements" (as he has been called) to some extent. In Saint Peter's in Rome, to the right and just behind Bernini's central Altar of the Chair, is the tomb of Clement XIII, sculptured by Canova. There are two inscriptions in Hebrew on this 18th-century work. One says *Kodesh Adonai*—God is Holy. The other words, on the waistband of one of the figures, are *Chesed We'emmes*—Benevolence and Truth.

Sabbathai's influence? Nehemiah's? or recondite iconography? Whatever the reason, the benevolent inscriptions were all there was to help the Jews of the Roman ghetto. Bankruptcy was still the rule of the day. The Vatican's economic and financial arrangements for the Jews were a network of inescapable restrictions. Between payments for the Homes of the Catechumen, interest on loans from the *Monte di Pietà*, charges by the Roman Senate, rent on empty apartments due to the *jus gazaga*, various compulsory church gifts, tax for nonparticipation in the long-expired carnival races, and several sundry items, they owed the Vatican close to 300,000 scudi. Considering that a liter of wine cost 5 *baiòcche* and a pound of meat ten, the debt was enormous.

Not even a Messiah, some despairing Jews thought, would have been able to extricate them out of this financial morass, unless he held the very purse strings of Heaven. What the Jews of Rome needed was still a miracle—would it be a real Messiah, or another form of liberation in the real world?

Chapter 24
Ghetto Life

In the daily humdrum life of the ghetto, worldly liberation seemed a wholly utopian prospect. During the two centuries preceding the French Revolution, the Roman Jews continued most of the time to live on a most depressed financial and intellectual level, with only an occasional piece of good fortune that would make them rejoice as if Paradise were beckoning. Wondrous times, they did not have to wear a pointed hat any longer—or a yellow sash, or a veil, or any other of the various distinctive discriminatory marks that disappeared and reappeared at irregular intervals. God be praised, they had managed to lighten by a little a heavy burden of indebtedness. Good news, they were now allowed to pull their push-carts all the way to the Piazza del Popolo to buy second-hand rags. Miracle of miracles, there were weeks when there were no accidents, no incidents of violence.

In the words of an old Jewish refrain, who would call this a life? It was just eking out an existence. The Jews of Rome were only barely tolerated, disagreeable fungus that had proliferated down there near the river, in the middle of a great city whose government recognized no universal civic rights, and whose church sedulously refused to practice what it preached—brotherly love, neighbourly kindness, the understanding of the heart, and mercy to all God's creatures.

Outside the ghetto the Jews would continue to do homage to every new Pope, some of whom would reign for a considerable number of years, others descending into their graves with startling alacrity. Between 1590 and 1592 there were four new Popes. Shortly afterwards Leo XI reigned for only twenty-six days, Gregory XV and Clement IX each just about two years. Each time a Pope was crowned, the Jews would decorate his inaugural route with precious rugs, banners, and costly bunting, mostly from the Arch of Titus to the Colosseum. For the rest, the contact between ghetto and Vatican would be fairly sporadic. Single Jews or small groups would visit the Pope on special occasions, either to praise or to plead.

The number of people who lived inside the ghetto fluctuated considerably. Between the middle of the seventeenth century and the end of the eighteenth, the figures go from a low of 850 families with some 4,500 souls to a maximum of about 8,000. On the whole there were so many children in the ghetto, that according to the remark of one visitor, "one was afraid of infanticide at each step." In this, of course, the narrow streets of the ghetto were not much different from the streets in any other Italian (and especially southern Italian) city where even today the children will crawl, run, and play in crowded places.

Yet with the years the rag-picking trade, which at times was the unique occupation of the ghetto, gave way to a variety of professions, many of which were started for ghetto consumption or sales only, then branching out beyond the walls. Towards the beginning of the eighteenth century there were not only tailors but also goldsmiths and jewelers, carpenters and ironmongers, makers of leather-ware, and traders in rugs and precious oriental cloth.

From dealing in rugs and furniture it was only a step to renting them to part-time residents of Rome; and soon there were Jews among the interior decorators of some of Rome's best-known palazzi. In 1686 the magnificent Pamphilij palace on the Piazza Navona (built in 1650, today the Brazilian embassy) was rented by the British ambassador for the Duke of Norfolk. It was half-empty, and Jewish dealers were requested to bring in the necessary furniture and other objects, which they did for the rental of one hundred gold florins a month.

There were even marginal professions beyond the fringe. Some inhabitants of the ghetto would also sell amulets and love potions. Love itself, wholesale or retail, was apparently also for sale; one Pope had Jewish girls forcibly removed from the Piazza Navona (as a marketplace it was frequented by Jews) where their presence was creating "an uproar at night." There are no details of *why* it caused such a turmoil; but a good guess may be that Christian prostitutes who considered the square their very own field of operation had protested against the Jewish competition.

Love and marriage among the Jews were usually less turbulent. Their period of betrothal was carefully watched, and such furtive meetings as would inevitably happen ignited bitter argument, for rules governing marriage at times were bizarre and even infuriating. One such case involved a girl called Rosa, the blossoming daughter of Mordehai Cohen; she had been engaged for about two years to Samuele Cohen (no relative). One evening another young man, Aaron Efrati, walked down Rosa's street in the company of two friends, whom he had asked along to be witnesses to his official betrothal.

The whistle love-call—it is still being effectively practiced in Rome today—shrilly emanated from Aaron's lips in the quiet of the evening; it soon brought the blushing Rosa to the other side of the front door, which happened to have one window-pane missing. According to the two witnesses, Aaron put his hand through the door opening and placed a ring onto Rosa's finger. Then they left, and claimed the next day that Aaron was now engaged to the unsuspecting Rosa: because in handing over the ring he had pronounced the official Hebrew engagement pledge.

Of course Samuele, who still considered himself properly engaged to Rosa, was rather upset by this unexpected interloping on the part of Aaron. So he and his parents, Rosa and *her* parents, Mordehai and his two witnesses, all went to put their conflicting arguments before the rabbi.

The Roman rabbi asked Rosa to give her side of the story. It was simply not true, said the shaken girl. She had *not* accepted the ring, and she had not even known that it was Aaron who had whistled. All she had heard was someone saying *"It's Samuele!"*—and at that she had rushed downstairs, only to feel something put into her hand. She had gasped a maidenly surprise, and when a servant arrived with a candle, what did they find? A ring—and Rosa promptly gave it to the maid, probably a Christian girl, who surely could not be in danger of a false betrothal.

As the story is told, while Rosa looked lovingly at Samuele and Samuele glanced furiously at Aaron, the rabbi kept on pondering. There was very little—in fact, nothing—he could do about it, he finally confessed. The holy words spoken by Aaron were binding, and the only conceivable way to undo the nocturnal episode of the ring would be for him to prepare a divorce document, so that Aaron and Rosa would be free again. Samuele expressed his gratitude to the rabbi and seemed pleased at the prospect. But no, said the rabbi, the case was *still* wide open, and would not therewith be able to be closed again. Because Samuele belonged to the family of the Cohens (or High Priests), and as such he would not be allowed to marry a divorcee which Rosa would technically become. The documents of the quarrel do not reveal what became of Rosa, balancing between her two husbands-not-to-be. But it is all too clear from the rabbi's decision that in order to be a Jew in those days, one needed more than mere human fortitude.

There is a second recorded case of "stolen love" which involved another Jewish girl. She was in the habit of lowering a small basket to pick up one of her betrothed's *billets-doux*, sending him at the same time one of hers. One night the string of the basket snapped, and somewhat in a panic she threw her letter out of the window. It twirled off in the wind, disappeared from sight, and was found the next day by a nephew of Cardinal Cuneo. After making inquiries, he discovered who the girl was; he found her young, gay, and pretty, and decided he wanted to marry her.

There was, of course, little hope for the poor man, the girl being a Jewess and he a good Catholic. But, as always, there were ways and means open to a man in a case like this, even if it would lead the girl into strange paths. The House of the Catechumen was called on for help, and the girl was dutifully and forcibly taken away from her parents and put through the usual forty days' training course. The method proved effective, for at the end of the indoctrination period she decided to accept the religion of her suitor and of the quite persuasive nuns, and to marry the young man with the cardinal's blessing.

What of the general hygienic conditions of the ghetto? They remained very sub-standard. One happy change early during the seventeenth century was the arrival of purer drinking water via a new acqueduct that had been built by Paul V; it brought the water from the Lake of Bracciano, about 25 miles north of Rome. It was a great improvement over the Tiber water which till then had been almost the only available source. The use of the acquaduct water was free; but the ghetto had to pay the Vatican six hundred scudi for the beautification of a far-away city fountain.

A ghetto suffers; a ghetto stinks. Around 1690 it was described as having "a penetrating stench," and Charles de Brosses, the French scholar who wrote extensively about Italy, said after a visit to the Roman ghetto in 1740 that he considered it an *archisaloperie*, a place that was nothing but a stinking, putrifying garbage heap. Another observer, possibly using his nose more than his brain, thought that he had discovered the secret of it all—"the *canaille* breeds too fast" (but given the population statistics of modern times this is just about as true for the *canaille* and non-*canaille* in every other country). All of it

made the ghetto sound like an unpleasant place to live; most
certainly it was not the Promised Land.

As an isolated religious community the Jews all through those
years remained true to their ancient customs. No doubt their
loyalties were constantly reinforced by the attempts, largely
futile, to subvert them by means of compulsory sermons and
forced baptism. The Sabbath remained holy. When dusk approached on Friday evening, an official night-caller, accompanied by a few ghetto notables, would walk around to bring
the coming day of rest to the attention of the inhabitants (and
the shops would close on time). After the small group had completed its third tour, the ghetto gates would be shut tight and the
Jews would be all on their own—with only the synagogue as
their consolation and hope.

Some of the ancient ghetto customs have died out. For instance, going barefoot through town was customary among the
Roman Jews on returning from a funeral. At other times, on the
last day of the Feast of the Tabernacles, everybody would walk
home with a lighted candle in his hand, and the spectacle used to
impress observers with its display of walking illuminations.

When humane Popes loosened the bands of prohibitions
every once in a while, conversation and companionship between
Jew and Christian could flourish in Rome; visits to each others'
coffee-houses would be frequent. Jews at times were allowed to
be served at a Christian establishment, and Catholics were often
visitors and customers in the ghetto. Benedict XIII, in 1728,
thought that the fraternisation had gone a bit far, and he
promulgated an order which "prohibited the Jew from serving
drinks to any Christian in his establishment at the occasion of
Jewish family celebrations or parties"; at the same time it forbade Christians from visiting these cafés or homes. Meetings
were to be limited to business appointments, the Pope decreed;
whoever did not comply would be fined twenty-five scudi.

Nevertheless, this did not mean that Benedict was a hostile
ruler, for the next year another decree would protect his subjects
in the ghetto during the Roman carnival time. A wall poster, put
up all over Rome, dealt in general "with masks and carnival

races," and ordered the Roman citizens "not to offend the Jews with words or deeds, under punishment of a prison term for adult males, and whipping for whores and young boys."

The atmosphere of slackening social tensions had, as usual, a salutary effect on the artistic development of the ghetto Jews. Of course, this did not result in a sudden blossoming of the Arts; yet it brought forth an excellent Jewish poetess, Deborah Ascarelli (a well known Jewish family name in Rome for ages). Elsewhere in Italy, away from the diminishing yet always stifling influence of the Vatican, writers would develop more easily. Among them was a rather fantastic individual who would die in 1838 in New York as a Jew, after having gone through a temporary stage of Catholicism—Lorenzo da Ponte. Under his own name Emanuele da Conegliano (from the city of Conegliano), he wrote the librettos for Mozart's *Marriage of Figaro*, *Don Giovanni*, and *Cosi fan Tutte*. But his cultural adventures were of no influence on the Jews of Rome who soon discovered that the papal glitter of freedom was not entirely eighteen (or as was then used in Rome) twenty-four carat gold.

By 1753 the comparatively mild régime of Pope Benedict XIV suddenly reverted to methods used by the old school—all Hebrew books were to be handed over. This evidently was a long and wearisome process, and the Vatican decided to enter the homes of the unbelievers and confiscate the books on the spot. Accompanied by *sbirri*, the papal delegates had the ghetto gates closed and then started a house-to-house search, picking up books wherever they found them. It must have been an all-night raid, for we know that towards morning some thirty-eight wagon-loads were hauled off to the Vatican. This time the organisation was better than previously. All bags were neatly labeled with the names of the owners who, notwithstanding this careful handling of their property, found themselves bereft of even an ordinary prayer book.

This action by the Pope was the more surprising because for thirteen years he had been a quite benevolent figure. In a power struggle with the Jesuits, Benedict had on several occasions opposed the monks in favour of the Jews; he felt that the persecution-complex of the *frati* was just a bit stronger than righteousness, justice, and his own interests ordained. More than a few Roman Jews, as a result of the turn of the tide, preferred to leave the city and look for a haven elsewhere—only to be persecuted even more violently by the Jesuits in those Italian cities that were not under the direct control of the Vatican. All things considered, it was at times better to stay home and abide with the troubles one knew.

Indeed, those Jews who did not emigrate from the Tiber under Benedict XIV soon discovered that the two Clements who now followed, the XIIIth and XIVth, were a great improvement: eleven years of the earlier Clement (the one with the Hebrew-inscribed tomb in St. Peter's), five years under his kind successor. The intra-Catholic faction fight with the Jesuits finally came to a head, and the Pope decided in the fourth year of his reign to suppress the order—to the joy of a good many European rulers, to the comfort of the Jews. The Pope, in the end, turned out to be weaker than the monks who quietly (and often not so quietly) continued to operate as if nothing had happened, protected by two powerful "Great" monarchs—Frederick of Prussia and Catherine of Russia.

As long as Clement XIV had his own troubles outside Rome, the Jews did well. Professions which time and again had been forbidden were once more open to them. Artisans, carpenters and tailors were able to find clients outside the ghetto walls. In 1764—still under Clement XIII—we know that the Jew Moshe Cohen received an order to deliver a large quantity of wheat from northern Italy to the Vatican. In 1773, a year of threatening famine, the same northern merchant continued his deliveries under Clement XIV. Grain wholesaler and banker, Cohen had substantial influence at the papal court; but this did not do the Roman Jews much good in the eyes of the non-Jews. There were circles within circles, and all of them seemed to be vicious circles. Whenever they were treated badly by the Vatican, nobody cared. When they were shown more tolerance and kindliness, jealousies would be rife.

During the next twenty-five years or so the Vatican found itself faced by many difficulties from many quarters. So did the

Jews. Ever since they had been shut behind the ghetto walls in 1555, their existence had a special precariousness. For over two centuries they had been told what to do, more often what they could *not* do. With what slowly was going to be considered a "typical Jewish character trait" of acceptance and non-violence, the Roman Jews continued obediently to walk the narrowest of permissible paths. Do this, don't do that; walk here, don't walk there; wear this, wear that; give me your children, abandon your books, surrender your money; persist and be forever damned, persist not and be eternally blessed; be poor, be poorer, be poorest. Pope Clement XIV died in 1774. The name taken by the new Pope, Pius VI, was taken by sign-sensitive Jews to be a bad omen, since the latest Pius before him, the Fifth, had been one of the most anti-Jewish Popes in history. Elsewhere in Europe there were rumblings of general dissidence and protest from a slowly awakening citizenry. The writings of Voltaire and Rousseau were preparing the world for what was going to be known as "The Age of Enlightenment." In America the first shots of the War of Independence were heard on April 19, 1775, and an historic battle for freedom was on. The following day, April 20, Pope Pius VI fired his own shots in Rome in a battle that would doom every last shred of freedom for the Jews. In America, during that fateful month of April, there was resistance and jubilation. In Rome there was—or could be—nothing of the sort. Once the Pope decreed, resistance was useless for the Jews of Rome.

Modernism, according to Pope Pius, was an idea that by all means at his disposal had to be stopped at the very frontiers of papal territory. If people in France and elsewhere thought that a time for change was approaching, then such changes were not to make any inroads on the prescribed ideas of life as were promulgated by the Vatican, emanating from there to all its citizens and obliging all the faithful to live according to the principles as proclaimed by papal decree.

Approximately a century-and-a-half earlier Galileo had tried to upset an established Catholic notion of how the world was made by proclaiming that the earth revolved around the sun (and not the other way)—and he was thoroughly denounced by the Inquisition for his dangerous and false thoughts. (Since by 1967 all kinds of man-made satellites were freely mingling with bodies celestial, Pope Paul VI during a short visit to Galileo's native city of Pisa finally had to admit that perhaps the great astronomer had not been entirely wrong, and that the ban pronounced in 1663 *perhaps* had been a bit precipitate. It suggested, more than three centuries after Galileo, and two centuries after Pope Pius VI, that the Vatican detests almost above all things hasty decisions and abrupt changes.)

But if, back in 1775, protests from abroad could not be endured within the Papal States, then protests from within (were there really any who dared protest openly?) were to be stamped out vigorously and immediately. One need not ask who would be the first to be so intimidated. The Jews, of course. They were on the side of those who thought differently (even if those who thought differently, including men of the Enlightenment, were not always on the side of the Jews).* But those who were not for the Vatican, were automatically against it, and in that category the Jews were certainly to be included. Moreover, the Roman Jews were the obvious targets just outside the windows of the Vatican; and if an example had to be set, it should be first set at home. So, as always had been the case, it was not down with the shoemakers, not down with the plumbers or with the fishermen along the Tiber, not down with the French and other nefarious free-thinkers, but—simply, conveniently—down with the Jews.

Pope Pius had been working on his edict of 1775 ever since he came to the throne. He only needed two months. On April 5 the draft had been finished, but it would take another two weeks before its decisions descended on the Jewish population of Rome, lulled perhaps into a false sense of security because of the happy times they had enjoyed so recently under Clement XIV. Consisting of forty-four tightly-composed paragraphs, Pius VI's *Edict on the Jews* obliterated with one huge sweep of the papal hand whatever rights the Jews had accumulated over the centuries. As we have seen, it was at times little more than

---

*For a critical historical study of anti-Semitism within the movement of Enlightenment and Revolution, see: Arthur Hertzber, *The French Enlightenment and the Jews* (Columbia University Press, 1968).

holding on to the hope and promise of papal goodwill. Had the Jews of Rome now come to the end of the road?

The Pope had not left a single item to chance. Every rule that had restricted the Jews through the centuries was excavated; every daily move was to be regulated and accounted for. They were told how to live, and where to live; whom to see, and (mostly) whom not to see; what to wear and what to read; and, above all, they were told that the Catholic religion was the best and that any interference with the efforts to make progressive Christians out of what the Vatican considered to be habitually retarded Jews would be a misdemeanor.

As to their Hebrew books—nothing in them should be contrary to Catholic belief, and no such items should ever be discussed. All books should, of course, be censored by the Vatican; no books could be freely imported from abroad (the Papal customs authorities would guard against that). The study of Kabbalah and Talmud was prohibited; it was supposed to have something to do with fortune-telling, and that was forbidden. As to clothes, the yellow dye was to be used again, and both men and women were to wear a yellow head-dress, and women were to wear *only* this yellow ribbon or piece of cloth, immediately attached to the hair. (What if a Jewish salesman dealt in hats? Then he was to exhibit these in his hands and to wear only the prescribed yellow one.) These orders were not to be restricted to Rome, but were to be applicable anywhere in the Papal States.

No one, of course, was to spend a night outside the ghetto, and no places of business were to be continued outside its walls without special permission. The Jews were allowed to buy milk, but for their private use only. Cheese was not to be made, and animals that were slaughtered by the Jews would serve exclusively for home consumption (the meat could not even be given away as a present). Nor could they sell or give away bread or *matzoth*. Thou shalt not: the Pope had turned an Old Testament injunction on its head.

As to Christian cameraderie—no more coffee, no more companionship, no ties, and no connections. Christians were not to enter synagogues, whether of their own free will or by invitation. Christian nurses and servants were things of the past. Jews were not to share meals with Christians, not to keep their company, nor to have dealings with them in any other way. Riding in carriages was as bad as sinning. If priests had any rags to sell, they could henceforth only sell them to "old Jews," not to young ones, and the transaction had to be consummated outside the Church.

As to association with anyone considered a Christian (even though he might be an ex-Jew) and with anyone who might want to become a Catholic, the old rules from now on would be applied with more vigour than ever. A baptized Jew was not to be found inside a Jewish home, and trying to "re-convert" such a person would be considered a crime, as would be the effort to prevent any soul from joining the Catholic Church. The entering of churches, convents, or monasteries became another *thou shalt not* rule to be reapplied in all severity. Quite naturally, the forced sermons were reinstituted and with an enthusiasm as if something new had been invented, for surely this was the only way to get rid of the Jews—to convert them all. If they would not yield to these churchly admonitions, they could perfectly well continue to live their miserable Jewish lives till the end of their days. At which time there would be three last restrictions—there was no longer to be any religious singing at funerals, and no more torches if the entombment took place late in the afternoon—and, finally, from 1775 on, tombstones were not to be allowed. What, after all, was a dead Jew but a dead Jew, who might as well be forgotten quickly by all and sundry, without any headstone to prolong the memory.

More rabid anti-Semitic priests immediately rejoiced, and many of the old stories of ritual murder were told anew with additional and amplified details. Forced baptism went through an upswing of popularity (or unpopularity, depending on what side of the font one said his prayers).

The Age of Enlightenment, with certain ideals of liberal tolerance, was starting, but not in Rome. A Frenchman, Charles Marguerite Dupaty, who visited the city in 1783, formulated the right historic question in his *Lettres sur l'Italie**: "The situation of the Jews in Rome is worse than anywhere else. People ask: when will all the Jews become Christians? I ask: when will Christians become more tolerant?"

Dupaty's impression of Rome was sharp in the new spirit of social criticism. He found that of the 36,000 houses in town, 20,000 were owned by the Vatican. He estimated that there were 10,000 beggars—"more than anywhere," he noted. The clergy amounted to one-sixth of the population, and among the rest of the citizens there were five women for every man, which made Dupaty conclude that this was "one of the reasons for the great *libertinage* in town." Security was scant, he wrote, because "the temporal power is reduced to a shadow of police supervision, exercized by priests." The papal *sbirri* "were privileged brigands who make war on non-privileged brigands," while "the courts are made up from prelates who are busy with all kinds of other things." No wonder that Dupaty could not quite comprehend why some people wanted the Jews to join this mélange of what he judged to be a rather debauched and unscrupulous crowd.

Pope Pius VI would die twenty-four years later in Valence, in 1799, brought there by Napoleon; his own Golgotha took him to France after forced sojourns in Siena, Florence, Turin, and Grenoble. By then that revolutionary movement of long-yearned-for worldly liberation had come for the Roman Jews. It was short-lived, for with the disappearance of Napoleon, the Popes would return—and the doors of the ghetto gates would be put back securely on their old hinges.

*Lettres sur l'Italie, écrites en 1885 par Dupaty (Avignon 1811, chez Jean-Albert Joly).

Chapter 25
The Bourbonic Plague

When on January 21, 1793, the Paris guillotine severed Louis XVI's head from his body, there must have been a nervous tightening of neck and throat muscles in Rome. One week *earlier*, or to be exact eight days, on Sunday January 13, the troubles which had started along the Seine four years *previously*, had exploded along the banks of the Tiber. On that day a Roman mob had spotted French Vice-Admiral Charles de Flotte driving down the Corso in the direction of the Piazza Venezia. Accompanying him in his carriage were the secretary of the French embassy in Naples who was on a mission to Rome, Nicolas-Jean Hugon de Bassville and his wife and young son—all of them prominently displaying that outrageous sign of *Liberté*, the tricolored French cockade.

The menacing crowd followed the carriage to the home of French banker Mout in the Palazzo Palombara, where the foursome had sought refuge. By now it was fully convinced that the French tricolor was a revolutionary sign that ought to be banished forthwith from their city. The unfortunate Hugon de Bassville was killed; the Mout residence was sacked.

The Vatican did not exactly applaud this outburst of Roman exuberance, yet the Pope surely felt relieved when he was informed that the first sign of revolutionary audacity had been nipped in the bud. In Rome *Liberté* was a treacherous word and political freedom an alien thought. If the French in 1789 in their Declaration of the Rights of Man had been willing to provide every human being with inalienable rights to individual freedom, including freedom of religion, then that was a strictly French affair. In Rome all rights remained with the Pope, and with the Pope exclusively; and the only valid religion was the religion of Christ and his Vicar on earth.

When the public wrath—which, though perhaps not instigated by the Vatican, was certainly approved by it—was spent, the Trasteverini wondered what could be done next. One did not have to wait long for an inspiration in Rome: the Jews. A rumor spread that four Frenchmen were hiding in the ghetto. It was also said that the Jews had manufactured large stocks of French tricolors, to be put on public display at some auspicious moment.

Papal soldiers already had searched the ghetto for the forbidden items, and had mounted a guard around its walls. That evening, there was an order to the Jews from the Vatican Secretary of State, Cardinal Francesco Savera de Zelada, to send their representatives to visit him. A committee of three appeared in the Cardinal's antechamber on January 14, and they were asked where they were hiding their arms. Tranquillo del Monte, one of the delegates, answered that the only "weapons" they had were "their measuring sticks for cloth" and that any talks they had had with the French were with traveling salesmen, who simply showed them their samples of silk.

Could this be believed? The French had been propagating their libertarian ideals for several years by now; and since the Vatican knew quite well that the Jews for obvious reasons would not turn a deaf ear to such propaganda, the Pope was not averse to holding the mob's pressure at a fairly high pitch so as to keep the Jews properly subdued, at the same time trying to placate that same mob sufficiently in order not to let their mass anger get entirely out of control. It appeared to be a policy of holding a flaming torch in one hand, and a bucket of water in the other.

The papal guard was doubled and then redoubled around the ghetto, until about 2,500 soldiers were deployed along its walls, with the Trasteverini milling around, looking for an opening. Spotting a lonely Jew, a certain Salomone di Segni, they gave him the choice: "*Die!—or* become a Christian!" Poor di Segni temporarily chose the Home for the Catechumen. But soon he proved so obstinate that after his forty days he paid 13 scudi and 35 *baiòcchi* for his food and board, and returned to the ghetto. It was not quite the same.

After di Segni's precipitate departure, three pushcarts and a broken-down horse had been hurriedly abandoned by some frightened Jews on the Piazza Mattei, near the charming Fountain of the Tortoises, outside the main gate of the ghetto and the Piazza Giudia. What else was there for the crowd to do but to kill the horse and set fire to the carts? Once the flames became visible in the distance, an inspiration came on the other side of the ghetto to a certain Decupis, who quickly rushed across to reconnoiter. He had the brilliant idea to set fire to the gate closest to him on his own side, for surely the doors would burn far more brightly than the pushcarts. "Gaetano!" he was heard to shout at a fellow enthusiast, "Gaetano—let's burn the place down! . . ."

They set fire to the Regola Gate, on the side of the Bridge With The Four Heads. The Jews inside the gate desperately tried to throw water on the spreading flames, being assiduously fed from the outside by Decupis and Gaetano and his friends. Reinforcements for the Trasteverini were soon under way. From across the Tiber more men rushed towards the bridge, carrying such wood as they could find for additional fuel. They were stopped by an officer who asked where they were going. "Going to burn down the ghetto!" they said. "Long live the Pope," they shouted, "Down with the Jews!"

"My children," said the kind officer (according to an eyewitness report,) "my dear children, the Pope is sure to be highly pleased by your attachment to his dignity, but he does not want the oppression of these poor people, because they are innocent. If you love the Pope, then let us together burn this wood in his honour, and this will be the sign and expression of your love for him." The extraordinary words had their magic and apparently succeeded in their purpose. The wood was burned right there in the square, in front of the small church of the Congregation of the Madonna of the Divine Pity, to the greater glory of the Pope.

Now to placate the Jews, still engaged in carrying their pitiful buckets of water to the gate and throwing it fitfully over the walls, the kind Marchese Accoramboni shouted at them above the din: "Don't be afraid! Trust in God and in your Holy Prince who only wants to protect you!" At which words, as it was reported, a tremendous downpour started. The Jews' puny efforts at fire fighting proved suddenly unnecessary. The Marchese was said to be highly pleased with the miracle. So, no doubt, were the Jews.

And what of the Trasteverini? Their love for bonfires was legendary, and they now saw their pyrotechnical efforts failing ingloriously in smoke. But for them, too, the good Marchese had a few kind words. "See, my dear children," he said, "see how innocent these Jews are. You want to set fire to their ghetto, and God instead sends water. Recognize the power of God, believe in the Pope, and go home in peace . . . "

A ghetto was saved, and they called it peace. Pius VI certainly had faith in the powers of the papacy, but the only solution he could think of was the renewal of the edict of 1775. He stubbornly tried to turn back history while the French feverishly were turning it forward. "Among the many sovereign acts which His Holiness Pope Pius VI constantly takes to maintain order in the city of Rome," his order read, "and to prevent any action which even in the least might disturb this order, His Holiness has judged it adequate to reinstitute the strict observance of the various rules which in the past have been adopted concerning the Jews, such as the measures that are included in the Edict published on the 5th of April of the year 1775." This had been the worst anti-Jewish measure of the century.

For a start, Jews were told on January 17, only four days after Hugon de Bassville's murder, that instead of freedom-badges they had best wear their yellow shame-badges again—this time not only outside the ghetto but inside its walls as well. The rule was strictly applied at once. Whenever people were hailed in the streets of Rome, they were asked to give a quick answer to the question *"Chi è viva?"** which in this case more or less meant "Who do you support?" or "Long live *WHO?*" The right answer was "The Pope!" Whoever did not come forward with this immediate retort was automatically considered to be a Jew, which conclusion would then invariably be followed by the standard punishment of kicking and beating.

During August 1793, as it happened, nobody less than the Prince of Wales was hailed with the same question in the dark of a Roman night. Being able in his puzzlement to think of only one person in all the world to whom he wanted to wish a long life, His Highness gave a naive answer to the nasty question. *"The King!"* The later George IV, in his embarrassment, barely escaped a beating before he quickly added *"The Pope!"* to the hoped-for longevity of his father. (George III, as it happened, would outlive Pius VI by twenty years.)

In England the Jews by now were quite advanced along the front of equal rights, ever since early in the eighteenth century John Toland had rallied effective support for the liberalizing cause with his *Reasons for Naturalizing the Jew*. In Holland the Jews were given equal rights in 1796; in Germany Lessing had helped their case eloquently with the publication in 1779 of his play *Nathan der Weise*. And all the while in Rome the Jews continued to wear their yellow badge—with those much-rumored blue, white, and red pieces of cloth perhaps ready to be made into tricolored cockades of freedom.

They waited for five more years. During this time echoes of the new European struggle reached more and more the nightly-closed gates of their ghetto walls. Napoleon's military advances

---

*Probably meaning to be *"Evviva chi?"* but faultily written down by the Jewish chronicler.

against the Papal States in the north had obliged the Pope to make a truce in Bologna in 1796, to be followed in February of 1797 by the arrival of Pius VI's emissaries at the victorious general's tent at Tolentino to sign a peace treaty. The Pope had miscalculated his diplomatic strategy, and paid as a consequence with losses in his papal territorial domain and treasury. Yet in Rome itself, although Napoleon's armies by now were positioned only 140 miles from the city, life went on as if not a single French flag were to be seen fluttering on the horizon; the Pope continued to regard the tempestuous European political events as if they were fought by strange creatures on another planet.

Soon, however, the new European reality would be knocking on the doors of the Vatican. Towards the end of 1797, a few days after Christmas, street skirmishes broke out in Rome; one of the French unofficial envoys to the city, General Duphot, was killed not far from the Corsini palace, at that time the French embassy, where he had been at lunch with Ambassador Joseph Bonaparte. This was enough reason for the French to have their army march on the Holy City, where they arrived early the following year. They halted at Monte Mario, the hill outside Rome where centuries before the Jews used to greet the arriving Pontiffs with their Torah and their prescribed words of submission. A delegation of Romans—all Catholics this time—went to see General Berthier, commander of the French troops, and asked him to occupy the capital. The general was perfectly willing to do so; after all, that was what he had come for. Yet his political acumen told him that such military penetration into the city might bring him into direct conflict with the Pope as ruler of the Church. He therefore suggested to the Roman delegation that they themselves declare Rome independent from Vatican rule. It was an idea that was transformed into reality within twenty-four hours. On the Campo Vaccino, just outside the ghetto, three hundred Romans solemnly voted independence from Papal rule. On February 15 the French entered the city, and five days later the Pope, having refused to recognize the popular decision, was taken prisoner by the French who sent him on his way into exile.

The Jews, of course, were jubilant. The ghetto gates became porticoes of freedom; the yellow patches were replaced by gaily-colored French emblems of liberty; the days of *apartheid* seemed over, one rule was there for all. After nearly two-and-a-half centuries, the ghetto walls built by Paul IV in 1555 no longer did a prison make.

All the old papal restrictive orders were immediately declared null and void. Since "according to the principles of the Roman Republic the laws must be general and equal for all citizens," the Jews "who possess all basic conditions prescribed for Roman Citizens" would henceforth be subject to the laws of the Republic only.

Three days after the victorious French troops' entry, Antonio Pacifici, delegate of the new Roman City Council, confirmed the joyous tidings. He stood under an illuminated Liberty Tree on the Piazza delle Scuole, in front of the building that housed the five synagogues inside the ghetto, now a place of confinement no longer. Having already made a vibrant speech to all Romans on the fifteenth under a Liberty Tree on the Piazza del Campidoglio, and having repeated his liberal manifesto that very morning of the 18th of February on the Campo Marzio where he had proclaimed that "not the French destroy religion, but it has been destroyed by the priests," Pacifici's words sounded to the Jews as if they were tidings from the angel Gabriel.

"You have been oppressed, O sons of Abraham!" cried Pacifici. "Now you too are free! Long live the God of Abraham and of Jacob, whose children have been liberated by the immortal Berthier from their long slavery under yet another Pharaonic tyrant! You are our brothers, our equals—the same law will judge us both. May this slavery be your last, and only remember that like your liberator Moses, the invincible French *Duce* has united us all, and that he has returned to you the ancient Liberty and Equality!"

The acclamation was deafening, for never before had such words resounded through Rome either inside or outside the ghetto walls. This was the new spirit of 1789, the liberating movement for universal rights and equality under the law, the vaunted modern sentiment of brotherly tolerance. Perhaps the

Jews were even more enthralled than the other Romans, for while these others—no, not "others," for now they were Romans all, without any distinction of race or religion—had won new civil liberties, the Jews had gained freedom of both body and soul. This was their city, for they had been there possibly longer than anyone, unmixed with foreign invaders' blood, untainted by foreign beliefs. The Jews had been there before and after the Caesars. They had been there when the Romans had yet to discover the meaning of monotheism. They already had been there when the first Pope arrived. And now they were still there when no autocratic Pope could despotically rule their lives, free men among free men, citizens among citizens, Rome an open city, with the free air of Italy and the whole world to breathe. Jews (or certainly Marranos) had gone with Columbus to discover America, Jews had roamed the other continents, and now they too, as free Roman Jews, would go forth and proclaim their liberty across the unrestricted lands and all the ocean seas. But not yet, not so soon. Times of troubles were not yet over. Seventy-two hours later the Trasteverini plundered the ghetto.

On that day, the twenty-first of February, 1798, full of their new emancipation and participating on an equal basis with all other citizens in the Roman celebrations, the Jews had gone to the Piazza del Monte Cavallo in front of the now-empty papal summer palace of the Quirinale. On their breasts they wore the proud French tricolored cockades, the signal of victory, the proof of equality, the symbol of freedom. Was it enthusiasm or reality, could it all be rhetoric and illusion? Weren't Romans Romans and Jews still Jews? Had all tensions, distinction and hostilities been eliminated at a stroke? The Trasteverini decided to wear a little cross on their cockades to make sure every Frenchman would understand that *they* were the real Romans, the Catholic ones, and quite superior to the Jews. Not quite so, thought one of Napoleon's soldiers. He seized a cross-decorated French freedom-emblem from the blouse of a barrel-chested Trasteverino and removed the holy insignia. In France religion was dead, and it better be that way in Rome too.

The men of the new order were already falling out among themselves. The Roman from the other side of the Tiber lashed out violently at the French soldier. He, in turn, felt it his sacred duty to defend his own honour and that of France. Other Trasteverini judged the moment ripe for their own intervention, and before long such a general brawl had developed, that it made the Trasteverini wonder about the real virtues of a foreign army of occupation. And whose fault was it? The Jews', of course! So down with their crossless cockades, and on to the ghetto! In an old familiar cry, the Trasteverini started shouting, "*Evviva il Papa! Evviva Maria!*" Fired by the unforgettable slogans of yesterday, they needed only a few hours to wipe out the one-week wonder of the Jewish enthusiasm.

Soon, however, Citizen Agretto made the new government's intentions clear to the rebellious Trasteverini. "Christ and the Venerable Fathers, they too lived among the Hebrews," read his proclamation that was posted on the walls of the city. "They wore no distinctive marks but their virtue. The obligation for the Jews to be distinguished by a badge is a papal law. Return to your homes and your duties, and let them live—let them live peacefully among you, this Nation which in the past has been so dear to God."

The antagonistic feeling would come to a head again with the mustering of men for the National Guard. Inclusion of the Jews was seriously opposed; yet the French governors and the new city fathers stood fast. The issue was resolved when a Jew by the name of Isacco Baraffael took his place as major in front of the troops, proudly sitting on a horse that had been presented to him by none other than Prince Marcantonio Borghese, father of Prince Camillo, who a few years later would marry Napoleon's beautiful sister Pauline. The prince soon would find more Jews in his company when Ezehiel Morpurgo, a prominent ex-ghetto inmate, was named a member of the Roman Senate, together with the illustrious Borghese himself.

The price of Jewish liberty, though, was high in money and goods. The only consolation was that it was high for the other Romans as well. The Jews had to raise 300,000 scudi in partial defrayment of the huge French occupation costs, half in cash and half in promissory notes. Beds, shoes, linens, blankets, pots, pans, household and other goods were constantly requisitioned in notices that were sent either to the *Cittadino Mandatore del Ghetto* (the Responsible Ghetto Citizen) or directly to individual Jews. Each notice, as were all French proclamations, were headed by the words *Liberté* and *Egalité*, but the third word *Fraternité* was conspicuously absent. If the required number of requisitioned articles or gold pieces were not delivered "by noon," then the indicated person's "disobedience" would be "punished with detention at Castel Sant'-Angelo." Liberty indeed had its price, and the endless stream of French requisition papers made one Jew sigh sadly, "It was better when it was worse. . . ."

The city was organizing itself, the Church appeared to be in disarray. All kinds of religious articles were put up for sale and were handled as so many useless objects by Christian and Jew alike, with the latter (accustomed as he was to dealing in rags, Gobelins, and furniture) often serving as the logical middleman. Some of the new zealots among the Roman Christian revolutionaries went even further. They took a leaf from the book of the French *Enragés* and proposed to brand all priests on the forehead and to designate the ghetto as their compulsory living space.

At this the Jews were not amused. Just the same they would gladly have continued to enjoy their liberties, if it had not been for the Bourbons in Naples. Ferdinand IV, a monarch of Spanish descent, in coalition with the Austrians and the British, had declared war on the French, and invaded the Roman Republic. Its government fled to Perugia. In the ensuing chaos, the Trasteverini, urged on by their natural instinct, made their move towards the ghetto. Whatever happened in Rome, whether the Pope was coming or going, the Tiber was high or low, the summer dry or wet, or the women virtuous or licentious, the one sure remedy in a time of trouble always appeared to be an attack on the Jews. This time, however, the National

Guard saved the ghetto from the worst; the beating and plundering were only nominal. The lull continued till the Neapolitans entered the city proper, about ten months after the French expelled the Pope. The Jewish paradise, as some had called it, had come to an end.

The Neapolitans, of course, made things rather unpleasant for the Jews, not unexpectedly. Things were now felt to be back to normal. But hardly had the coalition-army succeeded in convincing the Romans that the Bourbons were worse than the French, and hardly had the Romans begun to wish the French back, when indeed they returned. Off, again, went the Neapolitans; the ghetto gates were opened once more and then soon shut again. In October 1799 the Neapolitans, emboldened by the French defeats in northern Italy, reappeared in force.

The Bourbon commander in Rome, Don Diego Naselli, "Prince of Aragon, Inspector General of the Sicilian Army, Major Domo of His Sicilian Majesty" (Ferdinand was not only King of Naples but also of Sicily), "Cavaliere of the Holy Order of Jerusalem, etc.," did not take long in putting the Jews back where they belonged. At the same time he tried to recapture some of the disappeared church properties, for which the Jews—obviously—were blamed and were deemed to be more guilty than all others.

On October 20 Naselli ordered the Jews "not to leave the ghetto gates without the VISIBLE BADGE which they have always worn," or they would be immediately arrested. But as a conqueror, bent on order, he also admonished the other Romans that "whoever molests or insults the Jews will be punished."

Then, on October 28, Don Diego—touching upon the second subject—told the Romans what everybody actually already knew: "You have all seen the destruction by the atheists and the spoliation of the churches." He advised "anyone holding holy objects, to return these immediately to the Signor Vice-Regente." And if anyone refused to cooperate, then "unpardonable action would be taken against the transgressors and especially AGAINST THE JEWS." The words, as had been the case with VISIBLE BADGE, are in capital letters on the wall poster*, for quite obviously the Jews, no longer endowed with civic rights, could easily be punished more than the others.

Pope Pius VI having died in France in the meantime, Pius VII was elected in Venice in 1800, and the French allowed him to return to Rome and take over the government of the city and the Papal States—or what was left of them. The Jews, who thought that hardly anything could be worse than the Neapolitans, dutifully redecorated the Arch of Titus and the road to the Colosseum as of old, then greeted the Pope with the usual gifts, and hoped for the best. The new Pius turned out to be a fair monarch, even though all Jewish church taxes, as in days of yore, were automatically re-instituted.

As long as the French were having the upper hand in Europe, the fate of the Roman Jews was bearable. Along the Tiber the ghetto continued to exist, although it was now governed with slightly more lenient rules. But Liberty never ceased to beckon from beyond the borders. Some five thousand Jews responded and emigrated to more tolerant regions, leaving only just over three thousand of them behind, among a total Roman population of about 160,000.

Bonaparte would, of course, have been less napoleonic if he could suffer anyone next to him who continued to exert sovereign powers of his own. By 1808 Emperor and Pope were definitely at odds. The French occupied Rome in February; it exacerbated the tensions and by June of the following year Pius VII was regally kidnapped and on his way to France and Fontainebleau, the second time a Head of the Catholic Church had to bend down before a French emperor.

The Jews welcomed the news. It was not that they were pro-French or pro-Napoleon; they were just partisans of their own rights and liberties. Even though the Pope reluctantly had improved their lot a trifle, every papal half-graceful gesture towards the Jews made some of the cardinals (one of them, possibly, the next Pope) feel that Christ was being crucified anew.

*In the archives of the Jewish Community in Rome.

When Rome, just prior to the Pope's departure, had been made an integral part of the French Empire, the kind of freedom which till then had been enjoyed in other Napoleon-occupied or governed countries, had once more become the freedom of the Roman Jews as well. Many of the old invidious taxes—for the neophyte and Catechumen Homes, for the carnival races and other events—were cancelled; and for the first time in two hundred and fifty years Jewish prayer books were allowed to be printed in Rome.

Napoleon went a little farther. A year or so after the unite the Jews of his multiple lands into one body, with one set of rules. An international Sanhedrin, based on the ancient Jerusalem (part religious, part lay) Tribunal, had convened with the Emperor's blessing in Paris early in 1807. A month later the delegates, including Rabbi Joshua Segre from Italy, accepted the twelve main points of the new Jewish rights and obligations, which would also be binding for the Jews of Rome. The Jews, who politically were already equal to all, had to finish officially with such left-overs of polygamy as still existed; their divorces would have to be confirmed by the civil authorities; and every Jew was obliged to consider the country of his birth or chosen residence as his fatherland, to defend when called upon. To the Roman Jews, who had only one Jewish major on horseback to look back upon, the Paris decision sounded like the beginning of a strange new martial era.

Napoleon went a little further. A year or so after the Sanhedrin wound up its affairs in Paris, every Jew in his realm who did not yet have a proper first or family name, was given three months time to find one. This law of 20 July 1808 stipulated that names of cities or from the Old Testament were "not allowed," but that "those who already have these" could keep them. Anyone who would not comply with the Emperor's wishes might as well look for living space elsewhere, according to Article Number Seven.

It made the Roman Jews scramble for suitable names. If one can judge from Jewish names which exist in Italy today, then either a great many Jews already *had* chosen the names of cities, or they hurriedly made a quick choice and prayed that it would be allowed retroactively. The names Milano, Pontecorvo, Romano, Alatri, Senigallia, Ancona, Ascoli, Volterra, Terracina and many others copied from Italian cities, abound. Many of the Jews belonging to the ancient *Cohanim* (Cohen or Coen), the aristocratic priestly family, took the name of Sacerdoti—priest.* The name Bondi comes from the Hebrew *Yom Touv* and its Italian equivalent *Bon di*, still generally used as a greeting all over the country. Pincherle is derived from a colloquial Austrian word that indicates someone who travels with a bag of merchandise on his shoulder.

With their names securely coupled to their free and legal existence, the future of the Jews in Rome seemed to rest securely on the grand victories of a vast military campaign. In 1810, excommunicated and divorced, Napoleon married his second wife, Princess Marie Louise of Austria. The future seemed even more secure when the offspring of this union came into the world in 1811, destined by his erstwhile childless and now overjoyed father to be the King of Rome. But then the Emperor made his fateful move to the east, towards Russia, to return ignominiously from Moscow to Paris towards the end of 1812.

The Roman Jews could well wonder whether their future had already become their past. Their fellow citizen Abraham Vita Modigliani had made a forward-looking speech only a year-and-a-half earlier, when he had acclaimed the Emperor's proclamation which instituted a Jewish Consistory in Rome. On that occasion Modigliani had called Napoleon "a wise representative whom God had called to govern over all people," stating moreover that he and his co-members of the consistory accepted their duty "with gratitude." Now it began to look at if the gratitude might fall upon an empty throne. Napoleon was

*After 1870, Senator Alberto Treves de Bonfili (*Treves:* Italian for the German city of Trier, a former capital city of the Roman Empire and the birthplace of Karl Marx) once met a Polish Jew on a train who asked him how a Jew could get such an aristocratic name. "That's nothing," said the senator whose title of Baron had been bestowed upon his Venetian family by Napoleon in 1812. He pointed to his friend and co-Senator Israele Coen from Verona, who was sitting next to him, and remarked: "Look at *him*—he has been an aristocrat for over four thousand years already. . . ."

defeated at Leipzig, Paris capitulated before the coalition armies of half of Europe. By then French general Count Sextius Alexandre Miollis, Governor of Rome since 1808, already had handed over his last Roman fortress, Castel Sant'Angelo, to the Emperor's enemies. Nine days later, on January 23 1814, the Pope left his forced residence at Fontainebleau to set off for Rome. When the news of his imminent return reached the city, the Jews must have looked at the empty hinges of their doorless ghetto gates—with a shudder.

Chapter 26
Il Risorgimento

Before long Napoleon was out, the Pope was in, the ghetto doors were up, and the Jews were down. Indeed, even their worst fears turned out to have been too optimistic. The blow had fallen well before Pope Pius arrived back in Rome. He re-entered the capital on the 25th of April, nine days before Napoleon, his one-time captor, would reach his own destination—Elba. But already on the twelfth of that month the Curia, to whom "modernism" was worse than Protestantism, had taken care of the Jews in the only way the Vatican knew. To the cardinals Napoleon had never been, nothing of lasting importance had happened. They piously erased the twenty years of shattering revolutionary change from their minds, closed their eyes to the immediate past, and continued where they had left off.

Back into the ghetto the Jews went, its gates supervised as closely as before. Jewish students were evicted from the university, the ignominous excises were renewed, and seven years' back-taxes had to be paid up for the catechumen and neophyte institutions. Shops outside the ghetto had to be closed. Compulsory sermons became once more common practice. Within months the Inquisition and the newly-recognized Jesuits were back in full power. Soon afterwards it was decreed that all real estate acquired during the Pope's absence had to be disposed of within five years. The Pope's action was all the more surprising because in a number of other decisions he showed a certain measure of clemency and understanding. The making of his tomb in Saint Peter's was entrusted to Danish Protestant sculptor Thorwaldson, a unique event. There was a concern for a possibly more flexible interpretation of the Church's teachings, but the Jews had remained a very special case, and for them there was no straining the quality of mercy.

Napoleon's return from Elba in March 1815 electrified the Roman Jews for the next hundred days or so. The Pope might soon be back on the road to Fontainebleau. But Napoleon was on the road to Waterloo, and it was to be the definite extinction of flame of Roman-Jewish hope for the renewal of Liberty and Equality (even without the never-bestowed Fraternity).

By November the Pope seemed to be making a hopeful offer. Several papal cities were requested to address a miraculous petition to the Vatican for an improvement in their status. When the Jews read the fine print, they concluded that the effort would not be quite worth the ink. It was so familiar, so painfully boring, so dispiriting. Article Seven of the Vatican offer of improved rules stipulated that "the Jews may have their laundry done by a Christian woman, but if she is married, then the husband must be present when the washing is handed to her; if she is a maiden or widow, then the laundry must be given to her at the foot of the stairs. . . ." Under the circumstances it is understandable that the Jews decided to do their own laundry.

The happiest Jewish note struck during these years was of such pure musical quality that it would linger around the globe for the next century and once in a while its echo even continues to enchant listeners of our own generation. The Roman Jews were allowed to stare at a wall, but the Jews in France had gained notable personal rights and cultural opportunities. In 1819 the Prix de Rome for music was won by Jacques Halévy, whose real name was plain Levy—a Jew and a brilliant musician. Aged twenty at the time, he remained for three years at Rome's *Acadèmie de France.*

Halévy's interest in his religious brothers, still dumb-struck by the regressive obstacle race run by the Vatican was such, that several years after his return to France, in 1835, the Paris Opera brought his *La Juive* to the stage, a story (full of cardinals and conversions and anti-Semitism) that clearly was inspired by the plight of the Jews of Rome.

By the time *La Juive* was sung in Paris by Mademoiselle Falcon to the enthusiastic applause of the French opera-lovers, Pope Leo XII had come and gone. With him, at his death in 1829, had gone the doors of the ghetto, which the embittered Romans broke down to help liberate the Jews, an act in which the Jews themselves had taken the initiative. Leo had not exactly won the devoted love of his subjects, either Christian or Jew. The Pope's policy had in effect obliged the inhabitants of the ghetto to go back to their lives as ragpickers, with the result that ever more Jews left the Papal States. Their permission to leave was also worth money—it had to be bought with a fee for a form of exit visa. The Pope also added, as emigration continued, an advance payment of a capital tax for the full period of the following ten years, which in accumulated interest represented confiscation of well over half the amount of money to be taken along.

If the Jews had been bold and angry enough to haul down the ghetto doors, and if the Romans were sufficiently outraged to help them do so, the Christian anger directed at the late Pope quite soon went through that mysterious chemical-political sublimation process which separates one anger from another, turns one resentment into forms of traditional hostility. We have to record yet another case of a customary ghetto incursion. After all, why not? If the Jews were giddy enough to open the doors wide, then why should not Romans walk through them and do a free-booting bit of exploration?

For a chronicler, by now the much-used (and even more frequently mis-used) ghetto doors began to look like swinging
gates. Forced open in 1829, they were hurriedly closed by the
papal supervisors. But hardly were they shut again, and new
Pope Pius VIII had occupied the empty throne, when this rather
kind Pontiff—who was quite unable to stand up against his
bitterly reactionary Secretary of State Albani and the
Curia—died after hardly a year of fairly inefficient government.
Now the "first miracle" of the nineteenth century occurred. We
know that the Jews had broken down the doors by force; we
know too that on occasion the Trasteverini tried to burn them
down, sometimes in solidarity, sometimes in sadism. This time
the Vatican would make a move for a change, perhaps show a
willingness to make amends. Gregory XVI had been crowned in
1831 and could confirm that the doors should remain where
they were—off their hinges. The grand gesture was really not as
grand as it looked, for the actual second removal had already
taken place during the revolutionary upheaval that set Rome
boiling in 1830 after the death of Pius VIII. Yet for the first time
the Pope did not rush in to put the doors back in place, and that
in itself was quite a papal achievement, in hesitant goodwill.

But perhaps the Pope could hardly have acted differently.
What had set Rome boiling was not a local movement of in-
surrection, but was the result of the revolutionary high tide that
rolled across all Europe, a tide which the Pope obstinately and
quite unsuccessfully tried to stop. The French spirit of 1789,
first heightened and then dampened by the downfall of
Napoleonic grandeur, and further weakened, but on the surface
only, by the reactionary government of Charles X, had continued to ferment. The revolution of 1830 brought the "citizen
king" Louis Philippe to the throne, not entirely the choice of
French liberals and republicans. Yet if a king there had to be,
then even they preferred Louis Philippe to Charles.

In England the Whigs finally had overcome the Tory
resistance to democratic change, and had made it known that
the old autocratic way of governing was a thing of the past.
Elsewhere in Europe this modern liberalism, often mixed with
republicanism, was being stimulated by the eloquence and per-

sonal influence of Giuseppe Mazzini in France and Switzerland, where the young, radical anti-royalist Italian had fled after having spent some time in one of his country's prisons in 1831. In Marseille, in close collaboration with Angelo Usiglio, a Jew, Mazzini (then 25) had started the "Young Italy" movement, preaching intellectual, political, and social upheaval in the interest of the liberation of the masses, who were to be governed in a united Pope-less republican Italy with Rome as its capital. His ideas and sentiments were widespread and widely-shared; and among the Italians who became his ardent followers were obviously the Jews, who were trying to throw off their role as the eternal scapegoat of the world—and, in particular, the Roman Jews, for centuries the permanent underdog of the Vatican.

Mazzini was far from alone in his struggle for the liberation, democratization and unification of Italy. Political firebrand and agitator par excellence of the proliferating movement, often intolerant and uncompromising, he was seconded by another famous Giuseppe, the most flamboyant revolutionary of them all—Garibaldi, who for the greater part of his life would distrust and oppose Mazzini as a dreamer and schemer.

The third and least powerful figure in the new movement was Vincenzo Gioberti, a young priest who till 1833 had been court chaplain of Charles Albert of the House of Savoy, King of Sardinia. He was exiled after having been arrested for his advanced ideas which pleaded for a united Italy under a liberal Papacy, a plan which far from pleased the hold-on-to-the-past clerical authorities. He would for years be the pro-Vatican and anti-"Young Italy" theoretician and chair-born advocate of change; finally, with age and some experience of practical politics, he would totally lose his trust in papal temporal leadership.

The fourth participant on the changing Italian scene was Cavour, the suave and brilliant aristocrat and manipulator of men, a political architect who was prepared to construct his country's unity by the use of any means at his disposal.

And then, from 1849 on, there was of course King Victor Emmanuel II. He, too, was part of the national team, yet standing high above them all as the "central beacon," the rallying

point, the "homecoming," and "the harbor." Opposed by Mazzini, partly opposed by Garibaldi, and for reasons of unity
always inalterably supported by Cavour, Victor Emmanuel was
(as described by British historian Bolton-King) "a tough, un-
abashed licentious, good-natured, bad-tempered man of
phenomenal ugliness, absolutely fearless, plain, almost boorish
in his tastes, without a trace of genius, as excellent a cavalry officer as he was a bad general. . . ." Yet the king personified to
the masses the only honest man among the Italian princely
leaders. The Jews, rallying to the call for freedom, did not lag
behind in their acclaim.

The Jews' affinity for Mazzini was as close as Mazzini's affinity for the Jews. Moving to London in 1837, he found a
haven with the Italian Jewish family of the Nathans (the
feminine half, Sarina, was born a Rosselli). Both Nathan and
Rosselli were to become historic names in Italy. Sarina's son
Ernesto Nathan, born in London, would be the first and highly
acclaimed Jewish mayor of Rome (from 1907 till 1913); and the
two expatriate brothers Carlo and Nello Rosselli, militantly intellectual antifascists, in 1937 would be murdered in Bagnoles-
de-l'Orne by the French Cagoulards, Mussolini's henchmen.

The Italian Jews living outside the Papal States had joined the
freedom movement early on. To the Jews of Rome, however, it
was not the physical struggle that affected them—except, of
course, emotionally. In their open-door prison they were unable
to fight, and could only watch over political conflict from afar,
their anxiety increased by the waiting.

The purely orthodox Jews of the Roman ghetto, not capable
of or desirous of handling sabers and guns—thought that they
were also serving by sharpening their pens and their tongues instead. While other Italians, including the Jews, fought for
national freedom, some of the Jews of Rome, in the years
between 1826 and 1845, fought about vowels, two of
which—the Hebrew equivalent of the letters *a* and *e*—could find
no peace among the thousands of yellowing parchment pages
inside the five closely-joined synagogues. As if nothing more

important existed in their lives, these learned men could come near to blows on account of *patah* and *shewa;* in fact, on one occasion, the Pope had to send in his *sbirri* to re-establish order. It would seem that some of the Elders of the ghetto were as oblivious to reality as were the Elders of the Curia.

In 1846 the reactionary Gregory XVI expired, his slightly pro-Jewish attitude—which might better be qualified as not entirely *anti*-Jewish—to a considerable extent mollified by the not inconsequential influence of the Rothschilds. Prodded by Louis Philippe, the Rothschilds—as they had done ten years previously—visited Rome on several occasions, each time consenting to make a loan to the Vatican. During one of these visits the Pope actually agreed to set up a trade school for Jewish boys, where they would be taught by Christian artisans—perhaps, once again, a victory of funds over fanaticism.

The new Pope, Pius IX, started his reign under a scintillating star. A ghetto delegation, received shortly after he was crowned, was assured that all would be well. If Jews would like to live outside the ghetto, that would be fine—provided they did not move too far away. Forced sermons were annoying? They would be discontinued. The poor? They would be provided for in the same way as the Christians. The carnival ceremony at the Campidoglio? Nothing would be more simple than to order an end to it, so the rabbi would no longer be humiliated. On one condition, though—that the Jews would continue to pay pecuniary homage to the city. All this was wondrous change, the Jews thought. In his enthusiasm, Dr. Mosé Finzi composed a poem in the Pope's honor, *"Soft in punishment,/His pardon kind,/So strikes me Pius/In my mind."* And a richly illustrated album which the Jews offered him as a present, contained among others Psalm 72 (for Solomon), *"He shall judge thy people with righteousness, and the poor with judgment. The mountains shall bring peace to the people, and the little hills, by righteousness. . . . "*

A welcome new tone: could it last? The very year of the Pope's crowning, the Vatican Secretary of State prohibited an

Italian Jewish magazine published in Parma to be imported into the papal territory. Jewish "morals, religion, literature and variegated subjects" were not to disaffect the Jews of Rome.

In the meantime, however, Italian liberal and nationalist propaganda continued to flow freely across the papal borders, disaffecting Christian and Jew alike, with or without papal blessing. From Brussels, where he was now residing, Gioberti continued his quiet, theoretical but highly important writings on what should be done with Italy. Mazzini's inflammatory pamphlets put fire to young souls. That perfect gentleman but not always very astute politician, the Marquess Massimo d'Azeglio, with the promised backing of King Charles Albert, published a violent critique of papal government. He followed it up with a specific study of the Jews—partly copied from *The Christian Doctrine* as used by the Diocese of Turin—which must not have endeared him to the Vatican. In it he asked "why must we love all men in the world, whether Turks, Jews or others?" and gave the answer immediately himself: "Because God orders it so, because they are all creatures made in the image of God." And he added that "the only explanation" for the traditional accusations against the Jews was that "the oppression to which they are subjected" had been created "so as to try and make them accept the faith of Christ."

Cavour, in that same year of 1847, in order to have a voice in the unification of all Italy behind the House of Savoy, started his newspaper *Il Risorgimento;* henceforth the name of the publication would be written with fiery letters in the Italian sky, forever signifying the whole Italian freedom movement.

The broader Roman masses could all be enlisted in the cause of freedom, but we can rightly suspect with this proviso: if only the Jews did not have too much a part in it. The rumor that the Pope would let all Jews out of the ghetto created adverse sentiments among the populace, still not entirely prepared to accept the reality of *égalité.* Who could know what the Vatican actually was planning? Certainly not the Jews. Roman atmosphere became so tense that the Jews felt themselves obliged—out of self-protection—to beg the Vatican, whatever its intentions, to let them stay where they were for a while longer. Soon, however, the Trasteverini (and others) would switch their feelings in one of those spectacular popular swings of love or hate that can be created at the drop of a word by any forceful speaker who knows how to handle crowd psychology.

A fifty-year-old Roman by the name of Angelo Brunetti (whose profession variously is given as blacksmith, café-owner, and transporter of wood) was popularly known as *Ciceruacchio*, a word that in Roman dialect flatteringly-ironically means "Big ugly Cicero." He was a strong supporter of Mazzini, had a stentorian voice, was the undisputed master of the multitude, the organizer of and chief orator at every street demonstration. Living halfway between the Piazza del Popolo and the Tiber, *Ciceruacchio* during the afternoon of July 15 mercilessly harangued a crowd of over two thousand of his republican and anti-papist followers at Tor di Quinto, just outside Rome as it was then, across the Tiber from today's Olympic Village and the Flaminia Bridge. The way-out-of-center meeting place was most likely chosen so as not to be disturbed by the papal police.

Ciceruacchio alternately cajoled and thundered with admonitions and words of conciliation. He called for unity, for understanding, for help and support, and he specifically asked to unite with the downtrodden Jews, victims of the papacy. The phrases were shot at the crowd like winged words of Mazzini, and the words hit home. Enthused by the self-appointed tribune's peroration, the meeting broke up amidst shouts of brotherhood; and the thundering *Evviva's* for once were certainly not intended for the Pope. All men were brothers, friends, and children of the same fatherland!

That evening the Jews got the fright of their lives. A seething mass of six thousand Romans, all honest sons of the lower and middle strata of the population, took the ghetto by storm. Not to plunder this time, miracle of miracles, but to kiss their Jewish brothers on both cheeks and shake hands with their women (in some cases it was the other way around). The enthusiasm and goodwill were unmistakable. Under the influence of Mazzini ideals and the eloquence of *Ciceruacchio*, the impossible had been achieved. *De jure* there were still Jewish Romans and Catholic Romans, but *de facto* they now were all one.

Chapter 27
The First Liberation

The Jews had crossed a new frontier of freedom. All that winter of 1847/1848 their ghetto gates were non-existent, and to all intents and purposes they were able to do as they pleased, with the Pope looking on if this were a situation he had been expecting for long, and had been accustomed to indeed.

In the Church of Santa Maria in Trastevere a priest by the name of Ambrosoli preached with such conviction and vehemence about tolerance and brotherly love that some of his listeners were evidently ready to cross the Bridge With The Four Heads that very evening and tear down the walls of the ghetto. Massimo d'Azeglio's words were ringing in everybody's ears. "Let each of us therefore extend our hands to our Jewish brothers," he had written. "Alleviate their pains, and repair the damage caused by the outrageous insults they had to endure from—I would not say Christians, because such a name is unworthy of those who betray or falsify the highest precept of

Christ, which is Charity—but from those who on account of their persecutions do not merit the name of Christians . . ."

It was one of the harshest public condemnations of the Vatican's past anti-Semitism, and each of Massimo d'Azeglio's phrases rang in the ears of the Trasteverini. The Jews, too, heard the message, especially heart-warming one evening of April 1848, when they were all sitting home around the festively-laid and candle-lighted tables to celebrate the beginning of the Passover, commemorating in this one ceremony the delivery from Egyptian slavery and the Easter meal in Jerusalem before the city was destroyed by Titus' army. The prescribed prayer of hope was, as always, "*This year here, next year in Jerusalem,*" and "*This year slaves, next year free men.*" But they had already been rejoicing, because in this year of 1848 they were free men in a free Rome, and the gates in their ghetto wall were now permanently open.

Could one discern darker forces on the scene? No one, as yet, paid any attention to them. Thoughts were of the remains of the Temple wall in Jerusalem, and on this festive evening they tried hard to keep their spirits free from the depredations of the Roman past. The ceremony went on, and they came to the passage in the *Haggadah*, the ceremonial book, where it is said that "not one man alone rose up against us to destroy us, but in every generation do men rise up against us to destroy us. . . ." Could a slight tremor be detected in the voices of all the fathers in the ghetto who were reading to their children and family, and being reminded of the attacks on Jewish communities through the ages especially around Easter when horror tales of ritual murder sometimes resulted in the massacre of whole communities? But this was 1848, and it could no longer be. The Pope himself had given the Jews of Rome their freedom, and the Catholic Romans had celebrated their delivery from the ghetto with shared laughter and enthusiasm. And so they read on, the fathers, putting their faith in the Lord; and they read that "the Holy One, blessed be He, deliver us from their hands. . . ."

At that moment, ten o'clock, the blow fell. Like an explosion a huge chunk of the wall came down, and fear gripped the heart and soul of every Jew in Rome. They rushed out of their houses in panic, to flee or to defend themselves, imploring God to have mercy on them on this Night of Delivery, and not to let it turn into a night of destruction. But a night of destruction it was—but also a night of joy, of joy so great that the words of the *Haggadah* might well be changed from "deliver us from their hands" to "deliver us *into* their hands." For the hammer-blows were only too true, but they were blows of deliverance, of total deliverance from the walls of the ghetto, which came down under the picks and hammers of the people of Rome, led by *Ciceruacchio* and his men.

Unknown to the Jews, Pius IX had ordered the destruction of the wall. By sheer accident one of *Ciceruacchio's* friends had heard the news from one of the cardinals, and in their enthusiasm the Trasteverini had thought they might as well start sooner than later. It turned out to be one one of the greatest Passover celebrations ever; and working in shifts, the benefactors of the Jews two days later had leveled the greater part of the centuries-old enclosure. The last vestiges of separation between Jew and Christian had disappeared, and the Jew could freely walk into town, without even having to go through the doorless gate.

They could and they did—till a few evenings later a Jew was found wandering quite a distance away from the ghetto. It was a strange sight. For innumerable generations Jews had not been allowed in town after nightfall. Had the change come too quickly? The poor man was harassed at first, then pushed, then beaten, then killed. The wreckers came back to the ghetto to finish their work. But instead of continuing on the wall, they wrecked some of the homes of the Jews. Deliverance was only a few nights old, and already large detachments of police were needed to protect the Jews. A nostalgia grew for their comparative safety behind high walls and closed gates.

But this too passed, for the international situation began to involve Rome in far more serious problems than quibbling about the rights of a few local Jews. The Austrians, under Metternich, threatened to invade the Papal States, and in

August they occupied the city of Ferrara. Indignation ran high in Rome and elsewhere, and for once all the sympathy was with the Pope, because—even in a divided Italy—this was a foreign threat to Italian territorial integrity. From faraway Buenos Aires, Garibaldi offered his services to the Pontiff whose political influence he detested.

Italy was in turmoil. In the north Charles Albert called upon Gioberti to head the new government of his kingdom, which now comprised Sardinia, Savoy, Piedmont and Genova. In Rome the Pope had to accept the social reformer Mamiani as Minister of the Interior, who was determined to try and give the Papal States, where the Church ever since its inception had governed the people, a government in which the people would govern the Church.

It just could not be done that quickly. Mamiani wanted to fight the Austrians; the Pope became desperate under the threats of both moderates and liberals; and another Premier was named. Six weeks later he too had to make way, to be replaced by the decidedly liberal ex-French ambassador—since 1845—to the Vatican Pellegrino Rossi (he was Italian-born and had become a naturalized French citizen). The Pope was looking for a way to save his temporal power, but discovered that time was running out even faster than the hands on the clock of Saint Peter's counted the hours.

Rossi tried to subdue the crowds by a show of power, but the troops he brought into Rome infuriated the people instead. On November 15, on entering the Rome parliament building, Rossi was murdered. The next day a violent demonstration took place in front of the Quirinale Palace, and again nine days later, on November 24, the Pope hurriedly fled from Rome to the safety of the city of Gaeta, on the border of the Papal States and the kingdom of Naples.

The public demonstrations in Rome had not only been directed against the Pope. As usually happened when the Romans were populistically inflamed, the political sparks flew wildly. It almost seemed to be a law of political physics. Whenever the tension mounted in one direction, it would equal-

Scenes depicting various stages of the Seder ceremony.

(Courtesy Rosenthaliana Library, Amsterdam)

 עטרת צבי

כי־טים ההטוכעתהחיא
אצמיח לריר צמחצדיקה
ועשהמשפטוצדקה בארץ

Sabatai Zwi in his days of glory, sitting on King Solomon's throne.

The text reads, from top to bottom:

Zwi the King (or: The Crown Zwi)

On this day and in this hour

I shall plant in David the seed of goodness

And there will be order and charity on earth.

THE RULE:

One must read the Torah night and day.

(Courtesy Rosenthaliana Library, Amsterdam)

MONARCHI
NOVA

Another etching of Sabatai Zwi, made in 1666. The upper right corner shows him in jail, upper left is his ship with an Israeli-inscribed flag.

(Courtesy Rosenthaliana Library, Amsterdam)

The Jews of Rome offer the Pope a Scroll of the Law at the Colosseum.

*Roman Jews during a compulsory sermon in the Church of Sant'
Angelo in Pescheria, after a painting by Hieronymus Hess (1799-1850).*
(Above and facing photos courtesy Thourwaldsens Museum, Copenhagen)

בְּנֵי יְהֹוָה Υἱοί τοῦ Ἰσραήλ

Two Roman Jewish paintings by
Hieronymus Hess. Top "Dressed for the
Sabbath" Bottom "The Children of Israel."

יוֹם הַקֹּדֶשׁ

Three drawings by Bartolomeo Pinelli Romano, done in 1823 as illustrations for a book of poetry written in 1695 by Giuseppe Berneri, entitled "Il Meo Patacca." In it, Berneri described this popular Roman figure's feats and deeds in collecting funds to help fight Vienna against the Turks—money Meo Patacca subsequently spent on Roman festivities when he heard that the Turks already had been defeated. In the Twelfth poem Berneri described a fire that threatened the ghetto. Top A Jew is rolled down the street by the Roman riff-raff. Center Meo Patacca quiets a mob that wanted to put fire to the ghetto. Bottom The Roman Jews offer Meo Patacca a gift for having saved the ghetto.

(Sam Waagenaar)

Early photograph of the Ghetto. (Courtesy Musei Comunali, Rome)
The Piazza delle Scuole with the five synagogues under one roof.

A contemporary drawing of the Mortara case in Bologna.
In the center stands little Edgardo Mortara,
firmly held by a priest. Edgardo's father is holding
out pleading hands, asking for the
return of the kidnapped boy, while his
mother (right foreground) faints.

The Piazetta Rua (Courtesy Musei Comunali, Rome)
The Via Rua, looking in the direction of the Gate of Octavia
(Courtesy Musei Comunali, Rom'

Interior of the Gate of Octavia. (Courtesy Musei Comunali, Rome)
The fish market under the Gate of Octavia. (Courtesy Musei Comunali, Rome)

The Piazza delle Azimelle (Square of the Matzoth Bakers).

(Courtesy Musei Comunali, Rome)

The Via Capocciuto. (Courtesy Musei Comunali, Rome)

The international Jewish crew of the Sailors School at
Civitavecchia, organized in 1935 by Mussolini.

Rome publisher Angelo Fortunato Formiggini (in
background) guiding Mussolini around the bookfair in the
capital. After publication of the Italian Racial Laws in 1938,
Formiggini committed suicide.

Inscription in Hebrew and Latin (Isaiah 65/2) above the door of the church of the Congregation of the Madonna of Divine Mercy opposite the former ghetto: "I have spread out my hands all day to a rebellious people, which walketh in the way that was not good, after their own thoughts." The text, still there today, served as an admonition to the Jews to convert. *(Sam Waagenaar)*

שָׁלוֹם עַל־יִשְׂרָאֵל :

(cum approb. eccl.ca)

SUB PROTECTIONE

A card distributed by the Catholic "Friends of Israel" association, which aim it was to convert the Jews. Pope Pius XI stopped the organization's activities. *(Sam Waagenaar)*

A blank false identity card and a completed one, product of the cooperation between Stefan Schwamm and Father Maria Benedetto. No "official" French fiscal stamps being available, obliterated French postage stamps were used instead— visible under the photograph.

(Sam Waagenaar)

Sample of the first false identification card made in Rome by Stefan Schwamm during the German occupation of the city in 1943.

(Sam Waagenaar)

שמעו נא כל העמים וראו מכאבי
בתולתי ובחורי הלכו בשבי
(THRE:IH)

DEL POPOLO D'ISRAELE
SEI MILIONI
LE INNOCENTI VITTIME IN EVROPA
DEL BIECO ODIO RAZZIALE

IN TVTTA ITALIA
DAL FATALE 16 OTTOBRE 1943
OLTRE OTTOMILA
I DEPORTATI I MARTORIATI I TRVCIDATI

DA ROMA

DVEMILANOVANTVNO

I DEPORTATI

NON ARIDE CIFRE SON QVESTE
MA NELLA CIVILTÀ OFFESA
NELLA OFFESA ALLA SANTA LEGGE DI DIO
È QVESTO VN TRIBVTO DI LACRIME DI SANGVE

A commemorative stone slab on the outer wall of the Rome synagogue for the Jews deported from Europe, Italy, and Rome.   (Sam Waagenaar)

The author acknowledges photos and documents from the following institutions:
Musei Comunali, Rome;
Rosenthaliana Library, Amsterdam;
Thorwaldsens Museum, Copenhagen;
British Museum;
Museum of Fine Arts, Boston.

ly mount, as if contained in communicating vessels, against the Jews. The wall-less ghetto made the invasions easier. After a butcher shop had been plundered, a two-day battle raged through the narrow alleyways of the ghetto, till papal troops restored order. Two civil guards had been seriously wounded by desperately combative Jews, and before long a new attack took place. It started curiously. Scissor-armed barbers accompanied the insurrectionists to test their skill in cutting Jewish beards down to Roman proportions. More heads were cracked, but this time the Jews were better prepared, and the wounded were predominantly on the attackers' side. It soon became clear that *Ciceruacchio* and his men had had nothing to do with this demonstration, but that a few anti-Semitic priests who refused to condone the Pope's treatment of the Jews were—as so often had been the case—the instigators.

On 9 February 1849, the Roman Republic was proclaimed, comprising all territories still left to the Pontifical States, at which the eager Austrians had been nibbling constantly. The Pope, hanging on to his ecclesiastical powers while losing the temporal ones, promptly excommunicated all members of the newly-formed Roman Constituent Assembly. While hardly any of the elected representatives were unduly disturbed by this papal action, the only ones who were not affected by it at all were its three Jewish members. Other Jews were elected to the municipal council; and various community services included, for the first time ever, Jewish employees on their staffs.

The Pope, now on the side of the Austrians (Prince Metternich had promised Pius IX to restore his states to him) was waiting for these allies to defeat King Charles Albert in the north, so they could then move down on Rome. In the capital Mazzini and his men soon realized that the Austrians constituted the greatest danger, and plans were made to send troops to fight with Charles Albert's forces against their common Austrian enemy. When the soldiers were ready to leave, news arrived of the disastrous defeat the Austrians had meted out to Charles Albert at Novara, resulting in the King's abdication in favor of his son Victor Emmanuel. Suddenly Rome found itself adrift; and to save the situation a triumvirate was formed to govern the territory, with Mazzini as its leader.

There was still time left to re-organize. The Austrians were far away, the other pro-papal monarchies as yet undecided. In France, Louis Napoleon was wavering; not for long, though. On the 24th of April a French expeditionary force under Oudinot landed at Civitavecchia, the port which is only forty-five miles from Rome; and six days later his troops stood before the city.

Garibaldi and his legion rushed to the rescue, and there were Jews in the ranks. In the first encounter Oudinot lost a thousand men and retreated to the safety of Civitavecchia, where during the following month he waited for reinforcements. Early in June he re-attacked, this time with more success. In a furious onslaught the French were able to push the Romans back behind the city walls, only holding on to a farm called the Vascello. Here one of Garibaldi's bravest Jewish soldiers, Enrico Guastalla*, distinguished himself to such an extent that when a few days later he recaptured a Roman flag at the Villa Corsini below the Gianicolo Hill, Garibaldi acclaimed him as the "hero of Vascello." Other Jews fought as bravely, including Enrico's brother Cesare and corporals Isacco and Israele Levi. Three Jews were killed—sixteen-year-old Ciro Finzi, who lost his life on June 16 after five days of heroic fighting, and Dr. Giacomo Venezian, who together with Israele Levi fell while trying to hold the Villa Barberini.

In Rome itself other Jews fought in desperation for the preservation of the city and their freedom, well aware that a return of the Pope might mean a return of the old ghetto. Although totally unaccustomed to bearing arms, 350 Jews served among the three thousand Roman volunteers—an extraordinary high percentage (twelve per cent) considering that the less than four thousand Jews of Rome constituted only just over two percent of the city's total population, then around 170,000.

---

*Enrico Guastalla later on took part in the Garibaldi battles of Aspramonte and Mentana. He concluded his military career in 1867 as temporary Chief of Staff.

On the second of July, after nearly a month of fighting, it was all over. Oudinot and his soldiers entered Rome, and while Mazzini, indifferent to danger, roamed the streets and was scarcely in a position to escape the oncoming enemy, Garibaldi and his men—including *Ciceruacchio* and his young son—struggled their way out of town, to continue, always fighting, to the north*. One day before they fled, in a city practically overrun by the invaders, the members of the Constituent Assembly had finished their work. From the top of Capitol Hill a constitution had been promulgated which guaranteed the rule of law and complete freedom of religion. It would be of little use. A dream had come to an end, and there were dreamers who felt a bit nauseated at the brutal awakening.

Four months later, with the Pope himself still away from the Vatican, it was made clear to the Jews that a change had taken place in the heart and mind of Pius IX, who had started out so eminently as an understanding liberalizing Pontiff and who, without the revolution of 1848, might have gone down in history as one of the greatest Popes of the century. Kindly treatment of his Jewish subjects now was only a thing of the past. On the morning of October 25 an iron military ring was thrown around the wall-less ghetto, with three boats patroling the Tiber, so as to make escape impossible. All Jewish homes were carefully searched from attic to cellar by French troops assisted by papal police, looking for what were supposed to be "stolen religious articles." The search was thorough, but the results rather meagre, even though the raid continued for two days. Two worthless pushcarts which had belonged to the Vatican were found, plus some pieces of ancient handwoven cloth and a few small silver objects that apparently had belonged to priests, and which most likely had been sold in 1848. The "papal treasures" and the massive mountain of jewels for which the action was said to have been undertaken never materialized. It was

---

*On reaching Venice, father and son Brunetti-*Ciceruacchio* were summarily shot by the Austrians, then still masters of the city. In 1907, at the occasion of the 100th anniversary of Garibaldi's birth, a bronze statue of the two victims was unveiled in Rome. It still stands between the Passeggiata di Ripetta and the Tiber, near the Ponte Marguerita, with a simple inscription: "*CICERUACCHIO—The people*."

clear that the real purpose of the search, four months after the Republic had so tragically ended, had been an attempt by the Church to intimidate the Jews. When complaints were made to the French, they feigned innocence; and, throwing all guilt on the papal police, they advised the community's delegates to address themselves to the Vatican authorities. Cardinal Savelli did not even want to discuss the grievances but simply stated that it had been the fault of the Jews that the Republic had been established. Moreover, they had been instrumental in prolonging the siege of the city. In other words, without the Jews it all would never have happened. It was obvious from these rationalizations that the Vatican was out to take revenge; and since it was difficult to turn against *all* the citizens of Rome, the Church had fallen back on the age-old expedient. It had worked before, and it was sure to work again. If no one could be found to be pronounced guilty, then as a last resort there were always the conveniently guilt-ridden Jews. They had been kicked around for so long by the Vatican that to many of the cardinals the kicking had become second nature; and if the Jews did not exist, how could things go on without inventing them?

And now, of course, they had to be punished—which was easy. As usual, the Vatican rulers picked up the first edict against the Jews they could find and vigorously applied its rules. Very little had to be changed or added. There were so many of them lying around since 1555 that whichever one they dusted off would serve the purpose. The ghetto-rules were re-applied, and whoever lived outside the area of its former walls was compelled to return within the demarcated confinement. The university exclusions were made stringent once more, with the exception that Jews were allowed to continue their study of medicine, on condition that they would practice among Jews only. The servant problem became an issue; once again Christian help was not allowed. And so on down the line through the centuries of repression and pettifogging. The sojourn in Gaeta clearly had not exactly expanded the Pope's range of humanitarian feeling.

The Jews really hardly needed these added rules of deprivation for their misery. Their ghetto was a doorless dilapidated prison. Gregorovius, who was then visiting the ghetto for the first time, found it a charmless place. "The Tiber had just broken its banks," he wrote, "and its yellow flood gushed through the lowest ghetto streets, where the water entered the homes through the gaping cellars. What a melancholy picture to see the miserable Jewish area sunk below the sad waters of the Tiber. In Rome Israel is reliving year after year the biblical déluge, with the ghetto floating on the waters like Noah's ark. . . ."

In April 1850 the Pontiff returned to Rome: there was no Jewish rejoicing as had been the case on his first arrival in 1846. Two years later, in the northern kingdom, Cavour became Premier. Ably assisted by Isacco Artom, his thirty-year-old Jewish secretary and close collaborator, political pressure on Rome mounted. In 1854, perhaps to regain theologically where he was losing temporally, the Pope confirmed the dogma of the Immaculate Conception. Again, four years later, little Edgardo Mortara was kidnapped in Bologna, and the world made its agonized response. The Pope remained unmoved, for in its treatment of the Jews the Vatican would not relent.

In 1860 the northern part of the Papal States, including the Romagna, Umbria, and the Marche provinces, were incorporated into the Kingdom of Sardinia. When discussions with King Victor Emmanuel's government were proposed, Pius IX, his territory constantly dwindling, angrily reacted with the words, "We cannot talk." The Pope's inaction caused Garibaldi's action. He departed for Sicily with his *Mille* to invade the island—still part of the Kingdom of Naples—and to annex it in the name of King Victor Emmanuel. Included in Garibaldi's one thousand volunteers from all over Italy were eleven Jews (representing one percent of the invasion forces). The number of Jews in the whole country, including Rome, being just over 30,000 (or only one-eighth of one percent of the total population) the Jewish soldiers among the *Mille* were eight times the overall average. The first or so-called "Christian" names of the red-shirted Jewish *Garibaldisti* were mostly as Italian as any Catholic's—Donato, Giuseppe, Angelo, Antonio, Eugenio, Giulio. But their family names were definitely Jewish—d'Ancona, Goldberg, Luzzatti, Rava, Rovigho—many of them names of cities.

The taking of Sicily soon afterwards was followed by the King's and Garibaldi's entrance in Naples, bringing an end to the Bourbon 125-year reign. All that was now left to do in order to unify the country completely—and, incidentally, free its remaining Jews—was the addition of the city of Rome and its papal territory. Victor Emmanuel, to keep abreast of history and to be ready for this eventuality, in 1861 took the title of King of Italy rather than King of Sardinia only. The country became one in its ruler, but the Pope was still to be convinced of its reality.

Realities in Rome remained in ancient moulds. The idea of forced baptism once again came to the foreground. In 1863 a young girl by the name of Graziosa Cavagli was found weeping near the ghetto compound. She had been punished by her mother, and was kindly taken in tow by a charming and doubtless God-fearing lady. There was only one way to console the child, thought this angel of mercy. So the kind woman brought Graziosa *linea recta* to the Home for the Catechumen. Notwithstanding violent protests by her parents and the Jewish community she was baptised after the usual forty days of indoctrination.

The following year 10-year-old Giuseppe Cohen was held fast by a priest while on his way to the shoemaker who had promised to teach him the trade. A few minutes later a struggling Giuseppe found himself guarded by the masters of the Catechumen Home. Again protests by parents, and even the intervention of the French ambassador, remained fruitless. Giuseppe was baptised and was only liberated from his uncongenial religious surroundings seven years later, due to intervention of the government of the (by then) united Italy. In the meantime Giuseppe's 18-year-old sister had died from the shock caused by her brother's abduction, his mother had gone mad, and his father had left Rome in order to escape the Vatican's revenge (he had dared to protest).

These acts were the last convulsions of a papal temporal régime that saw itself doomed, yet had no wish to surrender. For seven centuries the Pope had reigned as a royal dictator, and Pius IX, Head of a Church which found it increasingly difficult to adapt itself to the exigencies of the changing world, was loath to relinquish these rights. As far as the Jews were concerned, a spontaneously kind papal gesture had been the rare exception. Everlastingly oppressed, the Jews had paid for every concession in human suffering or in money; the Jew had always been an Enemy.

On 20 July 1870 the Franco-Prussian War broke out. The following day the Vatican Council in Rome declared the Pope's infallibility. Soon France found itself more than hard-pressed by the Prussians, Louis Napoleon lost his throne, and nearly immediately afterwards Italian royalist troops decided to march on the stronghold of the Pope, infallible or not.

The Roman Jewish community had not been sitting still. As early as July, when Bismarck had engaged France in war, its governors had prepared a petition to be sent to the Pope. It was an interminable document in which they incorporated practically all the important events that had occurred ever since Rome had become the seat of the papacy, and was respectfully addressed to the "Holiest Father." Calling themselves "loyal subjects of Your Holiness" who "throw themselves down before Your exalted throne," they gave a detailed account of the difficult conditions the community found itself in, and they begged the Pope "to look mercifully at those who as Jews also belong to Your people."

The community's own description of living conditions in the ghetto confirmed Gregorovius' impressionistic account. In some streets the poorer Jews lived under the worst possible non-hygienic conditions. "Air and light" in those streets were "hardly available" and yet these places were "necessarily used as homes." There was a school in the ghetto (the governors wrote) but "at an early age children are obliged to give up learning, to assist their parents in trying to make enough money to buy a piece of bread." The only professions they saw open to them were those of "porters, ragpickers, salesmen of sulphur sticks, errand boys and night watchmen, buyers of old shoes and clothes, and that of water carriers, and never, never anything else! In his desperation," the document continued, "the Jew loses the consciousness of being human." Under these circumstances it was a miracle that the Jews "have retained a sense of duty and honor." Therefore "our prayer to Your Holiness," so ended the petition, "is the prayer of 4,800 of Your Jewish subjects."

It had been the intention of the ghetto fathers to add an extensive series of charts, figures, accounts of payments made through the centuries, and all kinds of other appendices to their petition; but time suddenly ran out. On September 20, 1870 General Cadorna arrived before Rome, and the governmental troops entered the city through a breach in the wall near the Porta Pia, led by a captain Giacomo Segre—a Jew.

A new day had arrived. The Jews had been liberated before, but now it looked as if it might be for good. Three days after the troops' entry, the Roman Jews handed a letter to General Cadorna to be transmitted to the King, thanking their new sovereign for their liberation. The nomenclature of Jew, they said in that historic letter, would henceforth be used in the synagogue only. "From now on," they concluded, "we will remind ourselves outside the Temple that we are Romans and Italians."

Chapter 28
Jews in Government

All fences were finally removed, and the Jews' activity in Italy developed as never before. They were not without political astuteness, and it was logical that they would be among the strongest nationalists of the new kingdom which had freed them. They had nothing to lose, everything to gain. Isacco Artom, one of the architects of the nation, would be the first Jewish member of the Senate. Even if he had wanted to, he could not have asked God to stand by him when he was sworn in to his new function. The government had banned all mention of *Dio* from the premises of the Senate and of other state organs, for theirs was to be a complete separation of church and state. Before he died in 1900, Artom would be ambassador to Denmark and permanent under-secretary of foreign affairs. His influence on Cavour had been great, and so was his influence on national policy.

Samuele Alatri—who had often pleaded for the Roman Jews' cause at the Vatican before 1870, and who would remain as the community's president after liberation—was one of the members of the Rome committee that handed King Victor Emmanuel the city's decision in favor of Italian unification. Alatri was soon one of the two Jewish members of Rome's city council, a position he was named to during the same month that nine Jewish deputies were elected to parliament.

In 1872 the violently anti-Catholic current in the municipal council led some of its members to propose removing the cross from above the entrance to the Campo Verano cemetery. Of all people, it was Alatri who fought the resolution. The Pope, with whom Alatri always had been on fairly good terms, is reported to have said on that occasion: "I always knew that *Sor* Samuele was the most Catholic of all city councilors." (And that same year the Pope, in an unexpected move, asked French Jewish sculptor Adam-Salomon to come and live for some time at the Vatican, to make a bust of His Holiness.)

Elected to parliament together with Garibaldi, Alatri remained a fervent supporter of liberal ideas, and a deeply religious member of the Jewish community. When he died in 1889 at the age of eighty-four, the mayor said of him that "the city of Rome loved the deceased greatly, and weeps for him as one weeps for a father . . . ." Even in the flowery language so common in the land, the mayor's tribute was sincerely meant, and was accepted as such by the Romans.

King Umberto I entrusted the military education of his son Victor Emmanuel III to Jewish General Giuseppe Ottolenghi. There never was any anti-Jewish feeling on the part of the royal family—on the contrary. During the Italo-Turkish War of 1911, when a small group of Italian anti-Semites spread the rumor that the conflict had been "engineered by the Jews," the King (whose grandfather, till fifty years previously had been ruler of Sardinia only) publicly made the statement that he "liked only two kinds of people—Sardinians and Jews."

There would be several other Jewish instructors for the royal children in later years, including the eminent jurist Vittorio Polacco, teacher of law to Crown-Prince Umberto. A strict Jew, whose name later on was given to the *Talmud Torah* school of the capital, Polacco took up a position in the Senate against a proposed divorce law, thus siding—although legally he had nothing to do with it—with the Pope.

A great many other Jews (as well as half-Jews or baptised Jews) became prominent in Italian life. The outstanding figure in the first category was undoubtedly Luigi Luzzatti. He was born in 1841; in his adult life he went through the whole period of the *Risorgimento*, the establishment of the Kingdom of Italy, the first World War, and the opening stages of fascism. A Jew married to a Jewess (Amalia Levi), he was a financial genius who during his long life would be seven times Minister of Finance; once Minister of Agriculture, Commerce and Industry; Minister of the Interior; Minister of State; Senator *del Regno*; and member of parliament for fifteen sessions. In 1910 Luzzatti became Prime Minister of Italy. As such he presided at the Palazzo Braschi, not far from Rome's Campo de' Fiori, the square which through the ages had been the place where Jews had been burned as mortal enemies of the Vatican.

Luzzatti died in 1927, aged eighty-six. He had the doubtful honor of being praised nine years later by one of the worst anti-Semites of the fascist régime, Giovanni Preziosi, who eulogized Luzzatti's "rare culture, idealism and effective realism," as well as "the harmony he effected between matter and mind." These were probably the last words of praise for a Jew ever published in Italy's fascist press.

Among other Jews, Leone Wollemborg, founder of the Rural Cooperative Savings Banks, would be Minister of State, Minister of Finance, and Senator. Austrian-born Salvatore Barzilai was member of parliament, Senator, Minister for the to-be-freed Austrian territories in 1915, and one of the five Italians who would sign the Versailles peace treaty. Austrian-born but baptised Carlo Schanzer would be Prime Minister after the first World War. Sydney Sonnino, a half-Jew of originally British nationality (he was born in Alexandria and educated in England), was twice Prime Minister. As Minister of Finance between 1893 and 1896 he would save the country from national bankruptcy, and as a political publicist he founded the

important Roman daily newspaper *Il Giornale d'Italia*. Still
another Minister of State was Ludovico Mortara, who also
headed the Ministry of Justice.

All this is, I think, worth recording. In other countries, of
course, it was nothing special during the latter part of the
nineteenth century and the beginning of the twentieth to find
such a comparatively significant number of Jews in high
government places. In Rome, however, the situation was
different. Most of the Jews who so suddenly had come to
national prominence were not born in the capital, with the exception of men like Alatri who already occupied a leading position in the Rome Jewish community. It is obvious that due to
papal restrictions on higher education, only a very limited
number of Roman Jews had been able to attain positions of
eminence in *any* field.

After their liberation the Jews for the greater part continued
to live in their miserable abodes inside the ghetto, free to leave,
but finding it difficult to do so. Freedom alone was not enough,
for the economic as well as the educational barriers posed
tremendous obstacles.

At times the Roman Jews had been upgraded from ragpickers to mattress-makers. This was an easy transition since
the rags would be used to fill the mattresses. They had gone up
in the business world every time one of the less disagreeable
Popes had been of the opinion that Jewish shops along the Corso would do no harm to the Roman economy. Some Jews had
become doctors and lawyers, most of the time practicing within
the confines of the ghetto only. But that was just about as far as
the liberation, if it could be called such, had gone. With
freedom, the governmental positions could only be attained by
the Jews from the north, for it was they who had had the
necessary education and the experience of free government.

The Roman Jews continued to group together in the ghetto
area. In fact, they had little choice, for the centuries-old *jus
gazàga* kept them confined to those few streets between the
Bridge With The Four Heads and the Piazza Mattei. The ancient
rental system was still in force and could not be set aside by the

simple incantation of the word *freedom*. The community remained responsible for the total of the rents on homes owned by persons living outside the ghetto—Italian Catholics all. If a Jew moved out, the rent still had to be paid; for, to the owner, this rent through the ages had become a permanent income, as solid as real estate. It was a situation that could only be resolved legally; and in Italy, then as now, matters involving the civil law seem to stretch into eternity. The Jewish Community started legal proceedings against the city shortly after King Victor Emmanuel had entered Rome. But it would not be until thirteen years later, in 1884, that the courts successfully had waded through the hundreds of legal documents and thousands of legal pages, and would come up with a verdict—in favor of the Jews. That same year a beginning was made with the destruction of the ghetto streets, of which in the end only few would remain. Yet the change took time. As late as 1899 only the first phase of the ghetto improvement showed results—at its center the ghetto had become a huge open space. Clearing had been started, but nothing new had taken its place. The poorer Jews were still living in what was left, running across and over each other "like ants on an anthill."

At the time the Pope had real estate problems of his own: At the inauguration of the Kingdom of Italy he had given up his summer palace of the Quirinale, which became the residence of King Victor Emmanuel. Pius IX, therefore, had to fall back on his regular home inside the Vatican, thoroughly restricted—by his own choice—in his movements. It was a somewhat paradoxical situation; even more, one of the ironies of history. For centuries the Vatican had kept the Jews shut up behind a wall, and now that the Jewish wall was gone, the Pope retreated behind a wall of his own, unwilling to come out. Neither Pius IX nor any of the Popes who came after him would leave the Vatican grounds until Benito Mussolini signed the *Concordat* of 1929, settling the relations between Italy and the Papacy. The Popes were angry at the audacity of the Italians who had taken away their livelihood, so to say, leaving them without any worldly possessions. Their direct hold on the Jews of Rome had also come to an end; and what happened outside its walls was far from pleasing to the Vatican as a whole, and even less pleasing to a great many of its ecclesiastical servants individually.

The Jews, having "caused the revolution"—at least as several cardinals had taught during the years preceding and even following 1870—could hardly be left in peace in a free Italy. While the Pope from within his 110 acres of independent Vatican territory would try to re-expand his influence on his religious subjects around the world, it seemed to become a necessity for a good many of his priestly activists to promote anti-Semitism. Leo XIII, who succeeded Pope Pius IX in 1878, succeeded brilliantly in his endeavor to strengthen his influence with certain foreign countries; he became a great friend of France (where he allowed the Catholics to recognize the Republic, only to see the various Church Orders forbidden by the French government in 1901). At the same time he imposed sanctions in his fight against the Kingdom of Italy, forbidding Italian citizens to take part in governmental life or to accept governmental posts. Moreover, all Italian Catholics—which meant the whole population—were papally forbidden to vote in elections. Successful in his foreign policy, the Pope was equally successful in his anti-Semitism. Perhaps to underline his friendship with France, Pope Leo took a strong anti-Jewish position in the Dreyfus case by declaring the Jews to be anarchists, freemasons, and enemies of the Church in general.

Encouraged by this papal attitude, the priests went quite a bit further, the Jesuits especially. Their anti-Semitic prejudices were printed with the ink of venom. They insisted that "Jews expect the realization of a dream, the dream of messianism, which will bring them universal domination." Thus the Jews, according to the Jesuits of that time, "were the sworn enemies of the countries they live in. . . . "

That frightening ancient canard of "ritual murder" was refurbished and disseminated once more with joy by the Jesuits. The Rome-published *Voice of Truth** wrote in 1890 that "it

*La Voce della Verità of March 9-10, 1890.

might be useful to remind the Jews that their barbaric and superstitious practices have been ascertained to be positive facts in the liturgy of the Church. Let us just mention Saint Simon of Trent, martyred by the Jews. If now they have abandoned this impious and sanguine practice, then every well-thinking soul will rejoice. But if they count on changing history to their advantage, then we would like to warn them that their plan will not succeed."

The theme was played and replayed in all hateful octaves. In 1892, fourteen years after Leo XIII had taken the reins of Catholicism into his hands, Father Rondina would write in the official Jesuit publication *La Civiltà Cattòlica* that the Jews "do not work, but profit from the work by others; they do not produce, but live and grow fat on the artistic and industrial products of the nations that give them shelter. The Jewish nation is a polyp that attracts and embraces all with its outsized tentacles."

During the reign of Pope Pius X, who was on far better terms with the Italian government than his two predecessors, the most notable event as far as the Jews were concerned was the arrival in Rome of Theodor Herzl. The founder of Zionism, shortly before his death, tried to interest Pope Pius in the work he had started in 1896 in his book *"Der Judenstaat."* The Pope was good enough to receive the promoter of the new Zionist interest, since on a personal basis he had no antipathy against the Jews. Popes, after all, had always (or, at least, often) been on perfectly friendly terms with Jewish doctors and others, as long as their influence did not spread too deeply—or, sometimes, even on the surface—among Catholics, and as long as the personal services of these Jews were needed for the well-being of the papacy. Just the same, Pope Pius X a few years later forbade the celebration of holy mass on the King's birthday in Mantova—because the year before on that day the mayor had visited the local synagogue!

Though after 1870 the Jews of Rome had become one with those of the rest of the country, the fate of the Italian Jews would continue to be decided in the capital. As the center of government, Rome also became the center of Italian Judaism as well. With their prominence in politics, industry, banking, and the sciences, some thirty Jewish families were ennobled by the King (as already had happened to Giuseppe Treves de' Bonfilli under Napoleon).*

A few years after the turn of the century, in July 1904, the huge new synagogue on the Lungotevere de' Cenci was inaugurated in Rome, honored by an early visit from King Victor Emmanuel III. Soon the five old synagogues-under-one-roof would fall under the wrecker's hammer. The King would continue to befriend Jews, both Italian and foreign. That same year would see the start of his friendship with David Lubin, a Russian-born American citizen who created the International Agricultural Institute in Rome. The King became one of its sponsors and was present when in 1908 its offices were inaugurated on a street near the Piazza del Popolo that carries the name of its founder, the Viale David Lubin. After the Second World War the Institute formed the basis for the Food and Agricultural Organisation of the United Nations, which took over its worldwide activities. It transferred its offices to the present FAO site near the Porta Capena—where two thousand years earlier Jewish beggar women, carrying their baskets of hay and straw (perhaps a prophetic sign of the agricultural events to come), would foretell the future to travelers leaving the city.

That future in the early twentieth century looked bright. If the arts did not yet find abundant protagonists among the Roman and other Italian Jews (with the exception of so rare a specimen as Modigliani, who went to Paris to find fame and death, and men like Graziadio Isaia Ascoli, who was one of the

---

*The Vatican, which had its own facilities to bestow honorific or noble titles on deserving Catholics, elevating them into its so-called "Black Nobility," once—before 1870—got its medals confounded. It honored the Tuscan Consul in Bordeaux, who had been instrumental in helping some shipwrecked Papal citizens. The Vatican did not receive a letter of thanks, and inquired what had caused the delay. The Consul sent back a polite note. He explained that his parents had always taught him never to boast about his virtues, his family, or his merits, and that therefore he had felt he should not pride himself on being a Jew who had saved some Vatican subjects.

most famous philologists of his time), new writers and musicians abounded. In the practical field of business Jews flourished. Camillo Olivetti started his typewriter factory which would develop into one of the most important of its kind in the world. Ernesto Nathan, that famous Jewish mayor of Rome, was one of the founders of the Dante Alighieri association, spreading Italian culture across the frontiers. The Galileo Ferraris Institute, which until a short while ago announced the time signal over the Italian radio, was started by a Jew.

In the armed forces, a profession for which the Jews were supposed not to have a natural proclivity, they would distinguish themselves, suggesting at an early date in Italy what would be confirmed so astonishingly half-a-century later in the Middle East. General Giuseppe Ottolenghi, a life senator, became Minister of War in 1902. During the First World War this same post would be held by Sydney Sonnino in the Orlandi cabinet, after which he figured as one of the Italian delegates to the Peace Conference of 1919. Between 1876 and 1924 about forty Jewish senators in all would be named by the King. The same personal mobility would be found in the armed forces. In 1869 there were only 87 Jewish officers among 14,000 Catholic ones. By 1900 the number had grown to 163, and during the 1915-1918 war there were fifteen Jewish Italian generals, an equal number of full colonels, and three admirals.

Through the years, the Italian Jews slowly and imperceptibly would fuse with their compatriots, till they were hardly distinguishable one from another. Only their names, at times, would indicate their religion. For the rest they melted unobtrusively into the multitude, more than in any other country in Europe. Being a Jew in Italy became a perfectly natural thing. It was neither remarked upon nor discussed. Jewishness was rarely mentioned. Except for some sick seeds hidden in the dusty old folds of moldy clerical robes, anti-Semitism, that virulent medieval disease of the dark ages—still so strongly alive in Eastern Europe—had virtually disappeared from the Italian scene.

Chapter 29
Jewish Fascists

When Mussolini's followers started their March on Rome in October 1922, he himself in an understandably agitated frame of mind taking the train a few days later, there were 230 enthusiastic fascist Jews among the participants. At least, that is the number who in later years could display the party membership card with the beloved declaration of "marching participation." They were the overflow of an even earlier Jewish love for Mussolini's life's work; when the party was formed in Milano in 1919, five Jews were among its *sansepolcristi*, those who were ready to give their lives for the new movement. Three indeed did die in the early struggles, and they were counted among the "fascist martyrs," while one, Cesare Goldmann, was the enthusiast who had arranged for the use of the hall on the second floor of a building on the Piazza San Sepolcro where that founding fascist meeting took place.

These Jews were the young revolutionary firebrands who believed in Italy with the same spirited love which had prompted Mussolini himself to break with the socialist party, and who were ready to set out with their leader on the conquest of the nation—the early *squadristi*. One of them, Aldo Finzi, the only fascist among the nine Jewish members of parliament elected in 1921, would a few years later turn Catholic and marry a cardinal's niece. In 1919 Finzi had been a pilot in the D'Annunzio's squadron that took Fiume when the fate of that city hung in the international balance after the First World War; and later he was elected a member of the Fascist Grand Council and became Under-Secretary of the Interior. Finzi finished his life miserably among the Roman hostages shot by the Germans in March 1944 at the Ardeatine Caves—forgotten by the fascists, loathed by the Roman Jews, and doubly execrated by the Germans.

There was, of course, no anti-Semitism among the fascists during those formative years, for the simple reason that there was no anti-Semitism among the Italians. Mussolini seemed a great man, a Hero of history, to a certain number of citizens, and the Jews were citizens like everybody else. Nobody held it against them that they had joined the fascist movement, except those who were against *all* fascists. And to them these Jewish fascists were plainly Italians-gone-wrong, in the same way as the Catholic Italians were beguiled and misled. Religion had no part in it—it was simply a matter of politics. It would indeed have been contrary to the statistical law of averages if some Jews had *not* taken Mussolini's side, because by 1922 most of them had stopped being Jews per se, and had become "very Italian."

Mussolini was quite impartial to Jews in those days. He had read Nietzsche whom he called his "favorite philosopher" and, perhaps, believed with him that "Rome was defeated (in Judaea) by four Jews—Jesus of Nazareth, the fisherman Peter, the rugweaver Paul, and Jesus' mother Mary," indeed that the Jews had used Christ as "the real tool of their hate." In 1908 Mussolini had declared that "the inversion of moral values had been the capital work of the Jews," another Nietzschean maxim. As a young socialist exile in Switzerland during the first years of the twentieth century, much of his political thinking had been molded by Angelica Balabanoff, a Jewish Russian-born socialist whom Mussolini had met at the anniversary celebration of the Paris Commune.*

Later Mussolini would find new and closer ties with another daughter of Israel, Margherita Sarfatti, an editorial member of the fascist magazine *Gerarchia*, the author (in 1924) of his biography *DUX* is which she referred to Catholicism as "the boat of the divine Jew Jesus," and a close very personal collaborator. Mussolini's after-thoughts on these two Jewish women who so strongly had influenced him were mixed. Of his early teacher Balabanoff he said later that she was "ugly, but with a noble and generous mind." Margherita came off less favorably; he called her "beautiful" but was of the opinion that she had a "greedy, guileful, and even sordid mind." Margherita, too, would outlive her lover; she died in Italy in 1961, after years of exile, persecution, and poverty, embittered against the man she had once so admired.

If there were Jews who were on Mussolini's side, there were also those—the vast majority—who opposed him, and there were those who were at first for him, only to turn as strongly against him when his political aims became more accentuated. Among the latter would be *sansepolcristo* Eucardio Momigliano, who soon—as one of the leaders of the Democratic Union—would be amongst Mussolini's most radical opponents. During the threat of the March on Rome, the army group designated to defend the city against the fascists was commanded by Jewish General Emanuele Pugliese. Neither he nor his troops were of any effective help. The King was afraid of the consequences of armed opposition, and at the last minute had refused to sign a declaration ordering the state of siege, resulting in Mussolini's unopposed arrival in the capital in the morning of 30 October 1922.

---

*Known in later life as "the Grandmother of Socialism," Balabanoff died, well over ninety, in Rome in 1967. She had been close to Lenin and Trotsky, was secretary of the Second International, representative of the Italian Socialist Party at the Third International, and a violent critic of Stalin. An opponent of Nenni when the left-wing of the Italian Socialist Party joined the Communists in 1947, she was thereafter close to Saragat; and when she died, the social-democratic President of Italy was named as one of the executors of her will.

The statements Mussolini had made on the Jews after he had donned his black shirt were usually of political significance only, although they contained sharp barbs. They had as yet, however, nothing to do with the Italian home front. In 1919, writing about the Russian Revolution, he had accused "the Jewish bankers in London and New York" (whom he said to be "bound by racial roots to the Jews in Moscow and Budapest") of wanting "to take revenge on the Aryan race which has condemned them to dispersion for so many centuries." The next year he predicted that "Bolshevism will cause the ruin of Judaism in Eastern Europe." Then came the announcement of the twelfth Zionist Congress in Carlsbad in September 1921, and the rabid Italian nationalist discovered a subject to be agitated about, and he did so in no uncertain terms. Writing in the *Popolo d'Italia* in August, Mussolini remarked that "the greater public will not be a little surprised to learn of the existence of a Zionist federation in Italy." This meant, he explained, that in a country "in which there never had been any anti-Semitism, there are Jews who are tired of being here"; and if they wanted to leave, then he would "gladly help them to complete the exodus."

Zionism started to take on a bloated enemy form in Mussolini's mind, because he saw the sinister hand of England behind the idea of establishing a British-dominated outpost in the eastern Mediterranean, which he considered *mare nostrum*, an Italian lake. In a speech in parliament in June 1921, he pointed out that the government should choose either the side of the Zionists, or that of Pope Benedict XV (who, of course, was against). No one should see "a hint of anti-Semitism" in his words, he added, for this "would be new in this auditorium. I recognize that the sacrifice of Jewish blood during the War has been great, vast, and generous, but here we have to examine a political situation." Zionism definitely became an ever-growing obsession, a movement that actually was negligible. It was, in Italy at least, exclusively theoretical and not practical. When Chaim Weizmann arrived in Rome the following year, he was surprised to find it even in existence. In his memoirs the future first president of Israel declared that "Zionism in Italy" for him held "the fascination of mystery." "The community was a small one," he wrote, and its members "were to all intents and purposes indistinguishable form their fellow citizens, except that they went to the synagogue instead of to Mass."

Weizmann, who was the newly-elected president of the Zionist Organisation, had come to Rome to make a speech at the *Collegio Romano* on the 6th of April. His statements gave rise to some pointed articles in the Vatican newspaper, the *Osservatore Romano*, which twisted his words. Weizmann had remarked that for the next ten years or so "no more land would be *bought*," which in the newspaper's version had become *expropriated*. It caused some controversy, perhaps only a storm in a Vatican fountain; but it was followed a month later by an anti-Zionist conference in Rome held by the Patriarch of Jerusalem, Monsignore Luigi Berlassina. Obviously, the hastily-called Monsignore had to refute Weizmann's statements. Zionism had caused "great damage" in Palestine, he said, for "the intolerable system of the present rulers has evoked the aversion and the disgust of the Arab natives, and above all the indignation of the Catholics," who should put up "an effective defense to protect the holy places of Christianity. . . ."

During his short stay in Rome in 1922, Weizmann wanted to gather some information about those holy places, and he talked about them to Jewish-descended Prime Minister Schanzer. Unfamiliar as he was with the ever-increasing Vatican influence on the Italian state, Weizmann was a bit taken aback to find himself placed so suddenly in the center of a problem which he felt should only interest the Vatican, and perhaps the British. When he saw Secretary of State Cardinal Gasparri after his lecture at the *Collegio Romano*, the Cardinal too brought up the question of the holy places and then remarked that the lecture had been "very interesting." Weizmann asked with a smile whether Gasparri was referring to his lecture "at the *Collegio Romano* or in the *Osservatore Romano*."

Weizmann did not note any anti-Semitism in Italy, yet the "Palestine issue" slowly was made into a religious football

which Mussolini (and especially some of his more rabid supporters) enjoyed kicking across the political field. Soon the
Jewish magazine *Israel* felt itself obliged to write that "anti-
Semitism, which seemed far removed from this civilized, gentle
and intelligent people, has found its obscure inroads in
Italy. . . . " Mussolini deplored its existence in various talks
with Roman Chief Rabbi Angelo Sacerdoti, stating that
"fascism never intended to follow an anti-Semitic policy." To
prove his point, the Italian government—that is, of course,
Mussolini—in 1925 appointed Giorgio Del Vecchio, a Jew and
one of the most respected international legal-philosophical
minds, as president of the Rome University. Del Vecchio immediately re-activated the university chapel which had been
closed since 1870. This started the rumor that he had been converted to Catholicism. The new dean quickly reacted, declaring
that nothing could be farther from his mind, and that he had
every intention to remain true to his religion. Thus, with the exception of a few peripheral complexities, everything seemed to
point simply to a happy politico-religious co-existence.

1926 was an Italian anti-anti-Semitic year of absolutely pure
vintage. Once again in Rome, Weizmann was received by
Mussolini who stressed his distrust of England's intentions in
Palestine and tried to win over his visitor to the ideas he himself
had in mind on the future of a Jewish state. "We could build
your whole nation," Mussolini is reported to have said; and he
suggested that the construction of the port of Haifa be entrusted
to the Italian-Jewish firm of Almagià (with main offices in
Rome and Egypt, and with construction facilities all around the
Mediterranean). Conversations along these lines shortly
afterwards did indeed take place with Almagià, but came to
nothing when the British decided to take on the job themselves
under the obligations they had as the mandate power. Yet
Mussolini's suggestion showed at least a commercial interest in
Zionism. Weizmann was not particularly responsive.

The tone of the conversation changed abruptly when the
Duce, elaborating on the construction job, suggested that the
Italians could build up the projected Jewish homeland from

"top to bottom." This remark prompted Weizmann to say, dry-ly, that he remembered how "the Romans had *destroyed* it from top to bottom." A rather glacial impression also resulted from the more political discussion of Zionism. "You know," Mussolini said, "that not all Jews are Zionists." "Of course," Weizmann answered, "I know it only too well, and not all Italians are Fascisti." According to Weizmann's understated account in his memoirs, Mussolini seemed disappointed by this answer; and one can wonder whether Weizmann who had done such outstanding work in a British laboratory during the First World War, was not a better chemist than a diplomat. Or could it merely have been the chair Weizmann had been offered in Mussolini's stadium-sized office in the Palazzo Venezia? The seat, we are told, was very hard, and neither the chair "nor the general atmosphere added any support" to the visitor's "physical or moral comfort."

At one point during that first conversation with the Duce, Weizmann felt "that he was skating on thin ice," and he wanted to end the conversation "as soon as I had spoken my piece on Jews and Fascism and Italy," but Mussolini "kept me for some time."

The Duce's favorable, if opportunistic, attitude toward Zionism continued to spread a fascist benediction on the efforts of the nearly-exclusively *non*-Italian Jews* who tried to es-tablish some kind of homeland in Palestine. In 1927 Mussolini told Nahum Sokolov of the Zionist Executive Council that he "could only repeat that in principle he had nothing against Zionism," and in 1928 he even allowed an Italo-Palestine Com-mittee to be organized on Roman soil. With the movement of-ficially sanctioned, a certain number of Jews were won over to fascist sympathies. They, too, seemed proud that the trains now ran on time, that the Italian sky was blue, that restless youth was kept in hand and in *balilla*-step, that food was cheap, and shining black boots impressive. They, too, were pleased that glassy-eyed visitors from all over the world came to be

*Between 1926 and 1938 only 150 Italian Jews emigrated to Palestine.

photographed with the Duce. These Jews were not alone in their awe of the golden calf of fascism. They participated emotionally in the nation's joys and disasters. The Italian explorer Nobile, in a spectacular trip that was followed by the admiring eyes of the whole world, flew over the North Pole in his own-designed dirigible *Italia*, only to crash near Spitzbergen on the way back. All Italians, including the Jews, were exhilarated and saddened, the latter especially when they heard that the prominent young Jewish physicist Aldo Pontremoli, who had been one of the expedition's brilliant scientists, had died in the crash. It did indicate, however, how the emancipated Jews were cooperating in every phase of Italian life; indeed if one collaborated and participated, then life in Rome had few difficulties.

Rome was not yet a cosmopolitan or worldly city in those days. In the 1920s the Italian capital was in many respects still a village—to many even an annoying and exasperating village where nothing ever happened except fascist parades. Of a Sunday the walkers in the city—a large number of strictly-chaperoned Catholic girls, a small number of Jewish families, a handful of tourists—would make their way through the Villa Borghese and on to the Via Veneto (from which the so-called *dolce vita* was still far removed). The Via Veneto was a pleasant, quiet street where the first sidewalk terrazza was still a thing of the distant future. The Excelsior Hotel, that modern mecca of the American tourist, was stoically guarded by doormen dressed in gold-collared cut-aways, black-velvet knickers, white stockings, and glacé pumps with silver buckles. Beyond its revolving doors, there was no crowded mass of talkative tourists; a museum-like sanctity would descend upon the intrepid intruder who out of sheer reverence would drop his voice to a timid whisper. One could still *walk* in Rome or take a clop-clop carriage; automobilism, Italian-style, was not yet a street-corner menace. The Victor Emmanuel momument stood on the Piazza Venezia, and the statue of Garibaldi on the Gianicolo Hill; but the Mussolini Forum near the Ponte Milvio, its name later to be changed to Italian Forum, was still on the drawing board. The Costanzi Theater had been closed in 1926 after a season that had seen the first performance of Puccini's *Turan-dot*, and was reopened in 1928 as the Royal Opera Theater with a glittering performance of Boito's *Nerone*, definitely a dictator's dream. Even the ghetto by now showed a new face. Its central open space slowly had been filled with new streets which bore names like the Via del Progresso and the Via Catalana (after the old Spanish synagogue); and from the Portico d'Ottavia the scene on Friday evenings, with several thousand Jews still living in the area, looked nearly as busy as at any time during the preceding centuries.

In the distant past the oppression by the Church had weighed as a tragic yoke on the Jews' shoulders. But now in the third decade of the progressive twentieth century, happy days seemed around the corner, so why not become faces in the crowd? The Jews did join in substantial numbers and about ten percent of them (or close to five thousand) soon were sympathizers, or believers, or in any case badge-wearing members of the party. Which still left another ninety percent, or 45,000 Jews, who carefully kept their distance from the fascist ranks.

To counteract the persistent anti-fascist charges about Italian anti-Semitism, the Italian embassy in Washington in 1928 issued a statement to the press to the effect that "Italy has always been the classic land of Jewish liberty." Mussolini's diplomats did not choose to look back any further than two short generations. The Vatican, having an equally short memory, also did a bit of historical rewriting when it announced that "it always had protected the Jewish people against unjust oppression. . . . " Propaganda thrives on historical amnesia.

In these general circumstances the Jews were joining the party in about an equal percentage with the rest of the population. During these same years of the latter part of the twenties Mussolini and the Pope decided that the time had come to bury their differences and join hands in ending the long animosity between Church and State. After three years of negotiations the Lateran treaty was signed in 1929 by Cardinal Gasparri for Pius XI, and by Mussolini as representative of the King. The Pope once again could venture beyond his self-imposed wall.

Immediately a cry went up, especially in the United States, about the future of the synagogues in Italy since, under the terms of the Concordat, Catholicism was specified as the official religion of the land. There was some concern too among the Jews of Rome; but Mussolini soon put an end to that momentary fear. On May 14 he reconfirmed total freedom of religion to an all-fascist parliament, stating that "it was ridiculous, as had been suggested, that the synagogues would be closed. . . ." He rummaged through history to sing praise of the Jews. "They have been in Rome since the time of the kings. . . ." he said. "Perhaps they supplied the clothes to the Sabine women after the Rape! . . . There were fifty thousand of them at the time of Augustus, and they asked to be allowed to weep near Caesar's body. . . . They will remain undisturbed, and undisturbed too all those who believe in other religions. . . . "

The reassurance was for the moment serious, even if the chronology was odd. In suggesting that the Jews had played kind Samaritans to the sorely tried Sabine virgins, Mussolini made the Jews residents of Rome about seven centuries before Judah Maccabae actually did send his two emissaries across the Mediterranean to talk to the Roman Senate about their trouble with the Syrians. To be sure, Mussolini (and a small group of violently anti-Semitic followers) would completely and conveniently forget about all this some years later, when the Italians were told that "the Jews do not belong to the Italian race" and that "the Fatherland does not admit adultery" by the Jews. The point was badly chosen, for had it not been rape in the legendary founding drama of Italian history, and had not the only protectors (as Mussolini had so ingeniously suggested) been the Jews?

Mussolini did not appear to be of two minds when "Jewish love" entered his *own* family; he reacted furiously. In the summer of 1929 his nineteen-year old daughter Edda fell in love with a Jewish young man while vacationing at Riccione on the Adriatic. As soon as he heard about it, the Duce wrote his sister Edvige, asking her to leave immediately for the summer resort and to do whatever she could to forestall the affair. "Such a step would raise an outcry in the whole world," wrote the evidently rather desperate Duce, pointing out to his sister that "ninety percent of mixed marriages go wrong anyhow. Such a marriage," Mussolini continued, "would be aggravated by the unhappiness it would cause. It would be a real and true scandal. It cannot and will not take place."

The letter—and Edvige's mission—apparently succeeded in preventing any untoward event, for Edda did not marry her Jewish young man. But while Mussolini had mentioned to his sister that he did not want to meet the young man or his family, a meeting between the father and the Duce did take place. Mussolini's paternal pride and fascist sense of honor must have received a rude shock. He was told that the boy would not be permitted to go through with the match in any event, because—according to Edvige—"the father would only allow his son to marry a Jewish girl! . . . "

Was this not something for which the Jews of Rome and of all Italy could be thankful? It was no doubt fortunate that Mussolini and the boy's father took such firm positions. The Duce might have promoted his Jewish son-in-law to be foreign minister (as he did with Ciano whom Edda subsequently married)!

Having thus deprived himself of getting a Jewish foreign minister, Mussolini sought out a Jew to head his Ministry of Finance, for whatever the vagaries of his attitude to the Jews, his sense of practical politics usually suspended the element of anti-Semitism. In 1932 he named Guido Jung as minister, stating that "a Jew should be at the head of finance." Perhaps Jung was a financial genius. His ethics, however, were hardly worth the buttons on a worn-out black shirt. When Mussolini six years later promulgated his racial laws, and left a loophole for those of little character, Guido Jung quickly made an exception of himself, signing a statement to the effect that his mother had had extra-marital relations with a Catholic and that the illegitimate offspring of that union was his own proud self; it is not often that a fascist has openly registered the claim to be a pure bastard.

Other Jews acted rather more honorably. One year before Jung's appointment, Mussolini required an oath of allegiance to the fascist regime from all Italian university professors. Of the twelve who refused, four were Jews—Vito Volterra, in the chair of mathematics in Rome; Giorgio Errera, chemistry; Fabio Luzzatto, professor of law; and Giorgio Levi. Yet that same year the Italian universities opened their doors wide to foreign Jewish students (many of them from Rumania) who could not study at home due to a religious *numerus clausus*. It seemed a policy in which the left fascist hand did not know what the right hand was doing; for, again during that same year 1931, Costanzo Ciano (Minister of Communications and father of Galeazzo Ciano who, in the meantime, had married Edda Mussolini) declared at the opening of the Jewish Museum in Livorno that "there are not enough Jews in Italy. . . . "

Thus, at a time when in Germany the anti-Jewish atmosphere became more and more venomous, Mussolini continued to pursue a quite pro-Jewish policy in his own country. The opening of the universities to foreign students was not the only pro-Jewish move he made. As a result of long conversations (started in 1932) with Vladimir Jabotinsky, the Russian-born Zionist revisionist who aimed at a Jewish state in Palestine which would be totally independent of Britain, Mussolini consented two years later to start a Naval School for Jews at Civitavecchia (and so unwittingly creating a nucleus of officers for the future Israeli Navy). Jabotinsky continued to have close ties with the Italian government, asserting that his young movement had much in common with fascist aims, a claim he would have to abjure a few years later. The Jewish Naval School obtained a first four-master training ship which was christened (so to say) the *Sara I*. She soon happily sailed her conglomerate crew of Rumanian, Polish, Czech, Hungarian, German, and Lithuanian Jewish sailors to such ports as Sevilla, where they did not hide—to the embarrassment of the Italian consulate—their anti-

Nazi feelings. Further training trips in the Mediterranean were thereafter carefully restricted to such safer political harbors as Nice and Marseille.

To be sure, Jabotinsky and Mussolini were following parallel courses of action, aiming at the removal of British influence from Palestine. But it would appear that Jabotinsky used Mussolini more than the other way around, since the Duce received no advantage whatsoever from his Jewish school. In 1937, while Mussolini mover closer to Hitler, the *Sara I* moved ever closer to Palestine. Later that year it entered the port of Haifa to the riotously jubilant acclamations of the Jews, after which the Civitavecchia center quite understandably was hurriedly closed.

In that same year of 1932 when Jabotinsky approached the Italian government about his Zionist plans, another Jew made contact with Mussolini—Emil Ludwig. The literary and political sensation created by the publication of their eighteen conversations between March 23 and April 4 made fascinating reading and was thoroughly regretted by the dictator's anti-Semitic followers. Mussolini's statements were clear and unambiguous. On the subject of race he said, "there are no more pure races—not even the Jews have remained unmixed. . . ." Nor did he believe that "one can biologically prove the greater or lesser purity of a race," and moreover it was his view that "national pride definitely does not need any racial delirium."

He reconfirmed the absence of anti-Semitism: "it does not exist" in Italy. To convince his interviewer, he focussed Ludwig's attention on "the high posts the Jews occupy in universities, in the army, and in banking. . . . A whole host of them are generals," he said, among others General Modena who was military commander of Sardinia.

Discussing anti-Semitism in Germany, Emil Ludwig remarked that the French used a name for it which he said they applied to a certain German abnormality (meaning homosexuality) and which should equally be used to designate anti-Semitism—*le vice allemand*. When Mussolini asked for an elucidation,

Ludwig said that "whenever something goes wrong in Germany, the Jews are supposed to be guilty, and just now things are going extremely wrong. . . . " It prompted a pithy comment from Mussolini. "Ah," he said, "the scapegoat."

Probably the most positive statement made by Mussolini during these conversations with Emil Ludwig came at the end of their last meeting. Mussolini remarked that "the belief had grown in him that there is a godly power in the universe." When Ludwig wondered whether he meant "a Christian power," Mussolini corrected it to "a divine power." He added that "people can pray to God in many ways—one should leave everyone to his own customs."

Needless to say, the Italian Jewish fascists were jubilant. The non-existence of an anti-Semitic movement was even acknowledged by those passionately anti-fascist self-expatriated Jews like Carlo Rosselli in Paris. Rosselli had started the publication of *Giustizia e Libertà*, which among its collaborators—some even from *within* Italy—counted such eminent Jewish writers as Max Ascoli (today living in New York), Carlo Levi (author-painter and until recently a member of the Italian Senate), and Leone Ginzburg, later publisher of the clandestine newspaper *"Free Italy."*

When the physical and economic persecution of the Jews started in Nazi Germany, the Jewish fascists would point to it as proof of the difference between the Duce's and the Führer's nationalist movements. Under pressure from Italian Jews (including the fascist ones) Mussolini sent his Berlin ambassador Cerrutti to see Hitler, who in turn sent Cerrutti back to Mussolini with a message that must have wounded the Duce's intellectual pride. "Mussolini does not understand anything about the Jewish Problem," Hitler had said; and the unhappy Cerrutti informed his chief that "the failure of the intervention could not be more complete." Yet Mussolini (so often a talker, not a doer) acted; at the request of Jewish Commander Federico Jarach, an important industrialist and a staunch supporter of the Duce, he decreed that German Jews would be welcome in

Italy, on condition that they had no political anti-Nazi affiliations.

That stirring decision was taken in April. Yet four months
later Mussolini suggested to Chancellor Dollfuss that he try to
mollify the Austrian Nazis and soften their increasing pressure
on the government by giving his régime "a slight touch of anti-
Semitism." With that move Mussolini's statements on the
Jewish question began to take on all the erratic signs of power-
political ambivalence, with a slight touch of megalomania in the
bargain.

Chapter 30
Jewish Anti-Fascists

Zionism was the issue that would cause a split in Italian Jewry. It was not that its activities or influence in the country were of any importance; but in the end Mussolini would use it as the stick with which to try and beat the English. To be able to make some audible noise about it, he had to beat the Jews at home as well, the more so because by 1934 he began to cast his eyes around the Mediterranean to see how far the Italian frontiers could be pushed across the sea in order to create the *Impero* that would recrown Rome with the glory of the early Caesars. On Zionism the Vatican saw quite eye to eye with the dictator. The possibility of having the holy places of Christianity—that is: Catholicism—"lost" into the hands of the Jews, was an everlasting pain to the Church. Cardinal Gasparri had already explained the problem to Weizmann in 1922; and with the accelerated emigration of Jews (especially from Hitler's Third Reich) to Palestine, the religious issues concerning the holy land became more clearly drawn. In 1929, seven years after Weizmann's first visit to Rome, the *Osservatore Romano* already had written that "Zionism has sown the wind that will reap the storm," to be followed in November of that same year by an article which implied that a Jewish peril was threatening the whole world. And now in February 1934 Weizmann returned for the third time to the Italian capital to have another talk with the Duce.

Outwardly Mussolini still seemed favorably inclined towards the cause that was so dear to Weizmann. In the north, Hitler was more and more emerging as The European Dictator in the centre of the world stage, which for years had been the exclusive role of Mussolini. If the Duce could enlarge his own territory and thus inflate his name and fame, the power and the glory might yet be his once again. Moreover, he was actually afraid of the heavy German hand which might try to seize all land, all power, all peoples, and even perhaps a bit of Italy.* The conversation with Weizmann, therefore, was heavily on the pro-Zion side, and Mussolini even told his visitor that he "should create a Jewish state," and in order to help him accomplish this he "had already talked to the Arabs." The difficulty was, he said, "the question of the capital city," because the Arabs had told him that the Jews "should place it in Tel Aviv."

Weizmann's answer was prophetic. "If Jerusalem does not become the Jewish capital, then under no circumstances can it become an Arab capital—on account of the Christian world. To the Moslems the holiness of Jerusalem is a rather recent invention. To the Jews it is the city of David, and to the Christians it is the center of their holy places." When he asked the Duce whether they might count on his assistance "when they would be ready for practical arrangements," Mussolini wholeheartedly answered "Certainly."

To cement the relations between the prospective Jewish state and Italy, Weizmann now made Mussolini an offer which

*There is a Roman story about Hitler propounding his war strategy to Mussolini. "You Duce, you will attack from the south—I shall attack from the north—and where our armies meet, there will be our new frontier." "An excellent idea, *mein Führer*, but don't forget," said Mussolini with emphasis, "that Milano always has been and always will remain an Italian city!"

countered the latter's previous suggestion to have the Italians build the port of Haifa. Weizmann proposed nothing less than to arrange and organize Italy's chemical independence from Germany, so Rome "would no longer be a German vassal in this field." The Jewish statesman and eminent chemist even offered to put "a large group of scientists" at Mussolini's disposal, with one clear purpose: "to help Italy and hurt Germany." If need be, added Weizmann, he could even "find the necessary capital." Mussolini seemed highly impressed; he held the suggestion to be "really very important." The meeting ended with words of kindness on both sides. Weizmann said that he and his wife would appreciate having a signed photograph of the Duce; he then went on to advise the Italian dictator to take good care of himself because he was "looking very tired" and the world "would still need him." Mussolini fully agreed, and said that he "hoped to go on working for a long time yet. . . ."

Soon, however, there was, in the phrase of Nietzsche, one of Mussolini's favorite philosophers, another "transvaluation of values." It was a change that was immediately grasped by the Jewish fascists.

The incident that proved to be the turning-point was the arrest at the Swiss border in March 1934 of Sion Segre-Amar, a 20-year-old Italian Jew who lived in Turin and "commuted" between France, Switzerland, and northern Italy. On this occasion he had returned with a large quantity of anti-fascist propaganda leaflets which he tried to smuggle into Italy, hidden in the tires of his automobile. He was a collaborator of the Paris-published anti-fascist *Giustizia e Libertà;* and he and some seventy to eighty others (all suspected anti-fascists but including many totally innocent people) were speedily arrested in Turin. Among them was Carlo Levi, then better known as a painter than as an author. Levi had been writing for the Paris publication since its inception and was, moreover, chief organizer of the intellectual anti-fascist group in northern Italy. The fact that he was a Jew was of no importance in his opposition to Mussolini. With the Rosselli brothers, who were editing the paper in Paris, Carlo Levi had been against the régime from the beginning; it was a matter of general political and moral principle. Before long the police had freed most of the prisoners, (among whom had been whole families picked up *en masse*) till only fifteen principal suspects remained.

Carlo Levi, today living in Rome (and until early 1973 a Senator) recalls how they were kept strictly incommunicado; the only newspaper he was allowed to read was the *Gazzetto dello Sport* because it never printed any political news. One morning, however, Levi was greatly surprised to find an enormous article on the front page of the sports paper, dealing with the Segre-Amar arrest and its aftermath. None of the Catholics who were still in prison were mentioned, but the names of the eleven Jews among them were given great prominence. It was, according to the newspaper, a tremendous Jewish plot—a story which already had been published the day before as a violent anti-Semitic article in the Roman newspaper *Il Tevere*.

The continuing campaign was totally out of proportion to the rather minor event itself. Anti-fascists had been arrested all along, without their detention being made into a national affair. It dawned on Carlo Levi that in all likelihood the régime was preparing ways and means to make the arrest of the eleven Jews (the four Catholics who were also in jail were soon entirely forgotten by the press) into a case of how "the Jews" had tried to overthrow the government; it might be presented as an organized coup and might indeed be blown up into the Italian counterpart of the Nazi-instigated *Reichstag* fire of February 1933. The convenient incident (it did not even entail the loss of expensive real estate as had happened in Berlin) might in its very modesty serve the new fascist line. Certainly no Italian in his right mind, not even a fascist, would ever think of putting fire to a building in Rome that had the importance of the *Reichstag*. For the moment all that happened was the publication of a continuous stream of invective in the press. Propaganda feeds on exaggerations, and on occasional sadistical ironies: "Next year in Jerusalem, but this year in prison. . . ."

It was too much for the Jewish fascists. Their good name as fascists first, Italians second and perhaps Jews last, had been

seriously attacked and harmed. While it should have been obvious to them that the eleven Jews among the arrested men,
possibly their mirror-images on the other side, could easily
claim that they were anti-fascists first and then Italians, and
perhaps Jews last, it was exactly the fact that they *were* Jews
which made the crime seem greater. The four Catholics among
the culprits were no longer of any importance—they were just
Catholic Italians like all the others. And so, if the non-fascist
Jews did not understand, then they, the fascists, would secede
from their central religious organisation, the Hebrew Union. Ettore Ovazza, participant in the March on Rome, *squadrista* and
president of the Jewish community in Turin, seconded by Commander Jarach who held the same position in Milano, decided to
publish a strictly-fascist Jewish publication of their own,
patriotically called *La Nostra Bandiera*—"Our Flag"—so as to
offset the sinister influence of the regular Union publication
Israel. In its first issue Ovazza explained its aims. "We are
soldiers," he wrote, "and we are fascists who feel equal to all
other citizens." As to the creation of a Jewish homeland in
Palestine (playing into the hands of the English?) their minds
were made up: "The creation of a Jewish nation in Palestine is
an historical anachronism which must be combatted," because
"in no European country have the Jews a fatherland that is so
equal and open to all as in Italy."

If the press inflated the Swiss border incident into an anti-
Semitic row, Mussolini appeared to remain more realistic. He
knew there were anti-fascists and he knew there were Jews, and
he also knew that the two often mixed. But it was equally
known to him, as he had explained to Weizmann years before,
that not all Jews were Zionists, nor that all Jews were anti-
fascists. He defended his point of view strongly when, three
months after the northern-border incident, he met Hitler for the
first time at the magnificent Tiepolo-decorated villa at Stra
between Venice and Padua, and pointed out the danger of
wholesale anti-Semitism as increasingly practiced by Hitler. His
arguments only reinforced Hitler's idea that Mussolini "did not
understand anything about the Jewish problem." The Duce, on

the other hand, did not understand the Führer, as he would explain heatedly to his collaborators when the fruitless meeting was over. "That idiot!" he fumed. "Instead of discussing pressing problems, he never stopped talking about that totally unreadable book of his, *Mein Kampf!* That man just doesn't understand *anything!* . . . "

Suddenly—and here I am following Carlo Levi's interpretation, as he put it to me—Mussolini, as the result of his negative Hitler interview, seemed to have lost all interest in his anti-Jewish campaign to arouse the indignation of the Italian people. For without any obvious reason all imprisoned Jews, with the exception of Segre-Amar and Leone Ginzburg, were called before the government's Commission on Banishments, which apparently had been given instructions to end the affair. They were treated pleasantly *all'italiana* (Carlo Levi even was complimented on his projected participation at the Venice Biennale's painting exhibit, a plan that fell through after his arrest). Most of them were freed. Others were sent to out-of-the-way villages where they spent their time under light surveillance. And Carlo Levi was given a year of house-arrest, meaning that he was not allowed to leave town without permission. (One year later he was re-arrested and banished to a miserable village, which forced sojourn would result in the writing of his famous postwar best-selling book *Christ Stopped at Eboli*.)

Segre-Amar and Ginzburg were sentenced to two years in prison, the first because he was caught in the act at the border, the second because incriminating anti-fascist papers had been found at his home. (In 1943, during the violent anti-Semitic Roman upheaval, Ginzburg was again arrested and sent to the Regina Coeli prison, where he died of the inflicted torture.)

Soon after the liberation of the Turin prisoners Mussolini's indignation reached a climax in July 1934 when Chancellor Dollfuss was murdered in Vienna, which the Duce considered within his sphere of influence. He gave vent to his anti-German indignation in an article he wrote for the *Popolo d'Italia* in August: "Science does not guarantee the purity of anyone's blood. The new civilizers in Germany may well have unknown relatives within the walls of Tel Aviv. Even if *Kultur* says no, the *Cultura* says yes. . . ."

His words were full of scorn, sarcasm, and bitterness when in September he spoke from a platform near the Palestine pavillion at the Bari Trade Fair. "Thirty centuries of history," he said, "allow us to consider with supreme pity the doctrines from across the Alps, which are being kept alive by progenies of the human race who did not even know how to write at a time when Rome already had Caesar, Augustus, and Virgil. . . ."

Mussolini met Nahum Goldmann, the president of the Executive Council of the Jewish Congress, who came to see him in the company of Roman Chief Rabbi Sacerdoti in November of that same year, and his feelings—or at least his promises—were still pro-Jewish. He told Goldmann that he would "force Germany to allow the Jews living in the German-occupied Saar to leave with their money," adding that he was "a friend of the Jews."

On the Americans, whom Mussolini half-respected, he had a biting comment when Goldmann informed him that "for the moment" he had been able to keep Americans, Jews and non-Jews alike, from demonstrating too openly against the recent anti-Jewish measures in Austria. According to the Duce, Americans "were always ready to protest and get mixed up in European affairs about which they did not understand a thing," carefully refraining from mentioning that he himself had advised Dollfuss "to add a slight touch of anti-Semitism" to his régime.

When Hitler came up in the conversation, Mussolini made some of his harshest remarks on the man he had met for the first time five months before. "He is an imbecile and a fanatical good-for-nothing," he fulminated. "To listen to him is sheer torture. Hitler is just a joke, who will only last for a few years." He advised Goldmann "not to fear him" because by the time "not a trace of Hitler will be left, the Jews still will be a great people." He added that he and the Jews "would bury Hitler together," and repeated the statement he had already made to Weizmann that "the Jews should create a Jewish state."

Elaborating on this, he surprised Goldmann with an astonishing affirmation: "I am a Zionist. You must have a real country and not that ridiculous National Home which the British offer you. I'll help you create a Jewish state. The most important thing is that the Jews have confidence in their future and that they not be afraid of that imbecile in Berlin. . . ."

According to the Jewish fascists this future lay clearly in a purely fascist Judaism, to which all those Jews would belong who were for Italy and its official political doctrine first. They should be nationalistic Jews with their eyes clearly fixed on Rome as its center, separated from any other nationalistic—that is, Zionist—aims. Its slogan should be *For Duce and Fatherland*. This was a hard pill to swallow for the great majority of Jews who felt themselves as Italian as anyone born under the sky of the Appenine Peninsula, be they Jewish or Catholic, but who could not go along with the extremist views of the Ovazza group.

Early in 1935 the objective of the dissidents was put down in *La Nostra Bandiera*. Their ideal was "to guide Judaism along tracks of clarity and Italianism" without following "Jewish internationalism." Zionism, which in Italy was blown up into an affair that seemed to decide the life or death of domestic political policy, should be considered "only from a philanthropic point of view."

Later on General Guido Liuzzi would explain more in detail what "the Jewish duty" would be "in a fascist Italy." It was "to have a Jewish soul that was not only Italian in the past, but that was also profoundly and securely fascist in the future."

Soon Mussolini would not only put the Jews to the test, but all other Italians as well. The war against Ethiopia prompted an international cry of indignation, and when the Duce had widened—as he thought—his historic frontiers forever, not only the churches but also the synagogues offered prayers of thanks, hailing the victory. The Duce's glorification of "fascist deeds" was then followed by a patriotic and clearly desperate appeal to deliver gold, wedding rings, and precious-metalled trinkets to the national coffers. The Rome synagogue, not wanting to be branded as anti-fascist and unpatriotic, delivered the golden key to the Ark and a large silver candlestick as its share in the national fundraising. If not all Jewish wedding rings were handed over, the community "as a whole"—that is, the synagogue—had upheld patriotism.

More patriotism was expected from the Jews when Mussolini thought that "international Judaism" had an important hand in the proclaiming of sanctions against Italy, as voted by the League of Nations. If international Jewry were indeed as powerful as Herr Hitler claimed, then surely the Jews would be able to stop the sanctions. So the Duce asked two of his most prominent Jewish countrymen to set out for England to see what they could accomplish. To London went Dante Lattes, one of the strongest proponents of Zionism in the country, accompanied by the poet Angiolo Orvieto. They talked to several important British Jews and non-Jews, including Weizmann, Lord Montefiore, a niece of Balfour, Italian ambassador Grandi, and—of course—a correspondent of the London *Times*. Quite naturally they returned home empty-handed, because the Duce's ideas about how the Jews could pull the strings of international diplomacy only existed in the mind of the leader of all the Germans.

Mussolini also kept an eye on events in the United States, wondering—and perhaps fearing—what the reaction of American Jewry might be. Speaking to a group of students from across the Atlantic late in 1935, he gave them a message which he hoped would tranquilize the heated feelings of the millions of Jews in America. Once again he tried to pacify the apprehensions of those who saw nothing but anti-Semitism in fascism. His régime did not want the Italian Jews "to renounce their religious traditions," he told the students. It only desired that "the Jews recognize the national ideal," and he reconfirmed that "a Jewish question does not exist in Italy" (or "I, at least, do not know of one").

Mussolini probably meant that officially he, the Duce, did not promote anti-Semitism, although he should have been aware that among his followers by now a small but vociferous group existed that aped Hitler and Streicher in their anti-Jewish feelings and statements. In his own family, of course, there certainly was one among his children who had not yet forgotten that summer-romance at Riccione seven years previously. When Edda Ciano-Mussolini visited Hitler in 1936, the Duce's "tall, very slender, and highly-elegant daughter" was not afraid to tell Hitler, when the Jewish question was brought up, that he "certainly could not punish anyone because his grandmother was Jewish," and "with passion she would defend a more human treatment of the Jews."*

If Edda in her own personal way protested against Hitler's extremism, Mussolini's feelings towards the Jews, or certainly towards their aims in Palestine, underwent a sudden change in the spring of 1937. He sallied forth to North Africa to make a remarkable speech on the Piazza Castello in Tripoli, then still an Italian colony. He broke all ties with Zionism in asserting that "fascist Italy assures the Moslems of its respect for the laws of the Prophet," and that "it wants to express its sympathy for the Mohametans of the whole world." And he added that the sword he had been given by the Arabs on that occasion would always be "among the most cherished souvenirs of his life," omitting to say that this very same sword had been made especially for him at his own party's orders by a theatrical costumer in Florence. Having thus proclaimed himself the greater protector of Islam, Mussolini could hardly continue to promise Weizmann, Goldmann, and the other leaders of Zionism that he would assist them in the establishment of a Jewish homeland.

At this time another ominous note crept into Italian politics—that of the purity of "Race." While emigration of Italians to Ethiopia and Tripoli was encouraged, the settlers and occupying soldiers were forbidden to mingle (sexually) with the attractive bronzed beauties of the area. Race-consciousness was not yet directed towards a hands-off policy with the Jews, but a racist start had been made.

The Pope, too, became concerned with the race problem. On

*According to Paul Schmidt, Hitler's interpreter, in his memoirs, *"Statist auf diplomatischer Bühne"* (Ullstein, 1950).

March 3 Pius XI published his *Mit Brennender Sorge* encyclical, in which he explained his "burning anxiety" about what was happening in Germany (specifically about what was happening to the Catholic Church, which was being combatted by the Nazis). It was, therefore, principally a pro-Catholic encyclical, which obviously was the Pope's good right and even his duty; but into it was read a great many of anti-Nazi, anti-fascist, and even some pro-Jewish implications.

The anti-Jewish storm was raging fiercely north of the Brenner Pass, and in Italy there were more signs of intolerance from journalists and editors, all of whom felt they had to support the government. Only the *Nuova Antologia* of 1 April 1937 put in a good word for the Jews, writing that "in Italy a Jewish problem cannot exist," because "our nation is too strong and too close-knit, and because moreover the Italian Jews represent one of the most homogeneous and most select groups of Judaism in general. . . . "

It was a lonely flower in the artificial fascist anti-Jewish wilderness. Insignificant weeds, nurtured by imported Nazi manure, were seeking to uproot the solid trees of religious compatibility among the Italian people.

Chapter 31
The Anti-Semitic Campaign

It was Paolo Orano, president of the University of Perugia, and in his younger days—at least judging from his writings—sympathetically inclined towards the Jews, who would cause the thunderclap that opened up the anti-Semitic deluge. His book *Gli Ebrei in Italia (The Jews in Italy)*, even though it did not have any direct influence on the larger mass of the people, became the standard work from which the Italian proto-Nazis would quote copiously, endlessly, and with increasing malice. According to Orano, "the Jews had no religion, because they lack the means to communicate with God . . . who refuses them because they refused Him." In other words, the Jews had no reason to exist as Jews any longer, and therefore they were not good Italians, for "the good fascist swears to serve exclusively the cause of the elected nation, which is the Italian one."

Orano warned the Italian Jews "to have a clear idea of this" and asked for "an act of condemnation" against the construction of "another Malta and another Gibraltar in front of the

Dodecanese Islands" (meaning Rhodes and the other Greek islands belonging to the group which had become Italian after the Italo-Turkish war of 1912). It was Orano's opinion that "Zionist activities should be considered as complicity with the enemy, because in Italy there are only Italians." Jews should become *real* Italians, not only Italians in nationality; they should be Italians of the purest Jewish-fascist feeling. "The hour has come," Orano threatened. "Rome, the Empire, Dante, and Caesar must be the same to all Italians. There is no room for any other myth in the Italy of the Blackshirts."

It has been suggested that Mussolini himself might have instigated the writing of the book. This, in my view, seems rather implausible; its writing would have had to go back to a period when Mussolini, at least outwardly, was not yet wholly anti-Jewish. But whatever the inspiration, the effect was sensational. The Italian Jews now were the official parents of Zionism and in that capacity they had caused—so claimed the controlled press—the anti-Italian development in the aftermath of the Ethiopian adventure, as well as the continuing British presence in the Eastern Mediterranean; the Jews would have to go, or at least would have to cease existing as Jews. The word was out. The Italian anti-Semites, who until now had been nothing but a deplorable little group that had howled a lot but had hardly gotten anywhere among the religiously tolerant masses, jumped at the opportunity that was offered to them. Within a short time a whole series of scurrilous publications flooded the market (and would continue to do so till the bitter end) giving the outside world the impression that Italy was anti-Semitic, while making the Italian Jews fear the worst. Yet nothing could have been farther from the truth. The people evidently continued to consider their fellow Italians as one and the same, whether Catholic or Jewish. But with money by now flowing freely from Goebbels' and Streicher's coffers in Germany, a certain number of Italians soon would outdo the Nazis in vilification.

"It is a question of the 'Italianity' of the Jews," wrote G. Natti Dubois. He conveniently forgot about the Saracens, the Arabs, the Spaniards, the Greek, and a half-dozen other races and tribes from elsewhere who had criss-crossed Italy through the ages, all of whom had left behind the traces of their origin. Which, as Mussolini once remarked of the Germans and Tel Aviv, made a good many Italians have "unknown relatives within the walls" of Athens, Alexandria, Tripoli, Malaga, Vienna, and Avignon—a mixture which, as in other countries, only had enriched the race.

Someone writing under the name of Abramo Levi, apparently a Jewish fascist, answered Orano with *Noi Ebrei* ("We Jews"). "A Zionist problem does not exist in Italy," he wrote, because there were "only Italians of the Hebrew religion" in the country, "one per thousand, who are thankful to the fascist régime for the free profession of their religion." The author said that there had to be "a precise question in the mind and conscience of the Jews: Do they consider themselves simply Jews in Italy, or Italian Jews?"

A certain Alfredo Romanini (the *Honorable* Alfredo Romanini, for the gentleman was a member of the fascist Italian parliament) wrote one of the most deplorable books ever, a clear echo of the anti-Semitic argument so viciously expounded by Streicher. Telesio Interlandi, editor of the daily *Il Tevere* and of two equally vitriolic weeklies, who at the time of the Segre arrest already had been walking the anti-Jewish beat, followed with *Contra Judaeos*. He stated precisely what he was after—"the indispensable and definitive separation of the Jewish element from our lives." He quickly made himself a laughing stock with his own presentation—only it was no laughing matter to the Jews—of the Jewish preponderance in Italian life; he stated that among the six thousand Italians mentioned in the *Piccolo Dizionario dei Contemporanei Italiani*, a sort of Italian "Who's Who," "there were one hundred-and-twenty-five Jews." Clearly a danger to society! He contradicted himself again when he proclaimed that "Italian racism needs to be brought directly to the attention of the people." Was he conceding that the people did not have an inkling of what the anti-Semites were after—that they had first to be taught? To prove his point, Interlandi then proclaimed in capital letters that THE JEWS DO NOT BELONG TO THE ITALIAN RACE, and "their intrusion into the pure Italian race is inadmissible and unbearable." Here was a man with a frightening (and frightened) inferiority complex, an undistinguished author and plagiarist of German racism, who wanted a final solution so that "the Jews among us will longer laugh at us."*

Roberto Farinacci, secretary of the Fascist Party, who would become Italy's official Jew-baiter, added his own bit to the growing literature with his degrading epic "The Church and the Jews." He discovered the real reason for fascist anti-Semitism, and for once the rabble-rouser seemed to have a point. He reasoned that the Church "till a few months ago had declared the Jewish religion to be profoundly corrupt, confirming that Judaism was out to dominate the world." The Jesuits especially, Farinacci wrote, had made it a rule that "it is absolutely forbidden to receive within its ranks anyone who descends from the Jewish race up to the fifth generation, which makes the Aryan racism of the Jesuits far more strict than that of Germany, where they only go back to the fourth generation. . . . " Continuing with variations on this theme, Farinacci came to this conclusion: "We cannot, in the course of a few weeks, renounce the anti-Semitic conscience that has been formed by the Church through thousands of years." He ended with the simple statement that "fascism obeys the lessons of history," by which he meant the anti-Semitic history as it had been shaped for centuries by the Vatican.

The worst book published during these years—in 1938—was undoubtedly *Ecco Il Diavolo (This Is The Devil)* by Piero Pellicano. He dedicated his opus to Giovanni Preziosi, who much later would become the head of the "Racial Office." Preziosi had been a prominent anti-Semite ever since the end of the First World War, when he announced that "Lloyd George is

---

*It prompted one Italian cynic who had read the book during the heyday of fascist racism at the Rome Public Library (I subsequently borrowed it) to scribble on the last page: "The true Aryan, *caro* Interlandi, must be as blond as Hitler, as tall as Goebbels, as slender as Goering, and his name must be Rosenberg."

of Jewish descent, Wilson is in the hands of the Jews, and Clemenceau is tied to a whole group of Jews. . . . " With news like that, Preziosi was on his way to outscooping the field. In 1934 Preziosi himself had to confess that anti-Semitic feeling was unknown in Italy, for "if by anti-Semitism we must understand the aversion against the Jews simply because they are Jews, then in Italy there never has been and there never will be anti-Semitism." It was certainly in great part due to Preziosi's own slanders that four years later Italian official (*i.e.,* governmental) anti-Semitism had reached a new malodorous level, and the dedication of Pellicano's book to Preziosi was entirely deserved. The two were in excellent company.

If the subsequent events in Italy had not taken such a tragic turn, then in retrospect the Pellicano book might be considered amusing, full of odd "boners." ("The Jews have no military spirit.") As Pellicano saw it, the Jews had caused the downfall of Italy, because "the Roman hierarchy had permitted the infiltration of the Jews and allowed them their subversive work." It was clear to Pellicano, as the Germans had already claimed, that "Roosevelt was a Jew, and among the British and the Czechs such figures as Anthony Eden and Benes." (His aphorism had a Third Reich copyright: "Where there is a Jew, there is a Jewish problem.")

In the face of this thickening, sickening stream of poison-pen literature, the non-fascist Jews could not help seeing the handwriting on the wall. Only a very few years had passed since similar accusations had been hurled at their co-religionists in Germany, whose misfortunes since then were running the gamut from the desperate to the tragic. The principal rabbis of the country met in Florence, where it was decided to compose a manifesto addressed to all Jews in Italy. Carefully worded in order not to offend the authorities, it essentially tried to encourage those Jews whose affiliations with the synagogue had deteriorated until they were attached to Jewish life with only a slender thread, to return to more active Judaism. "Everyone knows," the message read, "that the Jews of today are the children of the Jews of the Ghetto, who in turn were the

children of those who were dispersed after the destruction of the
Temple." As Jews, the rabbis wrote, they had nothing to fear
from themselves, because their "conscience was clear—so why
should we doubt?" Then they came quietly to the point. "Recent and even not-so-recent history teaches us that in some
countries there is an excess of anti-Semitic fervor. The cry *'Kill
Them!'* is resounding in too many places. The persecuted Jews
are human beings, but they are also part of us, they *are* us. They
are not against anyone, they only want peace." They concluded
in the prescribed style, asking God to hear their prayers "for the
prosperity of Italy, to help, defend, and protect Victor Emmanuel III, King and Emperor and his August Family, and
Benito Mussolini, Duce and Founder of the Empire." They all
signed—first the four chief rabbis of Rome, Milano, Livorno,
and Venice, and then the other twenty-six rabbis in alphabetical
order, ending with a strangely unbalanced man who then was
still called Israele Zolli, Chief Rabbi of Trieste.

Actually the contagion of the various anti-Semitic tomes did
not touch the public till the fascist press decided to carry the
virus further. And even then that public remained remarkably
immune. It became a journalistic battle of words which the
Italians with their basic common sense shrugged off as yet
another rhetorical exercise in political bravura. The man in the
street could not care less about who was a Jew and who was not.
But the Jews themselves, of course, were ultra-sensitive, and
well they might be. Some climbed on to the bandwagon to join
the fascists in earnest, defending the "pure pro-Italian" line of
thinking as prescribed by a handful of party hooligans; or they
wrote quiet manifestoes and hoped for the best while fearing the
worst.

The *Popolo d'Italia* early in June wrote that "no one wants to
subject the Jews to an inquisition. There has only been a
warning, especially to the leaders, that Zionism does not
rhyme with Fascism."

It was perfectly natural that the Jewish members of the party
could not sit still and let the rabbis rather timidly go to work. In
fact, they had anticipated the rabbis' action and had already

assembled some time earlier, also in Florence, to discuss certain "Jewish-fascist difficulties." At the end of their meeting on 30 May 1937, they published a memorandum; and again it was the *Popolo d'Italia*, the mouthpiece of fascism, which (on June 5) printed this *non mea culpa* declaration of the *camerati* or fascist comrades. Having read the Orano book, they said, and having constituted "the Committee of Italians of the Jewish religion in Rome on January 24, 1937," which they indicated by the fascist year XV, they declared themselves "strictly the enemies of whatever international Jewish or non-Jewish organisation that is masonic, subversive and, above all, anti-fascist."

The Milano newspaper *Corriere della Sera*, on the 3rd of June, had already written that it was "not a racial problem." Its editors even "denied that such a problem can be mentioned or discussed," concluding with the request to "the believers in Mosaic law" that they "consider themselves Jewish Italians and not Italian Jews." The next day the *Gazzetta del Popolo* followed suit, declaring that in view of "the menacing attitude of international Judaism, vigilance is needed."

The more the press discussed the subject which had been put so bluntly by Orano, the more the Jewish fascists tried to justify themselves. Especially the *Popolo d'Italia* opened its columns to all those who were out to get their names cleared from the dangerous taint of anti-Mussolinianism. Letters poured in from all over the country—three lines, four lines, ten lines. It was a case of *everybody is wrong but me.* Ettore Ovazza set the tone. He agreed with Orano. He was against any and all British "military ports, oil ports, and other colonialism" in the Middle East, against "protection of the Suez canal," against Zionism which created "a tower of Babel" in Palestine. He insisted that all this should "interest Italians of the Jewish religion only as an historical fact, in order to fight it."

The conformist hysteria went so far that the magazine *Israel* felt it needed to put the record straight. It took upon itself the defense of "a Jewish religion, which in order to exist would have to identify itself with Christianity, and would have to dis-avow itself." And they wondered why "the Jews must be con-

demned as a massed unit for two thousand years," because "the
religion of the Bible is [considered] a poor abortion, or as
Orano describes it 'an arrested development'."

The fear was so contagious it could be detected as far away as
the United States. Generoso Pope, editor of the largest
American Italian-language newspaper, made a trip to Rome to
establish the truth. Again Mussolini found the right words,
albeit that they were not quite honest words. "We authorize you
to declare and to communicate to the Jews of America that their
preoccupation with their brothers in Italy has no valid reason
whatever, but is simply the result of unscrupulous information.
We authorize you to specify that the Italian Jews have received
in the past, receive today, and will receive in the future the same
kind of treatment as is reserved for every other Italian citizen,
that there is not a single thought of racial or religious discrimination in my mind, and that I shall remain true to my
policy of equality as prescribed by law, and also shall remain
true to the freedom of religion. . . . " It could not be said more
clearly. Yet surely Mussolini knew that he was no longer telling
the truth.

Ciano (by now Mussolini's foreign minister, after having
headed the press and information office for several years) confided the Duce's real thoughts to his diary. On 6 September
1937, he wrote that Mussolini had been "raging against
America, country of negroes and Jews. He wants to write a book
entitled *Europe 2000*. The races that will then play an important part will be the Italians, Germans, Russians, and Japanese.
The other nations will be destroyed by the acid of Jewish corruption." Three months later he would add that in Italy an anti-
Semitic problem "does not exist," this being his own opinion
and not Mussolini's. "There are only a few of them, and with a
single exception all good. Again: the problem does not exist
here." After which Ciano finished his entry for that day on the
sardonic note that "maybe a small number of Jews are necessary
to society, as yeast is necessary to bread."

The Church went along with the new wave, or at least that
part of the Church which through the centuries, with or

without the Vatican's cooperation, had been its anti-Semitic whip. On 19 June 1937 the *Civiltà Cattolica* wrote that "even when the Zionist state is a reality, there will still be several million sons of Israel throughout the world, who will not be very different from what they are today: speculators who soak up gold, Messianics and revolutionaries." It then went on to say that "the tragic aspect of the Jewish question is that Israel everlastingly tries to assimilate itself" but never succeeds. The question was "insoluble and therefore it was useless to try and find a solution." Yet a kind of solution there was, the same solution the Jesuits had been after for centuries, using forced sermons, forced baptism, the myth of ritual murder, and burning at the stake as its weapons. By 1937 the methods might have changed, but the aim was still the same. "There is one hope left to the Christians," wrote the authoritative *Civiltà Cattolica*, "the conversion of Israel. That would be the final solution."

For once the Vatican apparently did not agree. Two weeks later the same publication had another unsigned article which began, "Every type of anti-Semitism is condemned by the Church." Was this the true word from on high?

Ettore Ovazza did not give up, and he too sat down to write a book, called *"The Jewish Problem—An Answer to Paolo Orano."* Ovazza thought it only right to sum up his qualifications, and these he outlined as "Captain of Artillery, Centurion of the Fascist Militia, *Croix de Guerre*, Fascist since 1920, decorated for the March on Rome." And so, he added with aplomb, "that is why I believe with complete serenity that I can shed some light on the tormented Jewish question. . . . " In an effort to glorify Mussolini, Ovazza argued that "the fascist laws have accorded the widest possible religious freedom." He was certain that the Jews of Italy would "always be among the first to follow the orders of the Great Chief, for the glory of the King Emperor, and for the Future of our Fascist Fatherland." For "we believe in Mussolini," he wrote, "the Author and Creator of the fascist rebirth and of the imperial Italian resurrection."

That was the year XV of the Fascist Revolution, in which (according to Ovazza) fascism was "opposed to religious violence." Six years later—on 9 October 1943—Ovazza, his wife and his 15-year-old daughter, sought refuge in the end-of-the-road Italian Alpine village of Gressoney-Saint-Jean, 60 miles north of Torino near the Swiss border. They were captured by Mussolini's friends—the Germans. Within 48 hours all three of them were shot, and their apparently not yet dead bodies were burned in the boiler room of the building's central heating system.

Chapter 32
The Scientists' Manifesto

Did Mussolini ever take the time to look into the results of his constantly vacillating statements on anti-Semitism? The press responded to his cues. It would have been simple enough to put a stop to the excesses of an official newspaper campaign; but nothing of the sort happened. It was no longer a matter of the left hand not knowing what the right hand was doing; because if anything ever was done openly, then it certainly was the anti-Semitic campaign led by the intellectual *Lumpenproletariat* of the party. It was as if the firemen, quietly playing cards while the house was going up in flames, were constantly reassuring the owner of the villa that in reality they were not playing games, but were doing their duty.

To calm the spirits, not only abroad but also at home where the flames were beginning to appear dangerous, Mussolini had a statement published in February 1938 declaring it "totally false" that the Italian government was "starting an anti-Semitic policy." If such an impression were given credence abroad, then

it only could have been created "by anti-fascist currents" which
were "entirely organized by Jewish elements." Even though he
had become anti-Zionist, Mussolini still tried to play a role as
the protector of the Jews. It was now his opinion that "the
Jewish question can be solved in one way only—by the creation
somewhere in the world, but not in Palestine, of a Jewish state
which can represent and protect through normal diplomatic
channels all the Jewish masses now dispersed in various countries."

Let the Jews be good fascists, and nothing would happen, for
"the fascist government [the official statement continued] has
never thought, nor does it think today of proclaiming political,
economic, or moral measures against the Jews. . . . and the laws
that regulate the lives of the Jewish community will remain un-
changed." It was ridiculous to talk about "a Jewish problem"
for, after all, "elsewhere Jews are counted in millions, whereas
here in Italy, on a total population of close to 44 million people,
the number of Jews is something between fifty and sixty
thousand" (including the Jews in the colonies). Only the last
phrase of the communiqué hinted at the possibility of some un-
pleasantry. The government "will watch . . . that the part
played in the national life of the country will not be dispropor-
tionate to the numerical importance of the community."

But this was Italy, and words did not mean much to those
who did not want to hear them (or even to those who *did* hear
them) and so much oratory had been disseminated by fascists
since 1922 which was devoid of practical meaning. The Italian
language is magniloquently full of words, and it was a national
pastime (as G. A. Borghese once argued in his *Goliath*) to string
them metrically together. If someone shouted "We Are
Strong!," then all right, then we may well be strong; and if
someone shouted *"Noi tireremo diritto"* (which can best be
translated as "We'll stop at nothing!") then good—we'll
probably stop at practically nothing. The people were perfectly
willing to accept the party slogan and to "Believe, Obey, and
Win"—on condition that they would not lose. And how could
action possibly suit the words in a real and complex situation

where some of the Jews had been among the best and first supporters of the Duce, where two Jews, Lieutenant-Generals Ettore Ascoli and Guido Liuzzi were in charge of the *Scuola di Guerra* (War College), where another Jew, Angelo Modena, held an equally high rank, where General Umberto Pugliese was in charge of all naval construction (with the title of Inspector-General of the Naval Engineer Corps), where Aldo Ascoli, Paolo Maroni, Renato Senigallia and Walter Hirsch were Rear-Admirals, where Guido Segre was Inspector-General of Naval Ordnance—Jews all—and where other Jews were in leading positions in so many fields? What—as Pirandello might have asked—was real, and who was absurd?

According to Ciano (and he had the word directly from the Master), Mussolini thought the February statement "a masterpiece of anti-Semitic propaganda." The Jews sensed the heat. The "Hebrew Union" and the secessionists had gotten together again; the pro-fascist Naval Commander Federico Jarach was now president of the original organisation. In May one of the principal figures in the reunified Union, Aldo Ascoli, a prominent Jewish lawyer, had an interview with Mario Montecchi, who was director of the Department of Culture at the Ministry of the Interior. Everything would be fine, Montecchi said soothingly, if only the Jews would accept "a national Hebraism" that would operate "within the terms of the law"; these had also been Mussolini's words. Montecchi added that if "the Jews would observe all the rules of the fascist government, they could live tranquilly. . . ."

That was an unimpeachable formulation, according to Mussolini. Yet, once again, his own actions belied his words. When the director of the Department of Health of Albania invited a Jewish professor, Maurizio Ascoli, to lecture on malaria in the capital city of Tirana, Mussolini penciled a footnote on the letter of request: "Pick a Christian from among the 44 million of them." This was wise counsel, thought the Jesuits, for was not (as they had written in *Civiltà Cattolica* in April) "the Jewish religion deeply corrupted as the religion of a deceiving messianism"?

Hitler, since March 1938 master of the so-called Austrian *Ostmark*, could look down from his eagle's nest at Berchtesgaden and watch how his recalcitrant former teacher and now pupil was doing. He was pleased with what the Jesuits said, but became rather impatient with the Duce's personal aberrations, the more so when on the second of July he elevated Brigadier-General Levi (a "pure Jew") to major-general. Another promotion was made in the case of Lieutenant-Colonel Giorgio Liuzzi (son of Lieutenant-General Guido Liuzzi) who was advanced to full colonel for reasons of "exceptional merit." It was brought to the attention of Mussolini that the younger Liuzzi—who would be named Chief of Staff in 1954—was, like his father, a Jew. The Duce inquired about his past military record, and was informed that Liuzzi had been a brilliant officer, who had seen serious active service during the First World War, had been three times decorated for *valore militare*, and that he had been twice seriously wounded. "*Promoted*," ran Mussolini's orders.

In retrospect it is far easier to see why some intelligent Jews supported the fascist movement (especially the military men who had started their careers way back when the evil tendencies of fascism were still hidden, and who, like the Liuzzis, never had become members of the party) than to analyse what went on in Mussolini's mind. Clearly he did certain things which seemed to value a Jew for what he was and contributed. Was this perhaps only a bandage on the wound so as not to see the deep incision he was inflicting underneath? He knew all the time that, at his own orders, a special university committee, supposedly composed of nothing but first-class Italian scientists, were actively discussing the wording of a governmental declaration on "*Race*"—this time not against the Ethiopians, but against the Jews. Eleven days after General Levi had been so blithely promoted, and just about the time when Liuzzi, the future top military man of Italy, had become a full colonel, Mussolini confided to his son-in-law that "an article would be published in the *Giornale d'Italia* dealing with a statement on the racial question." According to Mussolini it would look "as if it were written by a group of scientists, but in reality it was written entirely by him personally. . . ."

On the 14th of July 1938 the "Manifesto of the Racial Scientists" was there to open the Italian Jews' eyes wide, fascist and non-fascist eyes alike.

"Races exist," proclaimed Article Number One of the manifesto. But "there are great and little races." The concept of race "is purely biological" and, to be sure, "present-day Italy is of Aryan origin and its population is Aryan." The 44 million inhabitants of the country were "descendants of families who lived in Italy over a thousand years," which obviously meant that there was "a pure Italian race." This, in turn, made it imperative for the Italians "to proclaim themselves openly racists, as has been frequently propounded by the Duce in his speeches."

The most extraordinary statement came in Article Number Seven, where the "scientists" outdid themselves. "The conception of Racism in Italy must be essentially Italian of the Aryan-Nordic type." So could astonished Italians read on that fourteenth of July. Did this mean that "the theories of German racism" would be introduced in Italy? Far from it. It only meant that the scientists (and not only my translation is tortuous) wanted "to present to the Italians the physical and above all psychological example of the human race, which in its purely European characteristics were entirely separated from all non-European races, and which would elevate the Italian to an ideal specimen with superior knowledge of himself, and also to greater responsibility. . . ." The scientists must have worked with Teutonic diligence to get those phrases on paper. What could a peasant of the underdeveloped Italian south have made of such intricate verbosity from the north?

Then it came. "The Jews do not belong to the Italian race." The learned men of Mussolini's working committee had decided that "of all the Semites who through the centuries have set foot on the sacred soil of the Fatherland, no traces now remain. Not even the Arab invasion of Sicily has left more than a name here and there. The Jews represent the only population-group who never have been assimilated, because it is composed of non-European racial elements, different in every possible way from the elements that shaped the Italians. . . ."

Stupefaction struck the nation. The Jews were aghast, and non-Jews were speechless. The statements sounded totally incomprehensible, so incomprehensible indeed that Mussolini on the following day decided to have the secretary of the party, Farinacci, call the celebrated group of scientists together so as to explain in simple terms that all they really had wanted to say was *"discrimination—not persecution."* In the meantime the Jews tried to put aside political differences, wondering what it all meant; for till now there had only been statements, but what would action entail?

While the Jews wondered, the Pope made up his mind. His encyclical of 1937 on Germany had not been followed by deeds. Now that he saw a similar movement develop in his own country, Pius XI decided that it was time for the head of the Catholic Church to make a stand, openly and unequivocally. He had signed the Concordat in 1929; Mussolini, if he disliked what he said, could take away whatever liberties the agreement had brought him. In the face of the cruel intentions only too clearly visible before his eyes, the Pope believed that he had the moral obligation to disregard all possible consequences to himself, to his subjects, or even to the Jews who were not his subjects, but who were fellow human beings made in the image of God. A Pope, in brief, had to have courage, and Pius XI would show that he was fully up to the task which he had shouldered.

The Pope waited two weeks before he spoke his mind. The occasion was a meeting with the theological students of the College of the *Propaganda Fide*. It was held in private but was duly reported on July 30—obviously on the Pope's own instructions—in the Vatican newspaper, the *Osservatore Romano*. Pius XI said that he was "against the erection of barriers between men and men." He punctuated his speech by wondering pointedly "why, *disgraziatemente*, Italy had felt the necessity to imitate Germany!" The result of the Pope's words was that a furious fascist mob burned the *Osservatore Romano* in the streets of Rome.

Mussolini happened to be in Forlì in order to make one of his big speeches to a group of *avanguardisti*, when he was informed about the Pope's statement. His fury was boundless, and it was reflected in his words. Repeating one of his favorite phrases about "stopping at nothing," he said that his "listeners should know, and everybody should know, that also on the subject of race we'll stop at nothing!" Evidently his pride was especially wounded because the Pope had said that he had not been "original" but had been following the example of Hitler; and he exclaimed angrily that "to say that fascism is imitating anyone or anything is absurd!"

Galeazzo Ciano also went into action as soon as he had heard about the Pope's words; and his reaction was perhaps even more bitter than his father-in-law's. He asked the Papal Nuncio to come and see him immediately; and, as always, he took to his pen to record a diary item for posterity. "If the Vatican continues this way," he wrote, "the shock [for the Duce] will be inevitable, because Mussolini considers the racial problem as fundamental." After having spoken to the Apostolic Nuncio [Monsignore Borgoncini-Duca], he noted that "he (the Nuncio) seemed fairly convinced." The final phrase in Ciano's entry was tragically revealing: an eye-opener, for it disclosed one kind of tendency that prevailed in certain circles of the Vatican. As Ciano wrote: "I want to add that he personally revealed himself as very anti-Semitic." This was the man who had to inform the Pope about what was happening within the government offices of the Kingdom of Italy.

Within a week, on August 5, Mussolini would try to blur the issues. He had been for and against, hot and cold. Could anybody, Jew or Gentile, know where he stood? The repetitive formula was that "to discriminate is not to persecute." As far as Mussolini was concerned, all he wanted was to bring about a fine and clear-cut balance between Jews and Italians—for after all, the Jews were hardly considered as such any longer. "Let this be understood by the too many Jews in Italy and abroad who send useless lamentations up to heaven, creating a senseless state of panic." He reiterated that there were "only 44,000 Jews in metropolitan Italy, one in a thousand inhabitants." Consequently, as Mussolini wrote in the *Popolo d'Italia* (which usually published this kind of dictatorial message), "there can be no doubt that the climate is ripe for racism." The mask was finally completely off, and the Jews saw the trend—without knowing the fearsome details. It had been a cat-and-mouse game, played with agonizingly slow movements on the part of the cat.

If the government had "no intention to persecute the Jews," it did all it could to excite the population into a contest of a thousand against one. It was not a battle against some foreign enemy. It was against Italian nationals who had no weapons. They certainly did not want to overthrow the government, nor did they have any other "sinister" plans—with the exception of the small but vigorous group of Jewish anti-fascists, and these were part of the far-larger group of Catholic Italians who held the same convictions.

Notwithstanding the violent fascist reaction against his speech of July 29, the Pope spoke up once more. Once again the statement was made to the students at the *Propaganda Fide*, this time on August 21. His words were far more biting than three weeks previously. "Guard yourselves above all against exaggerated nationalism," the Pope stated. "There is room for a just, moderate, temperate nationalism, associated to all virtues. But keep away from exaggerated nationalism as you would keep away from a malediction, for it invokes the curse of divisionism, of conflict, which entails the dangers of war. . . ."

The Duce's reaction was swift. He was in Rome and he called Father Tacchi-Venturi, his Jesuit confidant, sometime advisor and personal intermediary with the Vatican, and told him—as reported by Ciano—that "contrary to what they think [at the Vatican], I am a patient man. But don't let them make me lose my temper, or I'll scratch the crust off the Italians: in no time they'll be anti-clerical. . . ." Having taken on the Jews, the Duce felt himself ready to take on the Vatican as well. Yet he could not intimidate Pope Pius XI, and one can only wonder how the Italian and the international crisis might have developed if this courageous Pope in 1938 had been younger than his eighty-one years, and would have been able to live through the 1940s.

The Duce appeared to be set to carry out his accumulated threats. His dependence on Germany and his personal ties with Hitler had been tightened ever since the signing of the Axis Pact two years previously. Early in July he had told Ciano that he intended to build concentration camps for political opponents, instead of simply banning them to some desolate villages off the beaten track. He was thinking of starting a new campaign against the anti-fascists with the burning of Jewish, Masonic, and French books, in an effort to show Hitler that he, Mussolini, was also a man of steel. A month later, on the 8th of August, he ordered Ciano to eliminate all Jews from the active diplomatic list. At the same time, in Ciano's presence, he unleashed his aversion against Pius XI's interference in the way he planned to run the country (and to run out the Jews). He re-emphasized his earlier threat to make the Italians anti-clerical, because (as he saw it) his countrymen had "found it difficult to accept a Jewish God," whatever that may have meant in a country where the God of the Jews was the same as the God of the Catholics.

By the end of the month the Duce's wayward mind turned back to his original plan of establishing a Jewish homeland away from Palestine. He would arrange to bring the Jews to the god-forsaken colony of Migiurtinia in Italian Somaliland. This would offer an immediate, important, and rather lurid advantage—there were lots of sharks along the coast, guaranteeing "the added benefit of a good many Jews being swallowed up. . . ."

On the second of September the Duce made arrangements for the possible first shipment of colonists to the planned Migiurtinian dreamland. He declared that all foreign Jews who had been naturalized after 1 January 1919 would automatically lose their citizenship. At the same time he ordered all these foreign Jews,

naturalized or stateless (a total of close to 50,000, mostly
refugees) to leave the country and its colonies within six
months. Was this another of the Duce's "humane" aberrations?
Did he still want to "protect" his beloved Italian Hebrew
nationals? Foreign Jews might as well be the first victims of the
sharks.

To some extent Mussolini, with his retroactive law, was really
a trifle more clement than Hitler, who struck out at Jews
without making any distinction between domestic and
naturalized ones. According to Mussolini, someone was a Jew
when both or one of his parents were of that religion, whether
the child had converted to Catholicism or not. The Duce in his
"Jew-tracing" might well have been tempted to go back to the
"third generation" of Jewish forefathers as Hitler had done.
Could he translate German racism literally into Italian? To
declare every Italian with a Jewish great-grandparent to be a Jew
would have disqualified perhaps a quarter of the nation's in-
telligentsia. However regrettable, it just could not be done.

On 3 September, one day after the decree concerning foreign
Jews was made public, another regulation came into force, this
one dealing with universities and schools. As of October 16, all
Jewish teachers and professors would lose their jobs, and all
members of state academies, of scientific and artistic institutions, would find all doors closed to them.

All through the rest of the month of September of that fateful
year 1938 Europe seemed to lose its balance. It was on the
tightrope of war and peace. The sudden crisis made the Czechs
wonder whether their allies would come to their rescue; and the
West talked, telephoned, and dithered. Chamberlain traveled to
Berchtesgaden and Bad Godesberg; Hitler remained adamant.
Didn't Mussolini have to do something to show his power too?
Three days after the British Premier had seen the Führer in the
Bavarian Alps on September 15, Mussolini journeyed to Trieste
to address the crowd about Victory, Empire—and Race. According to his new formula, by which he had to justify the
necessity of the anti-Jewish measures already taken, the Italian
leader explained that "the racial problem has not exploded

suddenly, but goes hand in hand with the conquest of Empire, and the Jewish problem is only one of the consequences of this phenomenon." He probably meant the conquest of Ethiopia— and the planned and hoped-for Empire elsewhere, for which he was building a huge Ministry of Overseas Territories that never would house any of the grandiose services.

"History teaches us," Mussolini said, "that Empires are conquered by arms but are maintained by prestige." What did this have to do with the anti-Jewish measures in Italy, which were lowering his prestige all over the world (except in Germany and Austria)? But if Hitler was shouting, then he too had to shout; and inside Italy the anti-Semitic campaign was deemed to be a counterpart of the propaganda value of Hitler's imminent invasion of Czechoslovakia.

On 30 September, Chamberlain, Hitler, Daladier and Mussolini signed the Munich Pact which handed the Sudetenland to the Nazis. The Czechs were abandoned by all, and by now Mussolini was convinced that Hitler was definitely on the right path (although he still hoped it would not be the war-path). What was there left for him to do except what Hitler had been doing so successfully all along? To strike out at the Jews, to discriminate, and to persecute, etc. The cry which the Vatican had employed for long centuries, to justify the tactic of Farinacci's brand of fascism—down with the Jews!

Chapter 33
The Racial Laws

Secrets were difficult to keep in Rome. Ever since the Mussolini-inspired discoveries by the so-called leading scientists were published and had been followed by the decrees of early September, the Jews of Rome—*especially* those of Rome, because they were closest to the government—had been out to gather as much information as possible. It was not too difficult in a society where in the right circles everybody knew everybody else, and where indignation among even some of the top fascists ran high about the plans their Duce was hatching. So it was small wonder that towards the first days of October the Jewish community had a fair idea about the first subject on the agenda at the forthcoming meeting of the Fascist Grand Council, to take place on the sixth. It was common knowledge among its participants that the major item to be discussed was "the Jews," and how to confront "the problem," deal with it, and solve it.

There was little the Hebrew Union could do about it, except to send a brief to the chief of government, reconfirming their "Italianism." The letter was brought to Mussolini on the 4th of October. It was a simple statement of fact, in which the men who were speaking for the forty thousand Italian-born Jews reiterated what everybody should have known—that they were not members of any "Jewish, masonic, or international movement, nor of any organisation that was Bolshevik, anti-fascist, or anti-Italian." And in the name of Italy and of Fascism (it was that kind of text, replete with collaborationist formulations) they asked "to be allowed to work in the dignity of peace and to die in the honor of war. We have never doubted your generosity," the message to Mussolini went on, "and with the purity of our fascist conscience we appeal to the spirit of Roman justice and humanity which has inspired your renovating and recreating activities." It was a declaration of people fighting for their lives. The few important fascists in the Hebrew Union, still guided by the spirit of men like Ovazza (who by now had left the group to remain a "real" fascist in his own right), had set the tone. But they now had little to hold on to but their fascist past, their fading fervor, their tarnished medals. The wings of their political convictions had been seriously clipped, and it was a fairly lame bird that tried to fly the ostracized coop.

The aversion among Mussolini's intimates to what was going to take place was not due to any pro-Jewishness. From a political point of view they simply considered the anti-Semitic move an absurdity. As Marshal de Bono put his thoughts in his diary: "It seems they want to create enemies everywhere! But if you knew for so long that the Jewish influence was harmful, then why did not you do something about it before? That, at least, is the way the public reasons. I seem to be the only stupid fool who realizes it! Apparently we have to discuss it at the *Gran Consiglio*. Even though I have always been anti-Semitic, I'll speak up. . . ."* And Ciano confided to his precious diary

*Other Italian anti-Semitic marshals, of course, did not "speak up." On 18 October 1943, when Marshal Graziani, the former Viceroy of Ethiopia, had become Minister of War in the fascist government formed after the fall of

that he "did not like the Jews," but that he "did not feel it was necessary to take such measures."

Marshal de Bono was well informed about the feelings of the Jews closest to him and under his immediate command. General Liuzzi, who on former occasions clearly had indicated his support of Jewish fascism, had in late September veered away from it and had communicated his anxieties to the Marshal. Thus when the Council convened at the Palazzo Venezia at ten o'clock in the evening of 6 October, De Bono, admittedly an anti-Semite, would be one of the strongest advocates of *not* going through with Mussolini's plans, and he was energetically seconded by Marshal Balbo. Others, to Ciano's surprise—as he would mention in his diary—were intransigent. Among them was the intellectually astute (and formerly a quite "liberal" minister of education) Giuseppe Bottai. "They loathe us because we have thrown them out," he said according to Ciano, and "they'll despise us if we readmit them." At the end of the meeting, which did not break up till several hours after midnight, Mussolini was jubilant. "We must push the problem hard," he said to his son-in-law. "The Italian blood by now has been inoculated with anti-Semitism. It will continue to develop all by itself. Even if tonight I have seemed occasionally to be moderately inclined, I'll be very tough in the preparation of the laws. . . ."

That same day Bottai informed schools and other institutions in the country about the first anti-Jewish decisions. Certain books by Jewish authors, which for as many as sixteen years had been on the reading lists, henceforth were not to be used any longer for educational purposes. This included books which even could not conceivably have had any political influence, *viz.* those written by professor of mathematics Salvatore Pincherle. Before long all Jewish names had to be stricken from the telephone books (although, with

Mussolini, he made the following remark to Cardinal Maglione: "The situation now is as follows. On the one side we have the Free Masons, the Jews, and the Communists, personified by England, America, and Russia. On the other side we have Germany, which is fighting these three dark forces of subversion. . . ."

typical Italian *lasciamo andare* nonchalance, most of the telephones remained connected).

Mussolini, for all his bravura about the planned Jewish exclusion laws and his personal satisfaction at seeing the Jews of Italy thrown into sudden disarray, was still concerned about the possible foreign response to his decisions, especially the reaction in the United States. In fact, he wondered what might happen to Italian exports if American Jews, certainly to be strongly supported by other Americans, were to start a boycott of Italian products similar to the one that had been put into effect against Nazi Germany several years previously. A confidential report, prepared in New York and dated 20 October 1938, did not quite reinforce his confidence. According to a 1936 survey by *Fortune* magazine, the report said, well over 54 percent of the population at that time held the opinion that a boycott of German products would make things difficult for Hitler's *Reich*. What would happen if such action now were to be extended to Italy? Of the fifty million dollars worth of Italian products bought by the USA during the year 1937, many could easily be replaced with products from elsewhere, the Italian experts in New York wrote. This was worrisome. Already, the report continued, "several New York departments stores, such as Macy's, Gimbel's, Saks, B. Altman, and Hearns" and similar companies elsewhere like "Bamberger and Marshall Field have decided to eliminate Italian products totally, or to a large extent, from their shops." And as to tourism, "American Jews make up about 50 percent of all tourist class passengers on the Italian Line, and about 30 percent of all first class passengers." The full report clearly seemed to be advising a go-slow policy.

In the end Mussolini was not impressed. Having crossed his own Rubicon, he addressed the members of the National Council of the party with his usual confidence on 25 October. It was a speech which, he said, was "not for publication," but which "could be repeated orally by the party functionaries." He started off in good humor, reporting that the "aristocratic" Roman middle class had been making fun of his decision to purify the Italian language of its slavish, class-distinctive personal pronouns. Having abolished the term *lei* (corresponding to the French *vous*) and having replaced it obligatorily by the age-old *tu* and *voi*, the Romans had been wondering, said Mussolini, whether in future instead of speaking about Gali*lei*, they would have to refer to him as Gali*voi!*

But his tone soon changed when he came to the main subject of his speech—Racism. It was of "incalculable importance" he said, because till now the Italians "had found themselves afflicted by an inferiority complex, being convinced that they were not one people" but a nation composed of "a mixture of races." That was a monstrous thought, Mussolini declared. "We should bear in mind that we are not Hamites, that we are not Semites, that we are not Mongols!" the Duce explained to his eager and adoring audience, who may have been prepared to follow him through the whole maze of racist pseudo-logic. For, said Mussolini without further ado, "if we are none of these races, then we are obviously Aryans and we have come from across the Alps, from the north." The next phrase was another masterpiece of incongruity. "Thus we are Aryans of the Mediterranean type—pure!" cried the happy Duce, who looked about as much like the blond Nazi ideal-type of an Aryan as did Dr. Goebbels.

Coming finally to his main topic, the Jews, the Italian dictator informed his listeners that all he wanted to say was that "those 44,000 who now make martyrs of themselves, never will have the strength to bring the glorious Italian advance to a halt." If they would try, he said, "we'll toss them into the gutter. And if really difficult hours will come, then this time we'll not hesitate to eliminate them forever. . . ."

Referring to the recent Munich conference, he made a remark that has gone down in history as a literally monumental *faux pas*. "What has happened in Munich is colossal!" Mussolini shouted. "I am using that word because it comes from us! Just think of the Colosseum!" Some of the more thoughtful party members probably did—and pondered perhaps why such a colossal structure had turned into such a colossal ruin.

The Vatican became more and more concerned with Mussolini's plan. For if the Jews somehow were to be restricted in their activities and occupations, then how would this affect those Catholics who shared their lives? It was important to safeguard the livelihood and family future of those who had contracted mixed marriages. Again it was Ciano who has given us a valuable account of the Vatican's preoccupied thoughts on the subject, as they were entrusted to him by Monsignor Montini of the Secretariat of State (later Pope Paul VI). The *reaction* of the Vatican was unfavorable, Ciano wrote, but "the greatest, not to say the only *objection* of the Holy See concerns marriages with converted—(or as yet unconverted)—Jews. . . ." This was an interesting observation to come from the Catholic hierarchy. The Catholic Church had always been *against* such marriages. Yet once they were transacted, the Church would valiantly jump into the breach to defend its own interests, *i.e.*, the converts, the possible converts, or at the very least the Catholic-born half of the mixed couple. (Actually, the unconverted other half did not matter overly much.)

There was, therefore, no "great" objection against the projected racial laws as far as they concerned the Jews themselves. There *was* fear for the possible consequences for the Catholics who happened to be married to them. It was a basic Vatican attitude that would be encountered time and again under far more tragic circumstances. It somehow brought to the fore a medieval Church axiom that Jews were only good when they were Catholics. This was an attitude that always had been strongly opposed by the Jesuits, who were generally of the opinion that Jews (to put it succinctly) were just no good at all, or ever.*

There are certain fanatical spirits which feed on cynical confusions. As Mussolini confessed to former senator Alexander Casati: "A Jewish problem? It doesn't exist. Race? Don't make me laugh. But there are political reasons I have to obey. . . ." *Raison d'état?* Was it the discovery he had made when talking to Emil Ludwig in 1932 when he called the German Jew the "scapegoat"?

On the 17th of November 1938 the details of the Racial Laws were put before the people. While propounding this racial

*One year after the application of the racial laws, there were 39,000 Jews in Italy, in some 11,500 families. Of these 6,820 were mixed marriages, of which

thesis, Mussolini had worked himself into a state of ever mounting antagonism against the Jews. According to Ciano, the Duce had by November 10 "unconditionally approved the reactionary measures taken by the Nazis. He says that in a similar case he would even act worse, and he has the intention to decree that Jewish children born in Italy will be declared stateless. . . ."

Mussolini's inspiration for the various articles of the new law, which fell upon the city like a storm, came from two sources. His greatest teacher was Hitler, whose sentiments the Duce had soaked up like a dehydrated sponge. Secondly, he must have gone carefully through the many Church edicts that had plagued the Jews of Rome since 1555 and even before, and which had persisted till 1870. There were a few differences with Hitler's own already executed plans (*e.g.*, the absence of concentration camps for the time being). "The existence of a racial consciousness has become a necessity," Mussolini had announced at the Grand Council meeting six weeks previously, and that racial consciousness was now given its basic guidelines, a series of ordinances destined to bring the Jews to their knees, by excluding them from any further active participation in the life of the country.

The twenty-nine judiciously subdivided articles of the "Legislative Measures for the Defense of the Italian Race" included some of the already published decrees on teaching and on foreign Jews. It also once again defined "a Jew" as a person who was born from either one or two Jewish parents. Its avalanche of rules and regulations decreed that mixed marriages from now on were *verboten*. So was service in the armed forces, teaching of non-Jews, ownership of factories that were working for the defense industry, or of any other factories that employed more than one hundred people.

As had been the case with earlier Vatican decrees, non-Jewish servants were out. The civil service and defense administrations had to dismiss their Jewish employees; banks and insurance

2,200 were childless. Of the remaining 4,620 mixed families with a total of 13,-000 children, 1,200 had oriented their 3,500 offspring towards a Jewish education; and 3,420 parents with approximately 9,500 children had opted for the Catholic or another religious faith.

companies (many of which had been started by Jews) had to find Catholics to fill the open places; and to do all this the leaders of industry, commerce, and the other organisations were given three months time. Needless to say, the party and other fascist groups had to send their Jewish members home. There were a few temporary exceptions for those Jews who had taken part in the various Italian wars and had received high battlefield decorations; for the Jewish fascists who had been wounded while fighting for The Cause; for pre-1922 members of the party; for those who had taken part in the battle for Fiume; and for the families of Jews who had been killed in the Libyan, Ethiopian, Spanish, or World War. (On condition, of course, that in the Spanish civil war they had fallen on the right side—the fascist side, fighting for Franco.)

Chauvinism would do its job. Before long the famous Roman Jewish artichokes, the delicious *carciofi alla giudia*, went the way of the American hamburger in World War One; they were aryanized, and indeed became *carciofi all'ariana*. Shortly afterwards the New Pocket Dictionary of the Italian Language was taken off the market because it suggested that the word anti-Semite referred to "a not very civilized person who is opposed to and who fights the Jews." If some German composers were not played in the United States during the First World War, and were banned in Israel after the Second, no one in Italy thought of putting Felix Mendelssohn (a baptized Jew who was born from Jewish parents and who, consequently, was a Jew according to the fascist rules) on the index—even though he had had the temerity to compose an "Italian symphony." Was it only because Italians are music lovers that Mendelssohn was not forbidden? There were many ridiculous after-effects which were, of course, of no importance. Other passing items of the day were rather more serious. There was the attack on the Roman Jewish community because on the commemorative stone in the wall of the synagogue those "fallen during the First World War" were remembered as having given their life "for a greater Italy." The accusation was a pure invention; yet the fascists, in their publication "The Defense of the Race" demanded to know why these Jews (formerly they had been called *heroes*) had not fallen for the *Fatherland?* The simple demagogic answer was given by the editors themselves: because Jews *have* no fatherland!

How did the people, the plain good kind Italian people, take the new laws? The leading fascists themselves, including Mussolini's sons, all had their own Jewish friends whom they tried to protect. The usual profession was an expression of regret. "It is awful," they used to say, "but believe us, we are your friends." It was a futile, if touching, gesture or speech. It had been made by so many other Italians who during the fascist era used to pin their party emblem on the reverse side of their coat lapels; and when showing it would say as an excuse: "I have to," meaning they *had* to be a member of the party, because it was a choice of survival or starvation.

Three days after the publication of the racial laws, the Italian Academy solemnly celebrated its tenth anniversary in the sumptuous Julius Caesar room on Capitol Hill, in the presence of King Victor Emmanuel. The eminent participating scientists took advantage of this occasion to laud the Duce, whom they called "the instigator and organizer of all the spiritual energies of the nation," after which the Academic Chairman, the Honorable Roberto Paribeni, was to read his essay on *"Judaism in the History and the Life of Ancient Rome,"* a highly educational treatise which would "naturally condemn" the subject it treated.

It was logical, said the president of the Academy, the Honorable Senator Luigi Federzoni, that "the Academy, called upon as it was to defend the national character of thought and culture, could not abstain from intervening in the discussion of such a highly important problem, even more important than problems of political, biological or historical value—the problem of *Race.*" And then the Honorable Roberto Paribeni went on to quote (among others) Cicero and Tacitus, and he indicated his agreement with the latter: ". . . the Jews declare profane what others hold sacred, and lawful what others consider wicked. . . ."

Curious things are fished out of the historical grab-bag by desperate propagandists. Mussolini had once used Tacitus in another connection. "They [the Germans]" Mussolini had written, "are still the way that Tacitus described them so perfectly. This Roman historian established a difference between the Germans and the British, which remains as true today as it was nineteen centuries ago. The British fight to defend their country and family, the Germans fight out of avarice and greed. . . . " But quotations are nothing if not manipulable. Paribeni's "address was greatly applauded." The King departed. The next day the newspapers obediently quoted all the quotations from Cicero, Tacitus, and the deplorable Honorable Roberto Paribeni.

Directed and edited by the truest among the party's literate (and sometimes even illiterate) stalwarts, the Italian press played up the proclamation of the racial laws as in a military campaign. By now not one paper dared make a remark which might be interpreted as a defense of the Jews; and from Turin to Catania it was just one anti-Semitic blackness of headlines that greeted the Italians morning and evening. The Sudetenland—which only recently had been occupied by Hitler, and which still received banner headlines elsewhere—had disappeared from the front pages of the Italian press. On the 23rd of November, three days after the Academicians had expressed their scientific opinion on the value of anti-Semitism, that most important newspaper of the country, the *Corriere della Sera*, had the following headlines in one single number:

> VERY SHORTLY THE REICH WILL HAVE SOLVED ITS
> JEWISH PROBLEM
> THE PRO-JEWISH HYPOCRISY OF THE GREAT
> DEMOCRACIES
> SEVENTY ITALIANS DISMISSED BY A JEWISH FIRM IN
> MONACO
> BARBARIC JEWISH VIOLENCE IN A PALESTINE VILLAGE
> POLEMIC IN THE USA: FATHER COUGHLIN DIS-
> APPROVES THE PRO-JEWISH HYSTERIA.
> JEWISH VILLAINY: TOO MANY PASSPORTS FOR HAITI.

On December 15 the same newspaper informed its countrymen that "one should feel oneself far removed—frankly, on account of its odor—from all that is Jewish in culture." The *Popolo di Roma* called Charlie Chaplin the "foulest, most disgusting, most inhuman and obnoxious" actor there was.

The effect on the Jews, of course, was one of extreme shock. Those who had actively opposed the régime had long since fled abroad. The silent opposers, who had refrained from becoming members of the party, now felt more than justified for their standfast viewpoint; yet at the same time they were indignant and terrified. But none of this could touch the sentiments of those Jews who had either supported the régime as the proud standard bearers of the Movement (like Ovazza), or who had been in the armed forces and had supported fascism because it was the State, the Government, the Established Power they had sworn to uphold. General Guido Liuzzi—now condemned to leave his post as one of the directors of the War College, a man who had devoted his life to the improvement of the Italian army—addressed himself bitterly to the King. His long letter went back over the history of the Jewish community to which he definitely felt be belonged. It reflected his active interest in the organization of a homogeneous Hebrew group that was to fight the non-alignment policy of the Hebrew Union.

"Today," wrote General Liuzzi, "our fault seems to be our non-belonging to a presumed Italian Aryan race. But this guilty situation apparently does not exist for other Italians who also belong to a foreign race, such as the Arabs, Slavs, Albanians, Armenians, and so on. This means that Italian racism is hiding behind a mask, in order to give anti-Semitism the appearance of having a logical foundation. . . ." Liuzzi, although a little late in his disillusionment, took off his uniform in disgust two days before Christmas 1938, on the occasion of Mussolini's order suddenly shortening the liquidation period of Jews in the armed forces (from three months to just over one month).*

The King read Liuzzi's letter with interest, and promptly sent

*General Liuzzi died in 1942 in Turin. His son hid out at his father-in-law's property near Modena, then tried to join the Allies in 1943 but could not manage to get through the lines with his pregnant wife. He went underground in Rome, and resumed active service after the liberation of the city. In 1954 he was made Chief of Staff of the Italian Army.

it on to Mussolini who was far from grateful. While the law was still under discussion, he had sent Minister Buffarini-Guidi, one of the men who would be in charge of the execution of the racial laws, to see Victor Emmanuel. At that time things had been smoothed out speedily. The King felt sorry for the Jews, but when he heard that "the special measures would be kind to those who had served their country well," he declared himself quite satisfied; he said that he "had been sure that the great sensibility, intuition, and generosity of the President would have followed this line of conduct." But when the Duce himself had gone to see Victor Emmanuel ten days after the racial laws had been promulgated, on 28 November, Ciano found him on his return from the palace "indignant about the King." The King had told the Duce that he felt "infinite pity for the Jews." He had mentioned to Mussolini several names of Jews he had been close to, such as the 80-year-old retired General Pugliese, "who, with so many decorations and wounds, must remain without servants." According to Ciano, the Duce had acidly remarked that "in Italy there are twenty-thousand people with rubber legs who are moved by the fate of the Jews. . . ." The King had replied that "he was one of them."

The Vatican kept officially silent. But Chairs at the Pontifical Academy were offered to Jewish mathematician Vito Volterra and to Tullio Levi-Civita, who was a member of the *Institut de France*, the Berlin *Akademie*, and of the Royal Society of London. There had been long negotiations between the Church and the Italian government, especially in order to try and protect the Jews who had converted to Catholicism, and whom the Vatican—contrary to Article Eight as it finally would be published—wanted to be considered full-fledged Christians. The Duce would not accept this point of view—to him a child born of Jewish parents was a Jew, converted or not. But for the rest the opposition of the Church's governing members (many of whose leading figures in the Curia were not at all opposed to a resumption of the centuries-old Vatican policy) was nearly exclusively concerned with *Race*, and only very little with anti-Semitism—certainly as long as there were no excesses to be deplored.

Pope Pius XI himself, contrary to many of his grey eminences, was quite explicit. Besides his earlier speeches to the *Propaganda Fide* students, he had told a group of Belgian Catholics early in September 1938 that "Abraham is called our patriarch, our forefather." These had been strong words while faced across Saint Peter's Square by a dictatorship that was gradually sliding down towards the sub-politics of inhumanity. Pope Pius XI had not in the least believed that such outspoken statements could "make things worse" for anyone—not for himself, not for the Church, and not for the Jews, as would be claimed after the war by the Vatican as an apology for and a defense of Pope Pius XII's silence when the fate of the Jews had reached the direst straits. Nor was this all from Pius XI. "Anti-Semitism is incompatible with the thought and the sublime reality which are expressed in these words," he had said, meaning the descent from Abraham. "Anti-Semitism is a repugnant movement, a movement in which we Christians can have no share," he had continued. And to make sure that no misunderstandings were left anywhere, Pius had repeated his earlier words in a new form: "Through Christ and in Christ we descend spiritually from Abraham."

Additional formulations like these apparently had been in preparation. For years it was rumored at the Vatican that the Pope had prepared another very strong statement on anti-Semitism. It was to be used in his speech on 11 February 1939, on the occasion of the tenth anniversary of the Concordat. Twenty-four hours before that day the Pope died; and it would take another twenty years before the contents of that prepared statement were to be made public.

Pope John XXIII, commemorating in February 1959 the 30th anniversary of the signing of the Lateran Pact as well as the 20th anniversary of the death of Pius XI, stated that "a great many stories have been invented at the time about the last thoughts of a mind and of a moral sensibility that could not have been anything but pure and noble. But the conditions that prevailed during those weeks, not free from feelings of bitterness towards the aging Pope, easily would have explained his expressing himself in terms and in a tone of voice of only too righteous resentment. . . ."

Pius XI's speech was referred to by Pope John as "a mysterious secret." It was still in the process of being written, he said, "when the angel of death touched him." There would have been enough anti-anti-Semitism in it to have made Mussolini—and Hitler—rather angry, if death had not intervened.

Having mentioned in his introduction that it would be "of great importance not only for Italy," Pius XI had intended to pronounce a strong admonition to the Italian people and to its Duce. "We have a press that can say anything it wants against Us and against Our causes," he had written, "even referring to and interpreting in a false and perverse sense the present and past history of the Church, even denying obstinately any and all persecution in Germany. . . .and no one objects, while our newspapers cannot even contradict or correct it."

According to the revelations of Pope John XXIII, his predecessor but one had intended to say more. "Call for a total and unflagging perseverance against all ambushes that threaten and oppose us from far and near," he had written. "And, finally, call for . . . order, tranquillity, and peace, peace, peace for the whole world, which even though it seems to be engulfed by a homicidal and suicidal madness of military armament, wants peace at all costs. . . ."

The indignation of the Jews, once they had read the details of the racial laws, took many forms. The weaker among them, others who were married to non-Jews, and a few dyed-in-the-wool fascists, took the easy way out and became Catholics. They hoped to save their lives and positions, notwithstanding the express statement in the racial laws that they would be considered to be Jews anyhow. The Church was accommodating, and by the end of 1939 between 7,000 and 8,000 Jews were converted, of whom approximately 1,800 in Rome alone.*

*Even though many of them converted out of pure expediency and without any religious urge, only between 400 and 500 would reconvert to Judaism when the war was over. Yet, according to the Chief Rabbi of Rome, Elio Toaff, "a good number of converted Jews these days, when they feel death approaching, call for the rabbi and want to be buried at the Jewish cemetery. . ."

Other Jews—not too many from Rome but mostly from the north—emigrated, especially of course those who could pay their own fare. Some of them would leave singly, then would make arrangements in the new country to have their families join them. The Vatican gladly supplied baptism certificates for those *converted* Jews who wanted to go to Brazil, where such papers were the compulsory key to entry into the country. Even some totally unbaptized Jews were given such certificates by humane and accommodating priests, acting without the Vatican's permission. All in all over 5,000 Jews and ex-Jews would thus escape a future which they felt to be hopeless. Among these fortunate ones were the Catholic physicist Enrico Fermi and his Jewish wife, daughter of retired admiral Augusto Capon.* Shortly after the racial laws went into effect Dr. Fermi traveled with his wife to Sweden to receive the Nobel prize. They did not return to Italy, but continued instead to the United States, where Fermi would use his knowledge to create an historic revolution in physics. His Jewish colleague Bruno Pontecorvo would also leave the country, first to join the Juliot-Curies in Paris, then to make a different kind of history and end up as a defector in Soviet Russia.

Angiolo Orvieto, the poet (in 1935 he had been sent to London by Mussolini to see what he could do about repeal of the sanctions) took to his pen with heavy heart and let his Muse cry out his anger in a poem he called *"The Yellow Hat"*:

No! I shall not walk with the stigma
of infamy and shame,
I will rebel.
They may hang me,
jail me, quarter me,
but I'll not put on the yellow hat.
I'll flee from Florence.
Like my fathers I too shall wander
from land to land,

*The aged Admiral was advised to leave Italy, but could not believe in the gravity of the danger. He remained at home—waiting. In 1943 the Nazis deported him to the gas chambers of Poland.

a wretched stranger, unknown,
breaking stones under the burning sun
with bronzed arms,
my hands hardened by bitter callouses,
but free, a man,
not a vile slave with a yellow hat!*

Other Jews chose other ways of escape. On November 29 the Roman publisher Angelo Fortunato Formiggini, who several years before had guided Mussolini around his display at the Rome Book Fair, returned quietly to his home in Modena and threw himself from the main tower of the city. It was, perhaps, a futile gesture, but many had preferred that way out before him, and many others would follow. When Achille Starace, the former secretary of the Fascist Party (who would be shot with Benito Mussolini in April 1945) heard about the suicide, he made a comment which can be taken as the epitome of fascist moral sentiment. Meeting with some of his cronies in the corridors of parliament, Starace said: "That Jew has committed suicide just the way one may expect it from a Jew—to save the money of a bullet he threw himself off a tower."

---

*Angiolo Orvieto, age 98, died in Florence in December 1967.

Chapter 34
Anti-Semitism
Within the Church

It was only natural and inevitable for the anti-Semitic members of the Fascist Party to blow their propaganda horns at every possible and impossible occasion. It was less natural to have the same thing happen among the Italian clergy. But since the higher priests were Italians who, in their own wise or unwise way, were as nationalistic as all others, the articles to be found in Catholic publications were often as violent—though perhaps couched in more civilized language—as those published in the fascist newspapers.

Only the simple parochial priests in the small towns and villages were indifferent to the anti-Jewish stridency from above (or, at least, many of them were). They themselves usually had come from everyday Italian homes; and while obviously loyal followers of the Church, their own unsophisticated way of looking at things made them consider anti-Semitism as a fly-by-night outgrowth of something strange and unfamiliar. But the higher one moved in the Catholic hierarchy, the more violent the opinions one would encounter. Little priests, if they were fascists, were only little fascists, and their influence, if any, was among their congregations only. The great priests, however, had a far wider audience and therefore a far greater influence. Outstanding among the leading clerics was Father Agostino Gemelli, president of the Pontifical Academy of Science and rector of the Catholic University of the Holy Heart in Milan. A frequent and important visitor to the Vatican, the good father made a memorable speech in Bologna on 9 January 1939. It was much commented upon and praised by the fascist press, and as such duly reported two days later in the powerful *Corriere della Sera*, as well as in the local Bologna newspaper *Il Resto del Carlino*, and of course in such purely party publications as the *Regima Fascista*.

The speaker spread his wisdom "in the presence of the authorities," the papers wrote, and those authorities underlined Father Gemelli's words with "particular applause" when he expressed his opinion on the Jews. He was "a courageous and sincere man," and the audience felt touched and moved by the priest's deeper thoughts when he explained how, when "we Catholic priests sometimes have criticized cardinals, bishops and Catholic newspapers, we were admonished that Catholics have only one duty—to obey without discussion." The kind father would not accept this point of view. He felt that the Church could not step aside when faced by such a high fascist mission. "In politics we have only one Chief," Father Gemelli cried out, "*Il Duce*—whom a great and august voice has called incomparable!." (He failed to add that the Pope, who indeed had called Mussolini *"incomparable,"* later on had said many other things about the Duce rather less eulogistic.) As a further patriotic admonition the good father exulted that it was necessary for the Italians to be "one in arms, language, religion, memory, race and sentiment!"

At this point an historian might well wonder why the Church, which can mete out the strictest discipline upon its spiritual advocates if and when it wants to, simply "admonished" this fascist and anti-Semitic priest, and then let him continue to distribute his inflammatory epistles among the multitude, knowing full well to what excesses such anti-Jewish zeal had led in Nazi Germany. For Father Gemelli had not yet come to the end of his Latin which he spread in his earthy Italian. The Jews had only asked for it, argued the rector of that great Catholic University in Milan, whose task it was to educate the younger generation in submissive humility and human understanding. "It is tragic to view this situation as we have seen it through the centuries," he preached, "a situation in which the sentence is carried out on the Christ-killing people, as a result of which they wander through the world, unable to find the peace of a fatherland, while the consequences of their horrible deed persecute them wherever they are and for all times. . . . "

In reality it was little wonder that priests like Father Gemelli spoke out as they did, considering the words of encouragement that came to them from far higher up, especially after the death of Pope Pius XI and the election of Pope Pius XII on 2 March 1939. The clergy was quite familiar with the former Pontiff's stand on the Jewish subject. Nothing as yet was known however about Pacelli's official attitude. Some of the cardinals, whenever an opportunity presented itself, publicly stated what so many of them had said privately for quite some time.

The Honorable Member of Parliament, Alfredo Romanini (whose scurrilous book *Jews, Christianity, Fascism* had been published, quite unnoticed, back in 1936) gave the cardinals the chance they had been looking for. By 1939 Romanini felt that his neglected doctrine should be dusted off and brought before the greater public. When the book first came out the Jews had still been full, if not entirely honored, citizens; now their official status was once more that of pariahs. The author, probably because his publisher did not want to risk any more money, decided to spend his own funds on a new and revised edition, this time making sure that important people, including cardinals, archbishops, and lesser priests would get a free reviewer's copy.

Thus, the Romanini book was published for the second time and inundated the literary field with its Streicheresque abominations. In 1936 he had written that "the League of Nations had come into being through (Jewish) inspiration," and that among Wilson's famous Fourteen Points "thirteen were based on Masonic-Jewish principles." The statements were now given fresh circulation. Jewish aspirations in 1939 were, according to Romanini, "to dominate Europe first, to be followed by the enslavement of the world." Already "banks, industries, newspapers, film studios, railroads and steamship lines were and are in the hands of the Jews," he proclaimed, and high Jewish finance had been "dominating European politics for over half a century."

It was almost amazing to find him putting in a good word for the Rothschilds. According to them, the Jews "want to live in peace and work in peace." Romanini found this quite noble, but then went on to say that "the Jewish leaders do not limit themselves to this program." In his view, "hatred, pride, and the unbridled ambition to dominate the world have caused the present situation." Romanini was certain there was only one way to counter this Jewish perniciousness and bring it to a halt; and quite obviously Mussolini was the man to guide this campaign. Mussolini, who was "the chief who raises himself powerfully and majestically against this malicious Israel, which thirsts after a Christian-Aryan *vendetta*, and which desires world domination with its gold, corruption, Masonic thirst and international organisations of various names and colors, having as its goal the brutalization of the masses. . . ."

The book in itself actually had little importance, being simply a monotonous repetition of old plagiarisms. Again it might have passed unnoticed. But with the uncertainty of Pope Pius XII's ideas hanging in the balance, the outspoken reaction of the higher clergy was astonishing. The free copies sent to the Italian cardinals were exchanged for applauding adjectives, which Romanini put to excellent use, quickly spreading the clergy-endorsed warnings to the masses before they were completely brutalized by the malicious Jewish conspiracy.

Cardinal Piazza, Patriarch of Venice, "blessed Romanini with all his heart," for his work was "most opportune to make known the grave danger that hangs over the world." Cardinal

Nasali Rocca, Archbishop of Bologna, wrote that the book treated "a vital argument with really considerable documentation," and sent his "congratulations for the difficult work, done with such commendable intent." From Sicily came the plaudits of Cardinal Lavitrano, Archbishop of Palermo. He found Romanini's book "excellent in substance and in form, and of an unquestionable usefulness in the understanding of the Jewish problem." Other archbishops too felt highly pleased with the worthy task undertaken by Romanini, whose opinions evidently so closely coincided with their own. His Excellency Giuseppe Nogara, Archbishop of Udine near the Austrian border, declared the book to be of "maximum importance," and he prayed the Lord "to prevent the triumph of everything that interferes with His Coming."

Even if Romanini's publicity campaign in spreading the clergy's encomiums did not have any direct effect or influence on the public at large, it is revealing to observe what kind of thinking prevailed in some of the Vatican's most august circles; such sentiments and opinions would, after the war, disappear from the variously repeated texts about how much the Vatican had done *for* the Jews of Rome, conveniently forgetting what some of its highest dignitaries had done *against* them, and against the Jews in general.

Anti-Semitic feeling was not restricted to fascists, cardinals, and Church officials. Some of "the best" among the other Italians were also creepingly (and sometimes even enthusiastically) won over to the idea of *Race*, even though this was not always directly connected with *Jews*. Yet it was quite impossible in the storm of sweeping fascist generalisations to make a difference between the two any longer. To the larger public, whether they understood it or not, *Race* and *Jews* were synonyms; whoever spoke of one was automatically understood to speak of the other.

The Jesuit publication *La Civiltà Cattolica*, distinctive as always, had kept running ahead of the pack, so much so that even the arch-fascist party secretary Roberto Farinacci had felt himself obliged to compliment the editors on their adroitness "to have known how to impose the Race problem so fascistical-

ly *avanti lettera*," well before the fascists themselves had even
dreamt of it. Yet by now they, the fascists, were organizing
frenetically to make the country "race-conscious." But even
though they were happily supported by a few of the high
figures in the Catholic Church, and were able to dispose of all
the money they wanted, collected either locally or supplied by
their brothers in Germany, it still turned out to be a constantly
uphill struggle.

The psychopaths were few, the cranks unreliable. Their most
brilliant idea was to organize "Centers for the Study of the
Jewish Problem" in all Italian towns. It sounded ingenious on
paper; the good populace would participate in large numbers,
and once the groups were organized, anti-Semitic orders would
be coming off the governmental assembly-line in ever-
increasing tempi. Unfortunately for the party bosses this hyper-
bolic bit of daydreaming did not take with the eminently sensi-
ble Italians. To be a member of the party and applaud the Duce
was one thing; to take leave of one's senses was quite another.
The Centers, which were to get their instructions directly from
the Ministry of Popular Culture so as to organize a national
crusade against the Jews, just did not materialize. The idea was
"ripe," the organisation at the top had its paperwork in
readiness; but when they sat back to observe how the people
would make a mad rush to sign their names on the membership
lists, it turned out that it was no rush, and not even a slow
crawl. After three years the die-hard fascist minister, Pavolini,
had to confess that the Italians had not responded to his clarion
call. Of all the planned centers only those in Ancona, Florence,
Milano, and Trieste had been organized—on a pitifully poor
basis. Rome, the capital, had none. Milano, which counted over
one hundred thousand Fascist Party members, had mustered 65
of them on the membership list of the Anti-Semitic Center. For
the whole country the expected recruitment showed even poorer
results—864 names out of four million party members. They
had made many calculations but had obviously not reckoned
with the element of common sense.

Was it the country which went berserk in June 1940? At least
Mussolini did. After Hitler had brought France to its knees,

Mussolini felt that the opportune moment had come for him to get his share of the spoils. He declared war on all and sundry, and occupied the southern part of France (his soldiers would have temperate sunshine at their disposal, and Monte Carlo was close by). The city of Nice, which the fascists had been shouting about for years in their claims for *"Corsica! Nizza! Savoia!"* now fell into Italian hands. The war—all praise to Mussolini—seemed to be going preciously well. In the German-occupied territories the Jews were already being rounded up with logistical priorities. Those Jews who had been fleeing to the presumed safety of France now rushed down to what was to be known as the unoccupied zone, and specifically to the part occupied by the Italians. Even in wartime the word *Italian* still had something sunny about it, something the Nazis definitely lacked. Notwithstanding all the top-heavy anti-Semitic bravura in Mussolini's dreamland, there had not been any reports of massacres of Jews from Rome, nor had there been any news about destroyed property. Even if there were a handful of hotheads, it appeared to be a safer bet to make one's way down to the French territory where the Italians were, than to remain up north where the Germans were sure to give no quarter.

These Jews turned out to be right. Their treatment under the benevolent or indifferent supervision of the Italian troops of occupation was not harsh. When Vichy policemen tried to arrest Jews in front of the registration office in Nice, Italian officers posted their men in front of the building and instructed them to arrest any Vichyite on sight if he tried to enter. In July 1942 the Italian vice-consul in Paris, Pasquinelli, contrived a so-called agreement with the Germans, which was then duly reported to the Nazis by Consul-General Gustavo Orlandini. "In agreement with the German authorities," he wrote, "the Italians themselves will check every Jewish case according to the Italian racial laws." The German to whom this was addressed was outraged, for there had been no agreement and the Germans were being deceived. In Teutonic fury he wrote in the letter's margin that it "is not true!," it was utter "insolence," and he had "never agreed" to it!

Mussolini himself knew only too well that the Italians as a

whole were too sober-minded a people ever to take on a Nazi-style ferocity. When German Ambassador Baron Georg Hans von Mackensen in 1943 mentioned the Italian army's laxity in enforcing anti-Jewish measures to Mussolini, the Duce explained that it really was "not a matter of ill will, but the logical consequence of their way of thinking," because "his soldiers did not have an exact idea of the Jewish problem." By then Mussolini must have been wondering about his own exact ideas. The war in general was now not going too well. Mussolini even might have been wondering why the Germans still clung with such murderous tenacity to the anti-Jewish question. It was only a stratagem which he personally must have considered from the beginning as a mere stick to beat a dog with—how artificial it all was, he understood more than most. After several years of reversals, Mussolini's anti-Semitic measures consisted mainly in confining some of the foreign Jews in concentration camps (where they were comparatively safe till the Germans came upon the scene), and in putting the Roman Jews to work on the banks of the Tiber, dressed in summery shorts, and with a lonely policeman, hands in pockets, as their rather disinterested supervisor.

Those fascists who had been shouting loudest before the war, were still shouting, for after all, if one could not win a battle, then at least one could make loud noises on the typewriter. Piero Pellicano (he, who in 1938 had opined that "the Jews have no military spirit") went on to say that *everything* that was wrong with Italy was the fault of the Jews—from the scarcity of oysters on the Roman fishmarket to the spate of accidental burnings of female hairdos under the beauty salon's dryer (since, according to him, the permanent wave was a Jewish invention).

But long before von Mackensen had complained to Mussolini—and long before the Duce had discovered that persecution of the Jews did not exactly constitute the grand strategy of winning of the war—disaster had struck. The date was 11 November, 1940 (twenty-two years to the day since the end of the First World War). The British Admiral Cunningham had been informed that the pride of Mussolini's fleet were lying at anchor in the Bay of Taranto, on the instep of Italy's geographic heel—and he decided that it was too tempting an opportunity not to try and cut the Italian Navy's Achilles tendon. In a devastating attack the British destroyed some of the Duce's most attractive units, including the battleship *Cavour*, which was sunk, and the *Littorio* and *Duilio*, which were seriously damaged. Mussolini was in despair, the Naval Ministry was in tears; the *mare nostrum* suddenly had become a *mare vestrum*.

There in the winter-grey waters off the Mediterranean coast lay the pride of Benito's sea power, like in an Italian preview of Pearl Harbor. As it was, it was nothing but a huge scrapheap, no good to anyone. Could it be used again? Perhaps—if someone were capable of raising the hulks. Who could produce the miracle? In all of Italy there was only one man able to do so—but unfortunately he was a Jew, a despised person, a parasite on whose head scorn had been heaped for years, and who back in 1939 had in dutiful disgust taken off his uniform.

The Naval Minister swallowed his pride and asked the 61-year-old ex-Inspector-General of the Naval Engineer Corps please to come and see him. Umberto Pugliese knew of course, as every Italian knew, what had happened down in the south. He had been in charge of all naval construction for years, was fully acquainted with the ships in question, especially with the *Littorio*, which he himself had designed and constructed. The confidential conversation between the minister and the ex-general was brief. The minister wanted to know how much it would cost him if Pugliese were to raise the submerged fleet, and how much did the general *personally* want to do the job? There is no report on how Pugliese (who died in October 1967) looked at the minister; only a report of his acceptance. "I want one round-trip ticket to Taranto," said the dismissed Inspector-General. After which he put his uniform back on, paid his own expenses while in the south, and raised the ships that had been so dear to him. The job done, he quietly returned to Rome and put his uniform back among the mothballs. The fleet had been resurrected, or at least surfaced—but with the exception of a few shame-faced insiders, no one in Italy knew who had done the job.

In Rome itself, of course, the story soon enough leaked out among the Jews. But if one of them had extricated the government from a difficulty, it did not change the situation for the rest of them, not even for General Pugliese himself. Life in the capital went on agonizingly slowly for those who remained. They had lost their work, and their joy in life; they had stopped living as individuals. Yet there was still no new ghetto in Rome, and they could reflect on what had happened through the centuries. The Jews of Rome had been the last ones to be freed from papal subserviency. Now they were practically, to all intents and purposes, back in that lowly position, but oppressed by a different master—fascism; and for the moment it did not look as if another liberation were close at hand.

Mussolini's flag was high. In Africa the Germans and Italians early in 1941 stood at the frontiers of Egypt. In June Hitler attacked Russia. By December of that same year the Japanese magnified the Taranto disaster at Pearl Harbor, bringing the United States into the war. There seemed to be no end to the Nazi-Fascist victories, and no limit to the suffering of the Jews. To the fascists, they had been "the cause of it all," together with a few other anti-fascist groups. In May 1943 *La Stampa* described, in a dispatch from Belgrade, how "Jews had kept their shovels at the ready to dig the ditch in which to bury Yugoslavia. . . ."

Yet if the Jews of Rome had lost everything or almost everything, they did not know how relatively lucky they were. If they ate wretchedly, at least they had something to stave off starvation. If they lived miserably and in fear, they had the small comfort of their own homes and apartments—and among Italians. There were no Germans to bully them, no daily threats to their very lives, and no cruel deportations—as elsewhere.

Then the war news changed. The Axis armies retreated in Africa. The Russian lines held at last, and the Red armies started to counter-attack. The Allies invaded Sicily, then the mainland,

and moved northward towards Rome. Mussolini's proud exhortations began to sound like the whimperings of a subdued animal. On 25 July 1943 the Duce was ousted as the head of government in a quiet coup d'état planned within the inner circle of the Fascist Grand Council. Six weeks later, on September 8, the terms of Marshal Badoglio's secret armistice with the Allies were made public.

That same day the Germans occupied Rome.

Chapter 35
The German
Occupation

The Jews of Rome were amazed. They had awaited the arrival of the Germans as masters of the city with a fear that had penetrated into the very depth of their souls, only to discover that it was "not true" what they had heard. In other countries the Jews had been sent to notorious labor camps; they had been tortured and separated from their families; in the German *Reich* persecution of the Jews had had an early start during the first years of the Nazi régime; and the Roman Jews had expected similar treatment. It just was "not true."

It was not that the Germans were suddenly full of the milk of human kindness; but Jews were for the moment not more seriously bothered than other Romans. After the first few upsetting days following the Armistice and the Occupation of September 8, life in Rome had returned to its usual (or, rather, unusual) war pattern. The aspect of the city had changed on account of the presence of German troops and the absence of automobiles which had been requisitioned. The extra-territorial enclave of the Vatican had become a partially closed or controlled area, with German sentries stationed at the entrance to the square in front of St. Peter's. Yet things were *korrekt*. Catholics wanting to enter the basilica were not hindered, and Germans had hardly any notion of who among the Italians were Jews or Catholics, since to them all cats looked grey in the dark. The Jews themselves felt greatly relieved; and quietly though not happily they continued to live their restricted lives, occupying themselves with their restricted activities.

Not *all* of the Jews though. The principal one in the community had suddenly disappeared.

61-year-old Chief Rabbi Italo Zolli—who had been born in Austrian Galicia, and who at an early age had come to Italy, later to be rabbi of Trieste for thirty years before being named in Rome late in 1938—was nowhere to be found. He had taken the place of Chief Rabbi David Prato because several Roman newspapers had considered the latter too conspicuously antifascist. The new rabbi's name first had been changed from Israel Zoller to Israel Zolli and then to Italo Zolli. Now the leading Roman Jew had gone with the prophet's breath, leaving no trace. It was a severe blow to the rest of the community, headed by president Ugo Foà, and seconded by Dante Almansi, president of the Hebrew Union in which all the Italian Jewish communities were grouped. Both presidents had a quite collaborationist past, which had brought them close to fascism; and Foà had been imposed upon the Roman Jews as their president during the height of the fascist régime. Rabbi Zolli had been constantly at odds with him on political issues—at least according to his own later statements.*

Still, September being climatically a delightful month in Rome, and with Mussolini gone—indeed audaciously freed by Otto Skorzeny on September 12 and taken to Germany—and the Allies somewhere to the south of the capital, it looked as if the war was moving to its final dramatic stages. The future

---

*Interview with Herbert L. Matthews in the *New York Times* of 9 July, 1944.

looked fairly hopeful for the Jews of Rome. Even with the Germans as their direct masters, partially governing via leftover fascist grouplets, the Jews felt that the worst was behind them.

This situation lasted for a few weeks, till Sunday 26 September, when the two Jewish community presidents received an invitation from Major Herbert Kappler, head of the SS (or *Schutzstaffel*) in Rome, to come and see him. That same afternoon, please. The two Jews found a German officer in his middle thirties, blond, quite good-looking, with an ingratiating smile and a dueling-scar on his cheek. The major had—Foà and Almansi could not know this—a female Italian teacher; she evidently was Jewish-born, but baptized, neither of which circumstances Kappler knew. The girl spoke fluent Italian and German, was holder of a Brazilian passport, and her connections with the German major were thought not to be restricted to the teaching of Italian. Moreover, this teacher during this period had contact with Father Antonio Weber of the *Good Works of San Raffaele*, whose task it was to help Catholic-baptized Jews of non-Italian nationality emigrate to Brazil; and on those occasions she would ask for his help in getting other baptized foreign Jews out of the country.

But neither emigration, nor charming girls, nor language lessons were on the mind of the polite major that afternoon of 26 September 1943. He was courteous to his two guests, apologized for disturbing them and chatted for a few minutes as any person might do who had asked someone to come and pay him a visit about an undisclosed subject. However, it did not take long for the real agenda of the invitation to be placed on the table. According to Ugo Foà, the tone soon changed. The blond major—now in the early 70s, older, greyer, religion his prime interest, and making frequent (and still polite) requests to be released from the prison at Gaeta south of Rome, where he is serving a life sentence—told the two representatives of the Jewish Community that he was not at all impressed by their Italian citizenship. "We Germans," he said, "consider you only as Jews and as such you are our enemy." He went on to explain, introducing his main theme of extortion, that it "was not his intention to take their lives or that of their children." He would take other things instead—gold, for instance, gold that would serve "to forge new arms" for his embattled fatherland. To be exact, "fifty kilograms" of gold (or just about one hundred and ten pounds). And it was to be handed over within thirty-six hours, "or otherwise two hundred Jews would be deported to Germany near the Russian border, or would be rendered innocuous in a different manner." *Guten Tag, meine Herren.*

One moment, please. The two Jewish emissaries wanted to have some more information. They wanted to know whether the intended hostages would only be Jews who were active members of the community, whether the major meant other Jews as well, and whether baptized Jews also would be included. And they pointed out that thirty-six hours was a rather short time to collect fifty kilograms of gold. Moreover, suppose they were unable to get the required quantity together, would the major take money instead? The major laughed. He would take dollars or sterling, he said, but *lire?* They were not worth the paper they were printed on; he could give instructions himself to print lire by the million. And as to the kind of Jews he had in mind, to him Jews were Jews, whether they were inscribed as members of the community or not, baptized or not, or married to non-Jews or not. "Everyone who has a drop of Jewish blood in his veins is a Jew—and thirty-six hours is thirty-six hours, with the deadline at eleven o'clock in the morning, Tuesday 28 September. *Sie können gehen.*"

So Signor Foà and Signor Almansi went, and assembled the wealthier members of the congregation, some of them summoned by the unlisted but still operative telephones, others called in person by Giuseppe Gay, a taxi-driver who had lost his license, and who as a religious Jew was a staunch supporter of the Temple. But who had fifty kilograms of gold hidden in his desk drawer? No one, of course. They had wedding rings, watches, cigarette cases, and bracelets; and here and there a gold cup or fork and spoon; and perhaps even some gold coins and a few dollars (which by then were worth around two hundred lire each on the black market, against an official but totally unrealistic rate of exchange of only eighteen or nineteen). But fifty kilograms of gold? Who had that? But wait a second—except the Vatican perhaps, someone thought.

Fifty kilograms of old gold in the Italy of today can be bought for approximately $50,000, its value (1971) being 550,000 lire or roughly $950 a kilogram for 18-carat quality. In 1943 it was, of course, non-existent on the open market, and its value on the black market had increased on par with the dollar—about tenfold. Turn to the Vatican? A good idea; the Vatican certainly might dispose of some gold when it was a matter of trading two hundred beings at 250 dollars a head. Cheap at the price, and considering the Nazis' usual greed, an actually ridiculously small amount to ask for—small, if one had it.

Time was pressing. Who could contact the Vatican authorities that quickly *and* get an answer? The leaders of the Jewish Community had a good many Catholic contacts in town, and Dr. Renzo Levi thought there was one man who might succeed—Father Borsarelli, Vice-Prior of the Convent of the Missionaries of the Holy Heart. The good prior immediately set off for the Vatican, and that same day (28 September) at two o'clock in the afternoon the answer came—the Vatican would indeed assist the Jews. Although the coffers inside the German-surrounded walls were probably well stocked, there was no offer to help out with the full amount or weight (which of course had not been asked for either); but under the circumstances it would have made things considerably easier for the hard-pressed Jews of Rome, and would have saved them many anxious hours. Still the offer was substantial. Any gold that was lacking by the time the deadline approached, up to a maximum of fifteen kilograms (at today's value roughly 15,000 dollars), would be put at the disposal of the community by the Vatican. And no reason for the Jews to worry—"they could refund it without any hurry when the community would be able to do so."* While the offer was generous, it somehow seemed to

*As recorded by Ugo Foà on 15 November, 1943 in his full report of German behaviour in Rome. The report was handed to a friend for safe-keeping in case Foà were to be taken away by the Nazis. Foà survived.

have its generous limitations, speaking so immediately of *refunding* in a case that involved hundreds of human lives.

The news spread quickly around Rome. Not only Jews but also Catholics started to come to the Temple along the Tiber in order to deposit their large and small donations at the offices of the community, an action in which several priests took an active part. So much so that the Vatican's offer could be declined politely with thanks, for the golden counterweight of Jewish flesh and blood had more than accumulated to its required quantity shortly before the thirty-sixth hour. On Tuesday morning President Foà had gone to ask the Germans for a slight extension of time, which was granted till four o'clock that afternoon. By then there was even a large surplus, between 28 and 30 kilograms over and above the requested weight.* Some two million lire in cash had also been offered; it remained unused in the office safe. They were certainly not to worry about buying gold from Rome's black marketeers who had assembled in front of the Temple as soon as the news of the German demand had circulated in the city.

The community leaders decided to play it safe with the Germans. They took along an extra 300 grams of gold—nearly 11 ounces—in order not to get a complaint of bringing an underweighted quantity. Then the question of transportation had to be considered; it posed a slight problem. None of the Jews of Rome had an automobile any longer. But there were still taxis in town, and Giuseppe Gay, who had helped to get the initial small advisory committee together and who had been helping out with the weighing of the contributions, was able to convince two of his former colleagues to take on the job. Two Roman policemen also came along to guard the precious cargo. They were joined by Chief of Police Cappa of the station closest to the synagogue, an old friend of the community, who for the occa-

---

*This extra gold, unfortunately, could never be used to help Jews who subsequently had to go into hiding in Rome. It was handed to one of the members of the community, who—together with most of the leaders—had to go underground himself. In 1948, after the State of Israel had become independent, the full surplus of gold was sent to Jerusalem as a contribution from the surviving Roman Jews.

sion had taken off his uniform and acted as if he were merely helping out with the carrying of the boxes.

Situated halfway between the basilicas of Santa Maria Maggiore and San Giovanni and close to the German embassy in the Villa Walkonsky, the SS headquarters in the Via Tasso housed upstairs the German office for Italian Labor Recruitment; downstairs was reserved for tougher, rougher assignments. Here the small group carried their cargo into Major Kappler's office. His second-in-command, a brutish Captain Schutz, took care of the operation of checking whether the required quantity of precious metal was all there. Using a five-kilogram pair of scales, the Germans went ten times through the weighing process, then to discover that there was a little gold left over—the 300 extra grams that had been added as a premium just to be on the safe side. Not so, said Captain Schutz; they had only weighed nine portions, and consequently the Jews were accused of trying to shortchange the honest SS out of their promised gold. With armed SS guards standing behind them, Foá and Almansi were involved in a tense argument. They had kept track of the weighing with mathematical precision, and they showed the Germans their figures. There was some shouting, much brave persistence, and then a recount. This time the fifty kilograms (plus the extra bit) were all present and accounted for, and without a receipt—which the Germans refused to give—the group left with relaxed and relieved hearts. The ransom had been paid, no Jews would be taken as hostages; and the members of the Roman community could sleep quietly. It had all been worth the money.

According to statements made by Major Kappler during his later trial in Rome, he entrusted the gold to a major from Berlin. He had it transferred to Ernst Kaltenbrunner, head of the German *Sicherheitsdienst*, who had followed Heydrich in this job after the latter had been murdered in 1942 in Czechoslovakia. But on that 28th of September 1943 it had been of precious little interest to the Jews of Rome what happened to the gold once it had been delivered; what mattered was they had been able to buy off the threat of deportation.

Again the Germans were *korrekt*. That is—for another twenty-four hours. Then, while a few armored cars parked along the Tiber, about forty armed men invaded the community's offices on the upper floors next to the Temple. In the presence of Dr. Foà, who had to act as guide, a minute inspection of the whole building took place. What they apparently were looking for were "secret papers," and in the absence of these they decided to take the over two million lire from the safe, which had been intended to buy the black-market gold, if necessary. The next morning (it happened to be Jewish New Year) some German Hebrew-experts came to see what documents of value there might be in the building's library. There were a considerable number, accumulated through the ages and including centuries-old manuscripts and first editions of books printed in Hebrew and *Ladino* (the Jewish-Spanish dialect spoken by the early immigrants to Italy after their deportation from Spain in 1492). On the Saturday morning following, the German experts returned once more. The day after that they broke into the apartment of the missing Chief Rabbi Italo Zolli *né* Israel Zoller. No secret documents here either, nor any indication of Zolli's whereabouts.

Such individual raids by the Germans had hardly any direct influence on the Jews dispersed throughout Rome. Yet whatever happened along the Lungotevere de' Cenci was quickly known in all four corners of the city. But the inspection of ancient books was no catastrophe, and since the gold had been paid, there was no reason to be alarmed. Even the attempt by the studious Germans to carry away some of the precious manuscripts was of no special importance, even if from a bibliographical point of view the collection's value was inestimable. The gold had been paid, the library had been plundered, the score was even.

It is amazing to look back—how could the Jews of Rome have been so confident? In retrospect their innocent trustfulness is stupifying. From the report written by Foà on that 15th of November 1943, the one constant impression one gets is his surprise at the Nazis' dishonesty. Their trying to cheat on five kilograms of gold had astounded him, and he speaks of *sconcertante malafede* (or "disconcerting bad faith"). And on leaving the German major's office he wondered whether the refusal to give a receipt for the gold had resulted from his "being conscious of the illegality of the accomplished action," as if that were of any consequence. When his secretary told him on 11 October that the Germans had been to the community's offices to inspect the library, he said to her—according to Miss Sorani's own diary—that "it would have been better if she had closed the library immediately and would have refused to give the key to anyone, even to him," as if not having the key would have kept the Germans out. One could almost have sympathy with Rabbi Zolli who had understood the Germans and had gone with the wind, if his desertion had not been the dispiriting act of a general deserting his troops or a shepherd abandoning his flock.

It was just over five weeks since the Germans had made Rome an occupied city. With the exception of a few arrests of some Catholics and some Jews, mostly for political reasons, there had not been any physical threats against the people in general.

Saturday morning it rained—a constant drizzle on one of those miserable coldish Roman October mornings when a slight fog hangs on the outskirts of town, and the Tiber looks like the most uninviting stream in the world. The Bridge With The Four Heads, crossing the river from the island, was deserted at the early hour, and the Jews living in the old ghetto area were asleep. To all of them it was the Sabbath, to many the day of rest. There had been sporadic shooting around Rome during the night, but no one actually knew who was shooting at whom. But by four o'clock all was quiet again.

By five the trucks arrived. They stopped near the Gate of Octavia, close to the church where in former years the forced sermons had taken place, and where on that other church the inscription in Latin and Hebrew insisted that the Jews were still in error. Quietly the men climbed down from the trucks onto the

wet pavements and then dispersed silently through the streets,
lists in hand. Five minutes later the first anguished cry was
heard—*"the Germans!"*

The heavy boots were noisy on the staircases. A knock on the
door—not everywhere, only for those people indicated in the
carefully prepared lists. Jews only. Upstairs there were running
feet too. Men trying to escape across roof tops. Children handed
out of windows. Women weeping, children crying, men
desperate. Germans methodical. Some Jews succeeded in getting
away, very few, saved by presence of mind. (When asked by a
soldier where a certain person lived, that certain person—a
woman—answered that she had moved, and walked past her
captors down the stairs to freedom.) The others were given a
notification to read: *"You are being transferred. Take along
food for eight days, blankets, money, and jewelry. Close the
apartment and bring the key. The sick can not stay
behind—there is a hospital in the camp. You have twenty
minutes to get ready."*

Some did not understand, others had nerve. Signorina Sorani,
the community's secretary, early on her way to the Temple to
check whether everything was all right, was warned by another
Jew not to continue on her walk along the Tiber. She persisted
and had to be warned twice more, then telephoned Foà. A
publisher, Luciano Morpurgo, went for an early morning stroll
with his brother—towards the ghetto, of all places. They walked
through the area, German soldiers standing watch near the
assembling groups of Jews in front of the small building that
houses the city's Antiquities Office. How could the Germans
have any notion who was a Jew and who was not? Everybody
looked thoroughly Italian. Those who were marked on their
lists were taken. Others, showing improvised false papers, were
left in peace. One man evaded arrest by joining a line in front of
a tobacco shop to buy cigarettes. (That, of course, must have
been an Italian, surely not a Jew; at least according to the Germans.)

Old women were caught, and old men; young children;
mothers nursing babies; and pregnant wives. Once the quota

was collected, the victims were herded into trucks or were thrown in, including the aged and the sick who could walk no longer. It had all happened hundreds and thousands of times elsewhere in Europe. But not in Italy, because it just could not happen there. Not in Rome. Not even a fascist would hurt or kill a Jew simply because he was a Jew. But the fascists were out; and only the worst elements among them, the equivalent of the German SS, swaggering along with the Nazis, were still in town—and active. The Jewish fascists had left the movement long ago, even those who had been such true believers. The plain, civilian, Catholic fascists who had remained in Rome instead of fleeing to Mussolini's republic of Saló in the north, had for two decades believed in the Duce, foolishly perhaps, stupidly perhaps. But they did not believe in the Germans, and they believed still less in the Nazis. To stand around the ghetto and the Bridge With The Four Heads on that Saturday morning was to learn a lesson. The Germans had acted, and the Romans reacted. They became pro-Italian as never before, and pro-Jewish—which for so many years they had not considered as a special religion, till Mussolini brought anti-Semitism to their attention, and failed.

One thousand and one hundred and twenty seven Roman Jews, of whom 800 were woman and children, were picked up on that Saturday between five in the morning and one o'clock in the afternoon—time, as one Jew remarked, for the Germans to have lunch. Most of the victims came from the ghetto area, a small number from elsewhere in town. Two days later, on Monday morning, their train departed for the north. In Chiusi, halfway to Florence, the body of the first dead woman was unloaded.

Major Kappler, from all the records of these events of 16 October 1943 (except those he personally provided), seems to have had an all-guiding hand in the proceedings. He added another heroic exploit to his career when on 24 March 1944 he had 335 Romans shot at the Ardeatine Caves outside the city. These were hostages for the killing of 33 German soldiers by a Roman partisan bomb-attack that had taken place the day before in the

Via Rasella, a side-street of the Via delle Quattro Fontane near the Piazza Barberini. At the official military exchange rate of ten to one, Kappler had not been able that quickly to find enough innocent Romans to be shot. To fill out the required number he had added 71 Jews who happened to be in prison or who were otherwise conveniently handy.

In 1961 during the preparations for the Eichmann trial in Israel, Major Kappler was interviewed in the Gaeta prison by a representative of Eichmann's lawyer, in the company of various Italian personalities, among whom was Jewish attorney Roberto Ascarelli. Major Kappler, living in "a plain, simple cell" (and, according to lawyer Ascarelli, behaving as "a distinguished person") was still polite but had changed his story. He now claimed that "on his own initiative" he "had asked the Roman Jews for fifty kilograms of gold *to avoid* their deportation." In other words, the major actually had tried to *save* the Jews of Rome.

According to reports which have since become available*, Major Kappler had not received the order to deport the Roman Jews till early in October, well after he already had extracted the gold from the Roman community—on his own initiative therefore. After seventeen years in prison and a bout of religious piety, Major Kappler, it would seem, still could not get the true story straight. In the meantime he has repeatedly asked the Italian government to reduce the term of his life imprisonment, a sentence based mainly on his complicity in the Ardeatine Caves murders. In his own view, Kappler feels that he is innocent. He testified that his orders for the Ardeatine killings actually had come "from above," or that they were executed "by others," and that it really had never been his intention to do harm.**

*Paul Friedlaender, *Pius XII and the Third Reich*, (Knopf, New York, 1966).
**In Rome, one Jew helped the Germans, or rather her lover who happened to be an Italian fascist policeman. She was a 19-year-old girl by the name of Stella di Porto. Known to her intimates as Celeste and to all others as *la pantera nera*—the black panther—she is said to have been paid 5,000 lire a head. She indicated her victims by greeting them in the street; if they returned the greeting, they would be picked up by the German SS who followed her at a distance. Once the Germans left Rome, Celeste was arrested—then freed, supposedly with the help of still influential fascists. Having taken refuge in a convent with the intent to become a nun, she soon left there and I have heard reports that she is supposed to be living on the outskirts of Rome in the section known as Acqua Bullicante, not far from the golf club on the Via Appia.

Between 16 October 1943 and 5 June 1944—the day Rome was liberated—nearly another thousand Roman Jews were arrested and deported, making a total of 2,091—about half of them men, and including close to three hundred children. Of these 73 men and 28 women returned after the war. No children.

Chapter 36
The Rescue Plan

Twenty-four hours after the Germans had made their first thousand arrests in Rome on October 16, there was not a Jew to be found in the city any longer—at least not officially. Over-night some eight thousand people disappeared—to the country-side if they could, others into the underground, changing homes and rooms constantly. The tribe on the Tiber, after centuries of concentrated living in the Roman ghetto, suddenly seemed to have vanished from the Italian soil, causing a "local diaspora" which the Papacy always had tried to prevent. For the next eight months Roman Jews lived under assumed names with false papers of every kind and description. Armed with these, some of them after a while even returned to the ghetto area. Here they mixed with Catholic refugees from the provinces, who by then had taken possession of the apartments freed by the sudden, mysterious disappearance of the Jews.

Help came from many sources. A spontaneous and highly in-dividual course of action was taken by a large number of priests and nuns, acting as Italians to help other Italians—who happened to be Jews. Churches, monasteries, and convents always had offered sanctuary to those who were seeking refuge; now they became the shelter for persecuted Jews. Those who had money, paid for their sojourn, not only in convents but also in hospitals, run by various religious orders, and even in lunatic asylums. In one of these the wife of taxi-driver Giuseppe Gay who had so actively participated in the gold collection, would spend part of the German occupation—even continuing to "act crazy" when her two young daughters came one day to visit her. The girls themselves were later given asylum in a convent, where Signor Gay paid for their keep (including an extra charge for the weekly bath that was punctually and carefully noted on the bill). "It was perfectly all right," Signor Gay told me in 1967, by then grey and seventy but a taxi-driver again. "The convents, too, were in danger of being detected by the Germans," he explained in retrospect, "and money from the Vatican was not forthcoming for any of these Jews, whether of Italian or other nationality. . . . "

As had been the case two thousand years earlier, the fate of the Jews living under Roman jurisdiction far from the Italian capital would once again be decided upon by the governing powers along the Tiber. When in March 1943 von Mackensen, the German ambassador in Rome, had complained to Mussolini about the Italian Army's benevolent treatment of Jews in Italian-occupied territories, the Duce had decided to do something about it. Having told von Mackensen that the Italian soldier "did not understand the problem," but simultaneously having promised—as the ambassador had cabled Berlin—"to solve the question according to German wishes," the Duce then went about it *all'italiana.*

Italian troops occupied parts of the Balkans and eight *départements* in France bordering on Italy—from the Rivièra to the mountains of Savoy, where the Fourth Army was on occupation duty. Inquiring into "the trouble," Commanding General Vercellini, who was headquartered in Menton, had informed Rome that he considered the Jews in his territory a civil responsibility, not that of the army. In the afternoon of 13 March 1943 the Duce had telephoned his Minister of the Interior, ordering a trusted gentleman from the police force to be sent to him, someone with knowledge—if possible—of France.

The minister called the chief of the Roman police, Carmine Senise, and Senise knew just the man—Guido Lospinoso, Inspector-General of the *Pubblica Sicurezza*, who had spent twelve years (from 1927 till 1939) at the Italian consulate in Nice in the capacity of police-attaché. But Lospinoso, whose day off it happened to be, had gone to the cinema. And since inspectors-general of the Roman police department had neither office nor staff, but simply reported to headquarters for assignments which took them all over the country as they turned up, Lospinoso's whereabouts had remained a day-long mystery.

At eleven o'clock that evening the inspector came home, found the urgent message to go and see Mussolini in person, and immediately set off through the blacked-out and deserted city for the Palazzo Venezia on foot; an inspector-general of the police did not then have an automobile at his disposal. He was in civilian clothes, and was promptly arrested when trying to enter the offices at such a late hour; it took some persuasiveness to get through to the Duce.

Mussolini came immediately to the point. He explained that the between 30,000 and 50,000 Jews (French and foreign) in the south of France "were politically suspect" and had to be sent "to the interior—at least one hundred kilometers from the coast," somewhere to Savoy or thereabouts. Lospinoso wondered how he was going to do this. Mussolini, to whom speech often was the equivalent of action, answered in two words of one syllable. *"Do it!"* he said.

The inspector, a bit taken aback, was as adamant as he felt his position would permit, and wondered "where they should be sent to live?" And he explained to the Duce that according to his information "there were no cars available," and *if* there were cars, he understood there was no gasoline. To the head of the

Italian government these were insignificant details. "You have my orders," said Mussolini, "execute them!" And with that Lospinoso plunged back into the uncomfortable darkness of the lonely Roman night, the sentries who had arrested him now smartly saluting—then to set off for the Rivièra, a place he dearly loved.

The Inspector-General had *carte blanche*, installed himself in a charming villa in the mountains above Nice, then went to see an old acquaintance of his, Angelo Donati, an Italian Jew who had been living for a great many years in France, where he had been director of the *Crédit Franco-Italien*, a bank in Nice. Donati had been very active in trying to save Jews from all over Europe who first had fled to the unoccupied zone of France, then filtered down to the Italian-governed provinces after the Germans took over the rest of the country in November 1942 (when the Allies had landed in North Africa and the French Navy had scuttled the fleet in Toulon): Donati felt that Mussolini could not have made a better choice in selecting his emissary. After their first conversation, he asked a French friar with whom he had been working closely, ever since June 1940, to pay Lospinoso a visit. This Capuchin priest, Father Marie-Benoit (or Maria Benedetto as he had been known in Rome before, and would be known again on his return there), would subsequently become a legendary figure in the Roman rescue activities in favor of the Jews.

The priest found Lospinoso "an honest person," easy to deal with. However, his impression of the inspector's knowledge of Jews and Judaism was rather meagre, especially when the Italian inquired how he, a priest, could take such an interest in Jews, then to ask whether the Jews and Catholics had the same God. (In Rome in 1967, Lospinoso told me that Father Maria Benedetto must have misunderstood him, because he knew perfectly well that God was the same for both religions.) The question having been answered in the affirmative, the two men separated amicably, after which Mussolini's envoy started to look for ways and means—making sure not to exhaust himself in the process—on how to resettle the Jews inland.

The war by now was not going too well for the Axis

partners. Angelo Donati saw a lurking danger in the possibility of having the Germans invade the Italian-occupied French provinces if and when Italy would be forced out of the conflict. The results of this certainly would be disastrous for the mass of Jewish refugees in southern France. So when Maria Benedetto was recalled to Rome by the father superior of his order, Donati decided to take advantage of this forthcoming trip in order to help his thousands of wards. He brought Father Benedetto in touch with the heads of the various French Jewish organisations who were hiding out in Lyon. Then, in June, the priest left for Rome—four suggested points of discussion with the Pope carefully hidden in his pocket, and full of hope to be able to get some results.

An audience with Pius XII was arranged. When Father Benedetto informed the Pontiff about the persecutions going on in the Vichy-governed territory, the Pope who openly never had done much to help the Jews anywhere, remarked that "one would not have believed France to act that way." Then Father Benedetto handed the Pope a carefully prepared memorandum, given to him especially for that purpose by the assembled rabbis in Lyon. It contained "clandestinely-obtained information on the concentration camps in Upper Silesia, and details on how deportations were organized in France." The concentration camps in Upper Silesia were Auschwitz and Treblinka, and the date this report was handed to Pope Pius XII was 16 July 1943. Father Benedetto told me that he "had only one copy of the report, which was left at the Vatican."

According to explanations made by the Vatican after the War, it had never been possible for the ecclesiastical authorities to "verify the veracity" of such reports on conditions in the concentration and extermination camps, which was the reason why no protest was made—an excuse frequently used by Vatican spokesmen to explain the Pope's inaction. It may be assumed that the detailed report handed Pius XII by Father Maria Benedetto was also considered unverifiable, and was added to the existing pile of similar papers that had been received by the Vatican from other sources on earlier dates.

The Capuchin priest left the four other questions, discussed in Lyon, with the Pope for study and consideration. The first item dealt with the possibility of "obtaining news on the fate of the approximately 50,000 Jews, both French and foreign, who had been deported from France." The second requested possible Vatican help in trying to obtain better treatment for those Jews who were in concentration camps in France itself. (Their condition was described in detail by the former chief rabbi of Strassbourg, Monsieur Hirschler, who had been able to visit these camps.) The third point dealt with the possible protection to be extended by Spain to those Jews in southern France who were of Sephardic extraction. The last and undoubtedly most important question submitted to the Pope was a request for cooperation in getting the Jews who were stranded in the Italian-occupied French territory out of there, and into Italy.

On points one and two there never was any action, and Father Benedetto in fact had not expected much, since all information or assistance had to come from the Germans. On point three there was action—too late though. By 9 September Father Benedetto was informed by the Vatican Secretary of State, Luigi Cardinal Maglione, that Spain (through the intervention of the Papal Nuncio in Madrid, Monsignore Gaetano Cicognani) had given orders to issue protective papers to any Jew in southern France "who somehow could prove his Spanish affiliation, even in the most embryonic manner." But by then the armistice between the Allies and Italy having been made public, and the Germans having taken the occupation duties out of the hands of the Italians, the stateless Jews in France who claimed Spanish nationality continued to be stateless Jews, and were treated accordingly by the Germans. On point four there never was any response from the Vatican at all, as Father Benedetto said bitterly to me in 1968.

But in the meantime the indefatigable Angelo Donati had started his own arrangements. Assisted by the Italians in Nice, he took off for Rome as if this were the most simple journey for a Jew, and arrived there on 24 July. Twenty-four hours later Mussolini was ousted; but Donati felt that instead of being detrimental to his project, it might even be a benefit. He returned to Nice, but was back in Rome by 15 August in order to deal directly with the Italian Foreign Office. Father Benedetto, by then solidly installed in the Capuchin convent in the Via Sicilia, told his friend that he could introduce him to the British ambassador to the Holy See, Sir D'Arcy Osborne, and to Harold Tittmann who (during the absence of Myron Taylor, President Roosevelt's personal envoy to Pope Pius) was in charge of American interests at the Vatican. The meeting was to take place in the apartment of another French priest and a close friend of Father Benedetto, Monsignor Hérissé; he lived inside the Vatican, where by now the British and American representatives, ousted from the city of Rome by war, also had their headquarters.

Donati talked with Guariglia, who headed the foreign ministry in the new Badoglio government, then spoke to Sir D'Arcy Osborne and Mr. Tittmann who promised to contact London and Washington on the subject. Donati's fertile brain, while these steps were being taken, had come up with an even shrewder idea—the Jews from southern France should be taken to North Africa, now in Allied hands. All eventual arrangements, said Donati, would be made by the Italian Jewish *Delasem** organisation, administered and organized in Genova by a Jewish lawyer named Lelio Vittorio Valobra, and financed via Switzerland by the *Joint* (the American Jewish Distribution Committee).

Communications between Tittmann and Washington had to go via Bern or Lisbon; but some progress was made. On 2 September the U.S. Secretary of State Cordell Hull informed the U.S. ambassador in London, John A. Winant, that (according to a telegram received from Tittmann via Bern, written on 25 August) "*Delasem* states that about 15,000 foreign Jews are at present in Italian-occupied France, waiting to take refuge in Italy to escape from Germans, should these replace Italians as occupants." The Italian government (Tittmann had informed Hull) "is willing to receive this fresh contingent of Jews, but

---

**Delegazione Assistenza Emigranti Ebrei*—Jewish Emigrant Association.

only in transit for another destination, since the country has not the resources to support additional burdens" over and above "the 14,000 refugee Jews [already] living on Italian soil."

Secretary Hull then went on to inform Winant (with a request to hand this matter over to the Intergovernmental Refugee Committee in London) about the plan evolved by Angelo Donati. "*Delasem* proposes," wired Hull, "that with the help of humanitarian organisations such as Red Cross which would supply ships, Jews now in danger in France be permitted by Allies to proceed to North Africa (Tunisia, Algeria, Morocco)." He further mentioned that they could be assisted with funds "already available in United States and Britain." Tittmann, in his telegram to Hull, had called the situation "extremely urgent." He had informed the Secretary of State that his "British colleague [at the Vatican] has reported foregoing proposal by telegram to London." Hull, for his part, expressed the hope of the State Department that "it will be possible for the [London] Committee to assist these refugees now in danger in France and Italy."

During the next few days Angelo Donati redoubled his efforts, and informed Father Benedetto that good progress had been made. Again he requested the priest to act as intermediary with the British and American representatives at the Vatican, and to make especially sure that all requests were transmitted in the name of the *Delasem* organisation, and not by Donati personally. Donati already had a copy of the identity card which the Italian authorities were to deliver to every Jew arriving from France on his way to North Africa. Some eighty trucks had been promised to bring the refugees in convoy from France to the Italian ports of embarkation. From there four Italian ships would bring them across the Mediterranean, all expenses to be paid by the American *Joint*. Informed of the arrangements, Harold Tittmann (on 30 August) sent a second communication to Washington, this time via Lisbon. Once more Secretary Hull sent it on the Ambassador Winant in London.

"The Italian *Delasem*," Hull wired, "reports Italian government prepared to provide steamships Vulcania, Saturnia,

Diulio* and Giulio Cesare which are capable of transporting approximately 30,000 Jews from Italy to North Africa in three voyages. Expenses would be 5,500 dollars per day while under navigation, plus insurance, fuel, lubricants, and food, to be borne by Jewish organisations in the United States. Fuel and lubricants to be furnished by British government against reimbursements. Color and personnel of ships which recently returned from East Africa with Italian repatriates, have already been agreed upon by British and American governments. Early action should be taken while ships are still in condition to accommodate refugees." And again Secretary Hull informed the American ambassador in London that the State Department "desires to commend the above to the appropriate consideration of the Intergovernmental Refugee Committee."

Another week passed, during which time things were almost organized. So much so that on 6 September Tittmann could send the most reassuring telegram of all to Washington via Bern. "Italian government," cabled Tittmann, "has authorized all French and foreign Jews residing in France in the zone over which it will not have control, to transfer their residence to the zone of the *Alpes Maritimes* Department, over which it will still have control. The Italian military authorities are in every way facilitating travel of these persons and their establishment in the new district. Some categories of Jews are provided with Italian police escort who have orders to prevent by force any opposition to their transfer."

There were three more significant paragraphs in Tittmann's telegram. In the first he explained that the Italian government "would have been willing to accept without conditions or guarantees the above-mentioned Jews as it did in the case of previous 14,000 from the Balkans, were it not for the fact that the localities to which it would have been possible to send them are already occupied by Italian citizens evacuated from the bombed areas. The purpose of the *Delasem* proposals is to

---

*An old passenger liner, not to be confused with the cruiser of the same name which in 1941 had been salvaged in the Bay of Taranto by the Italian Jewish general Pugliese.

relieve the Italian Government of this fresh burden and to avoid the possibility that the Jews might be deported in spite of the manifest wishes of the Italians."

Tittmann then asked for permission from Washington—as the British ambassador had requested from London—"to be authorized to contact the Italian government (which I am told is only too willing to cooperate) with a view of solving the problem at the earliest possible moment." And the American representative at the Vatican added, as his fourth point, that "a long delay in carrying out the proposals would compromise the desired results."

This last four-point telegram was received in Washington in the afternoon of 9 September. Why should there have been any further delay? Angelo Donati had been given to understand by the Italian authorities (and Tittmann obviously must have had the same impression) that the planned publication of the armistice, signed between the Badoglio government and General Eisenhower on 3 September would not be announced by the U.S. Commander-in-Chief till some time in October. This might have allowed the over-hopeful rescue organisation—Germans willing—to develop normally, and to have all Jews from France transferred to Italy and from there to North Africa before the Italians would stop hostilities. Most likely, the Italian authorities in Rome who informed Donati of the reassuring October date were actually ignorant about the day fixed for the announcement. Even those belonging to the innermost circle of the Badoglio government were groping in the dark. But they knew that it would not be later than 15 September, a date they implored Eisenhower to keep. The American commander, having fully organized the invasion of the Italian mainland from Sicily, and having promised to make the cease-fire arrangements public only a few hours before that invasion would take place, informed the world of the armistice on 8 September. That was two days after Tittmann had sent his enthusiastic last telegram from Rome, and twenty-four hours before it reached Washington.

By then thousands of Jews had assembled on the French Rivièra. They were waiting to be rescued, in vain. On that same 8th of September the Germans occupied all territory previously administered by the Italian army in France. The Italian troops were in a state of shock and chaos. Police inspector Lospinoso disappeared by walking across the border at Ventimiglia and removing his uniform. Donati was in despair.

Between 40,000 and 50,000 Jews were trapped in southern France. Most of them fell victim to Hitler's "Final Solution."

Chapter 37
Maria Benedetto,
"Father of the Jews"

The debacle of the Jewish rescue operation in France would have one beneficial result. Through a strange quirk of fate and a happy mistake made by the Germans, it would bring together in Rome a quartet of persons who, combining endless effort with infinite audacity and uncanny ingenuity, would subsequently be able to save the lives of large numbers of Jewish refugees in the Italian capital.

In the department of the *Haute Savoie*, there were over two thousand non-French Jews who had been living in comparative safety under the very loose control of the Italians. The greater part of these involuntary religious migrants had decided to try and get to the sea, from there to continue to Italy and the promised points south. The Mussolini-Lospinoso operation was going in reverse gear at this time. Younger men were left behind to join the partisans; some two thousand boarded trucks, put at their disposal by the Italians, and set off for Nice. A remnant of some two hundred, mostly old and sick,

were put on a train which also left in the direction of the
French Rivièra. Accompanying them were two members of the
Central Jewish Committee, Kasztersztein and Kott. An extraordinary ex-Viennese Jewish lawyer, Stefan Schwamm, a
man especially gifted with a practical sense (he "lived dan-
gerously" and had once spent three months in a French jail for
forging and carrying false identity cards and living under an
assumed name), accompanied the group as interpreter and all-
round manager.

Due to German troop movements—Hitler had in the meantime given orders to occupy Nice—the trains were sidetracked in
Grenoble and sent on in the direction of Turin. Now it was
Rome, thought to be safer from German interference, which
became the end-station of the homeless group. Schwamm this
time posed as a delegate of the Swiss Red Cross; he showed a
passport (with his own substituted photograph) of a dead
French friend by the name of Bernard Lioré, and told a German
lieutenant who had boarded the train that he "had to accompany these French invalids" to Nice. The lieutenant declared
this to be *"ja unmoeglich!"*—and ordered the train to continue
to Rome, where they had wanted to go in the first (or rather second) place anyhow.

One of Father Benedetto's friends among the refugees made
contact with the representatives of the Delasem in Rome, where
Settimio Sorani headed the local committee, who informed the
priest of the new arrivals. The Capuchin found several of his
old acquaintances from the French Rivièra among them, and he
not only continued where he had left off in France, but before
long—shortly after the Germans occupied the city—he became
the unofficial "president" of the Catholic-Jewish quandrum-
virate which would guide the destinies of all those who came to
ask for help. from the Delasem. Sorani remained the
organisation's president-in-name, for a time seconded by a Jew
from Yugoslavia, Joseph Levi. But the executive committee,
responsible for the fate of the refugees, soon was composed of
Father Maria Benedetto—from then on known to all as *Il Padre
degli Ebrei* or "the priest of the Jews"—Settimio Sorani, Aaron

Kasztersztein, and the incomparable Stefan Schwamm. With the exception of Sorani they were foreigners. But Sorani had his special troubles. He paid a visit to the cooperative Yugoslav consul Cyril Kotnik at his home, and found himself suddenly faced by the *Gestapo* who had come to arrest the consul. In vain Sorani tried to pass himself off as a Catholic who by mistake had wrung the wrong doorbell on the wrong floor; within the hour he was in prison. But the Germans accepted Sorani's false papers which "proved his Catholicism" for granted, and never discovered his religion. Tortured for almost two weeks, during which his captors tried to make him confess his complicity with the Yugoslav official, Sorani was surprisingly enough then freed—but had to go underground in order not to risk the lives of his Delasem co-workers. It made Father Benedetto more than ever the hub around whom the rescue activities were turning.

Native Roman Jews were hiding out in the country or in certain Catholic homes and institutions. Others simply moved into new apartments under false names. The situation with foreigners, hardly any of whom could speak Italian, was far more difficult, and it was further aggravated after the Nazis' *razzia* on October 16 had put the fear of Hitler into everybody. The refugees (many of whom, though they had French passports, could not speak the language) soon formed a community of over one thousand five hundred souls, daily augmented by Italian Jews who passed through Rome, trying to find a haven somewhere. All of them had to be housed, fed, and supplied with false identity cards. This brought hundreds of people daily to the new Delasem "headquarters" in the Capuchin convent in the Via Sicilia, where the committee began to meet after the closing of the Delasem city-offices on October 16. Not only were several convent rooms put aside to receive and process the refugees right under the noses of the Nazis and the Italian militia, but Father Benedetto had stored the principal papers from the Delasem archives ("six huge parcels," as he told me later,)" in the building's attic, till the convent became too suspect and we moved the papers to our neighbours, the Carmelite Fathers. . . .").

The backdoor of the convent had an exit on the Via Boncompagni, and it was always left open for a quick getaway. The courageous priest* today agrees that his activities were "rather compromising" for his Order. So did one of his fellow priests at the time, who went to complain to the Father-General, a Belgian named Donatus van Welle. The complaint received little attention from the head of the convent; his own country had been invaded by the Germans. "Do not worry," he said. "If anyone has to go to jail with Father Benedetto, it won't be you, but me."

The housing of the large number of refugees was solved by lodging them in small pensions and hotels, where—if necessary—extra payments and often large bribes made it possible to let them stay on without going through the compulsory registration with the Italian authorities at the *Questura*. Feeding these hundreds and hundreds of mouths posed an even greater problem. Food in Rome was severely rationed, and ration cards could only be obtained on presentation of a *permesso di soggiorno*, the official permit allowing a foreigner to reside in the city. Not one of the refugees had such a paper, obliging the Delasem committee to buy ration cards on the black market—a costly procedure. For a while an Italian, who claimed to be from the city's distributing office, was able to supply the necessary coupons—till it was discovered that he was obtaining them fraudulently, at which point the police became involved in the proceedings. Father Benedetto, the only member of the Committee of Four who was able to move freely around the city, saved the situation by explaining to the head of the Foreigners' Ration Bureau that they themselves had fallen victim to the forger. The official was sympathetic, accustomed as he was to the circumventing of the law in a city where everybody was conniving to stay out of the hands of the Germans; and he was able to ease the trouble with the police. For the moment the situation was safe. At least, it was as safe as it could be under the circumstances since, by now, not only living but even dying

*Born in 1895 as Pierre Péteul, he fought during the First World War as a warrant-officer, was wounded, and finished the war wearing the *Croix de Guerre* with five citations, plus the *Medaille Militaire*.

posed a problem. The corpses of dead Jews, Romans and refugees alike, had to be transported to the cemetery in Catholic hearses, and then surreptitiously transferred to the Jewish section on arrival. Thus a dead Jew became an even greater danger than a living one. His relatives and friends, conspicuously assembled near the grave, were in constant peril of being picked up by the fascist militia.

Till that moment, late November 1943, the Roman Delasem had been able to get along on funds that had been supplied from its original headquarters in Genova. On 8 September, when the German Army overran the country and occupied the city, the head of the Genova organisation, *Avvocato* Valobra, had handed the remaining funds (amounting to approximately five million lire, an enormous sum at that time) to Cardinal Boetto, Archbishop of Genova and always helpful in assisting the Jews. The Cardinal, in turn actively seconded by his secretary Don Francesco Repetto, had managed to send part of these funds to Rome by Raffaele Cantoni, a Venetian Jew who had acted as courier. But Cantoni was arrested (he later escaped from prison and was able to reach Switzerland), while trains and bridges were being constantly bombed by the Allied air force. Communications had dried up, and so (by January 1944) had the money.

Again Father Benedetto went to see Monsignor Hérissé, as he had during the fruitless efforts to get the American and British governments to intervene with the Refugee Committee in London and save the Jews from southern France. Another meeting with Harold Tittmann was arranged at the Monsignor's private apartment inside the Vatican walls. New cables were sent to Washington, this time requesting cooperation from the American *Joint* to supply funds. After weeks of agonized waiting an affirmative answer was received, and by mid-February 20,000 dollars were deposited with a bank in London. Father Benedetto and Settimio Sorani —freed from the *Gestapo* jail but moving only cautiously through the city—succeeded in getting Ambassador Sir D'Arcy Osborne's signature on a piece of paper, certifying that the money was indeed in London; and against this simple guarantee Sorani was able to obtain lire at the black-market rate of exchange from well-to-do Italians who were promised "refunds in London in dollars after the war." All transactions took place in Monsignor Hérissé's Vatican apartment, where Italian currency was handed over against receipts signed by the apartment's helpful occupant. For the moment the financial danger was averted.

During the first days of December, a new ordinance had come into effect which prohibited issuing residence permits —and, consequently, ration coupons—to any person who arrived in Rome after the sixth of that month. The application of this rule, and an expected house-to-house search by the Germans, would be catastrophic for the refugees, most of whom claimed to be French and Catholic, and hardly any of whom had any legitimate papers. Only a few had real French identity cards, obtained during their years of sojourn in France before the war. Armed with these, Settimio Sorani obtained protective letters from Monsieur Chauvet of the Swiss legation in Rome, a friend of his, certifying that these "French citizens" were under the protection of the Swiss (the government in Bern having agreed to take over the interests of the French in Italy when Mussolini had declared war on the Allies).

Schwamm's legalistic mind came to the rescue. Why not make *all* refugees French, and ask Monsieur Chauvet to expand his protection? Schwamm went to the Swiss legation, brought along a sample of a hastily and rather crudely manufactured "identity card," for which the "official" rubber stamp had been made with the inked dial of a man's watch, the text filled in with letters from a toy printing set. According to Schwamm, Monsieur Chauvet was "visibly embarrassed." He remarked that the card "really did not look any too good." Schwamm immediately promised to come back with a better one.

Hidden behind rubbish and old furniture in a deep closet of the Capuchin convent Father Benedetto found an obsolete printing press that had not been in service for years. A typographer among the refugees succeeded in producing a fairly decent-looking identity card with this rather archaic piece of machinery; a cooperative Roman manufactured half-a-dozen different rubber stamps with the names of various French cities, copied from the sets of false documents Schwamm collected. A slight difficulty was caused by the non-availability of French fiscal stamps, which always are affixed to these *cartes d'identité*. But a supply of used French postage stamps was bought from a philatelic shop in Rome, and these were cunningly affixed on to the faked documents. Father Benedetto blithely signed the cards in the name of the appropriate French authorities; Schwamm took care of attaching the thin pieces of paper to the required bits of folded cardboard. The final product looked very French. Monsieur Chauvet was duly impressed, and delivered the nearly two hundred required protective documents without further ado. Nor was he alone. Similar "adoption papers" for the Jews were supplied by Rumanian Minister Cameracescu, and by the consular agent at the one-man Hungarian Legation, Viktor Szasz.

As for *Italian* Jews who needed assistance, they could not be "alienized" like the Jews from abroad; but false papers were obtained for them from various Italian Resistance groups. One day Monsieur Yves Debroise of the French Consulate in Rome, who had gone over to the Allied side, came to ask for help, and Father Benedetto felt that things had run full circle. "This is really the end," he said, "when a French consul comes to beg *me* for French papers!"

With part of the group "legalized," it now became imperative to obtain the necessary ration cards for most of the others, who were still without any papers whatever. Again it was Schwamm who made the acceptable proposition. Their own executive group simply would become "official" and issue its very own pre-December-sixth-dated identification papers. Since the committee as a unit already existed, all it needed was a name—which was easily devised. Within a few minutes the *C.A.P.* was born, the *Comitato Assistenza Profughi*—Committee for the Assistance to Refugees. The papers this "committee" issued were small masterpieces of deceptive simplicity.

Schwamm, using a duplicating machine, rolled off five hundred sheets with the *C.A.P.* heading, dated 4 November 1943. Leaving space to fill in the applicant's name (which most of the time was also fictitious), the dual-language text in forthright Italian and German read: "This is to state that *SoandSo* belongs to the group of 500 refugees who are being assisted by our *Committee*, by the Swiss Legation, and by the Rome Section of the International Red Cross—for which group we have taken the necessary steps to procure a collective Residence Permit in the Open City of Rome." The signature at the bottom was that of the president—"*Maria Benedetto, Capuchin.*"

To give the simple sheet of paper some kind of official look, Schwamm suggested that Father Benedetto go to see the Secretary-General of the Roman Vicariate, Monsignor Umberto Dionisi, and ask him to certify that his signature was indeed *his* signature—in other words, to "legalize" it somehow. This was not a punishable act, because the Monsignor simply "declared as authentic the signature and qualification of Father Maria Benedetto, Capuchin, President of the Committee for the Assistance to Refugees." Affixed to the haphazard and improvised document, this statement and the Vicariate's rubber seal gave the impression that the Vatican itself sanctioned the committee. (The Vatican, and certainly the Pope, knew nothing whatsoever about the whole procedure, which would have horrified them.) The person to whom a certificate was issued stated on it in writing that he "had arrived in Rome on December 5th" (or any other date before the sixth), and that he had "no ration card."

The system worked like magic—thanks to the further connivance by Signor Charrier, director of the ration-cards office for foreigners. He glanced at the papers, and frankly could not care less. With a little bit of goodwill, any official-looking-paper was taken at face value at that time, when most Romans had some kind of fraudulent deal up their sleeve anyhow. As to native Jews who needed ration cards, Signor Charrier suggested that they pass themselves off as Italian refugees from North Africa. All they needed was a written statement confirming their arrival from the other side of the Mediterranean. The helpful Signor Charrier made things easy by writing out the required text for this new addition to the long series of Delasem-manufactured fakes. It made the total number of illegally-distributed ration cards supplied by Charrier finally amount to well over thirteen hundred.

Armed with all these papers, which with the exception of the ration coupons were all counterfeit, an effort was made to obtain genuine residence permits. It was important to have some kind of registration with the *Questura*, in order to have at least *some* official status with the Roman police. Dr. Angelo de Fiore, director of the *Questura's* bureau for foreigners, turned out to be a marvel at bureaucratic legerdemain. Papers were filed—disappeared—turned up again. It was not an unfamiliar Italian phenomenon, but in this case it was meticulously planned. Dr. de Fiore is a shy and totally self-effacing man who has been awarded some eighteen international decorations, including the French Legion of Honor for his work during the war. He told me that "what we tried to do was to give the impression that we knew nothing." He agrees that he "made such a *pasticcio*—such a mess—of the files" that the Germans never found the names they were looking for. There was a higher order in the Italian disorder, and it saved human life.

Chapter 38
The Delasem

The more the war started to go wrong for the Germans, the more the rescue activities expanded. When Jews were arrested by the fascist militia, the Delasem would rush to help. On one such occasion Schwamm went to the Mussolini Barracks near the Vatican, posed once more as "Monsieur Bernard Lioré, French delegate of the International Red Cross," and managed to get his "compatriot"—whose only connection with France were his false papers—promptly released. Another time Father Benedetto, with the help of the Count de Salis (of the *real* International Red Cross), was able to extricate a Jewish child out of the hands of the *Gestapo*.

Then things suddenly threatened to take a turn for the worse. Monsieur Chauvet at the Swiss consulate, who calmly had continued to issue the protective certificates, informed Father Benedetto that "the game was up," and that his usefulness had come to an end. Someone had informed the Italian Minister of the Interior that "there were over four hundred French refugees in Rome." If so, then the minister wanted to repatriate them all, and had asked for a list of the names.

Schwamm and Father Benedetto decided to try and convince the Swiss to overlook the requested list of the non-French French. If this proposition were not accepted, the whole Delasem operation would be jeopardized. And if, moreover, one of the more militant fascists at the Italian foreign ministry were to inform the Germans about what was going on, then the whole refugee rescue group might well be deported, including Father Benedetto.

Besides Chauvet, the two Delasem conspirators found three other officals waiting for them at the consulate—Carlo Sommaruga, who was the legation-counselor, and Messieurs Yves Debroise and François de Vial from the French consulates in Rome and at the Vatican, who of course had been cooperating without the knowledge of their Vichy government. Father Benedetto quite categorically refused to hand over any list, and the Swiss protection game obviously had come to an end. Yet for the Swiss, too, an honorable formula would have to be arranged. Schwamm found a way out.

With perfect self-assurance he advised the Swiss consular officers and their French colleagues to inform the Minister of the Interior that it would be far too much of an effort for the *Italians* to send the nearly five hundred refugees back to their "native France." It was not necessary at all, declared Schwamm solemnly, for "we can do it ourselves." The Swiss and French looked incredulous, and even Father Benedetto was disturbed. Schwamm calmly went on to explain that he had "the necessary trucks at his disposal," and that he and Father Benedetto "would take all required steps to repatriate the refugee Frenchmen." The fascist Minister of the Interior could be advised to sleep quietly, he said—for all would be well.

Of course, nothing was well, and as Father Benedetto explained to me later: "Not only didn't we have one single truck, we didn't even have a bicycle. . . ." Aaron Kasztersztein was the one to take the committee out of its embarrassing, almost desperate position. His plan was a grand play of ingenious double-dealing, in which the Hungarian counselor, Viktor Szasz (whose one-man consulate had now been placed under the protection of the Swedish legation) became the key operator. Kasztersztein simply suggested to *denaturalize* all so-called Frenchmen and make *Hungarians* out of them. Viktor Szasz agreed, and Schwamm once more went to work, this time to fabricate the required false Hungarian papers. Szasz* supplied the necessary rubber-stamps—these were the official ones—from his own and from the Swedish consulate; the photographs were neatly lifted from the false French papers to be dutifully glued onto the fake new ones. A week later Father Benedetto could safely return to the Swiss consulate with the invalidated papers of "the first group of repatriated Frenchmen." "The others—" was the closing line of the Capuchin's remarkable and eloquent explanatory speech, "—the others will follow as soon as the remaining trucks were ready." What he meant was, of course, that they would follow as soon as the feverishly prepared new Hungarian papers were fabricated.

As Father Maria Benedetto has said to me, "one must try to imagine the atmosphere we lived in, in order to be able to understand the hallucinating inventiveness of all these crazy ideas. We constantly visited the representatives of more than half-a-dozen countries accredited to the Vatican—Yugoslavia, Spain, France, Hungary, Poland, Belgium, Portugal, the Apostolic *Nunciatura*, and the office of the Secretary of State at the Vatican. We were in touch with the underground members of all political parties, with Pastor Anselmo Ammenti of the Methodist church, with the Quakers, and we collaborated with various religious and ecclesiastical Orders who supported similar actions. I believe I can safely say that we knocked on any and all doors where we hoped to receive help. . . ."

The committee's fame spread to all corners of Rome. One day, a foreign Jew presented himself at the *Questura* with a Spanish passport that obviously was not his. He became rather desperate

---

*Szasz would prove to be of even greater help later, when seventeen Jewish refugees were apprehended by the Italian militia. It was exclusively through his interference—boldly threatening "retaliations against Italian prisoners in Hungary"!—that the Ministry of the Interior gave orders to set them free.

when this was pointed out to him. The man behind the counter advised him consolingly "to go and see Father Benedetto in the Via Sicilia." As an afterthought he added: "Don't worry—father Benedetto fixes everything. . . ."

In their desperation to get help, Schwamm and his ecclesiastical accomplice even had gone to see Baron Sigismund von Braun, first secretary at the German embassy to the Vatican. Things after all were going badly for Hitler's armies, and they had heard that the baron was not over-zealous in his enthusiasm for the Nazi cause. The reception was friendly; but the moment Herr von Braun (brother of space scientist Wernher von Braun, and recently West Germany's ambassador to France) heard that the help was requested for French Jews, his warmth quickly cooled.

If the reception behind some of these doors was not always encouraging, Father Benedetto still is particularly saddened about the treatment he received from exactly those institutions where he had expected to be welcomed with open arms. Cardinal Riberi at the Nunciatura, when asked for financial assistance—not an outright gift, but a *loan*—answered curtly that "the Vatican does not lend money. *Se ha—da*," meaning that "if it *has* the money, it gives it outright." But in this case the Vatican kept its purse strings securely closed, and gave nothing. Another financial request at the Nunciatura was countered with the recommendation "to pray fervently and constantly." "That," as Father Benedetto has drily remarked, "was a bit of advice we were perfectly familiar with. . . ." Nor was any money received from the Roman Vicariate, although here Monsignore Dionisi *personally* had been most helpful in many other ways, including his attesting to the veracity of Father Benedetto's signature for the fake identity papers.

If the Vatican never gave any financial assistance to the Jews of Rome, Father Benedetto *did* receive several large bags of flour, 300 kilograms in all. On taking delivery, the priest who handed them over asked: "And who is going to pay for it?" Maria Benedetto refused to answer, but (as he later explained) his thoughts were: "*Vous en avez du culot!* (you have *some* nerve!)." And that, as Father Maria Benedetto has declared, closes as far as he is concerned the chapter on any and all the financial help from the Vatican for the Jews of Rome.

When the twenty thousand dollars was already spent in its counter-value of black-market lire, a second request was made to the Joint in New York, again via Harold Tittmann's American channels. This time the communications and arrangements took much longer; yet, in the end, a new and far more substantial credit was opened in London, amounting to one hundred thousand dollars.* But in the meanwhile what could be done without funds?

Father Benedetto and Schwamm decided to try and reach northern Italy on a two-fold mission. For some months they had been dispatching "identity cards" to cities in and around the Po Valley, taken there (as the Capuchin father described her) by "a courageous young Jewish woman." The so-called French, Hungarian, or Rumanian refugees then would emerge from their hiding places and make their way down to Rome, using whatever transportation available. Their arrival placed an ever heavier burden on the Rome Delasem group. Would it not be much easier if they could get to Switzerland instead of coming south? The purpose of the mission was, in the first place, to check possible escape routes through the mountains; secondly, Father Benedetto would see Cardinal Boetto in Genova, and possibly return with some of the funds that had been deposited with him early in September.

There was no train service between Rome and Florence, and the two men set off during the second week of April 1944 in an automobile which Schwamm had been able to scrounge from a friendly police captain (who in turn had "liberated" the car from the Germans without, alas, license plates for civilian use). Schwamm, still posing as the Frenchman Bernard Lioré, obtained a letter from the International Red Cross, identifying

---

*Of this second credit from the Joint, only $16,000 were eventually changed into lire. The black-market transactions were long and complicated because Italians who did have lire available were loath to make quick deals, with the lire-dollar rate severely fluctuating on the black market. The unchanged dollars in the London bank finally were returned to the Joint after the War.

them as "persons on a mission to bring spiritual comfort to the French prisoners of war in the Italian and German camps in the north," and requesting the authorities to assist them as much as possible. To obtain the necessary gasoline, Schwamm brazenly went to the German *Kommandatura*. The Red Cross letter worked; in Florence the procedure was repeated at the Excelsior Hotel, occupied by field-grade German officers, where the two "Red Cross envoys" were also given rooms for the night.

In Milan, on April 15, Schwamm made a mistake. Telephoning his contact at her apartment, he told her to come and see him at a restaurant where he and Father Benedetto were to have lunch. His contact had been under suspicion and was arrested that day by Mussolini's militia; within half-an-hour Schwamm himself was picked up at the restaurant by the police.* Fortunately Father Benedetto was able to escape and find refuge at the Capuchin convent in the city.

After hiding out for a week, Maria Benedetto took the train to Genova, where at Cardinal Boetto's residence he was informed that for the moment it "was difficult to get hold of the hidden money, which would be sent as quickly as possible. . . ." It could be, Father Benedetto remarked later, that "they didn't trust me."

He returned to Rome as best he could (for the two Italian chauffeurs of the car which had been used to drive to Milan had decided to visit girl-friends in Verona). He took a train as far as Florence, hitchhiked from there to Rome.

The Capuchin convent in the Via Sicilia had been warned about what happened in Milan, and all incriminating papers were burned. The Belgian head of the convent now felt it prudent for Father Benedetto to disappear from view till the situation improved. It was alarmingly clear that the priest's life was in danger. Since the Germans had occupied the city in September, he had been interrogated for three hours by the fascist militia, denounced to the *Gestapo* and to the Roman tribunal dealing with anti-fascist activities, and blackmailed for

---

*Schwamm spent three months in prison, and then was sent to a German forced labor camp in Poland. There he was liberated by the Russians. Traveling via the round-about way of Budapest and Bucarest, he subsequently rejoined his family in Rome.

twenty thousand lire (which were never paid). He was, moreover, informed that an order for his arrest was on Major Kappler's desk.

A month later, on 4 June 1944, the Allied troops entered Rome. The end at long last came to a time of horror—and of secret fraternity. "So many good Romans," as Stefan Schwamm has said, "most of them poor, and with family troubles of their own, have been at our disposal—without ever asking anything in return....." At the beginning of the occupation, on 8 September 1943, "just over one hundred foreign Jews were assisted by us," as Father Benedetto wrote in his private notes (20 July 1944). "By 4 June 1944 their number had grown to 4,000, of whom 1,500 were foreign Jews and 2,500 Italians. During that time we spent twenty-five million lire, and even this sum had proved to be insufficient...." There had been much human solidarity, too little money, too many victims.

Official recognition for the heroic work done by Father Maria Benedetto came several years later. In Milan on 17 April 1955, on the occasion of the tenth anniversary of the Italian liberation, he was awarded a special gold medal by the Hebrew Union of Italy. This was followed (on 30 November 1967) by the *Medal of the Righteous* from the *Yad Vashem* in Jerusalem—the Martyrs and Heroes Remembrance Authority, a medal that symbolically expresses the Talmudic thought: "He who saves a single life, saves a whole world."

At the Milan ceremony Father Benedetto was not alone. The same gold medal was awarded to twenty-two other Catholics (seven of whom were deceased, including Yugoslav consul Cyril Kotnik who had died after the war from prison injuries inflicted by the *Gestapo*.) Among those present were two who came from Rome—Father Maria Benedetto and Dr. Angelo de Fiore of the *Questura*.

On the medal were symbols of the Ten Commandments and the seven-armed candelabrum, and the words *"From the Jews of Italy—In Gratitude."* Father Benedetto was given a citation which read in part: "Incomparable in his rescue work, he succeeded in bringing his great arduous task to a successful end—contemptuous of danger, with strong will-power, and a noble joy in the helping of others—deserving of everlasting gratitude. . . . ''

Present with Father Benedetto to receive their medals were three other priests, including Don Francesco Repetto and Don Carlo Salvi (who had succeeded the former as secretary of Cardinal Boetto in Genova when Don Repetto had to go into hiding to escape from the *Gestapo*). *Il Popolo*, the daily newspaper of the Christian Democratic party of Italy, headlined the ceremony as ''The thanks of the Jews who were saved by the Christian courage of the people.'' There was no mention of the Vatican.

Chapter 39
Vatican Claims

On 30 April 1943 Pope Pius XII wrote an important letter to the Archbishop of Berlin, Monsignor Konrad von Preysing.* In this letter he discussed the problems of both "Catholic non-Aryans and real Jews." The Pope remarked that he had "no intention to speak of the large amounts of money in American currency which we have appropriated for the overseas trips of the emigrants." But of course, although not wanting to speak about these large amounts of money, the Pope certainly did; for had he *not* wanted to speak about them, then he would not have mentioned the subject in the first place. Pius XII went on to say that he had given these sums "gladly, for these people were in distress; we have helped them for the praise of the Lord, and

*Two years previously, on 17 January 1941, the Archbishop had written an important letter to the Pope, in which he said among others: "Your Holiness is undoubtedly familiar with the conditions of the Jews in Germany and adjacent countries. As a matter of interest I would like to mention that both by Catholic and Protestant groups the question has been put to me whether the Holy See might not be able to do something in this matter—perhaps to make an appeal in favor of these unhappy people?"

have done well not to count on earthly thanks." The Pope then informed his bishop in Berlin that "for the Catholic non-Aryans as well as for the Jews themselves the Holy See charitably had done what has been in its power, both economically and morally . . ." It was the first time the Pope had mentioned any money he presumably had spent for the Jews; and if the letter to von Preysing had not been secret at the time, but could have been brought to the attention of the Jews of Rome, the air along the Tiber certainly would have been filled with exclamations of surprise.

By the end of the war a good many apologists were moved to defend the Pope's attitude during the many years of European suffering. Most of these Vatican spokesmen dealt with Pius XII's refusal to speak up on behalf of the Jews. Some argued softly; others used megaphones.

The case reached its climax after the premiere in Berlin on 17 February 1963 of Rolf Hochhuth's play *"Der Stellvertreter"* (*The Representative*), and the ensuing world-wide controversy. The Vatican took note of the new polemical stage of the argument, and slowly but surely began to fight back with the publication of a series of books on "Acts and Documents of the Holy See, dealing with the Second World War" (the aforementioned papal letter to Monsignor von Preysing among them). Pius XII himself referred to his feelings about those who had been slavish disciples of Hitler and Mussolini, when on Easter Sunday 1945 he spoke to the assembled believers on the Piazza San Pietro.

"Those who let themselves be seduced by the instigators of violence and who followed the band so unwisely, now finally begin to wake up from their illusion, astonished to see how far their servile docility has led them," he said. "For them," the Pope continued, "there is no other way of salvation but to repudiate once and for all the idolatry of absolute nationalism, of pride in the superiority of race and blood."

These were sound words and showed humane judgment, but unfortunately the words were uttered at a rather late date—once the holocaust had happened. An historian must get the impression that the Pope himself also finally "woke up" from "illusion," for it was indeed a statement that somehow echoed the brave words spoken by his predecessor, Pius XI. But the latter had had the courage, the presence of mind and heart, to admonish the Italians and the world while Mussolini and Hitler were still present; Pius XII made his first unequivocal public statement only once the danger was past.

Shortly afterwards, the Pope once again referred to his fairly concealed attitude and feelings during the world conflict when, on 2 June 1945, he spoke to the College of Cardinals. "During the war," he said, "we have never stopped, especially in our messages, to oppose ourselves to the ruinous and relentless applications of the National-Socialist doctrines, which made use of the most refined scientific methods to torture and to do away with people who often were innocent."

This attitude by the Pope appears to contradict the subsequent apologies by others—and even by himself—that the Vatican had *not* known *for certain* about the consequences of those "ruinous and relentless applications" of Nazi doctrines. Of course, there was a substantial difference between what the Pope *thought* he had conveyed in his various messages, and what the rest of the world actually had understood about them. In an article in the *Osservatore Romano* of 25 October 1943, seven days after the first eleven hundred Jews had been deported from Rome, the Pope's willingness to help was described as "having increased, knowing neither frontiers, nor nationality, religion, or race." According to the Vatican, this was a highly significant, clear, and perfectly plain protest against the deportations. According to Ernst von Weiszäcker, German ambassador to the Vatican (as reported in his cable three days later to the Foreign Office in Berlin), the Pope's message was nothing like that at all. It was couched, he radioed, "in the typical style of the Vatican newspaper, which means [that it is] richly meandering and unclear." And von Weiszäcker was of the opinion that it was not even necessary for the Wilhelmstrasse to make an official protest against this article because "only very few people will take it as containing anything that deals with the Jewish problem. . . ."

The Pope *was* concerned, and at times he *did* speak out about

Jews who were Jews no longer *i.e.*, Jews who had converted to Catholicism. But in the Catholic Church, of course, the principle of once a Catholic always a Catholic is strictly applied; and any words spoken in defense of converted Jews were words spoken in defense of Catholics. The Pope had mentioned this in his letter to Cardinal von Preysing, stating that "our fatherly love is greatly concerned with the non-Aryan and half-Aryan Catholics, who are children of the Church as all others." And on 18 November 1942 the then Secretary of State Maglione, writing to Cardinal Bertram of Breslau on the subject of the suffering of Polish priests in German concentration camps, had indicated that the Pope "is greatly concerned about them and about the suffering of all those who are oppressed, whose sufferings are also his." It could be that this included the sufferings of the Jews.

The Pope, as the Vatican apologists explained later, hesitated in his condemnation precisely because he was so interested in those who suffered—in other words he hesitated . . . in order to promote their well-being. Harold Tittmann, on 7 July 1942 (in a cable to Washington that was received four days later), informed the U.S. State Department that he had reminded the Vatican of the possibility that its "failure to protest publicly against Nazi atrocities" would undermine "faith both in the Church and in the Holy Father himself." According to Tittmann, the answer he invariably received was that the Pope in his speeches and messages "had already condemned offenses against morality, and that to be specific would make things [only] worse." In answer to another "reminder" by Myron Taylor in September, the Pope replied on 10 October 1942—the answer once more being sent to Washington by Tittmann—that the Vatican itself also had received reports "of severe measures taken against non-Aryans," but that the Holy See was not in a position to verify their accuracy. Tittmann was informed, however, that the Vatican was "taking advantage of every opportunity to mitigate the suffering of non-Aryans."

The only way to verify these sufferings would have been for some high authoritative person at the Vatican to visit the German concentration camps in person. Although a good number of very brave and very outspoken priests were inmates of these camps, none of them had gone there of his own free will and none were at liberty to confirm or deny.

To the mass of information accumulating at the Vatican was added an appeal made on 2 January 1943 by the president of the Polish government-in-exile in London, Wladislas Rackiewicz. He wrote in his letter to the Pope: "The extermination of Jews, and with them of many Christians of the Semitic race, has only been a test for the systematic application of scientifically organized mass murder. . . . Divine laws are violated . . . Hundreds of thousands of people are killed without due process . . . This is how Poland appears to us from reports which we receive. The Polish people strongly believe that the divine right does not admit any compromise. . . . It does not ask for diplomatic or material aid, but for a word that would clearly and distinctly indicate where the evil resides, and which would brand those who serve it."

Another important appeal was made seven weeks later, on 22 February 1943, by the Apostolic delegate in London, Monsignor William Godfrey, explaining that Cardinal Hinsley (Archbishop of Westminster) and Dr. William Temple (Archbishop of Canterbury) suggested that "the English Catholic bishops should humbly offer a petition to the Holy See in favor of the Jews of Eastern Europe and in the occupied countries."

But the most saddening proof that the Vatican did actually know about what was going on in Eastern Europe, was a letter sent on 8 July 1943 to Monsignor Montini (the present Pope Paul VI) by Monsignor Roncalli (later Pope John XXIII). Roncalli at the time was Papal Nuncio in Turkey, and Montini was serving as Pope Pius' Secretary of State.*

Reporting on a conversation he had had during Easter in Ankara with German Ambassador Franz von Papen, Roncalli,

*See footnote on page 420.

expressing himself in his usual plain language, informed Rome that von Papen had spoken at length about the mass grave of Polish officers found at Katyn (the massacre at the time was ascribed to the Russians). The German envoy, Roncalli reported, was of the opinion that the Poles now better turn to the Germans instead of placing their hopes on their neighbors to the east. The Papal Nuncio had his answer ready.

"I replied with a melancholy smile," Roncalli wrote to Rome, "that before anything else it would be necessary to make the world forget the millions of Jews sent to Poland and exterminated there."

The later Pope John did not elaborate on the subject, undoubtedly because he was convinced that the Vatican was as aware of what was going on as he was himself. In other words, he knew that it was old news. For had he thought that it would indeed be news to the Pope and his closest collaborators (of whom Montini certainly was one of the most important), would he not have added some details about the information concerning these "millions of Jews who were being exterminated?" The story, quite obviously, notwithstanding all the later excuses, was known at the Vatican.

The impression in the world press caused by the recent publication of Roncalli's letter was one of a mild sensation. The *New York Times*, in an article by its Rome correspondent Paul Hoffmann, headlined its story on 5 April 1973 "THE VATICAN KNEW OF NAZI POGROMS, ITS RECORDS SHOW," and the Roman morning paper *Il Messagero* wrote that Roncalli's letter "is new testimony—beyond suspicion—that already in 1943 the Vatican knew about the killing of the Jews in the extermination camps in that part of Poland that was occupied by Germany." The reaction in other newspaper was much the same.

In addition to written reports and petitions to "speak up" or to "speak out," it may be assumed that verbal statements were added to the growing mass of papers accumulating at the Vatican. President Roosevelt's envoy Myron Taylor made three trips from Washington to Rome, and sojourned for the last time in the Holy City from 17-28 September 1942. Cardinal Spellman, who had left New York on 9 February arrived in Rome from Barcelona on 20 February 1943, to remain till March 4. The British minister to the Holy See Sir Francis Godolphin d'Arcy Osborne was able to leave the Vatican on 8 April 1943, to return to Rome nearly three months later, on 29 June. All three were able to, and did, supply the Pope with verbal and written information emanating from their governments.

Several months before his departure to London, the British minister—in a conversation with Cardinal Maglione (on 14 December 1942)—had asked "why the Holy See does not intervene against the terrible slaughter of the Jews?" The Cardinal had replied that "the Holy Father in his messages has already claimed the right to live . . . for all men, to whatever race or religion they may belong." But, as Cardinal Maglione has written in his private notes dealing with this conversation, "the Minister insisted on this point: it was necessary for the Holy See to intervene in order to stop the massacre of the Jews."

In 1940 Cardinal Tisserant had sent his quite explosive letter (made public only in 1964 by Professor Jaeckel of the University of Kiel) to his compatriot Cardinal Suhard, Archbishop of Paris, in which he said he had requested the Pope "with insistence to publish an encyclical on the individual duty to obey the command of one's conscience." Tisserant, moreover, pointed to the danger that "history tomorrow should not be allowed to reproach the Holy See with having followed a line of political convenience which was serving its own advantage exclusively, and not to have done much else. . . ." On the other hand, Cardinal Montini (the present Pope Paul VI) in June 1963 pronounced Pius XII's silence to be absolutely just, because "an attitude of condemnation and protest not only would have been useless, but even dangerous."

Historians have wondered whether the Pope's silence—and his defenders' apologies for not speaking out against the Nazi régime and its "unverifiable" atrocities—might somehow have been connected with the possibility of Hitler's abrogating the

Concordat, by one of which articles the German government
collected (and still collects today) the compulsory domestic
church tax from all German citizens. Under the terms of this
Church-State agreement the governments of the various German *Laender* collect an extra percentage of the overall internal
revenues from salaries as a religious tax, and deliver this money
to the ecclesiastical authorities. In 1943 (fiscal year 1 April 1943
to 31 March 1944) this church tax amounted to just about 450
million marks.* This money was divided approximately fifty-
fifty—according to the population's church-membership
—among the various Protestant groups and the Catholic
Church. A furious reaction by Hitler against a pro-Jewish papal
pronouncement might well have left the Catholic Church in
Germany without an income—an income that at the time reached the sum of 225 million marks, half of the total amount
collected. It would be difficult, if not impossible, to believe that
financial considerations could have entered the mind of the
Pope himself in deciding on matters of humanity. Yet in view of
the huge amount of money involved, and the disastrous results
its stoppage might have had on the already severely-plagued
German Catholic Church, the influence of this material dilemma might possibly have received a certain consideration in other
Vatican circles.

But all these justifications and apologies by Catholic
spokesmen, especially after the world-wide repercussions
following the Hochhuth play, can to some extent be rational-
ized. It was, after all, the Church's good right to defend itself
against what it believed or declared to be wrong accusations.
The Vatican spokesmen did not usually brand these accusations
as false; their defense was based on the assumption that silence
and inaction had been the *better* policy because an outspoken
opinion might have made matters *worse*. Although spokesmen
for the other side of the debate (including the present chief rabbi
of Rome and priests like Father Maria Benedetto, who so in-

---

*According to the Finance Ministry in Bonn, the Church Tax collected by the
German government in 1971 was about 5 billion marks, or more than 2 billion
dollars.

timately knew about suffering of the Jews) are still wondering "How much worse could it have been?," the Vatican's opinion still has certain value in its own line of defense.

The story changes, however, when one leaves the problem of international Jewry, and focuses attention on the Jews of Rome. Even before the Hochhuth play brought endless discussions *pro et contra* into the open, there were some churchmen who judged it necessary to defend the Vatican against the accusations of inaction in Rome proper or, even more, to laud the magnificent help which the Vatican had, as they saw it, given the Jewish Community along the Tiber during its time of greatest need. Among these priests who have heaped praise on the Vatican and on the person of Pope Pius XII are two outstanding figures, Fathers Leiber and Hudal, both German Jesuits (and Leiber especially was a close collaborator of the Pope).

Monsignor Ludwig Hudal was rector of *Santa Maria dell'Anima*, the home church of German-speaking nationals in the holy city. He intervened on 16 October 1943 with General Rainer Stahel, commander of the German troops in Rome, in an effort to make him stop the deportation of the Jews which had started that morning. In the urgent letter he sent to the general, apparently written at the request of a close collaborator of the Pope, Father Hudal suggested that the suspension of the deportations was necessary in order "not to harm the good name of the Germans abroad." He, moreover, informed the German general that "the Pope might make a public statement against the action, which might then become a weapon in the hands of our enemies."

According to the apologetic account of the French author Paul Duclos*, General Stahel telephoned Father Hudal the next day, stating that he had informed Heinrich Himmler of the father's letter, and Himmler had given orders "to stop the arrests immediately." The French author claims that this caused "the *Gestapo* not to effect any further *razzia* of that kind in Rome."

*Le Vatican et la seconde guerre mondiale (Editions Pedone, Paris, 1955).

This suspension of further arrests must have been a source of great relief to Father Hudal and to the other Vatican officials involved. Yet none of them made even the slightest further effort to save the lives of the 1,127 Jews who already had been arrested and who were still in Rome. Nor did they try to prevent the Germans from sending all these unfortunates on their way to certain death two days later.

It is noteworthy that Austrian-born Father Hudal indicated to the German general that the Pope's possible speech "might be a weapon in the hands of *our* enemies." It is perfectly possible that Father Hudal, as an Austro-German citizen, carefully and tactically chose his words in order better to influence the general, and that for that very same reason he alluded to "the good name of the Germans abroad." To be sure, the *razzia* was not "stopped"—neither as the result of Father Hudal's letter, nor on instructions from Himmler. It came to a momentary end simply because most of the remaining Jews suddenly had disappeared, and the Germans could not get at them so easily any longer. For the deportations from Rome continued with clocklike regularity till the very end of the German occupation—till two days before the liberation of the city in June 1944. Though tracking down the Jews had become more difficult, close to another thousand victims were sent to the extermination camps during the next thirty-three weeks: an average of four a day.

There is a surprising contradiction in Father Hudal's and in the other apologists' statements, when they claim that the letter to General Stahel stopped the deportations—even temporarily. For if this indeed were true, then it seems disingenuous to claim in the same breath that a public statement by the Pope only would have made things worse. If a simple monsignor could obtain such results, how much more effective might have been words from the Pope himself! "If Pius XII would have said *'Liberate the Roman Jews,'* the Germans probably would have given in." This is the opinion of Chief Rabbi Toaff. Weiszäcker, he believes, "was simply waiting for the sign." All the same, Father Hudal's statement is a straightforward one. He protested—and for the moment the Nazi roundup came to an end, whether or not as a result of the father's action. At least he had tried.

The strange case of Father Robert Leiber is, however, of a totally different nature. Till he took hold of his pen, the Vatican statements had been made in self-defense, without trying to re-write the actual, tragic course of events. Father Leiber went one step further. He was a professor of ecclesiastical history at the Pontifical Gregorian University, who had entered the Order of the Jesuits in 1906 and who was private secretary and, possibly, the closest confidant of the Pope. On 4 March 1961 he publish-ed an article in the Jesuit monthly *Civiltà Cattolica*, entitled "Pius XII and the Jews of Rome 1943-1944." At the same time the original German text of this dissertation was printed in *Stimmen der Zeit*, a magazine published by the Herder Verlag in Freiburg-in-Breisgau. As harsh as it may sound, the article written by the eminent scholar twisted the course of events and turned history upside down, calling white what was black, and black white. It resulted in the creation of a myth composed of untruths that are a staggering evasion of history, and they have been quoted and requoted ever since as the real course of events as seen through the eyes of the Vatican. Father Leiber repeated some of his statements five years later in a taped interview with the American magazine *Look*, when it published excerpts from a book by Paul Friedlaender* in its number of 17 May 1966. The excerpts previously had been submitted to the Jesuit Father in Rome, and his comments were published in the magazine un-derneath Friedlaender's documentary evidence.

According to Father Leiber there had been "two special ecclesiastical or pontifical organisations" in Rome which assisted the Jews. One of these was the Delasem and the other one the *Opera di San Raffaele*, which had been started in Ger-many in 1871 as the *Raphaelsverein*. In 1941, when Hitler ordered its Hamburg office closed, it had been moved to its Pallottine headquarters in Rome. As Father Leiber told it, the Delasem had started out as "a Jewish organisation in Genova."

---

*Pius XII and the Third Reich (Alfred A. Knopf, New York, 1966). The original edition was published by Éditions du Seuil (Paris, 1964).

But when the Germans occupied that city, the Delasem became a Vatican institution, because "about five million lire were handed to Cardinal Boetto, who delivered this money to the Apostolic *Nunciatura* in Rome." And the Jesuit father added in his article, "the *Nunciatura* [then] distributed the money to help the Jews. The practical work was confided to the Capuchin Father Benedetto . . . through whose hands passed, till 1945, with the help given him by Pius XII, 25 million lire, about one billion 250 million in today's [1961] currency."

"Where did the money come from?" Father Leiber then asked. He admitted that some Jews who were hidden in convents and other church institutions in Rome "still disposed of funds"; for those Jews who were without money, *"even though their number was small,"* these church institutions "provided the funds themselves." And, the Jesuit father continued, "the rest was totally donated by Pius XII." In his *Look* comments Father Leiber supplied the additional information that "the Pope spent his whole private fortune" to help the Jews, although this "was not an enormous sum of money."

When the executive members of the Jewish Community in Rome and Genova read these astonishing statements by Father Leiber in the *Civiltà Cattolica*, they decided that a note of protest was required. Signed by Lelio Vittorio Valobra in Genova, and by Settimio Sorani and Renzo Levi in Rome, the Letter to the Editor pointed out the total untruths contained in Father Leiber's article. The writers specified that the Delasem had never been "an ecclesiastical or pontifical institution," but had been, and remained till the end, "a Jewish organisation." They explained that the five million lire entrusted to Cardinal Boetto via his secretary Don Giuseppe Ripetto, had never been handed—unless by mistake—to the *Nunciatura* in Rome. Nor, wrote the three Jewish leaders, "was any of the Delasem money obtained from Pope Pius XII." It was received instead from Italian citizens "against the promise of reimbursement in dollars after the liberation" in London.

The corrections in the counter-statement were never published in the *Civiltà Cattolica*; they were printed—in a shortened version—in *Israel*, the weekly of the Italian Jewish communities. Father Leiber answered with a curt note. He said, in essence, that all this really had taken place *so* many years before, that by now it was not worthwhile to discuss the matter any further. . . .

Father Maria Benedetto, too, had some words to say on the subject. He addressed himself to *Avvocato* Valobra, confirming that the Delasem during the nine months of the German occupation had indeed "spent about twenty-five million lire" but that during this period, while he was acting as president of the organisation, "no money whatever had been received from the Vatican." And he went on to recall the answer from Monsignor Riberi at the *Nunciatura* when he (and Schwamm) had gone there to ask for a loan, a request that received the retort that "if the Vatican has money, it gives it" (*se ha, da*) "after which we left without having accomplished anything." Recapitulating, Father Benedetto reminded the Genovese lawyer that the countervalue of the money received from the Joint via London "may or may not have amounted to twenty-five million lire, but this is of no importance. The fact is that the money did not come from the Vatican."

But Father Leiber had claimed more when he fashioned the useful myth of the huge amounts spent by the Vatican in the interest of the Jews. There was much more, especially on the subject of the second "ecclesiastical or pontifical organisation" he had mentioned, the one known as the "Good Works of Saint Raphael." This organisation, then headed in Rome by the 34-year-old German Pallottine Father Anton Weber, "facilitated the trip to America of 2,000 persons who had sought refuge in Rome, of whom 1,500 were Jews." A highly laudable accomplishment, and partly true—but only partly. For the *Opera di San Raffaele* (according to statements made to me in Rome in 1967 and 1968, and repeated once again in April 1973 by none but Father Weber himself) "only took care of Catholic-baptized Jews of non-Italian nationality, never of *real* Jews." The Vatican, Father Weber explained, had received three thousand immigration visas from the Brazilian government to be used ex-

clusively for converted Jews; and these cases were handled by
San Raffaele. Actually, Father Weber added, they had used only
2,000 of the available visas, of which about 500 were given to
other people, including some young priests who had to leave
Rome with a valid foreign entry visa—for which the Brazilian
one was used—in order to reach their posts abroad, usually
traveling from Rome via Lisbon. Only 1,500 visas therefore
were handed to converted Jews, and to *converted* Jews *exclusively*.

Father Weber's figures may even be slightly inflated, for in
1973 the Vatican revealed* that "the number of non-Aryans
who thus could be helped were only several hundred, the total
amounting to hardly more than one thousand."

The initiative to obtain a Brazilian "haven" had been taken
on 31 March 1939 by Cardinal Michael Faulhaber of Munich,
together with the Bishop of Osnabrueck, Wilhelm Berning. In
letters to Vatican Secretary of State Cardinal Luigi Maglione,
the two German prelates had pointed out the great pressures on
the Catholic non-Aryans "who equally belong to the diocese-
children of the German bishops"; and they had suggested that
the Vatican make an appeal to President Getulio Vargas of
Brazil. Consequently Maglione (on 5 April 1939, in a letter to
the Papal Nuncio in Rio de Janeiro) asked the Brazilian government that "over and above the already exhausted permits for
1939, immigration visas be issued to three thousand non-Aryan
German Christians." The permission was granted on 23 June
1939—with some strings attached. As Father Weber had indicated, 2,000 of these visas were put at the disposal of Saint
Raphael, while the remaining thousand were to be handled by
the Brazilian embassies themselves. In granting the visas, the
Brazilian government specifically pointed out that they should
be used exclusively—as indeed Cardinal Maglione had asked—to
serve "sincere Catholics, who deserve to be helped," and for

---

*These and other details about the Saint Raphael operation are taken from the
two volumes of hitherto secret documents which were published in book form
(Volumes 6 and 7) by the Vatican on 4 April 1973 under the title *"Actes et
Documents du Saint Siège relatifs à la seconde guerre mondiale."*

which the Brazilian government required a deposit per family of "20 contos Reis" or one thousand dollars. Thus the *Raphaelsverein*, at that time still in Hamburg, was told that the money for this purpose should be spent "above all" for the emigration of "German non-Aryan Catholics."*

Where did the money come from for this surely noble work, which may well have saved the lives of many persons who once had been Jews? According to Father Leiber this money also came from the Vatican.

"That gives the wrong impression," Father Weber has said, explaining that the funds for his work simply *passed through* the Vatican. The funds had been put at his disposal by Americans, he said, especially by those Americans belonging to the Catholic Refugee Committee. The war made direct transfers of money impossible, so the funds quite naturally had to be channelled *via* the Vatican, which consequently served as a transfer office or clearing house only.

As has now become evident from the secret Vatican papers published in April 1973, Father Weber himself was not accurately informed about where the money he used actually did come from. During a papal audience on 26th August 1939, Monsignor Bernard Sheil, Bishop of Chicago, had offered $125,000 as a gift to the Vatican from the Chicago section of the United Jewish Appeal. The money was to be used "for distribution through Christian agencies to help victims of persecution without regard to race or religion." At the same time the Bishop explained that the American Jews were willing to finance a Chair in Jewish History at the Catholic University of America in Washington, D.C., and at the Seminary of Saint Mary of the

---

*There were several other Catholic plans for foreign settlements for . . . non-Jews—and sometimes even Jews—elsewhere in the world. Dom Odo (Duke Carl Alexander of Württemberg, who could call Britain's Queen Mary his "aunt") lived in the United States till 1949 after having been expelled from Germany in 1934 by the *Gestapo*. In October 1940 he had detailed talks with former German banker Max Warburg. He wanted to settle millions of Jews and non-Jews (but principally the former) in Australia; later he suggested Venezuela and the Virgin Islands as possible immigration havens. Amazingly, this undoubtedly intelligent priest would, in his letters to Cardinal Maglione, whenever he mentioned the President of the United States, refer to him as "President Roosfeld."

Lake in Chicago. Cardinal Maglione informed Bishop Sheil by mail on September 8 (and reconfirmed his message by telegram on 31 December 1939) that the Pope was pleased with the "conspicuous charitable offering." As to the two proposed chairs on Jewish history, he was of the opinion that "study . . . at the theological seminaries teaches the students enough about the Jewish people, and hence makes the installation of the offered chairs superfluous."

It was furthermore suggested to Bishop Sheil that $50,000 be given to American Catholic Aid Societies. Thus the eminent Chicago Bishop transferred (on 6 February 1940) the remaining $75,000 via American Express to Rome, where $30,000 were put at the disposal of the Saint Raphael organisation in order to "facilitate the emigration to Brazil of German Catholic refugees." Another $7,000 was sent to Holland, and $3,000 to the Papal Nuncio in Switzerland. Cardinal Pietro Boetto, who had repeatedly asked for financial help in order to succor "converted Jewish refugees living in Genova," was sent 20,000 lire or one thousand dollars, followed by another 25,000 lire in May 1940.

Thus, the "large amounts of money in American currency which we have appropriated for the overseas trips of the emigrants," as Pope Pius XII had written to Cardinal von Preysing in Berlin, actually were not *appropriated* by the Pope for this purpose. They had been *put at his disposal* exactly *for* such a purpose by the United Jewish Appeal in the United States.

It was not till April 1973—when details of the $125,000 offered to the Pope by Chicago's United Jewish Appeal became known from the documents published by the Vatican—that it became totally clear how the *Raphaelsverein* at that moment had been practically penniless, and how the money from American Jews was going to enable it to make a new start. In his letter to the Pope on 21 February 1940, the *Raphaelsverein's* secretary-general (Grösser) had informed Pius XII that "from the funds put at our disposal by German and American Catholics, we cannot possibly pay the passage for any more refugees . . ." And notes from the Secretariat of State (written on 4 January 1940) mention that "if the *Raphaelsverein* could have a sizable amount of money at its disposal, the emigration of German Catholic refugees to Brazil will be facilitated, because one of the heaviest conditions posed by the Brazilian Immigration and Colonization Council is the deposit of 20 *contos de Reis* for every person." Furthermore, on 17 October 1940, Monsignor Domenico Tardini (Secretary of the Congregation of Extraordinary Ecclesiastic Affairs), checking whether any of the United Jewish Appeal money could be used for "pure" Catholics as well, wrote the following in his private notes (these were also first made public in April 1973): "I have personally checked Monsignor Sheil's telegram of 28 December 1939. The doubt which I expressed yesterday, is now a certainty. The telegram says that part of the money collected by American Jews should be reserved for distribution through Christian agencies to help victims of persecution without regard to race or religion. The text is clear. From it can be deduced that: (1) Aryans can be helped with these funds; (2) if till now it has, on the whole, been preferred to help those who were Jews by race but Catholic by religion, then there is no reason whatsoever to continue along these lines. . . ."

A veil of mystery still covers some of the other money which the Vatican claims it spent. While Father Weber was hard at work trying to help his converted Jews,* he received one day a visit from Monsignor Emilio Guano, later Bishop of Livorno. Neither Father Weber nor Bishop Guano, who has fully corroborated the Pallottine priest's story, can recall with exactitude the date of their meeting. The monsignor arrived from Genova, and to Father Weber's immense surprise brought along what both priests recall as being close to two million lire, received from Cardinal Boetto. The Cardinal had informed Monsignor Guano that this money came from and belonged to the

---

*According to Father Weber, several years later (most likely "around 1950") "about five" of Martin Bormann's children arrived at the Pallottine Order's monastery in Rome. They carried either German or American passports—Father Weber does not remember which—made out in a false name, supplied "by the Americans in Germany." The children stayed with the Pallottine Fathers for several days, then left for South America.

Delasem organisation. Being "Jewish money" destined for purely Jewish purposes, Father Weber declined to accept it for his non-Jewish activities. Instead he had suggested to Monsignor Guano that he deposit it temporarily with the *Nunciatura* in Rome—which was done.

When I asked him for his opinion on the matter, Father Maria Benedetto said that in his mind "it is clear that Monsignor Guano, in addressing himself to Father Weber, did not know where to go, and I fully understand therefore that Father Weber advised the monsignor to bring the money to Monsignor Riberi at the *Nunciatura*. But what happened to it then? My surmise is that it remained there, for Monsignor Riberi knew nothing of our activities. In any case one thing is sure—*we* certainly did not get it."*

There is a possibility that Father Leiber, if he knew about this money, considered it part of the other funds he claims were spent by the Vatican. It is an assumption that would be fully in line with his claims that *everything* that had been done in Rome by those lonely admirable priests, strong in a laudable religious devotion (and a certain national pride), had been done on orders from the Vatican. Such as, for instance, the housing of Jewish refugees in convents and other religious buildings in the capital (where—if we take the information imparted by Father Leiber for granted—half of the Jewish population of Rome is supposed to have found permanent shelter).

"Pius XII had made it known," Father Leiber wrote in 1961, "that the religious homes could *and should**** give the Jews refuge." This is in quite flagrant opposition to the statements made by all those priests who—individually, spontaneously, on their own—were so active in helping the Jews of

---

*In an article published in the *Civiltà Cattolica* of August 1972, American Jesuit Father Robert A. Graham, one of the four historians who compiled the Vatican documents published in April 1973, tried to ridicule this story (which I have previously recounted) of the two million lire, making it sound—by the use of irony, sarcasm and even innuendo—as if I had invented a tale, although (as reported) it had been told to me by Father Weber, and was confirmed to me in all its details by Bishop Guano.

**Italics added.

Rome, and who had never heard of any of these papal instructions. The help given to these human beings, hunted like animals, may well have had the Pope's silent consent; but it is certain that, contrary to Father Leiber's contentions, the initiative never came from the Vatican. Father Giuseppe de Zotti, one of the five priests who in 1967 received the Yad Vashem medal, called their movement "utterly spontaneous," started by "Italians and Christians"; and he added that "never, not once had they been given orders from above."

Enlarging on the myth, Father Leiber claimed that close to four thousand five hundred Jews were hidden in the various clerical homes in Rome. "To these one should add," he explained, "all those who were hidden in the Vatican, the number of which is quite difficult to specify, because, hidden illegally, no one ever talked about them." This is an interesting point, and to prove it Father Leiber supplied a detailed list of the numbers of these hidden Jews to Italian historian Renzo de Felice, who published it in his book *Storia degli ebrei italiani sotto il fascismo.**

It is true that Father Leiber had nothing to do with the compilation of this list. According to information he himself supplied, it was prepared by Swiss Father Ambord, who had done excellent work in Rome in helping both Jewish and ex-Jewish refugees with money—as he has declared in a letter to the present author—"received indirectly from a Jew in Switzerland." The list was then handed to Father Leiber by Miss Iris Rub-Rothenberger (a German half-Jewish refugee from Frankfurt who had been baptized at an early age, and who after the liberation of Rome worked as an assistant to Father Ambord in the preparation of German-language broadcasts over the Vatican Radio).

Some of the figures indicating the number of refugees on the list seem highly inflated. It would, for instance, have been totally impossible for the Church of San Bartolomeo on the Tiber island to hide for months on end four hundred Jews; this is the

*Giulio Einaudi Editore (Torino 1961).

figure mentioned. There simply was not enough physical room for such a permanent crowd. (Perhaps it was meant that the priests of the church over the full period of the German occupation had helped a *total* of 400 Jews, many of whom changed their shelter every night, or every few nights.) According to Father Ambord, "the figures mentioned on the list give no detailed information on single nights." (This could mean that, all in all, a total of four hundred nights were spent at the church by the aggregate of a number of people—perhaps one hundred Jews four nights each, fifty Jews eight nights, or as an extreme example—one Jew four hundred nights.) The list seems to conform to other equally bland assertions by Father Leiber on the tremendous help the Vatican meted out to the Jews of Rome, including that great crowd hidden inside the Vatican, the number of which could not be ascertained because they were there "illegally." But the Jews who found protection in churches and convents certainly were not hidden any less "illegally" than those supposedly given shelter inside the Vatican. If Jews *were* hidden within the Vatican walls in those large numbers not indicated by Father Leiber, then it may be assumed that they were not the butcher, the baker, and the candlestick-maker, but that they were Jews of a certain importance who had close connections with Vatican authorities—professors perhaps, or lawyers, doctors, and other important persons. However, it is surprising that after much research it has been possible to discover the trail of only one family of eleven Jews who found a four months' "illegal" haven within the Vatican walls. From all indications, it seems to have been a special case, in which one of the daughters—in a group that included parents, grandparents, children plus an uncle and aunt—had been engaged to be married to a Catholic youth who was befriended by a priest living inside the Vatican. To be sure, the fact that "Catholic-Jewish love" was involved in no way diminishes the great merit of the two priests, Monsignori Fioretti and Nichini, who were so splendidly active in this rescue operation. Yet neither the chief rabbi of Rome, nor any of the other important members of the Jewish community along the Tiber have ever heard of even a

single Jew who was hidden inside the Vatican itself. I must except Dr. Renzo Levi, who tells me that one of his uncles was
there.*

A priest who spent the whole of the war inside the Vatican
has informed me that during the German occupation of Rome
approximately forty men had been housed in the building he
lived in; but as far as he knew—and he was well informed—"they were all Italian officers." Mademoiselle Solange
Pinzauti-Fivé of the French consulate, who did more than most
in the diplomatic community to help Jews and other refugees in
Rome, declares that she "never, *never* knew of Italian Jews who
were in the Vatican during the war, and I can assure you that I
have known a few. Yet I have never even met *one*. . . ."

Moreover, the assistance—especially in the case of convents
belonging to German nuns—had not always been as spontaneous, or free from financial charges, as Father Leiber would
like us to believe. Fräulein Rub-Rothenberger herself—who in
1942 had arrived from Frankfurt with a valid German passport
"obtained with the help of certain influential people"—hid out
in Rome at the convent of the German *Sisters of Nostra Signora*
in the Via Como. She found their protection at times "tough
going," since the nuns suspected her of not being "one hundred
percent Catholic," as she had claimed to be. With her at the convent were two young Italian Catholic girls, refugees from the
north—and every lira spent for them was reimbursed. Some
payments, as in Fräulein Rub's own case, were covered with a
loan from Father Ambord which was duly repaid after the war.
When Rome finally was liberated, the two young Italian
Catholic refugees from northern Italy turned out to be two little
Jewish girls, born and bred in Rome. On hearing this horren-
dous news, as Fräulein Rub relates, "the Mother Superior
fainted dead away. . . ."

---

*The uncle, however, was no longer a Jew at that time, since he had converted
to Catholicism in 1938. He was, moreover, an extremely rich man, the first
Italian who had manufactured ready-made clothes on a large scale in his plant in
Turin, and who—by then a Catholic for eleven years—in 1949 left all his
possessions to Pope Pius XII.

Father Leiber had several more argumentative arrows in his bow to demonstrate the Vatican's selfless help for the Roman Jews. There was the matter of the money from America. "Nor should one forget," he wrote, "the considerable sums of money which the American Jews put at the disposal of Pius XII to help the victims of the persecution, and which he used according to the desires of the donors. . . ." By which the Pope's apologist must have meant the $125,000 offered to Pius by the United Jewish Appeal, and the money put at the disposal of Father Maria Benedetto and the Delasem by the American Joint—the counter-value of which changed hands on Vatican territory in the apartment of Monsignor Hérissé, but which neither the Pope *nor* the Vatican had anything to do with. And to make a simple calculation of what the Vatican had done financially for the Jews, Father Leiber summed up the whole matter in a single phrase: "The total amount of money distributed by the Pope for the Jews till 1945, amounts according to a careful calculation to at least two-and-a-half billion of today's lire." The Jews of Rome, who were "the Pope's Jews," his closest Jewish neighbors, are still wondering where their share went.*

Towards the end of his article Father Leiber tried to establish "how grateful the Jews were to the Pope for the help they received from him during the war." He described how in 1945 a group of Jews who returned from concentration camps came to

---

*In June 1972, when the Italian edition of this book was published by Mondadori in Milan, the important daily newspaper *La Stampa* formulated a list of seven questions, all based on statements contained in my final chapters, requesting the Vatican for clarification and comment.

The answers, written by two anonymous Vatican *studiosi,* came back within a few days, but none of them touched upon the questions submitted. Instead, the two *studiosi* talked ambiguously around the subjects, explaining matters that were never raised at all. They alleged that "Father Maria Benedetto reported to Monsignor Riberi," without adding—as Father Maria Benedetto himself did when the Vatican's answers were submitted to him for comment—that he (Father Benedetto) "had made only one report to Monsignor Riberi, on 24 January 1945, after the liberation of Rome. It was a report on the assistance I gave to converted Jews. . . . It was totally independent of the Delasem action, which organisation by then had begun to function again, form which moment on I had had nothing more to do with it. . . ."

Asked for clarification of another question by *La Stampa,* this one dealing with the mysterious disappearance of the two million lire that were deposited by

thank the Pope for his help; how the Israeli Philharmonic Orchestra gave a concert at the Vatican on 26 May 1955; how the Chief Rabbi of Rome, Elio Toaff, wrote (on the occasion of the Pope's death) in an article requested from him by the *Osservatore Romano*, how "more than anyone, we have had the occasion to appreciate the great compassionate goodness and magnanimity of the Pope during those unhappy years of persecution and terror, when it seemed that there was no escape for us. . . ."

The orchestra did play, the Jews were thankful—and still are—but they are principally thankful to those brave men of the Church who acted without waiting for moral leadership or any special orders from the Vatican. Since it was impossible to thank every known and unknown priest individually, the Jewish expressions of gratitude went out to the one man who represented the Church in general—the Pope. Father Leiber omitted to mention (or perhaps he did not know) that the *Osservatore Romano*, in publishing the warm words by Dr. Elio Toaff, had decided *not* to publish the second part of the article, in which the Chief Rabbi of Rome in a few carefully chosen phrases had expressed the opinion that so much more *could* have been done. On another occasion he had expressed these thoughts, gently and discreetly, by saying: "We prefer to remember what the late Pope *has* done for the Jews, instead of thinking about what he has *not* done. . . ."

This critical note was not deemed to be in the interest of the Vatican, and consequently the passage was censored out of the article. It was also cut out of the same article when it was

Monsignor Guano at the Roman *Nunciatura*, the Vatican replied that "this is not a correct interpretation of the nature of the funds received from the Vatican." After which the two *studiosi* curiously directed their non-reply to an issue that was totally unknown to everybody, except, apparently, to the Vatican itself. "The money had been given directly to the Pope," the *studiosi* wrote, "but it was destined for a specific purpose. Such, for example, was the case with the $150,000 given to the Pope in 1940 by a group of American Jews to help the persecuted." Asked for comment, Father Benedetto wrote to the author of this book that "these 150 thousand dollars astound me. . . .and if the Vatican really received these 150 thousand dollars from American Jews in 1940, it would be interesting to discover what use they made of it. What remains clear is that the Delasem received nothing from the Vatican." The money alluded to was, of course, the $125.000—not $150.000—offered to the Pope by Chicago's United Jewish Appeal via Bishop Sheil.

republished in the special edition of the *Osservatore della Domenica* (the Vatican's Sunday paper) on 28 June 1964—an edition that was entirely devoted to what the Vatican claimed it had done for the Jews. Most of Father Leiber's erroneous statements were sedulously repeated in this eighty-page glorification of papal assistance—about the 1,500 "Jews" who were helped to emigrate by Father Weber (which item was published under a headline that reads "A PONTIFICAL ORGANISATION FOR THE EMIGRATION OF THE JEWS"; then about the "new organisation called the DELASEM of which Father Maria Benedetto took the leadership"; about the money spent, and the reasons for the Pope's benevolent silences.

In the end, as an historian must conclude, one gets the impression that the Jesuit father tried to put to the credit of the Vatican every individual act of charity ever bestowed on the Jews of Rome, that he set out to prove that every beneficent move had been instituted by the Pope; and that, consequently, Father Leiber, at the expense and to the detriment of those modest, magnificent, and self-effacing Italian and French priests, had hoped to give a color of official whitewash to a very discolored story.

Chapter 40
More Vatican Claims

Some of the tales which were so grossly invented by Father Leiber live on and on. In April 1973 a book was published in London* in which the author, Anthony Rhodes, while launching a devastating attack on Rolf Hochhuth's play *The Representative* (known in the United States as *The Deputy*), once again tries to justify the Vatican's and Pope Pius' action—and inaction—during the war years, quoting from a good many sources to prove that Pius XII was immensely interested in the fate of the Jews.

As Rhodes attempts to tell it, the Pope had confided as follows in Don Pirro Scavizzi (who, according to the Vatican's press office, was "a simple parochial priest" who died around 1967). Said the Pope, as retold by the priest: "I realize that my condemnation [of Hitler] would not only fail to help the

*Anthony Rhodes, *The Vatican in the Age of the Dictators, 1922-1945* (Hodder & Stoughton 1973).

Jews, it might even worsen their situation . . . No doubt a protest would have gained me the praise and respect of the civilized world, but it would have submitted the poor Jews to an even worse persecution."

As a further example to prove his point about the danger to the Jews resulting from an eventual papal protest, Rhodes relates what happened in Holland, where the Reformed Church and the Catholics in July 1942 "protested in a telegram to the German *Reichskommissar* against the deportation of Dutch Jews, and threatened to make the protest public if the deportations were not discontinued." The Germans replied that if the churches remained silent in this matter, they would continue to make a special exception of the *baptized* Jews. "The Reformed Church," Rhodes continues (describing an event that indeed did take place, although not exactly as he tells it), "agreed to this and let the matter drop. But the Catholic Archbishop of Utrecht refused and issued a Pastoral Letter sharply condemning the Nazi persecution of the Jews. Whereupon the Germans arrested all the baptized Catholic Jews and deported them to the death-camps of the East. The baptized Protestant Jews on the other hand were not touched."

When I asked Dr. L. de Jong, director of the Netherlands Institute for War Documentation for a comment, he replied that in his opinion Rhodes "treats what happened in Holland far too simplistically. Indeed the reading of the pastoral letter caused the deportation of a certain number of Jewish Catholics, but not of all of them, for a fair number remained. But no one knows how many Jews were *saved*—because precisely as a result of this protest, many Catholic families opened their homes to Jews who wanted to go into hiding. The non-reading of the protest in most of the Protestant churches created in fact a profound feeling of guilt among these various Protestant groups of the Reformed Church."

Rhodes also refers to Adolf Hitler's plan, as it has been described by various authors, to remove the Pope from Rome. For, he writes, "we now know that Hitler planned at one point to kidnap the Pope."

Historians are not supposed to "speculate," but it can't be helped here. Now suppose the Pope *had* spoken up and suppose he *had* been kidnapped. Would not "the civilized world" indeed have protested, including most likely millions of devout Catholics in Germany and German-occupied territories? Might this not even have changed the whole course of the war? In September 1943, when the Germans had occupied Rome and there was fear at the Vatican that the Pope might be forced to leave, the Brazilian ambassador, as dean of the diplomatic corps, reported to Cardinal Maglione on the 16th that on the previous day "all diplomats . . . had declared their . . . desire to remain with the August Person of the Pope *always* and wherever."* And two days later, on September 17th, Maglione was informed that "all those present, without exception, associated themselves with the proposal that in case the Germans dared to seize the person of the Sovereign Pontiff to take him along as their prisoner, all the Chiefs of Mission inside the Vatican would judge it their duty not only to protest against such outrage, but they would also ask to accompany His Holiness."

SS-General Karl Wolff, in an interview with the German weekly *Der Stern* which was published on April 16, 1972—three weeks after Wolff had been heard by the "Consistory and Metropolitan Court of Munich and Freising" in connection with the listing of facts and events that may lead to the beatification of Pius XII—declared that Hitler had ordered him on September 12, 1943 "to occupy the Vatican, kidnap the Pope, and to bring him and the Curia north." Later in the interview with *Der Stern* Wolff stated that he had planned to escort the Pontiff to Liechtenstein, adding that the intention to kidnap the Pope had been "an *idée fixe* with Hitler."

During a subsequent meeting between Wolff and Hitler around the middle of December 1943, once again at the Führer's "Wolfsschanze" headquarters in East Prussia, Wolff—always according to the interview with the German weekly—said he

---

*Original italics by Cardinal Maglione.

had informed Hitler that "kidnapping the Pope might lead among the German Catholics at home and at the front to exceptionally negative repercussions." As explained by the German general, Hitler then allowed him "to do what he thought right," and the plan was abandoned.

Wolff told *Der Stern* that up till Mussolini's ouster on July 25, 1943—in which ouster, Hitler presumed, the Vatican had had an active hand—the Führer had been extremely in favor of Pope Pius, who as Monsignor Pacelli had been Papal Nuncio in Munich for twelve years, from 1917 till 1929. Based on this pro-Pius opinion, Hitler in 1941 had confided in Wolff that "If I could nominate a German Pope for German Catholics, I would without any hesitation choose Pacelli."

Four days previous to the first meeting between Hitler and Wolff, when on September 8, 1943 the armistice between General Eisenhower and Marshal Badoglio was made public, Hitler had ordered Wolff from the eastern to the southern front with the newly created rank of "Highest SS and Police Führer in Italy," a job in which velvet gloves were notoriously absent.

Once in Rome, Wolff—as told to *Der Stern*—repeatedly had tried to get in touch with the Pope. Finally on May 10, 1944, a private audience was arranged for him by the German Father Superior of the Order of Salvatorians, Monsignor Pankratius Pfeiffer. In June 1973, inquiring after Father Pfeiffer, I was told by the Order's Postulator General, Father Leonard Gerke, that Pfeiffer had died in 1945. And, added Father Gerke, "we have no information on that Papal audience, for when the Allies approached Rome, Father Pfeiffer burned all his private papers."

Yet some information seems to have survived, perhaps via Wolff. For we are informed by *Der Stern* that the SS-general—who in 1964 was condemned to fifteen years *Zuchthaus* for having been "the eyes and ears of Himmler" and as such having had knowledge of the mass murder of "at least 300,000 Jews" in Poland—at the end of that private audience with Pope Pius XII was given the Pope's blessing.

Had Wolff not abandoned his plans, and had the Pope indeed been kidnapped, Pius would have become a martyr. But as the Vicar of Christ on earth, might this not have set a magnificent example to others, including many priests who openly were opposing the Nazis? Anthony Rhodes quotes from the Pope's letter to Archbishop Konrad von Preysing in Berlin, stating that Pius XII expressed his "paternal gratitude and profound sympathy for Monsignor Lichtenberg, who asked to share the lot of the Jews in the concentration camps, and who spoke up against their persecutions in the pulpit." These are words of justified papal mental turmoil, caused by the exemplary courage of Monsignor Lichtenberg and so many other priests; but surely this was, on the part of the Pope, words only.

As I have suggested earlier, there was always a significant difference between what the Pope *thought* his words meant, and what others made of them. Once again quoting from Pius XII's letter to the archbishop of Berlin, Anthony Rhodes reminds us of the Pope's statement that "in Our Christmas message, We said a word concerning the Jews in the Territories under German control. The reference was short, but it was well understood." Yet Harold Tittmann, President Roosevelt's representative at the Vatican, after talking to the Pope a few days later, said the following (in his telegram of December 30, 1942 to Secretary of State Cordell Hull in Washington) about this "well understood reference": "He seemed astonished when I told him that not all people were of his opinion."

The "short, well understood reference" pronounced by the Pope on that 24 December, 1942 came towards the end of a radio speech which was over 2,500 words long and which must have lasted between twenty and twenty-five minutes. Referring to a number of "solemn oaths" which all "magnanimous and honest people" should take, the Pope mentioned "the solemn oath which humanity owes to the hundreds of thousands of persons who, without any personal guilt, but only for reasons of nationality or race, are destined to die or to waste away slowly." The Pope, as Tittmann cabled, felt that "it must have been clear to everyone that he meant the Poles, the Jews, and the hostages."

Rhodes, an energetic defender of papal policy, considers the Christmas message "a clear enough reference to the Jews." Yet Rhodes himself adds elsewhere in his book that "several

governments, including the Belgian, British, Polish, and
Brazilian made a joint protest to the Vatican that the Pope
should have stigmatized Germany by name for its persecution
of the Jews." The "clarity" of the reference to the Jews,
therefore, finds on the one side the Pope and a few apologetic
authors, and, on the other side, the four mentioned
governments, Harold Tittmann, and even the German ambassador to the Vatican. The protests made by the four
governments, Rhodes writes, "grieved the Pope who believed he
had met all possible demands for plain speaking."

As I have pointed out previously, the German ambassador to
the Holy See, Weiszäcker, thought that the Pope's words as
published in the *Osservatore Romano* of 25 October 1943 were
so *unclear*, that he informed Berlin not to worry, "because only
very few people will recognize it as having anything to do with
the Jewish problem."

Elsewhere in his book, Anthony Rhodes cites the letter sent
by German Father Hudal to Hitler's commander in Rome,
General Stahel, hoping that this written intervention might
cause the Germans to stop the arrest of Roman Jews on 16 October 1943. As we have seen, it was not this letter that stopped
the German action, but the fact that the Germans for the moment had run out of names on their list. But then Rhodes adds a
report from the British minister to the Vatican, Sir Francis d'Arcy Osborne, to the Foreign Office in London. According to this
message, "the Cardinal Secretary of State summoned the German ambassador (Weiszäcker) to protest against the arrest of
the Jews. The ambassador took immediate action, *with the
result that a large number were released. . . .* *

For the sake of historical accuracy I believe it is necessary to
quote the *full* text of D'Arcy Osborne's message, as I found it in
the Public Record Office in London: "As soon as he heard of
the news of the arrest of Jews in Rome, Cardinal Secretary of
State sent for the German ambassador and formulated some
sort of protest. The ambassador took immediate action, with the
result that large numbers were released. It appears that only
German and Italian Jews were retained and that those who had

*Italics added.

one Aryan parent or were themselves parents of children were released. Vatican intervention thus seems to have been effective in saving a number of these unfortunate people. I inquired whether I might report this to you, and was told that I might do so, but strictly for your information, and on no account for publicity, since any publication of information would probably lead to renewed persecution."

There is a remarkable marginal note on the cable as received in London, hand-written apparently by the director of the Refugee Department of the Foreign Office. It is not reported by Rhodes, and it reads: "This is all rather indefinite, as we aren't told how many Jews have been released."

Now it is quite clear that the Osborne report to London resulted exclusively from what he had been told by the Vatican's Secretary of State. Osborne, a British subject who himself was hiding inside the Vatican, had no opportunity to check the Vatican's report personally. He simply *listened* to the Vatican's account and *reported*. The news he cabled to London contained, in my view, less hard facts than elements of fantasy and wishful thinking on the part of the Vatican. Nor did Rhodes apparently consider it necessary to check the story's veracity with the Jewish authorities in Rome. Without further inquiry he too accepted the Vatican's statement. One begins to wonder about the re son why the Vatican had insisted that the story should be exclusively reported to the Foreign Office "and on no account for publicity." For the Vatican's story does not square with the known facts, as has been confirmed and reconfirmed time and again by officials at the Office of the Roman Jewish Community, including its Chief Rabbi Dr. Elio Toaff: "*Not one single Jew was liberated by the Germans once they were caught on that October morning.*" Some 1,127 Jews were rounded up on that fateful Saturday, and 1,127 were deported to Nazi concentration and extermination camps in Poland two days later.*

---

*It is surprising to discover that in the secret documents which were published by the Vatican on 4 April 1973, there is nowhere even the slightest mention of the October 16 round-up of the Jews. One might assume that, in view of the claimed intervention by the Pope, *someone* inside the Vatican walls had made

In defending what he believes to be, or perhaps what he would like to be, the truth, Rhodes—as so many others before him—does little more than repeat certain rationalizations devised by the Vatican. The tragic truth is bitter, and there is no hiding place behind the Osborne telegram. For it is all a circular argument. In the Introduction to the seventh volume of the secret documents published by the Vatican, we read that in dealing with Maglione's protest to Weiszäcker "it seems that Weiszächer did act. Some days later, the British minister Osborne, in a telegram to London dated October 31, informed his government about the intervention by the cardinal, mentioning that 'a large number of those unhappy people were released' . . . " Thus the Vatican, not having verified its own wishful reportage, now hides behind Osborne's report *on what he heard from Maglione* in order to "prove" the truth of its own claims!

History is too important to be left to unhistorical methods. In the "Conclusion" to his book, Anthony Rhodes makes the sweeping statement that "the charge against Pius XII has already been disposed of." It would seem that it is exclusively disposed of in the mind of the author himself. Arguments are never, or not for long, reinforced by unconfirmed reports or unchecked statements by third parties. Thus, in his chapter on "Pius XII and the Jews," Rhodes mentions that the British Jewish author and Member of Parliament "Mr. Maurice Edelman, President of the Anglo-Jewish Association, who had a private audience with Pius XII after the war, declared to the London Council of the Association that the intervention of the Pope was responsible during the war for saving tens of thousands of Jewish lives." Is this so? Has it been checked? As Mr. Edelman explained to me in May 1973 when I inquired about the veracity of the statement attributed to him: "It was

notes on the events of that day for posterity, or might have transcribed a message for Cardinal Maglione or for Pope Pius himself. In view of the importance of the *razzia* in the modern history of the Church, one would have thought that the four priests who edited volumes 6 and 7, might have included at least *one* documented reference to it. Yet among all 930 carefully selected and reproduced papers there is not a single one that deals with the events of that tragic Saturday in October.

only a quotation of what the Pope actually had said to me. . . . "
The circles in the circular argument get smaller and smaller.

Comment is free (as a great *Manchester Guardian* editor, C.
P. Scott, once said), but facts are sacred. What about the gold
which the Germans had asked for from the Roman Jews in
September 1943? Rhodes records that the Nazis had requested
"fifty-five kilograms of gold," and that otherwise "300
hostages would be taken." (The details are, again, quite in-
correct, for it was fifty kilograms and 200 hostages.) "As this
amount could not be raised so quickly, the chief rabbi approached the Vatican, which contributed immediately fifteen
kilograms towards the sum." It was not the chief rabbi who was
involved, and the fifteen kilograms of gold were never "contributed." They were only *promised* in case the full weight of
gold could not be collected; it was, and hence the fifteen
kilograms of gold were never contributed at all.

Myths are made to be believed, but historians are called to exercise sceptical judgment. The Vatican myths, to some extent,
are to be used by the Church to strengthen the motives and
reasons for the sanctification of Pius XII, the preliminary
research for which was completed by Jesuit priest Paolo
Molinari in Rome early in 1973. The decision to begin was
made on 8 November 1965 by Pope Paul VI to the bishops
assembled in Saint Peter's: "I have decided to start the process
of beatification of my two predecessors Pius XII and John
XXIII."

Among the thousands of documents and testimonials
assembled by Father Molinari are many which in the witness'
opinion deal with proofs of Pope Pius' strong interest in the
fate of the Jews. Pius' housekeeper for some forty years, the
famous German Sister Pasqualina, has stated, for instance, that
Pius (during the war) distributed to the Jews all the money
which he received in gifts. Therefore, as Father Molinari told me
in April 1973, "the discoveries made will throw a new light on
the acts and gestures of Pius XII."

We are further informed that Pius XII, on a note submitted to
him by the then Secretary of State (the present Paul VI) dealing
with Nazi abominations, had annotated in his own hand-

writing: "We should speak words of fire against such things." But he is also said to have declared to the Italian ambassador to the Holy See: "I demand my freedom and my right to speak. If I remain silent, it is only to avoid worse." The fiery words next time.*

And thus, while six million European Jews died, including over eight thousand from Italy and two thousand ninety-two from Rome, Pope Pius XII, to avoid worse, remained silent.

There is no escaping history. The Vatican—which has had a millennial history of true saints and martyrs, and whose moralists have disseminated so much theological insight into the nature of sin and the shortcomings of men—will simply have to learn to live with the bitterness, with the chagrin and the pity, with the ineradicability of this tragedy.

---

*That the papal silence was dictated by the perennial fear of doing anything that might provoke Adolf Hitler's ire, has been made very clear by the Vatican itself in some of the recently-published documents from its secret files.

In 1942 the Netherlands government-in-exile in London wanted to renew its diplomatic relations with the Vatican, which had been served in 1927. By 1943 all arrangements had been made, and the Vatican had accepted the name of the to-be-appointed Dutch ambassador. Then the Germans occupied Rome. and a rather frantic telegram from the Vatican to its nuncio in London requested total secrecy about the relationship with the Dutch government.

Yet one year previously (in 1942), the Vatican had also agreed to establish diplomatic relations with Japan, notwithstanding furious protests by the British and American governments. On 5 March 1942 Assistant Secretary of State Sumner Welles cabled Rome that "If Japan waited for 20 years before taking this step, then the Holy See could postpone the matter till after the war. . . ." Cicognani himself cabled the Vatican two days later (on March 7) that "It seems inconceivable to him [Roosevelt] that at such a critical moment one can conclude and publicize such a step."

Chapter 41
The Converted Rabbi

I want to return to one fascinating item in Father Leiber's scriptures with which he had tried to convince the world of the veracity of the proclaimed pro-Jewish beneficial deeds the Vatican had performed. This item dealt with what he considered the ultimate proof of loving-kindness to "the Pope's Jews." It concerned the strange affair of Chief Rabbi Italo Zolli, who had disappeared shortly after 8 September 1943, when the Germans overran Rome. When they left in June 1944, Zolli emerged from his hiding place. According to many stories still going the rounds of Rome, his refuge was supposed to have been the Vatican. In reality Zolli had been hiding out at various places in the city—first (for only a few days) in the Via del Mascherino at the apartment of a fellow Jew, Dr. Angelo Anav, who had already fled the city. Then he was hospitably received by Amadeo Pierantoni and his wife in the Via delle Alpi 32, and he moved from there to the apartment of a young couple by the name of Falconieri. Both Pierantoni and Falconieri were

Catholics. Quite obviously none of these hiding places were in-side the Vatican, nor even anywhere near it.

Sixty-three years of age on his return, Zolli wanted his old job back—and did get it back with the assistance of Colonel Charles Poletti, the American military governor of Rome—against great opposition from among the Jews in the community. They felt that their chief rabbi had abandoned them when they needed him most.

To shift Zolli away from the active leadership of the con-gregation, he was promoted to head the newly-to-be-established Rabbinical College, which had ceased to exist in Florence, and which now would be reopened in the capital. In the meantime Zolli continued to officiate at services.

On 12 February 1945 he adjudicated a divorce* at his rab-binical offices. The following day, February 13, Zolli and his wife were baptized in a small chapel next to the Church of *Santa Maria degli Angeli;* his daughter Miriam followed in her parents' footsteps some months later. (Dora—a daughter by Zolli's first wife, Adele Litwak, who had died in 1917—re-mained a Jew.) In Father Leiber's opinion this was the supreme evidence of the goodness of the Pope, since Israel Zoller "out of gratitude towards Pius XII, took the name of Eugenio"—the Pope's first name.

How strange are the ironies of history, how many twists of fate and faith have we seen in the history of the Jews of Rome! In 1280 Spanish-born Abu'lafia had tried to convert the Pope. Now, almost seven centuries later, the Vatican captured the conversion prize of the millennium and baptized the chief rabbi of Italy.

Some Vatican spokesmen assert that Zolli had made a vow to convert if God would guide him safely through the holocaust. I was told by another priest that he had already been attracted to Christianity as a little boy, and this same priest affirmed that

---

*In Italy, where divorce at that time did not yet exist, a Jewish divorce had no legal value. However, if the divorcee later on had children by another man, the mother—according to Jewish law—was not considered to have committed adultery, as was the case in similar circumstances with Catholics.

"Zolli had the goodness of heart which is so eminently Christian." Yet this was the same Rabbi Zolli who ten years previously, when many Jews gave up their membership in the Jewish Community or even converted to Catholicism, had written from Trieste to Chief Rabbi Angelo Sacerdoti in Rome: "Israel feels, and always has felt, that there is one God only, one and indivisible. The souls of the Patriarchs, Moses, the prophets, the martyrs, and the heroes—they all will tremble before the degrading spectacle of these deserters who repudiate the Torah, the source of their spirit and the inheritance of their fathers. . . ."

It was also the same Rabbi Zolli who in 1935 had written in his book *Israele:* "And the Lord of the Universe had entered into this soul that has shrunken from nostalgia as if it were an august temple. And this temple will remain His forever. Israel has . . . consecrated its life, its soul, to the only God, after which the only God in His turn has consecrated Israel as a people."

Would it be more reasonable, as some claim, to presume that Zolli (who after his conversion became professor of Hebrew and Testamental Literature at the Pontifical Biblical Institute of Rome) converted "out of spite"? The troubles that beset him on his return were grave. He was intensely resented by the members of the community. His refuge at the Vatican might have been the human context of his claimed vow of conversion; but the fact that during all these months of his disappearance Zolli had set foot only once inside the Vatican, and then for one hour only, entirely nullifies this story.

Zolli was a complex spirit, a Jew who was totally and nearly exclusively immersed in theological knowledge. According to his daughter Miriam (in a statement made to me in 1970), he was a man who all his life had been seeking the Universal God, and who, when he died in 1956, still was seeking the secrets of the divine.

He was one of six children, and Zolli's deeply religious parents back in Brody had destined him to become a rabbi, a profession or calling (as Miriam felt) for which he was totally unfit. In our conversation, she characterized her father as "a profound *studioso*, an intensely good man, a great humanist, sensitive but weak and *pauroso*"—frightened. In his daughter's eyes "he was certainly not a hero."

Having finished his rabbinical studies, and while officiating as rabbi in Trieste, Zolli taught Old and New Testament theology at the University of Padua. The idea of establishing some kind of a "bridge between the two faiths" was apparently strongly in his mind, although the thought of abandoning the religion of his forefathers appeared totally alien to him. Yet somehow flirting with this "religious bridge" idea, Zolli published in 1938 a book entitled *The Nazarene* ("An exegetical study of the New Testament based on the Aramaic"), dealing with Christ *as a Jew*. Three years previously, in 1935, he already had approached the bridge between the Old and the New Testament in a dissertation which he called "The Holy Alliance between the Ancient and New-Testamentary Literature."

It is Miriam Zolli's view that from the very beginning there never was a feeling of harmony between Zolli and the Roman Jewish Community; according to her, "there was no contact." This feeling became acute when Zolli reappeared upon the Roman scene in 1944. He found the Jewish Community solidly opposed to him.

He became more and more embittered, and Zolli's "tremendous inner struggle"—Miriam's words—slowly seemed to carry him away. Yet from all evidence at hand it is more likely that, in the end, Zolli's conversion, which so deeply shocked and scandalized the Jews in Rome and elsewhere, was indeed more a matter of spite than of scripture.

There is a dramatic bit of proof about Zolli's continued Hebraical feelings in the contents of his writing of that period. While hiding out from the Germans, Zolli—indeed a *studioso* as Miriam had characterized him, a *studioso* with more than a dozen substantial works of Judaism to his credit—had spent those months in writing another book. This one, its subject undoubtedly prompted by the *Zeitgeist*, was entitled "*Antisemitismo*," and it deals with the history of this religious plague through the centuries. The book, as Zolli himself mentions, was nearly finished during the last months of the German occupation of Rome, thus only about eight months before his conversion in February 1945. Yet in this long treatise Zolli recorded ideas and thoughts which surely did not reflect the spirit of someone who was "already attracted to Christianity when he was a little boy."

"To promise a complete assimilation, a perfect fusion with other races, is a responsibility that no representative of the Jewish race should assume; because Israel, from ancient times onward, from the moment it acquired the conscience of its interior unity, has given to humanity all it could give: the Bible, the Talmud, and many other contributions in the field of thought and literature. . . . "

The book, which as we have noted was practically finished by June 1944, was published a year later by the A.V.E. *(Anonima Veritas Editrice)*, a Catholic publishing house in Rome, as is evident from Zolli's inscribed preface date: 23 July 1945. The intermediate months had given Zolli the opportunity to add a last chapter to his work, dealing with matters on his mind. It shows that some of the Vatican's senior disciples, many years before Father Leiber became their spokesman on the subject of the Church's presumed pro-Semitism, had already become firm believers in these very same myths. For, in his very last chapter, Zolli repeated the information he had received from Father Gozzolini Birolo; it dealt with the splendid work done by the Pallottine Father Antonio Weber and his *"Opera di San Raffaele."* Zolli simply accepted Father Birolo's misinformation, which was consequently included in his work exactly as his informant wanted it.

The last chapter was entitled "H. H. Pius XII and the Jews of Rome during the Period of the German Invasion," and Zolli wrote: "Here in Rome during these recent stormy times, under the auspices of the Holy See, the great deeds performed by 'The Good Works of San Raffaele' were carried through for the benefit of the emigrants; it was consecrated nearly exclusively to the protection and rescue of persecuted Jews, who took advantage of it by the thousands." Before ending his chapter, Zolli added the details about the expense involved in all this good work to save the Jews: "The Reverend Father Antonio Weber, secretary general of San Raffaele . . . helped between 20,000 and 25,000 people; among these were 1,500 Jewish emigrants. The expenses involved amounted to 4,995,000 lire, of which 2,079,000 lire were contributed by the Vatican and by the Reverend Pallottine Fathers. . . ." None of this, as we have already seen, was the case; and it was Father Weber himself who clarified the true story.

The only Jew in Rome who during the first few weeks of the desperate German occupation—up till the end of September 1943—knew where Zolli was in hiding, was Giorgio Fiorentino. He was a young lawyer who was a close friend of Miriam Zolli, and through her of her father. Fiorentino, moreover, was close to some of the principal members of the Jewish community, and he acted as a go-between for Zolli in his relationship with these leaders (some of them with former fascist leanings, but all of them by then as much in danger of their lives as Zolli himself). Any messages exchanged between Zolli and Messrs. Foà and Almansi at the community's offices were transmitted through Fiorentino. He would then refer the answer either directly or by telephone to Zolli's daughter (she had found refuge elsewhere in Rome) who in turn would contact her father.

After the liberation of Rome, Fiorentino who (as he testified in 1945) had heard that Zolli "was not liked by the members of the community, had advised him that it would be better for him to look quietly for some other arrangement or solution." Zolli "reacted violently" to this suggestion. He stated—as Fiorentino said in his testimony before the community's investigating committee—that "if the Roman Jews would insist on putting him out to pasture after having spent forty years of his life on behalf of Judaism, they would pay dearly for it."

This, then, seems to be the clue to Zolli's subsequent behaviour, although in an interview with a correspondent of the Israeli newspaper *Maariv* in 1950, Zolli gave a different version of the reasons for his conversion.

"Heaven is my witness," he told his interviewer, "that what I did was not done out of self-interest. I simply became a convert to Catholicism as the result of a profound religious conviction that developed in me over a period of years." Which, of course, might logically have been a compelling reason for him to abandon the post of chief rabbi instead of continuing to serve as the leading Jew in the community. However, according to Zolli, "the knowledge of Catholicism and my love for Christ and for the Gospels could merge in my soul without any contrast." When the Israeli journalist asked Zolli whether on the eve of the principal Jewish holidays he "did not feel the vibrations of some Hebraic sentiment," the former chief rabbi answered: "No—that whole period never seems to have existed in my soul; I feel as if I were born a Catholic. . . . " He seemed to have forgotten, or to have repressed completely, the fervent letter full of vibrant Hebraic feelings and passion which he had sent to Rabbi Sacerdoti in Rome only ten years previously.

Perhaps *Avvocato* Valobra's opinion about Zolli, as he put it to me, is closer to the truth. "He was an extremely learned man," the Genovese lawyer said, "but basically he was an atheist. . . . He was a man intensely *interested in religion*, but not a religious man."

Whatever the personal explanation, here was rich material for myths to feed on. Cardinal Bea's private secretary, Father Stefan Schmidt, declared in a conversation with me that it had been Zolli who had contacted the Holy Father in order to get the gold that might have been missing from the quantity the Germans had ordered from the Jews in 1943. Father Schmidt insisted that he was "absolutely sure of his facts." "Zolli came to see the Holy Father," he said, "and the Pope immediately agreed to put the gold at the disposal of the Jews." He went on, trying to piece together fragments of a lapsed memory: "I think the Germans had asked for five kilograms, but the Jews had only been able to get together two. Therefore Pope Pius promised that next morning he would take care of the missing three kilos. That evening Monsignor Montini said to the Pope: 'Tomorrow may be too late.' So the Pope that very same evening sent the

package with the three kilograms of gold to Rabbi Zolli's
private apartment.''

There is *some* basis to Father Schmidt's story, for Zolli did go
to the Vatican to try and get assistance for the hard-pressed
Jewish community, a story which he himself mentioned in
writing to the community's offices after the war. On 27
September 1943, in the company of Giorgio Fiorentino and a
Catholic lawyer-friend by the name of Giuseppe Dieci,
Zolli—the only time he had come out of hiding—had gone to see
some Vatican dignitaries with whom Dieci was closely befriended, in order to try and get a papal contribution to the 50
kilograms of gold which Major Kappler had requested from the
Roman Jews. The news they received was not disappointing;
but by the time Zolli—via his daughter and Giorgio Fiorentino—had sent a message about it to the community's offices,
the same information had already been known to its leaders for
twenty-four hours via Father Borsarelli and Renzo Levi.

As if Zolli in his various statements, seconded so strongly by
priests who felt that his conversion was a fine feather in the
Vatican hat, had not sufficiently confused the whole affair to
his conversion, Zolli in 1953 started to complicate his case even
more. By then he was a man who had thoroughly repudiated his
former religion. For years he had been installed as professor of
Hebraic studies at the Pontifical Biblical Institute of Rome.
Zolli was invited that year to the United States to give a series of
summer lectures on Christian liturgy at the University of Notre
Dame in Indiana. In Washington he met Archbishop Amletto
Giovanni Cicognani (at that time Apostolic Delegate in the
American capital and later Secretary of State at the Vatican),
and he discussed with him the possibility of writing some kind
of autobiographical memoir in which he would elaborate on the
circumstances of his conversion. The project grew, and the
result was a book entitled *Before The Dawn* that was published
a year later by a Catholic firm in New York. Zolli did not know
any English, and the book had to be translated. It was evidently
intended to serve as an example and inspiration to American
Jews, justifying and possibly stimulating ''religious transition.''

The book, which turned out to be nothing but a long personal apology, was never published in Italy.

Monsignor Cicognani was kind enough to write an introduction for Zolli's *apologia*. He praised the former chief rabbi for his ardent Catholic feelings and for "the mysterious attraction he felt for Jesus Christ from childhood," which resulted in "the talent and genius of Zolli reaching its fulfillment in his conversion to Catholicism."

As Zolli tells it in *Before The Dawn*, he began to meditate on Christ at the age of twelve when visiting a young Christian school-friend in Stanislavow in Austria where he and his family then lived, having moved there from Galician Brody. There was a crucifix on the wall of his friend's house, Zolli wrote, and he "would raise his eyes and look for a long time at the figure hanging there. This contemplation, if I may call it that without exaggeration," he continued, "was not done without a stirring of my spirit. . . . "

Having thus laid the cornerstone for his conversion that was to take place more than half-a-century later, Zolli reminisced on the years during which he had been chief rabbi of Trieste, remarking that during this time "the seed of the Christian life that the invisible hand of God had cast in my soul began to grow with greater vigor." Yet this did not disturb him in the least for "I still did not observe any conflict between this development and my part as a member of the Jewish religious community."

Then Zolli started to strengthen his arguments. "The Old and New Testaments were blending into a harmonious whole." Occupied on a certain night "of 1917 or 1918" with the writing of an article, he put down his pen "and as if in a trance began to invoke the name of Jesus." Apparently he was transfixed, transfigured, and fascinated, for he "found no peace until I saw Him, as if in a large picture without a frame, in the dark corner of my room." Zolli felt at that moment that "Jesus had entered into my interior life as a guest."

One gathers that even now Zolli was not particularly worried that this new passion might possibly mix improperly with the

pieties of a practicing rabbi. For, he insists, "my intense love for
Jesus and the experiences I had, concerned no one. Neither
Hebraism nor Christianity seemed to interfere in my love for
Jesus. Jesus was present in me, and I in Jesus."

Then Zolli makes a great leap forward in his book from 1918
to 1944, a jump that brought him to the day some four months
after he had reappeared on the Roman Jewish scene and—after
those controversial discussions—had been reappointed as chief
rabbi. This day, on which Zolli claims to have had an all-
deciding vision, was a very special occasion—the holiest day in
the life of a Jew—Yom Kippur, the Day of Atonement.

This is, in Zolli's own narrative, what happened. He was
standing, he explained, in the big Roman synagogue after a long
day of fasting and praying, so that God might purify mind and
body of the sins of the previous twelve months, and might offer
forgiveness. "The day was nearing its end," Zolli wrote, "and I
was alone in the midst of a great number of persons. I began to
feel as though a fog were creeping into my soul; it became
denser, and I wholly lost touch with the men and things around
me. A candle burned on a candlestick near me. As the wax li-
quefied, the small flame flared into a larger one, leaping
heavenwards. I was fascinated by the sight of it. I said to
myself: 'in that flame there is something of my own being.' But
I felt so withdrawn from the ritual that I let others recite the
prayers and sing. I was conscious of neither joy nor sorrow; I
was devoid of thought and feeling. My heart lay as though dead
in my breast. . . . And just then I saw in my mind's eye a
meadow sweeping upward, with bright grass but no flowers. In
this meadow I saw Jesus Christ clad in a white mantle, and
beyond His head the blue sky. I experienced the greatest inner
peace. . . . Nearly an hour later my wife, my daughter and I
were at home for supper at last. When I was tired I went to my
bedroom. The door of my daughter's room was shut. Suddenly
my wife said to me: 'Today while you were standing before the
Ark of the Torah, it seemed to me as if the white figure of Jesus
put his hands on your head as if He were blessing you.' I was
amazed but very calm, and pretended not to have understood.

She repeated what she had said, word for word. At that very moment we heard our younger daughter, Miriam, when she called from afar: 'Papàààà!' I went to her room. 'What is the matter?', I asked. 'You were talking about Jesus Christ,' she replied. 'You know, Papa, tonight I have been dreaming that I saw a very tall Jesus, but I don't remember what came next! It was a few days after this that I resigned my post in the Israelite community and went to a quite unknown priest in order to receive instruction. An interval of some weeks elapsed, until the 13th of February, when I received the Sacrament of Baptism and was incorporated into the Catholic Church, the Mystical Body of Jesus Christ. . . . "

Zolli's confession of faith reads like a dream within a dream, with the whole family separately and jointly witnessing the same apparition. And as reported by Zolli in his book, it reads most convincingly: he resigned his post "a few days after," meaning a few days after this Day of Miracles on the Day of Atonement which, in 1944, fell on September 27th. After which, as he records it, "a few weeks elapsed" before he was baptized on February 13th. Yet notwithstanding Zolli's chronology of the quick succession of events between inspiration and consummation, he did not wait *a few days* and *a few weeks;* he waited for nearly five months.

Things had not been developing favorably for Zolli during this period. After his reappearance, Zolli had found a letter from the community's offices (sent to him on 2 April 1944 when a clandestine meeting of leaders of the community had taken place). It turned down his request for payment of his salary while hiding, a demand he had made the previous February 3rd. Instead of salary, he was offered financial assistance as many others received who had also been in hiding. Zolli answered that while he retained "the widest possible reservations on the defense of my rights," he "would continue to exercise" his duties; he did not consider himself "bound by a decision" that he could "not accept as being valid."

As the days passed, the opposition to him among the members of the congregation only increased. Shortly

afterwards, on 7 July 1944, the wartime leaders of the community—including the vaccilating Foà—had been dismissed by
order of Colonel Charles Poletti in his capacity as the regional
commander of the American Military Government. He "ordered
the dissolution of the Council . . . and entrusted the temporary
administration of the Israelite Community to *Avvocato* Sergio
Ottolenghi" (an anti-fascist lawyer) "with the task to proceed,
at a date still to be determined, with new elections." Then, as the
result of Colonel Poletti's intervention and the special support
he received from some American Jewish army chaplains, Zolli
was reinstated as chief rabbi on September 21st. His nomination
was officially confirmed on that date by the Italian Minister of
Interior.

At this, the vociferous dissent among the Jews of Rome, instead of abating, went into crescendo. Zolli's conduct had
violently upset the mood and mind of his flock. As Giorgio
Fiorentino already had pointed out to Zolli during that summer,
it might have been advisable for him to look for some other
position within the Hebrew Community. Zolli, however, was
adamant, as he proclaimed to several people at the time: he *was*
chief rabbi, he was going to *remain* chief rabbi. Sergio Ottolenghi, during these difficult days—as confirmed by various
people who were close to him, including today's president of the
Union of Italian Israelite Communities, Judge Sergio Piperno—was having a hard time of it. He tried to explain to the
recalcitrant Zolli that perhaps he was right in saying that he had
done "nothing wrong." After all, he had simply gone underground as had so many others, to save his life. Zolli
remonstrated during these many meetings that this was indeed
the case—"his job did not impose the duty on him to risk his
neck" (a statement he also made in writing). But this did not
change the attitude of the Roman Jews, whom he now once
again had to lead in their religious services.

Giorgio Fiorentino was at that time working at the law office
of *Avvocato* Ottolenghi, and he himself stood right in the middle of the controversy that raged through the community. According to Fiorentino, Ottolenghi explained to the recalcitrant

rabbi that if he waited till the new board of directors of the community were elected, he would definitely be voted out of office. In order to forestall so drastic and painful an event, Ottolenghi suggested that it would be best for all concerned if Zolli were to resign of his own account. He would then be offered the post of director of the Rabbinical College, which after its closing in Rome in 1938, would now be reopened—a post which would take Zolli away from the members of the congregation, and where moreover his erudition would be fully appreciated. But Zolli continued to insist that he saw no reason whatever to resign after a rabbinical career of over thirty years, and became ever more obstinate. "Why," he insisted, "why *should* I resign?"

Yet even Zolli understood at last that perhaps the proffered way out might well be the best way out. Thus, on 19 January 1945 he sent a letter to the administration of the Israelite Community in which he explained that "as I already informed you verbally, my health does not allow me any longer to perform my duties as chief rabbi." To strengthen the impression that his letter was a simple request for an ordinary transfer, Zolli sent along a medical certificate (obtained from a neighbour, Dr. Augusto Calonzi), recounting his various physical ailments, some of which certainly might have existed at his age. According to Dr. Calonzi, Zolli was "suffering from cardio-aortic sclerosis which already had caused him on various occasions circulatory discompensation, with edema, frequent dyspepsia, and paroxistic attacks of tachiarhythmia," all of which made it necessary for him "to follow a more restful kind of life, and definitely to avoid any and all physical and mental exertion."

Zolli's resignation was made official one week later, on 26 January, to be effective 1 February 1945. In the same letter the amount of his pension was fixed according to the Italian government's retirement regulations—"you will be paid a monthly pension of a gross amount of 2,507.86 lire." This amounted to approximately sixty percent of his salary, which in 1939—on his arrival in Rome—had been fixed at 4,000 lire a month.

On the same date came the offer to take up the new post of director of the Rabbinical College. But (according to sworn statements made by witnesses before the community's committee which, shortly afterwards, was appointed to investigate Zolli's behavior) Zolli "hesitated to accept and on February 6th 1945 he refused the offered solution, declaring that there were other possibilities open to him for his scholarly career. . . . "

Although by now he had stopped officiating at the Temple services, Zolli (according to these same statements by some twenty witnesses) continued "to visit his offices of chief rabbi," where he could exercise those duties that are allowed to any chief rabbi, such as marriages and other ceremonies. Thus, on the morning of 12 February 1945, he proceeded to call for the religious *minyan*, the necessary quorum of ten men—counting himself—to constitute a Rabbinical Tribunal. Among these men were the assistant rabbis Alfredo Ravenna and Marco Vivanti. And as these men testified during their interrogation, confirming the official entry in the register of the community, Zolli "officiated at a divorce ceremony" between two Yugoslav nationals, "Jacob, son of Abraham (Altarac) and Sultana, daughter of Moses Levi."

Twenty-four hours later, apparently (as it then seemed) having made his decision on the "other possibilities open to him for his scholarly career," Zolli and his wife were baptized—to the considerable and understandable surprise and indignation among Jewish communities around the world. These feelings were naturally far stronger in Rome itself, where the Jews of the city got their first inkling of what had happened from the articles in the newspapers on the days following the baptism—February 14 and 15.

Action followed quickly. A meeting was called of the Council of the community, which deliberated on two technical problems of the day. In the first place they wondered whether the divorce pronounced by ex-Rabbi Zolli was valid, because at the time he acted in this case he was considered to have left all idea of Hebraism behind, and already to have mentally embraced Catholicism.

Secondly, they wondered whether the community would have to continue the payment of Zolli's pension. The decision on the first issue was left open; but there was no hesitation as to what measures to take on the second. In its final report the Council decided that Zolli had "perpetrated the most deplorable act a man can morally and religiously be blamed for; and Professor Zolli's responsibility is all the more serious because, with his uncommon talent and culture and specific competence in Semitic knowledge and in the study of comparative religion, he more than anyone else could measure the gravity of the impropriety he consciously has committed."

The Council was, therefore, of the opinion that "these facts are so serious, that we shall have to authorize, nay to *impose* the revocation of his appointment, with all its moral and legal consequences." It was also decided that Zolli was to lose his right to a pension.

Zolli dissented. He was of the opinion that he was legally entitled to his pension, and he protested in no uncertain terms. Early in March he complained to the Prefecture of Rome that he had not yet received his pension for the month of February; and on the 14th of that same month the Prefecture wrote to the community's offices, ordering them to pay forthwith, a request that was repeated by the Prefecture on the 23rd. Payments were not made, and Zolli did not give up. On the 22nd of May 1945 he addressed a strongly-worded letter to the "President of the Israelite Community of Rome." He explained that he considered the arrangement proposed by Ottolenghi "on the 26th of January 1945" as absolutely binding. For the rest he had "various reasons seriously to scrutinize the spurious, fabricated, and arbitrary accusations contained in the indictment." He contended that "the whole paper is nothing but the result of an odious and useless labor, which is incapable of presenting juridical evidence concerning a factual and legal position that already previously had been worked out and agreed upon."

Neither side would relent. The Council appealed the Prefecture's decision; and finally, on 18 May 1946, the tribunal of Rome declared itself incompetent in the case, referring the matter "to the jurisdiction of the Council of State." At the same time it ordered Zolli "to pay all legal expenses suffered by the community." Zolli evidently decided that he was fighting a lost cause. He did not appeal; no pension was ever paid.

By then fifteen months had elapsed since his conversion. The *Osservatore Romano* had announced it at the time (in its edition of 15 February 1945) as having taken place two days previously in the presence of various patricians of the Church—"Father Dezza of the Gregorian University, Father Bea of the Pontifical Biblical Institute," and others who together with "Monsignor Cosimo Bonaldi, rector of *Santa Maria degli Angli*, have instructed the Zolli family in the Christian religion." The baptism itself had been performed by Monsignor Luigi Traglia—today a cardinal.

Father Paolo Dezza, in a conversation (2 March 1972) with the author, declared that Zolli had already told him in August 1944—six months before he was baptized—that he had wanted to convert. Father Dezza recalled that Zolli's decision had not been prompted by any material gain, for Zolli had told him: "I am asking for the water of baptism only, I am asking for nothing else. . . . " The date of this conversation, as Father Dezza said he clearly remembered it, was the *Ferragosto* holiday of that year—August 15. That was the very moment when Zolli's future looked immensely bleak, when he was fighting so desperately to be reinstated as the chief rabbi of Rome. It was also the moment when he had told Giorgio Fiorentino that "if the Roman Jews would insist on putting him out to pasture after having spent forty years of his life on behalf of Judaism, they would pay dearly for it. . . . "

The payment was made, but what good books were balanced thereby? There is, in theological matters, no double-entry bookkeeping.

Chapter 42
The Present

In 1555, when Pope Paul IV ordéred the creation of the ghetto, he declared that "God has imposed servitude upon the Jews until they shall have recognized their errors." Four centuries later the Church finally decided that something had to be done about that statement, as well as about a few other matters that involved the whole or partial condemnation of the Jews, including the not infrequent Church-inspired anti-Semitism.

In March 1938 Pius XI had taken a first important step towards the eradication of the *"only-Catholicism-is-good-for-the-world"* attitude of some priests, when he decided to suspend the "Friends of Israel" (*Amici Israel*)—an organisation, which for many years had been trying to convert the Jews. The wording of the papal decision did not leave any doubt about the Pope's thoughts and intentions. "Inasmuch as the Holy See disapproves of all hatred and all animosity between people," the order read, "it most categorically condemns the hatred against the people who once were chosen by God, a hatred which nowadays is commonly indicated by the word anti-Semitism."

Taking up where Pius XI had left off, Pope John XXIII* (on 18 September 1960) instructed 79-year-old Cardinal Bea to prepare a text on the relationship between the Catholic Church and the Jews; this would be discussed during the Ecumenical Council which was to convene two years later, in October 1962. When during the 1963 session the prepared text was read for the first time, the world heard officially that the Vatican had requested a discussion and a vote on a proposition which proclaimed that the chosen people "were unjustly called a cursed people . . . or, alternately, a god-killing people." The moment this news had reached the press, the echo of the words against *"deicide"* started to provoke feverish feelings in the hearts and minds of a great many Jews, especially those belonging to lay organisations in the United States. Meetings were held, delegations were sent off to Rome to promote the idea among the participants of the Council, and innumerable articles were written. As an antidote to this enthusiasm, the Roman Jews remained conspicuously indifferent; they, frankly, could not care less.

In Rome the Jews were of the opinion that their centuries-old association, often too close for comfort, with the Catholic Church had taught them a few things about the Vatican. Yet, undeniably, even they were thankful that a thaw had set in. But they had seen so many pro-Jewish papal decisions changed, in a casuistic dialectic of opposites, into exactly the other extreme by subsequent Popes, that they were not ready to cheer the Council delegates on from the sidelines on the Tiber.

The way they saw it, the verdict on who did or did not kill Christ was a matter for the Catholics to agree upon among themselves. They, the Jews of Rome, already had concluded long centuries before that they had not—even though for about fifteen hundred years, ever since the papacy had started to

*Pope John's sense of honesty and straightforwardness has been conspicuous throughout his life. In his report of 20 May 1943 from Instanbul—it was sent to Cardinal Maglione on the occasion of Cardinal Spellman's visit to the city on the Bosphorus—he wrote that he remained confirmed in "the judgment of those who claim that in order to confound diplomats, journalists, and small fry, nothing is more effective than the simple truth. . . ."

govern their lives, the Popes had told them the contrary. For after all, they argued, who could still seriously discuss a matter that had not been settled during two thousand years of polemical debate? So they looked on, in a mixture of coolness and concern and some confusion, while the world press reported every move and nuance of the slow theological proceedings, as if the subject under deliberation was the trial of a crime that had been committed only yesterday.

In the beginning Pope John seemed to be short of support. There was great opposition, especially from the Catholic representatives who had come from the Middle East, and occasionally from other quarters. Finally, during the Fourth Council Session in 1965, a vote was taken on a revised formulation, from which the loaded word *"deicide"* had disappeared. By now the assembled Fathers gave their nod to a text which said that "if it is true that the Church represents the new people of God, the Jews nevertheless must not be represented as being rejected by God, or as damned." In essence the details of the articles meant that the Jewish people, now or in the past, were not collectively guilty for the action of those among their leaders who had delivered up Christ to the Romans for crucifixion.

Some of the American observers in the Italian capital rejoiced. To them it was quite a victory; the new text, as taught in Sunday schools in the United States, could well have a significant influence on American youth and on American Catholics in general. Yet, in the end, the watered-down version made no one very happy; and to the Jews of Rome it made scarcely any difference. To them it was ancient history. To them the maxim remained: a good Pope was a good Pope, and a bad Pope would always be a mortal problem.

Even though the Council finally had accepted the articles, it had not been easy going—far from it. Toward the end there had been a bomb scare in Saint Peter's where the meetings were held, and during the third and fourth sessions the assembled 2,300 Fathers had received some unedifying literature in the form of a handful of anti-Semitic booklets and pamphlets, written and distributed by people who had done their best to influence the bishops, to hold fast to the anti-Semitic spirit of yore.

The first of the two publications, called "The Jewish-Masonic Action in the Council," was "exclusively reserved to the Reverend Councillory Fathers." Its text quoted from an even earlier anti-Semitic effort that had been handed to the Catholic Fathers in 1962, called "A Plot against the Church," "published by eminent prelates of various nationalities" under the pseudonym of "Maurice Pinay."

Cardinal Bea, fighting valorously for his ecumenical principles, came off badly in this frightening example of still virulent anti-Jewish feelings. The German-born cardinal was vaguely accused of being of Spanish-Jewish ancestry, the name *Beha* in Germany and Austria "being the equivalent of the Sephardic *Beja*." The Cardinal's proposal, moreover, was castigated as suspiciously "crypto-Hebraic, like those emanating from the many Jews who through the centuries have succeeded in penetrating the Catholic clergy. . . ."

The other venomous publication, from the pen of a certain "Bernardus" had been written in 1963. It was entitled: "The Jews and the Council as Seen in the Light of the Holy Scriptures and of Tradition." It tried to rally the support of the loyalist to the tradition of anti-Semitism. "Bernardus" insisted that "unfortunately [sic] all the measures taken by the Church against Judaism for the Defense of the Christian people are as necessary today as they were in the past."

Apparently the Council was not unduly influenced by the voices from the past. As to the Jews of Rome, they took the anti-Semitic rantings in their stride. They had heard them before, and will not even be surprised if, propagated by similar cranks, they hear them again. That is why they had watched the long drawn-out sessions of the Council, as one of them put it to me, "like spectators at a theater. We asked for nothing, and did nothing—because one does not argue things with the Vatican, and one does not pressure the Vatican. Let any responsibility for any decision taken by the Catholics be the *Vatican's* responsibility, and theirs only. . . ."

By the time the Ecumenical Council finished its work, the Roman Jews had gone through more than twenty postwar years of liberal and peaceful co-existence.

They had been able to pick themselves up from the tragic depths of ruin and degradation in which they had found themselves in 1944. There had been times of intense joy and moments of bewilderment during those ensuing years. There was joy when Chief Rabbi David Prato, who had been exiled under Mussolini, returned in 1945 from Palestine to take up where Zolli had left off. There was puzzlement a few years later, when the Roman Jews watched the arrival of a group of ex-Catholics from the city of Sannicandro Garganico in the spur of Italy, who before the war had thought they had discovered an extinct race called the Jews, in whose religion they believed to have found something which their own Catholicism never had given them. Under the guidance of an exalted invalid by the name of Donato Manduzio, they had started to practice what they thought the Old Testament preached, and by 1949 about forty of them gradually arrived in Rome on their way to Israel. To the members of the Tribe on the Tiber, who learned about the strange addition to their family from the morning newspapers, the whole episode sounded like something out of ancient and medieval scrolls.

Soon, shops that for years had been closed and abandoned were reopened along the streets of Rome; and today once again hardly anyone knows, or cares, which place is owned by a Jew and which by a Catholic. It is a discovery that can only be made on the Day of Atonement, when a good many shops in the center of Rome have their shutters down, with a simple note announcing that they will be "open as usual" only on the following day. The Romans pass by and take no notice—let everyone live and work and worship as he wishes.

In 1959 the Rome newspapers announced that one of the Italians who under Mussolini had emigrated to the United States had received the Nobel prize for physics—Emilio Segre, an old friend and colleague of Enrico Fermi. To the Italians it was all the same. Other Italians before him had done equally well in America. This one was a Jew? Most newspapers did not even note it, and if they did, it was mentioned in a flattering way.

During one of the more recent meetings of the Hebrew Congregations of Italy in Rome, one of the speakers registered some of the accomplishments—and a few of the fears—of the Jewish community. Among the fears was the possibility of assimilation—which he called "a grave and urgent problem." Some people believe, he said, that centers of Judaism may disappear in Italy in two or three generations. The opinion was shared by Rabbi Elio Toaff, when he remarked that the smaller centers indeed may become extinct within the century. On the other hand, said Rabbi Toaff, the centers of Milan and especially Rome were thriving. Rome had a Jewish population of well over 12,000 (an increase that is partly due to Jewish migration from the provinces to the capital, partly due to larger families, and also the result of increasing pride in their Judaism among the Romans). There are fewer mixed marriages in Rome than ever before, said Rabbi Toaff; and he noted that there has not been a known conversion for years.

On the wall above the door of the church near the former ghetto one still can read the inscription about the erring Jews; and if, with courage, one is able to cross the street in between the onrushing automobiles, one reaches the Bridge With The Four Heads, tranquilly as ever leading to the Island in the Tiber. At one end is a hospital; in the center stands the Church of San Bartolomeo; and behind it, in happy harmony, slumbered till recently the Jewish Home for the Aged, now removed to a brand-new modern building on the outskirts of Rome. On all sides the Tiber flows by as it did two thousand years ago, its level rising and falling with the seasons, its waters caressing the walls of the Catholic and Jewish buildings without prejudice.

Inside the former ghetto, in its mixed population still inhabited by some five hundred Jews, a shop with Israeli-manufactured souvenirs has made its appearance, hoping to attract the tourists. Next to it is a Jewish restaurant which claims to have *carciofi alla giudia* every bit as good as the long-existing non-Jewish *trattoria* a bit closer to the Portico d'Ottavia. On a late Friday afternoon the population congregates in the streets, as do all other Italians in a thousand other cities, with the difference that here a good many of them move on to the synagogue to take part in the services that celebrate the approaching Sabbath.

In the upstairs offices above the synagogue, one can find Jews who come to announce a death in the family, and young radiant couples who have decided to get married. "When?" is the stereotyped question of the secretary, just to make sure the chief rabbi is available on that day. I watched recently a young man and woman consult each other a second time before pronouncing the fateful date, which in this particular case happened to be "June 29." One of the women present in the room looked up at this announcement, and said "That's a lovely day—I also got married on *San Pietro e Paolo.*" What did a nice Jewish girl have to do with the celebration of that Catholic holiday, which commemorates the apostles Peter and Paul? Nothing, or perhaps just a little. It was proof that two thousand years of close Roman association between Jews and Catholics, notwithstanding all the ups-and-downs, have left their mark on the minds of the Jews, as it has been left on the minds of their Catholic fellow citizens. To everyone in Rome, after all, June 29th is a holiday, Saint Peter's and Saint Paul's, a day on which no one goes to work along the Tiber. Surely, as good a day as any, if not a better one, to get married.

That same day, down in front of the old building, a Roman father with his son—perhaps Jews, maybe not—were reading the inscription on the stone embedded in the wall of the synagogue, commemorating the six million Jews who died during the last World War, the more than eight thousand deported from all over Italy, and the two thousand ninety-one from Rome who perished in the concentration camps. After a while they slowly walked over to the other stone slab with the names of the seventy-one Jews who were shot in the Ardeatine caves. Could they have known someone called Sonnino, Fornari, De Segni, Limentani, or Milano? Perhaps these names meant something to them—maybe not.

Interrupting the silent contemplation, the boy turned to his father. "Father," he asked, "how long have the Jews been in Rome?" The father took his eyes away from the wall. He took the boy by the hand and walked off in the direction of the Bridge With The Four Heads, and his answer could be heard for some distance along the Lungotevere de' Cenci. "Son," he said with a kind of rhetorical certitude that had more than a grain of truth in it, "son—there have *always* been Jews in Rome. . . ."

Bibliography

Actes et Documents du Saint Siège relatifs à la seconde guerre mondiale, Volumes 6 and 7 (Libreria Editrice Vaticana 1973)

Alberti, Angelo, Il Messaggio degli Evangeli (Massimo, Milano 1956)

Albrecht, Friedrich, Der Gewaltsame Kinderraub zu Bologna (Verlag Gebrueder Ruedling, Ulm 1858)

Andreotti, Giulio, La Sciarada di Papa Mastai (Rizzoli Editore, Milano 1967)

Angelis, Guido de, Garibaldi Romanziere de "Il Mille" e gli Ebrei (in "Israel" November/December 1959)

Ascarelli, Attillio, Le Fosse Ardeatine (Fratelli Palombi Editore, Roma 1945)

Ausubel, Nathan, A Treasury of Jewish Folklore (Crown Publishers, New York 1948)

Azeglio, Massimo d', Gli Ebrei sono Uomini! (Organizzazione Editoriale Tipografica, Roma)

Bedarida, Guido, Ebrei d'Italia - Societa Editrice Tirrena (Livorne 1950)

Bedarride, I., Les Juifs en France en Italie et en Espagne (Michel Levy Frères, Paris 1861)

Berliner, Dr. A. Geschichte der Juden in Rom (J. Kauffmann, Frankfurt am Main 1893)

Berliner, Dr. A., Aus den letzten Tagen des Roemischen Ghetto (Rosenstein & Hildesheimer, Berlin 1886)

Blanshard, Paul, On Vatican II (Beacon Press, Boston 1966)

Blustein, Dott. G., *Storia Degli Ebrei in Roma* (P. Maglione & C. Strini, Roma 1921)

Bos, L. van, *Wegh-Wyer door Italien* (Isaak Stangniete, Amsterdam 1665)

Brod, Max, *Rëubeni, Fürst der Juden* (Kurt Wolff Verlag, Munchen 1925)

Carpi, Daniel, *The Catholic Church and Italian Jewry under the Fascists* (Yad Washem Studies IV, Jerusalem 1960)

Catalano, Franco, *Luigi Luzzatti-La Vita e l'Opera* (Banco Popolare di Milano, Milano 1965)

Ciano, Galeazzo, *Diario 1937-1938* (Cappelli Editore, Roma 1948)

Civiltà Cattolica, *La Questione Giudaica e le Cenversione*
                    La Questione Giudaica e l'Apostolato Cattolico

Cohen, Israel, *Israel in Italien* (Louis Lamm, Berlin 1909)

Crawford, Francis Marion, *Ave Roma Immortalis* (Macmillan & Co. Ltd., London 1899)

Deakin, F. W., *The Brutal Friendship* (Weidenfeld & Nicolson, London 1962)

Debenedetti, Giacomo, *16 Ottobre 1943* (Edizioni del Secolo, Roma 1945)

Dupaty, *Lettres sur i'Italie* (Jean-Albert Joly, Avignon 1811)

Egesippus, *Van de Verstooringhe der Stadt Ierusalem* (Jan Paedts Jacobszoon, Leyden 1607)

Elle Di Ci, *Le Religioni non Cristiane nel Vaticano II* (Elle Di Ci, Torino 1966)

Elmo, Luciano, *La Condizione Giuridica degli Ebrei in Italia* (Baldini & Castoldi, Milano 1939)

Epstein, Isidore, *Judaism, A Historical Presentation* (Penguin Books Ltd., London, Middlesex 1959)

Falconi, Carlo, *Il Silenzio di Pio XII* (Sugar Editore, Milano 1965)

Fanfani, Amintore, *L'Impulso Politico all'Economia* (Revista Internazionale di Scienze Sociali, May 1939)

Fano, Enzo, *Brief Historical Survey of the Jewish Community of Rome* (The B'nai B'rith Association of Rome, Roma 1961)

Farinacci, Roberto, *La Chiesa e gli Ebrei* (Roma 1939)

Felice, Renzo De, *Storia degli Ebrei Italiani sotto il Fascismo* (Giulio Enaudi Editore, Torino 1961)

Frey, Jean Baptiste, *Corpus Inscriptionum* (Ponteficio Istituto di Archeologia, Roma 1936)

Friedlaender, Paul, *Pie XII et le III Reich* (Editions du Seuil, Paris 1964)

Gabrieli, G., *Italia Judaica* (Fondazione Leonardo, Roma 1924)

Geiger, Ludwig, *Johann Reuchleins Briefwechsel* (Literarische Verein, Stuttgart 1875)

Graetz, Dr. H., *Geschichte der Juden* (Oskar Leiner, Leipzig 1876)

Graves, Robert, *I, Claudius* (Penguin Books, London, Middlesex 1966)

Gregorovius, Ferdinand, *Der Ghetto und die Juden in Rom* (Schocken Verlag, Berlin 1935)

Harris, M. H., *Hebraic Literature* (Tudor Publishing Co., New York 1939)
Heriot, Angus, *The French in Italy* (Chatto & Windus, London 1957)
Hochhuth, Rolf, *Der Stellvertreter* (Rowohlt Verlag, Hamburg 1963). *The Representative* (Methuen, London 1963). *The Deputy* (Grove Press, New York 1964).
Hudson, E. H., *History of the Jews in Rome* (Hodder & Stoughton, London 1884)

Interlandi, Telesio, *Contra Judaeos* (Tumminelli & Co., Roma 1938)

Josephus, Flavius, *Van den Joodschen Gheschiedenissen* (Jan Paedts Jacobszoon, Leyden 1607)
Josephus, Flavius, *Gheslacht Afcoemste ende Leven* (Leyden 1607)
Josephus, Flavius, *Van den Jodischen Crijgh ende Verwoestinghe der Stadt Ierusalem* (Jan Paedts Jacobszoon, Leyden 1607)
Josephus, Flavius, *Tegen Apionem Alexandrinum* (Jan Paedts Jacobszoon, Leyden 1607)
Jüdisches Lexikon, *Five Volumes* (Jüdischer Verlag, Berlin 1927-1930)
Juster, Jean, *Les Juifs dans l'Empire Romain* (Librairie Paul Geuthner, Paris 1914)

Kastein, Josef, *History and Destiny of the Jews* (Garden City Publishing Co., Inc., Garden City N.Y., 1933)
Katz, Robert, *Death in Rome* (Macmillan, New York 1957)
Katz, Robert, *Black Sabbath* (Macmillan, New York 1969)
King, Bolton, *A History of Italian Unity 1814-1871* (Nisbet & Co., London 1934)
Kirkpatrick, Sir Ivone, *Mussolini, Study of a Demagogue* (Odhams, London 1964)
Kisch, Egon Erwin, *Geschichten Aus Sieben Ghettos* (Allert de Lange, Amsterdam 1934)
Koddige en Ernstige Opschriften op Luyffels, Wagens, Glazen, Uithangborden, en andere Taferelen (Jeroen Jeroense, Amsterdam 1731)

Lapide, Pinchas, *The Last Three Popes and the Jews* (Dutch edition, by Nederlands Uitgeverscentrum N.V., Hilversum 1967)
Lattes, Dante, *Letture del Risorgimento Ebraico* (Casa Editrice Israel, Firenze 1948)
Lattes, Dante, *Benedetto Croce e l'Inutile Martirio d'Israele* (Casa Editrice Israel, Firenze 1948)
Leiber, R., *Pio XII e gli Ebrei di Roma 1943-1944* (La Civiltà Cattolica, 4 March 1961)
Leon, Harry J., *The Jews of Ancient Rome* (The Jewish Publication Society of

America, Philadelphia 1960)

Les Etapes du Racisme Italien (Manifeste du 14 juillet 1938, etc.)

Leti, Gregorio, *Het Leeven van Sixtus den Vyfűen* (Amsterdam 1722)

Lettres de Pie XII aux Evèques Allemands 1939-1944 (Libreria Editrice Vaticana 1966)

Levi, Abramo, *Noi Ebrei* (Casa Editrice Pinciana, Roma 1937)

Levi, Giuseppe, *Cristiani ed Ebrei nel Medio Evo*

Loevinson, Ermanno, *Roma Israelitica* (Kauffmann Verlag, Frankfurt am Main 1927)

Loevinson, Ermanno, *Gli Ebrei dello Stato della Chiesa nel Periodo del Risorgemento Politico d'Italia* ("*Israel*", April/May 1937)

Loevinson, Ermanno, *Gli Israeliti dello Stato Pontificio e la loro evoluzione nel periodo del Risorgimento Italiano fino al 1849* (Rassegna Storica del Risorgimento, 1929)

Manfrin, J., *Gli Ebrei sotto la Dominazione Romana* (Fratelli Bocca Editore, Roma 1888)

Marie-Venoit (Maria Benedetto), *Resumé de mon activite en faveur des Juifs persecutes (1940-1944)*, in *Livre d'or des Congregations franaises*, DRAC Paris, 1948)

Massa, Aniceto Del, *Razzismo Ebraismo* (Mondadori, Milano 1944)

Michaelis, Meir, *On the Jewish Question in Fascist Italy* (Yad Washem Studies IV, Jerusalem 1960)

Milano, Attilio, *Storia degli Ebrei in Italia* (Giulio Enaudi Editore, Torino 1963)

Milano, Attilio, *Gli Ebrei in Italia nei Secoli XI e XII* (Tipografia arti Grafiche, Città di Castello 1938)

Milano, Attilio, *Ricerche sulle Condizione Economiche degli Ebrei a Roma durante la Clausura nel Ghetto (1555-1848)* (Città di Castello 1931)

Milano, Attilio, *L'impari Lotta della Comunità di Roma contro la Casa dei Catecumeni* (Città di Castello 1950)

Milano, Attilio, *I 'Capitoli' di Daniel da Pisa e la Comunità di Roma* ("*Israel*", November/December 1935)

Milano, Attilio, *Il Ghetto di Roma* (Staderini Editore, Roma 1964)

Momigliano, Eucardio, *Storia Tragica e Grotesca del Razzismo Fascista* (Arnoldo Mondadori Editore, Milano 1946)

Montaigne, *Journal de Voyage en Italie* (Société des Belles Lettres, Paris 1946)

Moppurgo, Luciano, *Caccia all'Uomo* (Casa Editrice Dalmatia S.A., Roma 1946)

Morrison, W. D., *The Jews under Roman Rule* (T. Fisher Unwin, London 1890)

Mussolini, Edvige, *Mio Fratello Mussolini* (La Fenice, Firenze 1957)

Natali, Ettore, *Il Ghetto di Roma* (Stablilimento Grafico della Tribuna, 1887)

Natti Dubois, G., *Ebrei e Cattolici in Italia* (Arti Grafiche Friulane, Udine 1937)

Newman, Louis I., *A "Chief Rabbi" of Rome Becomes a Catholic* (The Renaissance Press, New York 1945) *'t Oude Romen* (Jacob van Meurs, Amsterdam 1661)

Orano, Paolo, *Gli Ebrei in Italia* (Casa Editrice Pinciana, Roma 1937)

Orvieto, Angiolo, *Il Vento di Sion e I Canti dell'Escluso* (Fondazione per la Gioventù Ebraica, Roma 1961)

Ottani, Giancarlo, *Un Popolo Piange* (Spartaco Giovane, Milano 1945)

Ovazzo, Ettore, *Il Problema Ebraico: Risposta a Paolo Orano* (Casa Editrice Pinciana, Roma 1937)

Pallenberg, Corrado, *Vatican Finances* (Peter Owen, Ltd., London 1971)

Pellicano, Piero, *Ecco il Diavolo, Israele* (Baldini & Castoldi, Milano 1938)

Peyrefitte, Roger, *Les Juifs* (Flammarion, Paris 1965)

Poliakov, Leon, *Il Nazismo e lo Sterminio degli Ebrei* (Enaudi Editore, Torino 1955)

Poliakov, Léon e Jacques Sabille, *Gli Ebrei sotto l'Occupazione Italiana* (Edizione di Comunità, Milano 1956)

Preti, Luigi, *I Miti dell'Impero e della Razza nell'Italia degli Anni '30* (Editoriale Opere Nuove, Roma 1965)

Reinach, Theodore, *Textes d'Auteurs Grecs et Romains relatifs au Judaisme* (Ernest Leroux Editeur, Paris 1895)
Histoire des Israélites (Librarie Hachette, Paris 1901)

Rezasco, Giuilio, *Segno degli Ebrei* (Tipografia del R. Istituto Sordo-Muto, Genova 1889)

Rhodes, Anthony, *The Vatican in the Age of the Dictators 1922-1945* (Hodder & Stoughton, London 1973)

Rodocanachi, Emmanuel, *Le Saint Siège et les Juifs - Le Ghetto a Rome* (Librairie de Firmin-Didot, Paris 1891)

Romanini, Alfredo, *Ebrei, Cristianesimo, Fascismo* (Roma 1936)

Roth, Cecil, *The History of the Jews of Italy* (Jewish Publication Society of America, Philadelphia 1946)

Sartre, Jean-Paul, *Portrait of the Anti-Semite* (Secker & Warburg, London 1948)
Anti-Semite and Jew (Schocken, New York 1948).

Schaerf, Samuele, *I Cognomi degli Ebrei d'Italia* (Casa Editrice Israel, Firenze 1925)

Schoenberger, Gerhard, *Der Gelbe Stern* (Ruetten & Loening, Hamburg 1960)

Schuerer, Emil, *Die Gemeindeverfassung der Juden in Rom in der Kaiserzeit* (J. C. Hinrichs' sche Buchhandlung 1879)

Serafian, Michael, *The Pilgrim* (Farrar, Straus & Co., New York 1964)

Sereni, Enzo, *L'Assedio del Ghetto di Roma nel 1793 nelle Memorie di un Contemporaneo* ("Israel" June/July 1935)

Synan, Edward A., *The Popes and the Jews in the Middle Ages* (Macmillan, New York 1965)

Toaff, Elio, *Il Carnevale di Roma e gli Ebrei* (Sally Mayer Foundation, Milano 1956)

Tompkins, Peter, *Italy Betrayed* (Simon & Schuster, New York 1966)

Valabrega, Guido, *Gli Ebrei in Italia durante il Fascismo* (Quaderni del Centro di Documentazione Ebraica Contemporanea, Milano)

Vogelstein, Herman & Paul Rieger, *Geschichte der Juden in Rom* (Mayer & Müller, Berlin 1896)

Volli, Gemma, *Papa Benedetto e gli Ebrei* (Città di Castello 1956)

Weizmann, Chaim, *Trial and Error* (Hamish Hamilton, London 1949)

Wielek, H., *De Oorlog die Hitler Won* (Amsterdamsche Boek- en Couranten Mij., Amsterdam 1947)

Yourcenar, Marguerite, *Memoirs of Hadrian* (Secker & Warburg, London 1955)

Zoller, Israel, *La Vita Religiosa Ebraica* (Tip. Sociale, Trieste 1932)
    L'Alleanza Sacra nella Letteratura Antica e Neo-testamentaria (Trieste 1935)
Zolli, Israele, *Israele* (Istituto Delle Edizione Academiche, Udine 1938)
    Il Nazareno (Istituto Delle Edizione Academiche, Udine 1938)
    Cenni di Psicologia Religiosa Ebraica (1938)
Zolli, Eugenio, *Antisemitismo* (AVE, Roma 1945)
    La Carità di Cristo Nel Cuore di Pio XII (1947)
    I Salmi, Documenti di Vita Vissuta (Ed. Viola, Milano 1953)
    L'Ebraismo (Ed. Studium, Roma 1953)
    Da Eva a Maria (Studium Cristi, Roma 1954)
    Before The Dawn (Sheed & Ward, New York 1954)
    Guida all'Aniitico e Nuovo Testamento (Garzanti, Milano 1956)
    Il Talmud Babilonese (Laterza, Bari 1958)

Index